SUDDEN FURY

LESLIE WALKER

SUDDEN FURY

A True Story of Adoption and Murder

ST. MARTIN'S PRESS   NEW YORK

Design by Judith A. Stagnitto

Library of Congress Cataloging-in-Publication Data

Walker, Leslie.
    Sudden fury/Leslie Walker.
        p.   cm.
    ISBN 0-312-03436-9
        1. Parricide—Maryland—Annapolis—Case studies.   2. Adoption—
    Maryland—Annapolis—Case studies.   3. Swartz, Larry 1966–   .
    I. Title.
    HV6534.A4W35   1989
    364.1'523'0975256—dc20   89-34900
                                                                      CIP

First Edition

10 9 8 7 6 5 4 3 2 1

For Lew and Angela

The names of Larry Swartz's foster parents and natural parents have been changed. The names of three other minor characters also are pseudonyms: Christine Monroe, Susan Barker, and Phyllis, who briefly dated Michael Swartz. All the other names are real.

PROLOGUE

His memory of life began here: A house by the water. He lived in a house by the cool shimmering water. Another little boy lived there, too. They were three or four years old. He couldn't remember how long he lived there, and he only remembered one event.

Awaking suddenly, he got out of bed, tiptoed to the kitchen, and opened the refrigerator. He carried some food back to his room and hid it in the dark slit under his bed.

Soon they moved him to a new home.

Before the house by the water, everything was a blank. Unlike his friends, he had no one to fill in the blanks, to tell him stories about his childhood. He never stayed with one family long enough to build that kind of history.

He was born in New Orleans and then moved somewhere

with his mother. He thought he lived with his grandparents for a while. He got his parents confused; there had been so many, he couldn't remember them all. He never knew the name he was born with, and couldn't recall much about his real mother. She used to visit him long ago. Each time she came, he hoped she would take him with her when she left. But she never did, and eventually she stopped coming to see him altogether. Slowly, painfully, she faded into the nooks and crannies of his memory, taking with her a slice of his heart.

Other mothers stepped in to replace her, but he remembered only one clearly. She had gray-brown hair and seemed older than the rest. She was always mad at him for wetting his bed. She'd scrunch up her face and scream at him, "You're too lazy to get up and go to the bathroom!" Sometimes that was true; he didn't feel like getting up. Other times, however, it was too late by the time he awoke. He was miserable in her home and thought he'd never be able to leave. He did leave, though. He complained to a social worker; suddenly, he was moved again.

He often wondered about his first parents. Now that he was nearly a man, he wanted to know his mother, to put a face on the ghost that haunted him still. But how could he track down someone whose name he didn't know? Where would he start?

He hadn't a clue.

SUDDEN FURY

ONE

January 17, 1984

1.

"I think my parents are dead."

Gracie Day nearly dropped her mug of fresh coffee.

"You think your parents are dead?"

"Yes."

Carefully setting down her mug, Gracie, a police operator, unhooked her feet from the ledge beneath her desk and leaned forward in her black swivel chair. She shoved a complaint card into the metal box on her left. The box punched the time—0713 on January 17, 1984.

"What is your address?"

"Twelve forty-two Mount Pleasant Drive," the caller said in a low monotone.

"And your name, sir?"

"Larry Swartz."

Gracie, a plump woman in her thirties, frowned in concentration. Double fatalities were rare, at least during her nine years of manning the emergency line for Anne Arundel County, Maryland. She had been up all night working the graveyard shift, and this was her first call since she had agreed to stay on that morning to fill in for a sick coworker.

"And what do you think is wrong with them? Do you think I need to send an ambulance? What do you think is wrong with them?"

"I have no idea. I just saw them lying down there. My mom is outside."

"On the ground outside?"

"Yes."

"Okay, I'll send an ambulance, too." Gracie was puzzled by the caller's extraordinary composure. He sounded grown-up, not childlike at all. His tone was so matter-of-fact he could have been talking about his breakfast. "Do you want to stay on the phone with me a few minutes?"

"Okay."

She put Larry Swartz on hold while she called the dispatcher handling the county's eastern district, to send a patrolman. Then she called the fire department to send an ambulance.

Gracie returned to her caller, who seemed less flustered than she. His voice was so devoid of emotion that she wondered whether he was in shock. Could this be a hoax? Gracie considered keeping the line open—she often did that to reassure distraught callers and children while help raced toward them—but she decided against it. This caller sounded as composed as a business executive who had everything under control.

"Okay, sir," she finally said. "I'll let you go and I'll get an ambulance started, and an officer. Okay?"

"All right."

2.

Like a box full of shoestrings dumped on the ground, the streets looped crazily through the riverfront community of Cape St. Claire. Up, down, left, right, the roads ran erratically, dangerously, without apparent design. On this freezing Tuesday morning, they were even more treacherous than usual, still coated with snow and ice from a storm the day before.

The dispatcher warned the firemen to take it easy because of the roads. Yanking their navy overcoats from metal lockers, one man hopped into an engine, and two hopped in an ambulance, and warily began negotiating the maze. Tom Heckner, a fireman and emergency medical technician, was skeptical because the dispatcher had told him the caller was calm on the phone. "They said there's a good possibility it was a prank call," he told the firefighter riding with him in the ambulance.

Tim Tryon, Heckner's partner, nodded. He doubted the call would amount to much. Although residents jokingly called the place Cape Despair, the sprawling community six miles northeast of Annapolis was a conservative, middle-class subdivision seldom bothered by murder or mayhem. Maybe the kid's parents had been up all night partying. Could they be buried booze-deep in sleep? Or, Tryon wondered, was this just another prank?

Throughout the Cape, ice hung from tree limbs and snow blanketed the wooded lots and hodgepodge of homes. Two inches of snow had fallen yesterday afternoon, on top of the three inches that had fallen the week before. It had been so cold in between that little of it had melted. Today a thick cloud cover hinted of more snow to come, and the morning sun was nowhere in sight. Everywhere the firemen looked—roofs, cars, treetops—they saw a lightly crusted white powder.

It took the firemen just over five minutes to make the one-mile trip. Taking one look at the driveway that sloped down to the house at 1242 Mount Pleasant Drive, they parked in the street. Leaving the third man with the engine, Tryon and Heckner grabbed a bag of medical gear and dashed past a pale blue Chevette parked outside the driveway. Two bumper stickers hung on the car: EVERYONE DESERVES ADOPTION and EQUAL RIGHTS FOR UNBORN WOMEN.

In the yard, Heckner dodged a large brown and white mutt that yapped furiously and circled his ankles. He glanced at the white house on the slope of a hill. Snow dusted its small front porch. A green wreath and red foil still hung on the door, nearly a month after Christmas.

Heckner and Tryon hurried toward the side entrance under a carport, where a screen door stood ajar.

Larry Swartz, barefoot and silent, met the firemen at the kitchen door. The trim youth stood five feet nine. He wore blue jeans, a half-buttoned pajama shirt, and no expression. He looked as if he'd just awakened; his curly black hair stuck out in all directions and sleep still clung to the corners of his eyes. He had olive skin, high cheekbones, and a strong square chin. His almond-shaped eyes, dark brown and wide-set, looked mysterious.

"Where are your parents?" Tryon asked.

"Downstairs," said Larry.

A dainty Asian girl stood beside the boy, clutching his hand. She didn't quite reach his shoulders. She appeared to be eight or nine, and her narrow eyes looked frightened. She wore her dark hair pulled back and had a cute face, like an Oriental Barbie doll.

Heckner stopped briefly and asked the boy, "What happened?"

"I don't know," Larry said. "I just came in and found them downstairs."

Larry bent to take the girl into his arms. She wrapped her legs around his waist and nuzzled his neck.

Walking through the kitchen into a dining room, the firemen found a stairwell and descended to a landing that opened left into a large basement recreation room. From the landing, they scanned the room: Ping-Pong table, curved bar, upright piano, brown corduroy sofa, two black vinyl armchairs—but no sign of people. While his partner headed left toward a sliding glass door across the room, Heckner turned right and opened a door on the stairway landing.

Right away, Heckner saw the feet. They were spread unnaturally far apart. To see the rest of the body, Heckner had to enter the tiny room—an office off the stairway landing—and turn right. A stocky man lay sprawled on his back between an ironing board and an overturned typing stand. One arm was twisted back underneath his hip. He looked as if someone had dumped a bucket of blood on him. There were big red blotches all over his short-sleeved beige shirt, brown pants, and wide gaudy tie. His tie, loosened, lay askew in his armpit. Blood streaked the man's bald head and face, forming blackish deposits in his graying beard.

Everything was in disarray around the body. A gooseneck lamp lay sideways on the brown shag carpet. Books and papers were scattered everywhere. The man had a brown buckle loafer on his right foot, but his left foot was missing its shoe. Apparently kicked off, the shoe was balanced oddly on its toe, leaning up against a shelf across the room. As Heckner crouched to check the man's pulse, he noticed blood-ringed holes in his shirt. Gunshot wounds, he figured. On the carpet near the body, he saw a pair of blood-smeared bifocals and a gold and pearl tiepin.

There was no pulse.

In the distance, Tryon shouted, "I found one out here."

Heckner walked into the recreation room and saw Tryon standing outside, beyond a partially open sliding glass door. Tryon motioned for Heckner to join him. As he approached, Heckner saw a large pool of red slush outside the door, a grotesque mingling of blood and snow. Beyond it, he spotted a naked woman stretched out on her back in the snow.

Her body was bony and elongated, and her skin appeared a sickly gray against the starkly white snow. She wore only a green kneesock pushed down around her right ankle. Her thin arms were bent and pulled up to her ears, and her legs were pushed so far apart, like her husband's, that the firemen suspected she'd been raped. A white eye patch hung over her left eye. Across her neck were a series of bloody gashes, and on the crown of her head was a gaping wound, matted with hair and blood.

The firemen had seen death and dismemberment before, but this was sickening. Turning to his partner, Tryon said softly, "Looks like somebody put a gun in her mouth and pulled the trigger."

Silently, Tryon surveyed the backyard: Tan moccasin upside down in a dog-food bowl. Green tarpaulin over a small oval swimming pool. Blue flannel pajama suit, red-stained and rumpled, in the snow. The house sat halfway down an incline, with a carport and main living quarters upstairs facing the street and a large recreation room downstairs opening into a fenced-in rear yard. Beyond the backyard stood a woodland.

Heckner led Tryon back inside to show him the man's body. Standing in the small study, Tryon and Heckner eyed the bloody corpse, and each other, nervously. Dropping his voice to a stage whisper, Tryon said, "You know, someone could still be in this house."

Heckner started. Wishing the police would hurry up, he decided to go upstairs and check on the children. In the kitchen, the girl clung tearfully to Larry.

"They're going to be okay, Annie," Larry kept telling her. "They're going to be okay."

"Where were you last night, if you weren't here?" Heckner demanded.

"I was here," Larry said.

Heckner was puzzled. "I thought you said you came in and found your parents."

"I woke up and couldn't find them, then went down and saw Mom outside." Larry shifted uncomfortably from one bare foot to the other.

Heckner raised an eyebrow. "You mean you were here all night and didn't hear all that shooting?"

"No."

The little girl began to wail, and Heckner decided to leave the children alone. As he went outside to radio police headquarters, two paramedics arrived. When the trio walked back down the tree-lined driveway toward the house, the Swartz's large brown dog made a beeline for Heckner. This time he was unable to dodge the mutt. Heckner yelped as the dog seized his pants and bit his leg. After shaking free, the firefighter pulled up his pants leg and saw red teeth marks but no blood.

The paramedics examined both bodies for signs of life, and felt embarrassed for the woman lying naked in the snow. Ignoring orders from county police never to touch murder victims, a paramedic retrieved a green wool blanket from the ambulance and gently draped it over her.

While waiting for police to arrive, the men went from room

to room inside the house, opening closet doors, peering under beds, making sure that whoever had committed the slayings wasn't still lurking, ready to pounce again. In each room, however, instead of a murderer, the firemen found a jumble of soiled laundry, food wrappers, and assorted papers—the kind of mess that suggested sloppy housekeeping, not a robbery or struggle.

The phone rang. A neighbor, Joan Folderauer, was wondering about the ambulance parked out front. When Larry said he thought his parents were dead, she couldn't believe it. She insisted he take Annie across the street right away.

Larry pulled on his black nylon windbreaker and his hightop wrestling sneakers, without bothering to lace them up, then walked across the street. He carried Annie like a tiny child, her legs wrapped around his waist and her arms hugging his neck.

When he returned, Larry spoke with the first uniformed police officer to reach the house. He told the officer he had awakened at seven o'clock—fifteen minutes after his sister—and she told him their parents were missing. When he went looking for them, he said, he spotted his mother's body through the kitchen window and phoned police.

After the cop asked Larry a few questions, one of the paramedics noticed the boy was in a daze. Worried, the paramedic led Larry outside to the carport, figuring a little privacy might help him vent his emotions. The paramedic stood with his hands in his pockets, waiting for the youth to speak.

After a minute, Larry said in a low voice, "They're dead, aren't they?" His face betrayed no emotion.

"Yes, they are." The paramedic was at a loss for words. Afraid Larry was in shock, he inspected him closely but saw no sweat or pallor, none of the symptoms that generally denote shock. If Larry was in some kind of emotional stupor, what would it take to bring him out? "Why don't you cry some? It might make you feel better. You know, things like this are hard for anyone to take."

Larry leaned against a wooden post and stared vacantly into the brown and white treeline behind his house. "This all seems like a dream," he said dully. "Like it never happened."

The paramedic waited for Larry's defenses to crumble, for tears to flow or anger to flash as the youth reacted to losing both parents at once; but the boy remained detached, his smooth olive-skinned face a blank. He seemed not to register the fact that his parents were dead. It could have been someone else's family—not his and Annie's—coming unraveled.

3.

Father Kevin Milton, pastor of St. Mary's Catholic Church in Annapolis, stuck his head in the doorway of the rectory dining room and saw Father Ted Heyburn sitting with a group of priests. "Ted, I need to see you for a minute," he called out.

Leaving his half-eaten breakfast, Heyburn, a stocky man with big ears and an oversized nose, excused himself and joined Milton in the hallway.

"There's been a tragedy," said Milton. "Someone killed Bob and Kay Swartz."

Heyburn pushed back a lock of gray hair, and his flaccid cheeks went pale. The fifty-year-old priest suddenly looked his age. Bob Swartz dead? Heyburn had seen him just two days ago, the ever-smiling, iron-willed, "let's change the world" Bob. On Sunday morning, he had taught his tenth-grade Sunday school class, then helped pass out communion wafers at afternoon mass. Heyburn could not imagine Sunday at St. Mary's without Bob and his charming wife, Kay.

Heyburn's bright blue eyes welled with tears. "What happened?"

"I don't know. Eileen Smithmyer called and said Larry called her. At this point, I don't think anybody knows anything. We should get out there."

Heyburn nodded. While he ran upstairs to grab his overcoat, Milton went to the church office and asked his secretary to phone Ron George, another parishioner and close friend of the Swartzes.

The two priests said little during the fifteen-minute ride to Cape St. Claire. Each was preoccupied with thoughts of Bob. A lay leader in the large affluent parish, one of the core members upon whom the priests leaned heavily, Bob was much beloved for his personal charm. He would flash a smile behind his bushy beard whenever he saw one of the ten priests who lived at St. Mary's. They all enjoyed the bald, stocky parish leader, who had vitality and a delightful sense of humor. There was no denying that he was a stubborn, outspoken man. But why would anyone want to kill him?

Bob's antiabortion picketing sprang to Heyburn's mind. At eight o'clock every Saturday morning, rain or shine, Bob picketed the Planned Parenthood clinic on the south side of Annapolis. He hadn't missed a Saturday in three years. Occasionally, Heyburn would join him. Bob would take placards in the back of his Chevette and pass them out to protesters. ADOPTION, NOT ABORTION, one said. IF BABIES COULD VOTE, ABORTION WOULD BE OUTLAWED, said another. Clinic workers often complained to police that the protesters harassed pregnant women who entered the clinic, but police made no arrests, and usually, the picketing remained peaceful. Heyburn doubted Bob's picketing had anything to do with his death. No, the slayings had to be the work of a robber or a lunatic.

When the priests reached Mount Pleasant Drive, a dozen people had congregated in the street beside the Swartz's driveway. A television crew aimed its bulky camera at two detectives wearing dark glasses who marched up the driveway, ignoring the reporters' questions, and entered the house across the street.

Father Milton approached a uniformed policeman who stood guard in the Swartz's front yard, barring reporters from entering the property. Milton introduced himself. "Bob and Kay were very active in our church," he said. "We came to anoint them and do whatever we can for the children."

The officer hesitated. "We're not letting anybody go down there. I'm sorry."

"Where are the Swartz children?" Milton asked. "May we see them?"

"Not now. The detectives are taking care of them. They're fine."

Retreating reluctantly to the street, the priests joined a crowd of neighbors, reporters, and school-aged children. Minutes later, the police officer pointed out the priests to a detective, who pulled them aside. "May I talk to you? I'm Detective Roland Mitchell." He told the priests he was canvassing friends and neighbors to find out what kind of people the Swartzes were, whether they had any enemies.

Eager to help, Milton and Heyburn sketched the Swartzes' church life. Yes, the priests knew the Swartz children. Larry was a steady boy. Both he and his younger sister were adopted. They had another adopted brother, Michael, who had been in some kind of trouble and no longer lived at home. Michael had gone to reform school somewhere in the mountains. As far as the priests knew, no one harbored ill will toward the Swartzes. "Bob and Kay weren't the kind of people who made enemies," Heyburn offered.

Mitchell jotted down the priests' telephone number on a yellow legal pad and thanked them both.

A half hour after they arrived, disappointed they hadn't been able to anoint the bodies or see the children, the two priests left. For Heyburn, the snowy scene would long evoke an empty feeling, as though he'd been shut out, cut off from something significant. All four family members had been within sixty feet of him, yet Heyburn never knew where Bob and Kay's bodies were, or where the children had been. Heyburn only knew what he felt—a haunting silence, a vacuum colder than the frigid January air, a hollow spot in his heart left by the sudden death of two dear friends.

4.

Detective Gary Barr was strolling out to his car when his wife leaned out the front door of their home in Severna Park, seven miles north of Cape St. Claire, and shrieked, "Gary, you have a double homicide!"

Barr turned abruptly and went back inside. Another detective was on the phone: Two people had been found dead in Cape St. Claire. After calling the radio room for details, Barr sprinted to his unmarked cruiser. With lights flashing and siren blaring, he pulled onto Ritchie Highway and headed south, snaking his way through the early-morning traffic.

The slim, handsome ex-Marine handled his cruiser with the same military precision he displayed toward everything else in his life. His rectangular face, framed by short brown hair, a neat brown mustache, and brown-rimmed glasses, often looked somber. He was only thirty-one, yet there was a stiffness about him that made him seem older. Even in blue jeans, checking his crab pots or puttering around in his speedboat, Barr always looked as though he was about to salute. His natural stance was straight as a steel door, and once he made it up, his mind was just as firm.

Barr liked to project a cool image, but this morning he felt uneasy. He had been a full-fledged homicide investigator for less than a year, and had handled only a few murders. Although his two years as an evidence technician helped, allowing him to work alongside some real pros, Barr realized that taking charge of a case was different; you never knew where it would lead, yet every twist and turn were your responsibility. Barr was the kind of man who enjoyed a challenge. Indeed, he often created challenges, then toiled painstakingly to meet them; but Barr also liked to know at all times where he was going. He was not the kind of man who liked surprises.

Already, Barr suspected the murders were drug-related. The few details the radio room gave him reminded him of the Carback murders, a sordid case that Anne Arundel County's homicide unit had cracked a year and a half earlier. A relative had found John and Donna Carbacks' bullet-riddled bodies in the dining room of their home. Barr, then an evidence technician, had worked the scene. Prosecutors later proved that a drug dealer had contracted to have the Carbacks killed because he had confessed to them that he had murdered someone and feared they would snitch.

Yet even before Barr reached Cape St. Claire, he changed his impression of the Swartz murders. Listening to his police radio, he heard a police officer at the scene ask a supervisor at headquarters to call a psychiatric hospital to find out whether they had a patient named Michael Swartz. Had Michael Swartz left the

Crownsville Hospital Center last night? the officer wanted to know. Barr began to suspect that a domestic dispute had triggered these murders. The uniforms already were checking the alibi of Michael Swartz, who apparently was a relative of the victims.

When Barr arrived, a commotion was under way in the front yard. A county dogcatcher zigzagged through the snow, chasing two dogs. The smaller one went straight to Larry, who scooped him up and carried him to the dogcatcher's truck. The larger brown and white mongrel ran after Barr, who managed to dodge him. "Here, Herc. C'mere, Herc," Larry cried, but the dog turned on his master and growled. Finally, the mutt calmed down and allowed Larry to put a leash around his neck. Earlier, a police officer had pulled his gun on Hercules when the dog had assumed an attacklike stance. Now the officer asked Larry what the police should do with his dogs.

He shrugged. "Put them to sleep, I guess."

The patrolman stared at Larry. Something seemed to be wrong with him, but he wasn't sure what. After telling the dogcatcher to keep both mutts at the animal shelter, the cop turned back to Larry and ordered him to sit in his cruiser. Then he strolled over to Detective Barr.

"You got a bad one," he declared. "There's a nude woman out back and a dead man in the basement. But before you go down, take a look at that boy." The patrolman motioned toward Larry. "He's the one who reported it. I'm no homicide detective, but something's wrong with that kid. He's too calm."

Barr glanced sidelong at Larry, trudging slowly to the cruiser. The patrolman was right about one thing: He was no homicide detective. Barr knew it was not unusual for relatives to react with stunned silence—especially a boy who had just lost both his parents.

A fireman approached Barr and pointed to a small patch of woods across the street from the Swartz house. "There's some spots in the snow that look like blood over there," the fireman said. Barr glanced in that direction but didn't go over, figuring one of the firemen had tracked the blood over on his boots. After he asked the patrolman a few questions, Barr walked around to the right side of the house, descended a set of wooden steps, and looked over the green chain-link fence into the backyard. He saw a forest-green blanket in the snow, two feet protruding from beneath it.

"Look here." A uniformed patrolman approached and pointed at the cone-shaped metal gatepost next to Barr. "It's blood, don't you think?"

Peering at the red smear on the silver gatepost, Barr agreed. It looked as if someone had touched the gate with a bloody hand. Glancing at the woods behind the backyard, Barr wondered, Had the killer fled through this gate and escaped into those tall old oaks and pines?

When Barr returned to the front yard, he authorized Eileen Smithmyer, a friend of the Swartzes who had just arrived, to take Larry across the street to join his sister at a neighbor's house. As Barr stood talking to the woman, a black Chevy pickup maneuvered through the crowd of onlookers and stopped in front of the Swartz house. Sergeant Bill "Tank" Tankersley, the red-headed supervisor of the county's homicide unit, climbed out.

Tommy Mock, Barr's partner, arrived a few minutes later, irritated that he had driven all the way to his office in Crownsville before he learned he was wanted at a murder scene twelve miles away. Dressed in a three-piece gray suit, trench coat and shiny black loafers, Mock stepped cautiously down the Swartz driveway. He stood five feet nine but seemed shorter, maybe because of his slight build. His gray hairline was receding and his sideburns were white. His eyes, tinted aquamarine by contact lenses, jumped out at you. He wore a diamond pinky ring on his left hand and carried a lit cigarette in his right. At forty-seven, he was a veteran cop with twenty years on the force, nearly half of them in homicide.

Barr sketched for Mock what little he knew. The uniforms had given him conflicting reports: One said the Swartzes had been shot; another said they'd been stabbed. Before examining the bodies for themselves, Barr and Mock decided to question the children.

"Christ, why did I put on these goddamn shoes?" Mock grumbled as the detectives walked up the driveway with their supervisor. Mock looked down at the loafers he had just bought the weekend before. "I can't get traction. How am I supposed to walk on ice?" Halfway up the driveway, Mock slipped and fell, picked himself up and dusted clumps of snow from his trench coat. No sooner had Mock struggled to his feet and taken a few steps, than down he went again. "Guys, if nobody's lookin', how about holdin' on to me?" he pleaded.

Chuckling, Barr and Tankersley pulled Mock up and held his elbows as he scaled the driveway. Ignoring questions called out by reporters, Barr and Mock crossed the street and climbed the steps to the neighbor's front porch.

Joan Folderauer ushered them into her kitchen, where Larry sat beside his sister, with one arm draped across her shoulder, comforting her. The detectives instantly sensed a bond between brother and sister. After introducing himself and Mock, Barr asked Larry, "How do you feel?"

"I'm all right," Larry said tonelessly.

"I know this is difficult for you, but we have to ask you some things." Barr looked at Annie, who leaned against her brother and watched the detectives with anxious brown eyes.

"Do you mind if we talk to your brother first? He'll be right back," Barr told her.

When Annie said nothing, Larry and the detectives went downstairs to a family room. Sitting with Larry on a couch, Barr led him through the preliminaries. He was seventeen; his father, Robert Swartz, fifty-one; his mother, Kathryn Swartz, forty-three. His mother taught English; his father repaired computers. Larry was a junior at Broadneck High School, where his mother taught.

Barr could hardly believe the calm even tone of the boy's replies. Trying not to be obvious, the detectives examined Larry from his curly black locks down to his well-worn hightops. His skin was dry and its coloring looked healthy. His breathing was steady. No sign of shock. No stains on his sneakers or clothes. Nothing unusual about his appearance at all.

Mock noticed an inflamed area on the back of Larry's right hand and leaned forward to inspect it. "What's that spot on your hand?"

"What? Oh, nothing. Just something I got in the kitchen the other day."

Barr caught Larry's eye. "How long have you lived here?"

"Since I was six."

"And before that, where?"

"I didn't live with them. Mom and Dad adopted me when I was six."

Barr jotted that down, then touched the rear tip of his pen to his mouth, remembering his own childhood. He, too, had been adopted, and there had been many times he wished his adoptive parents had never taken him in. Looking at Larry, he wondered fleetingly whether Larry's adoptive life had been any better.

Barr rolled his eyes toward the staircase. "Your sister, she's adopted, too?"

"Yeah." Larry looked at the floor, then volunteered that he also had an adopted brother, Michael, who had gone to reform school at age thirteen and no longer lived at home. Recently, Michael had been placed in the state mental hospital in Crownsville.

"What kind of trouble did Michael get into?" Barr asked.

"I don't know. He broke into some homes. He's pretty heavy into drugs. Lately he's been worse, doing PCP, stuff like that. I heard his friends smuggle it in to him in Crownsville."

Mock leaned forward. "Who are Michael's friends?"

"I don't know."

"You don't know the names of the guys smuggling stuff in to him?"

"No."

Barr waited a minute, then said, "Why don't you tell us everything that happened, starting yesterday."

"Well . . ." Larry's eyes shifted around the room; he appeared uncertain how to begin. Finally, he said he'd gotten out of school early the previous day, Monday, because of mid-year exams. He had gone over to his friend Craig Casey's house, played chess for a while, then gone sledding with Craig. Shortly after five o'clock, he had gone home and studied in his bedroom. He'd eaten with the family at seven o'clock.

"Anything happen last night?" Barr asked. "Any arguments or problems?"

Larry crossed his arms. "Dad got mad because I messed up one of his computer disks. I had been fooling around with a friend, and we must have messed it up. It wasn't a big deal."

"Michael has been calling me a lot lately," Larry added, abruptly changing the subject. He said his brother was undergoing psychiatric testing at Crownsville under a court order, and "hates Mom and Dad." Michael had rarely spoken to his parents since they sent him away to reform school. "Mom told me she was afraid Michael would come home one day and kill her and Dad."

Larry added that his parents had no idea he talked to his brother on the telephone and would not have approved of it. His brother had made threats against his parents on the phone to Larry. "Michael is emotionally disturbed," he concluded.

Barr found the boy's rambling monologue puzzling. Did he really think his brother could have murdered his parents? After a pause, Barr nudged Larry back to his chronological tale.

He said his sister had heard screaming the night before and awoke him at eleven or eleven-thirty to tell him about it. "I told her, 'You're dreaming. Go back to sleep.' She came and slept in my room with me. She does that a lot."

"So you slept in the same room," Barr repeated, taking notes. "Okay, what happened this morning?"

Larry said that when he awoke at seven, Annie told him that she couldn't find their parents. Then he changed his story slightly about what happened next. "When I went to call the dogs, I looked out the dining room window and saw Mom outside. She was lying in the snow. I grabbed Annie and covered her eyes." Earlier, he told the uniformed cop he saw his mother through the kitchen window, and he told the fireman he went downstairs. As soon as he saw the body, he said, he phoned the police and his mother's friend Mrs. Smithmyer but couldn't talk to her, so he handed the phone to his sister.

"Did you go downstairs at all?" Barr asked.

"No."

"You didn't go in the backyard to check on your mom?"

"No. Annie and I stayed upstairs and got dressed while we were waiting."

An evidence technician arrived to test Larry's hands for gunshot residue, a standard police procedure in suspected shootings. Using a solution of nitric acid, the technician carefully swabbed Larry's hands and fingers, front and back. Later, the swabbings would be sent to the FBI laboratory for analysis.

Barr resumed his questioning after the technician left. "Last night, other than what Annie said she heard, did you hear any noises?"

"Only our dogs barking out back, but they do that a lot," Larry said. The dogs had been in the backyard when he went to bed but were running around the neighborhood in the morning. Although Sandy, the small dog, didn't bite, Hercules occasionally bit strangers. "Michael could get around him, though," Larry added. "Herc knows Michael."

"Has anyone in your family been arguing lately?"

"No. Everyone gets along, but there are some big arguments. Dad gets irritable."

"Who has these big arguments?"

"Me and Dad don't get along very well. He's always yelling at me."

Barr wrote that down. "Okay," he said, putting down his note pad and looking at Larry. "Thanks for helping us. We need to talk to your sister now. Could you get her?"

Larry disappeared upstairs but quickly reappeared with his sister in tow behind him. "She's scared to talk by herself," he said. "Is it okay if I sit with her?"

Barr glanced at Mock, and the detectives assented. Appearing pale and frightened, Annie sat in her brother's lap and spoke so softly that Mock repeatedly had to ask her to speak up. Although Barr had taken the lead with Larry, Mock, a cunning interrogator with a ready smile for children, shepherded Annie through the questioning. He knelt beside her, patted her arm, and said it wouldn't take long.

Annie said she was nine years old and attended third grade at Cape St. Claire Elementary School. At eleven-thirty the previous night, she had heard her dad making strange noises and screaming "Help. Help."

"Are you sure about that, Annie? How do you know it was eleven-thirty?" Mock asked in his loud gravelly voice.

"Why, I looked at my watch," Annie said. "As a matter of fact, it was eleven-thirty-four when I woke up."

"You looked at your watch?"

"Yes, I did."

Mock smiled. "What a clever girl! What did you do then?"

"I ran outside to the carport. There was a guy in the backyard walking away. He had a shovel over his shoulder, and it was dripping blood." Annie buried her head in Larry's shoulder, as though she'd said all she could bear to say.

"What did this guy look like?" Mock asked gently.

Annie looked up. "He had black hair, curly on the top. It came down to his shoulders. And, uh, he was humming—like he was glad, or happy."

Barr glanced at Larry. The youth had curly black hair, long and bushy, and it came down almost to his shoulders.

"What did his face look like?" Barr asked.

Annie said she hadn't seen his face but had noticed that he wore blue jeans and a gray sweat shirt—one with BROADNECK printed on the back.

Larry asked Annie whether it was like a gray sweat shirt that Michael owned. Annie seemed unsure.

Barr wanted a better description of this man. "How tall was he?"

Annie looked at Barr, confusion pinching her round face. Barr, who was six feet, rose and walked over to a Ping-Pong table. "As tall as I am?"

"He was taller," Annie said.

Larry, who was only five nine, looked at Barr. "Michael is real tall," he volunteered. "He's six four."

"Was he as tall as Michael?" Barr asked.

"Uh-huh," Annie affirmed. "He looked like my brother," she added.

"You mean Michael," Larry said quickly.

"Yes," Annie agreed.

"Michael does a lot of drugs," Larry added.

Barr and Mock exchanged glances, unsure what to make of Larry and Annie. Was Larry coaching Annie or merely trying to help her remember? And why was he volunteering all this information about Michael?

"You told us your brother is at the Crownsville Hospital," Mock said. "If he's in there, he can't get out, can he? I mean, he's locked up."

"He can get out," Larry assured him. He related how Michael recently had left the hospital and had come by the neighborhood for a visit. Again, Larry told the detectives that Michael had been able to get drugs in and out of the hospital.

Neither officer found Larry convincing, but they were anxious to examine the crime scene and decided not to press the children yet.

Mock reached out and patted Annie's arm. "You've been a really good girl," he told her. "Thanks for helping us out. Maybe you and I can talk again later, okay?"

Annie snuggled against her brother's chest. "Uh-huh," she said softly.

5.

Detective Jim Moore took the telephone call at his desk.

Detective Barr asked Moore to shoot over to Crownsville Hospital Center and check out a suspect named Michael Swartz. His adoptive parents had been found slain an hour ago, and his sister thought she had seen him outside their house last night. Barr wanted to know whether the kid could have slipped out last night and gotten back in. Also, Barr wanted a rundown on everything the kid was wearing.

Another detective volunteered to accompany Moore and trudged with him through the snow to the hospital, located directly behind the Criminal Investigative Division offices of the county police.

Quickly, the officers tracked down the dormitory that housed Michael Swartz. Two nurses in the dorm asserted that Michael had been there all last night.

"How can you be so certain?" asked Moore.

"Simple," one nurse replied. She showed him a log listing the patients' names and hospital locations. Checks appeared beside each location where staff members had seen a patient at specified times. Moore saw that Michael had been checked off at regular intervals all evening, including bedtime.

A veteran investigator, Moore glanced at the two nurses and smiled. "You don't really mean every patient is seen every single time they are checked off, do you?" Moore asked. "Sometimes you must check them all off, when maybe you didn't eyeball each one?"

With a shrug, the nurse in charge conceded that this might be true, there was a certain routine to the checkoffs. But both nurses insisted that Michael could not have left the hospital at night without someone on the staff detecting his escape. And certainly he could not have slipped back in undetected: Security in Michael's ward was tighter than in the other wards. It had wire meshing on the windows and locks on each door.

Michael was listening to rock music in a room with several other patients. He stepped into the hallway to speak to the detectives. At six foot six, the gawky youth towered over both officers. He had dark bushy unkempt hair that stuck straight out from his ears and touched his shoulders at the back. He had a sparse goatee and the faint beginnings of a mustache over his full lips. He wore a plaid flannel shirt, blue jeans, and Nike tennis shoes, so white they looked as though he'd bought them that morning.

"Where were you last night?" Moore demanded after introducing himself and his partner.

"Where do you suppose I was?" Michael snickered. "Here."

"Did you go out at all?"

"Go out?" Michael cocked his head and looked at Moore. "Oh, man. You can't just walk out of here."

"Do you have a gray sweat shirt?"

"No. Why are you asking me these questions?" Michael asked peevishly.

Moore deflected Michael's curiosity with a lie. He claimed they were investigating the theft of a motorcycle that had occurred the previous night. Moore didn't want to give Michael one iota of information about the death of his parents. That way, he reasoned, if Michael made any incriminating statements, he could not argue later that the detectives had led him to do so.

But their conversation was brief, and Michael's tongue never slipped. Obviously a rebellious youth, Michael treated the detectives playfully, with deliberate disrespect, as though their visit was a joke. Moore had a hunch the kid knew nothing about the murders. If he did, Michael must be quite a con man, for Moore could hardly believe anyone could be so casual and flip about the murder of his own parents.

6.

It was almost noon, and Anne Klyman, a Spanish teacher at Broadneck High School, was looking forward to watching the students pile onto the buses and head home, leaving their teachers behind to grade midyear exams. She stepped outside her classroom, where the students were still working, and saw two other teachers down the hall. One of them appeared to be weeping.

Anne approached to offer whatever help her fellow teacher might need.

"I don't know if I'm supposed to say anything, but Kay Swartz and her husband were murdered," said Cindy Campbell, an English and Spanish teacher. Her voice was choked, and she hesitated before adding that Larry had told a neighbor that he'd stayed up late studying, then had awakened early and found his mother's body.

Anne was both bewildered and puzzled. "That doesn't sound like Larry," she said, frowning.

Larry was a late sleeper, and Anne, his homeroom teacher, more than once had discussed his habitual lateness with his mother. His lateness was especially odd because he and his mother had only a five-minute walk through the woods behind their house to reach the eighty-four-acre school grounds. Anne also thought it odd that Larry had stayed up late studying. Maybe he was doing better in his other classes, but he was flunking Spanish. Anne attributed his poor performance to a lack of interest. Larry seldom bothered to do his homework, and his mother had suggested that it may have been a mistake for him to take Spanish.

Lawrence Knight's voice suddenly blared over the school's public-address system. The second and final exam for the day was over, and Mr. Knight, the principal, had decided to address the awful buzzing he knew was going on up and down the school's cinder-block hallways.

"I regret to inform you that we have suffered a great loss," Mr. Knight announced. His voice was calm, controlled, deliberately reassuring. Yet Anne knew him well enough to detect an edge of sadness. "Mrs. Swartz and her husband have both been killed. At this time, we have no details on what happened. I ask you to join me in a moment of silence. Let us show that we share the grief the Swartz family feels for their tragic loss."

7.

Ron George knew at once he had to go to the house.

George, a jeweler and sometime actor, was president of the Annapolis Right to Life chapter. Bob Swartz was the treasurer. They had known each other barely two years but had developed a strong friendship through their battle to save the unborn.

As he left the jewelry store where he worked on Main Street and headed for Cape St. Claire, George fought back tears. A small man with shiny black hair, a dark mustache, and pale porcelain complexion, George struggled to comprehend what the secretary at St. Mary's Church had called to say. Of all people, why did this happen to Bob Swartz, the man George looked up to, the spiritual mentor whose faith awed him, the jolly jokester whose high-pitched chuckle had so brightened George's life?

What would happen to Larry and Annie? It seemed so unfair. These kids already had lost one set of parents. Why would God let something like that happen to them twice?

The cold air jolted George as he left his warmed car, walked down the Swartz driveway, past the carport, and looked over the rear fence. There was Kay's body, feet protruding from under a blanket. George felt numb. Staring at the dark green sock on her foot, he told himself that Kay's spirit lived on, and Bob's, too. Death was a beginning; the afterlife, real. The Swartzes had believed that, and so had George. He believed it now more than ever.

He walked back to the street and stood by himself, off to one side of a growing crowd. A woman approached, identified herself as a reporter, and inquired whether he knew the Swartzes.

Reluctantly, George said he'd known Bob Swartz through Right to Life. "He was the blood of our group. He was a beautiful person." George spoke slowly, in a flat tone. He remembered first meeting Bob at a Right to Life event. For years, they had picketed the Planned Parenthood abortion clinic together. Bob, not George, was the zealot. He never missed a Saturday, not even for vacation.

"Did he make enemies on the picket line?" the reporter asked.

"Not enemies. A couple of times, just being in front of Planned Parenthood, people yelled at him, or even hit him."

"Do you know of anyone who hated him? Anyone who might have wanted to kill him?"

George was adamant. "Absolutely not." He was convinced the Right to Life movement had nothing to do with the murders. He shut his eyes, recalling a promise he'd made to Bob. George had agreed to join Cursillo, a group of lay people who get together for religious fellowship, in the spring. Cursillo had meant so much to Bob that he had wanted to share it with George. Now Bob wouldn't be there to sponsor him.

In pained tones, George struggled to explain what Cursillo was, who Bob was: "Bob was an absolutely beautiful person. . . . They both gave themselves . . . so much . . . to the community, to the church . . ." His voice trailed off; he buried his hands in his coat pockets, reflecting on his loss. Although he had known Bob well, George knew little about his friend's life before they had met. Now he wondered how Bob had developed such a deep faith. What had driven him and his wife to become such good Christians?

And who, he wondered, could destroy such beautiful, good people?

TWO

Fall 1968

1.

As Bob Swartz threaded his way between endless rows of cars in a University of Maryland parking lot, the short, bald graduate student saw a tall woman leaning against a rust-bitten Ford Falcon. She appeared to be pasting paper on its roof.

Bob stopped and watched in quiet amusement. "What are you doing?" he inquired.

Looking up, the woman smiled. "I'm wallpapering my Ford," she said matter-of-factly. She explained that she could not tolerate her car's beat-up appearance, nor could she afford body-shop repairs. So she was hiding the ugly rust spots under yellow and green floral contact paper.

Bob was tickled. "Fan-tastic," he said, shaking his head at the bizarre effect the bright flowers created on her white car. As they chatted, Bob found he enjoyed the young woman's style—

original, witty, friendly. Her lilting voice especially delighted him.

She was Kathryn Ann Sullivan, Katie or Kate to friends. At age twenty-seven the year before, she had decided to quit teaching school for a while to earn her master's degree. Looming over Bob at five feet eleven, Katie was thin as Twiggy, the British fashion queen, and her brown hair was cropped short. When she smiled, her lips stretched wide and lit up her face. She occasionally wore contacts but usually wore large brown glasses over her long hooked nose, giving her face a stark expression.

After watching her for a few minutes, Bob excused himself and went on to class.

He didn't forget her, and when he got a glimpse of a lanky woman in the college cafeteria several months later, he walked right over. Sure enough, it was Katie Sullivan. He joined her for lunch and soon discovered they had several things in common.

Both had moved to Maryland from points west. Bob had come last year from Ohio, but he had spent most of his youth near Pittsburgh before he dropped out of college to hop around the world. Katie had come from Colorado, where she'd been teaching high school for the last few years. Actually, Katie was a Midwesterner, born and reared and college-educated in the Hawkeye state of Iowa. Both were the children of schoolteachers, and both were going for their master's degrees in education. And at the moment, both were GRs, graduate residents, earning room and board by living in the dorms and advising undergraduates.

Bob liked to talk more than he liked to listen, but he found himself listening at length to this fast-talking woman who seemed so bright and vivacious. On most topics they discussed, they shared deeply conservative beliefs. Katie talked a lot about Catholicism, her religion. That fascinated Bob, who was a Protestant. When Katie talked, she was direct, even blunt, and looked him right in the eye. Bob wasn't strong on eye contact. He wasn't keen on female relationships in general, even though his friends had always considered him rather aggressive.

The truth was, no one would ever accuse Robert Lee Swartz of being a ladies' man.

Standing just under five feet eight, he was noticeably short of hair. His hair had fallen out in his twenties, leaving him with a bald dome, which he wasn't happy about. At age thirty-six, he still had brown tufts over his ears and big bushy sideburns reaching halfway to his chin. An active swimmer, Bob kept his weight around 160 and liked to stay in shape. He had a triangular, ragged face with bushy eyebrows arched high over small hazel eyes. On the left side of his face was a long dark patch that looked like a birthmark or scar. It started on his left temple and extended down below his cheekbone.

Few people mentioned the mark, and when anyone asked, Bob couldn't be counted on to tell the truth. He told some friends it was a scar from a motorcycle accident. In fact, he had incurred it in infancy when he fell and wedged himself between a couch and a steam radiator. The radiator had severely burned his face and permanently darkened the skin. As he grew older, the scar had lightened, but it still was the first thing many people noticed about him.

Katie, however, was not the kind of woman who judged a man by his looks. She judged people more by their character and personality. And Bob, with his jolly laugh and boundless repertoire of trivia, seemed to have more than his share of personality. His character seemed to have depth, too, for even though he laughed a lot, Katie could tell from his conversation that he was serious about life. He talked about principles and ideas and took an interest in everything around him.

Although he rarely dated, Bob soon asked Katie to go to the movies. Katie rarely dated, either, but she accepted. They went to see *Finian's Rainbow,* a film adaptation of the whimsical Broadway musical that was alive with fantasy, magic, and legends of love. An Irish girl through and through, Katie knew the music well. She so loved the beautiful and lilting "How are things in Glocca Morra?" that when the overture began, she cried.

Katie confided to a friend that she had met an older man who came across as a know-it-all. "She said what bothered her more was that he really did know it all," Sally Hayes recalled years later. "She said, 'You can't even go for a walk with this man but what he doesn't have to name the leaf on every tree and what's growing on the ground.' He'd go on and explain all this stuff. She just wanted to enjoy it."

Katie was in the final year of her two-year graduate program and told friends that her first priority was getting her degree. She saw Bob occasionally during the remainder of the school year, but their relationship stayed cool and casual. Bob spent most of his time bumming around campus with his best friend, a blond-haired younger man whom Katie considered shallow and full of himself.

In the summer of 1969, Katie proudly left the University of Maryland with a master's degree in education, but with little money and no job. She moved off campus into an efficiency that her friend Sally had rented outside Washington, D.C. Although Sally had a summer job with the city park service, she, too, was seeking permanent employment. Together, Katie and Sally embarked on an intensive hunt, applying for positions in such exotic places as Samoa and the Philippines. After studying education for years, Katie had begun to think that maybe she didn't want to be a teacher, after all. She took qualifying tests for the air force, then decided not to enlist. She studied real estate and obtained her sales license, then decided real estate wasn't for her. At one job interview, Katie stood up to leave and felt a blast of cold air on her back, then realized she'd forgotten to zip her dress. At the end of the summer, when neither she nor Sally had found work, they began substitute teaching to pay their rent.

Katie had seen little of Bob over the summer but began dating him again in the fall. Bob had abandoned his studies at Maryland without earning a graduate degree and was living in Beltsville, northeast of Washington, near his new job as an electronics instructor for the Bendix Corporation. He recently had broken his leg in a motorcycle accident but managed to hop around in a cast. He hopped after Katie a lot. And he stopped calling her Katie, a name he considered too girlish for a woman who had just turned twenty-nine. Bob decided to call the woman he planned to make his wife Kate. Sometimes he even shortened it to Kay, a name that would eventually stick.

As her bills piled up, Kate grew more determined than ever to find a job. One morning, she called every school district within driving distance. Although no one needed an English teacher, she found a school that needed a gym teacher, and Sally was certified to teach physical education. When her friend came home, Kate announced, "Tomorrow morning you go over to Falls Church, Virginia. You have an appointment. I've just talked them into listening to you. They're starting a new position in phys ed." Delighted, Sally went and was hired the next day.

It took awhile longer for Kate to find a job, and then it was two hundred miles away at Atlantic City High School in New Jersey, where an employment agency finally located an English teaching post. Kate went to work the week after Thanksgiving.

In November and December, Bob kept in touch with Kate by phone and saw her several times. By now, there was no doubt in his mind: Kate would be his wife. He told her so several times. She still had doubts, but they weren't as strong as they had been a year earlier.

At Christmas, Kate took Bob home to meet her mother in Hinsdale, Illinois. Shortly after the Christmas break, Kate phoned Sally and asked, "Will you be around in June? I want you to be my maid of honor." Kate had agreed to marry Bob and move back to the Washington area in the spring.

Bob called his brother Joe in Pittsburgh and asked him to be his best man. They set the wedding for June 20, eight days before Bob's thirty-eighth birthday. It would be a Catholic ceremony, and a first marriage for both bride and groom. Although he was only a year older than Bob, Joe had been married for seventeen years. Bob, on the other hand, had never even come close to the altar. "I was actually surprised," Joe was to say of his brother's announcement. "I don't remember hearing anything about a girl."

Although they were surprised, Bob's family was nevertheless delighted. Of course, Joe would be best man, and the whole Swartz family would attend the wedding.

For Bob, the marriage that was to moor him in Maryland was a voyage into his past. His own father, a lifelong Protestant, only last year had married a Catholic woman in a Catholic ceremony. Joe had been best man at that wedding, too. And the state where Bob had met his fiancée and where he planned to make his home happened to be his father's birthplace. It was also the place where his father had met and married his mother.

That link was not lost on Joe, who later would remark that Bob, like so many sons, seemed to go out of his way to follow in his father's footsteps.

2.

Father to the Swartz boys was Joseph Franklin Swartz, Jr., a bright, aloof man born in 1905 in the small riverfront town of Denton on Maryland's Eastern Shore. Standing just over five feet nine, Joseph Jr. had deep brooding eyes and a protruding mouth. *Who's Who in America* listed a string of degrees under his name, ending with a Ph.D. in education. He was the eldest son of Joseph Sr., a short man with a handlebar mustache who had migrated to Maryland from the Shenandoah Valley before the turn of the century. Their ancestors were Mennonites with thick German accents. After he attended college in Virginia, Joseph Jr. returned to Maryland's Eastern Shore to teach high school. There he met and married Gladys M. Bowden, a happy-go-lucky girl born and raised on Chincoteague Island.

They married on August 4, 1930. Exactly nine months later—to the day—Gladys gave birth to Joseph Franklin Swartz III.

The trio soon packed up and moved to Clairton, a suburb of Pittsburgh, where Joseph Jr. began teaching at Clairton High School. There, on June 28, 1932, Gladys gave birth to their second son, Robert Lee.

Depression babies born almost fourteen months apart, Bob and Joe spent their early years in a red pillbox home with a high hill in their backyard, which dropped precipitously down to a hollow that ran wide and deep and straight into the industrial jungle. The tangle of smokestacks and steel darkened the town's soul, not to mention the sign that greeted visitors: CLAIRTON: THE CITY OF PRAYER.

Clairton was a sooty mill town, harder than diamonds around its edges. Bars with names such as The Hollywood Club sprang up near the main gate of the massive Clairton Steel Works, owned by the U.S. Steel Company since 1904. Most of Clairton's homes sat high on a plateau overlooking the Monongahela River and the mills that lined its shores. Clairton was full of narrow streets and alleyways, many of them hugging hillsides, giving the town the feel of a pinball machine on "tilt." A railroad ran beside the river below the town. Stretching for several miles along the tracks were smokestacks, stockpiles of coal, railroad cars, and monstrous mills. The steel mill spewed out a fine black ash that wind gusts lifted up to the residential part of town, blackening cars and clothes hung out to dry. Sometimes the ash created a smog so malodorous and dense that it turned day into night, requiring the Swartzes to keep their house lights on until past noon.

Joseph Jr. built a brick home on one of Clairton's highest points in 1938, giving him a splendid view of the town's hills. They moved in shortly before the birth of their third son and youngest child, Jacob William. Although the Great Depression slowed steel production and idled thousands of workers, Joseph Jr. belonged to that fortunate class of Americans who managed to hold on to their jobs. He taught high school math straight through the thirties and completed work for a master's degree in education at the University of Pittsburgh in 1939. When the Japanese bombed Pearl Harbor two years later, Joseph Jr. enlisted in the navy and sailed off to war.

His boys sorely missed him, for he was the emotional center of their lives. Although they loved their mother, a warm, bubbly woman, they craved approval and attention from their dad. While he rarely raised his voice and almost never hit them, Joseph Jr. seemed strict and stern to his sons. He always held himself slightly apart. Throughout their childhood, the boys longed for more contact with him. He invited students over for special tutoring sessions but seemed unable to connect emotionally with his sons. Joe later speculated that his father was simply a shy man. "I never saw much affection between my dad and mother," he said sadly. "My dad was just not one who could show his affection."

Joe, an academic achiever, brought home A's and B's, but Bob either could not or would not compete. From the start, Bob brought home a disappointing pile of report cards. Fatherly pep talks did little good; Bob continued, year after year, to earn mediocre grades. His older brother watched in silence, believing that Bob was bright enough but had chosen a course of laziness at school.

Bob displayed laziness at home, too, and battled his father over every little chore. While Joe, eager to please, automatically performed tasks assigned to him, Bob had to be told again and again. Even then he'd balk.

The two older boys fell into roles: Joe the obedient, dutiful son, Bob the stubborn boat-rocker. As if his nature required it, Bob dug in and refused when anyone ordered him to do anything. Their mother's sister, nicknamed Bets, came from Chincoteague to live with them during the early war years. She and Bob often sparred, and one minor fight stuck in Joe's mind. It began when Bets ordered her nephew to pick up a pile of trash that had spilled outside on the ground beside their garbage pail. With a defiant edge to his voice, Bob refused.

Bets insisted, saying, "You're going to pick it up!"

"No I'm not!" Bob boomed.

"You are!" Bets shrieked.

"No!"

"Yes!"

Nobody was going to push Bob Swartz around, even at the tender age of ten.

In 1944, Gladys took the boys to Miami, where the navy had stationed her husband ashore. When her father died a few months later, however, she and the boys went north to Chincoteague and stayed there with her mother for the next fifteen months.

The family reunited in Clairton in 1945, then moved 120 miles north to Erie, where Joseph Jr. went to work for the Veterans Administration.

In high school in Erie, Bob took a sudden, almost obsessive interest in biology. He displayed a knack for absorbing incredible amounts of minutiae about microorganisms, and loved to show off his newly acquired knowledge. His family for the first time noticed that he possessed an extraordinary memory. Like a child learning his native language, Bob retained and rolled off his tongue the long weird names that other students took one look at and forgot.

Mindful of his German name and ancestry, Bob impressed his

family again by spending hours seated at a desk, studying German and teaching himself the painstaking art of writing in florid German script. If he decided he wanted to do something, very little could deter him; his willpower hardened like cement to whatever purpose he chose. That unswerving will often worked to his advantage, enabling him throughout his life to accomplish things that other people might not even try. Unfortunately, the same trait had a dark underside, one that would turn tragically and violently against him.

As the boys matured in adolescence, Bob displayed a fondness for debate, which his father shared, but which young Joe detested. Joseph Jr., a Republican, often discussed the issues of the day—from Red China to the hydrogen bomb—over dinner with his sons. When the conversation exploded into arguments between Bob and his father, Joe would shrink from the talk. "For some reason I figured out you don't gain anything by just throwing words back and forth," Joe explained. "So I did the opposite thing: I just shut up. And a lot of times, you know, Bob would sort of lord it over me because he knew something that I didn't, and I just, you know, ignored it."

Throughout high school, Bob had little trouble making male friends, yet he displayed faint interest in the opposite sex. He saw only one girl regularly. She sang with him at the United Brethren Church in Erie, where Mrs. Swartz took the boys because it was the closest Protestant church. On their own initiative, Bob and Joe formed a mixed quartet with two girls and sang anthems in church on Sunday. Bob liked Nancy Zimmer, a plain, quiet girl who sang in the quartet. He usually asked her out whenever he and Joe double-dated. Their relationship was casual, and Nancy penned only a few brief lines in Bob's senior yearbook, concluding, "Keep up the good work! From a modest friend."

After his graduation in 1950, Bob enrolled at Youngstown University in Ohio, where his dad had become an associate professor and where Joe was completing his freshman year. The family moved across the border to Ohio, halfway between Erie and Pittsburgh. Taking the family's slate-blue '39 Ford every morning, Bob and Joe drove to classes together for two years.

By now, Joe knew what he wanted to be: an engineer. Despite

his father's insistent prodding toward a teaching career, he plodded straight through college and became a mechanical engineer.

Unlike Joe, Bob seemed undecided about his future; yet he followed his brother and took engineering courses at Youngstown University. While he spoke of becoming an engineer, he also spoke of becoming a preacher. That surprised his family; he had never been very devout. Bob earned abysmal grades in his engineering courses and dropped out of college after only two years. Then, instead of becoming a preacher, he joined the navy, as his father had done a decade before.

After studying electronics for nine months, Bob was dispatched to turbulent French Morocco to help maintain electronic equipment at the naval base in Port Lyautey. Since he had seen little of the world, Bob spent his leaves traveling. During his two years there, he frequently sent letters and photographs home. One summer, he returned home accompanied by a young Frenchman, handsome and blond, whom he had befriended and wanted to show around the States. Bob earned four promotions during his enlistment and a perfect 4.0 conduct rating. Although the navy wanted him to reenlist, he declined. In May 1956, he went home and struck out on his own.

For the next decade, Bob's career ran a zigzag course as he darted in and out of school, in and out of jobs, trying to figure out what to do with his life. At various points during the fifties and sixties, Bob managed a laundromat in Milwaukee with a partner, taught manpower training courses in Youngstown, and did radar maintenance for a defense contractor in the Arctic Circle.

The latter was by far his most adventurous job. When the North American Air Defense Command began operations in Colorado Springs in 1957, one of its projects was the erection of a massive radar system around the North Pole. It was called the Distant Early Warning line. The ring embraced thirty-one radar outposts from Alaska to Greenland and soon became America's northernmost "trip wire" to warn of bomber attacks. Based on Bob's navy electronics training, a contractor hired him to help maintain the electronic listening equipment. First, he underwent survival training in the midwest, then he flew to Canada's

Northwest Territories for an eighteen-month assignment. He was stationed on Baffin Island, a thousand-mile stretch of ice-coated rocks north of the Hudson Bay. Because few qualified technicians were willing to work in the frigid air and social isolation of the Arctic, Bob drew extraordinary pay—three times what his brother was earning with his college degree.

For that reason, after Bob went home, his company pestered him with letters and telegrams until he agreed to sign up for another eighteen months. This time, he went to Point Barrow, as far north as you can go in Alaska. For the rest of his life, Bob would enjoy recounting to friends how he swam like a polar bear in the icy Arctic Ocean.

Between his Arctic wanderings, he took courses for three years at the Milwaukee School of Engineering, but he quit in the summer of 1961 without earning a degree. A few years later, his father, now a full professor and dean at Youngstown, persuaded him to return home. Dutifully, Bob transferred his credits back to the college where he had started and changed his major from engineering to education. Finally, in 1967—seventeen years after he had started college—Bob earned a bachelor's degree.

Still uncertain what he wanted to do but certain that he didn't want to do it at home, Bob moved into the waterfront vacation cottage that his father had purchased outside Cambridge on Maryland's Eastern Shore. In the fall, figuring he would become a career educator like his dad after all, Bob moved to College Park and enrolled at the University of Maryland.

3.

When he finally decided to marry, Bob chose someone whose path in life had been somewhat more conventional than his own.

His bride-to-be was one of those brainy girls destined to be a high school valedictorian, who then plows straight through college. She had none of Bob's North African adventures or his tales of the Arctic. Her early childhood in Iowa had been so boring and isolated that she defended her sanity by burying herself in books.

Kate was the fourth and youngest child born to Leonard and Teresa Sullivan, who were working a farm in Iowa when they had Katie in July 1940. With sisters seven and nine years older and a brother ten years older, Kate had a hard time finding playmates on the farm. She learned to read and lost herself in books at an early age. In elementary school, after her family moved from the farm into town, Kate would go home from school and plop on a chair to read. Hours later, someone would wander in and turn on a light. She became so engrossed in her novels that she never noticed when the sun went down. By the time she left high school, Kate had devoured hundreds of novels. She proclaimed her all-time favorite to be *The Grapes of Wrath,* Steinbeck's sentimental tale of sharecroppers displaced from the Dust Bowl.

The choice was natural, considering that Kate's relatives were poor tenant farmers descended from Irish immigrants. Although both her maternal grandparents came directly from Ireland, Kate's parents were born and reared in Iowa. After they married, her mother taught school briefly, then stayed home while her husband tried to squeeze a living out of an eighty-acre farm in Dunlap, Iowa, a small agricultural community sixty miles northeast of Omaha.

Shortly before Kate was born, her parents moved to a 280-acre farm outside Dunlap. All the Sullivan children would retain fond memories of that farm. Although the family was poor and lived in a house with no indoor plumbing, electricity, or telephone, they raised their own food and the children had fun. Dad was hard-working and quiet. Mom was more outgoing, but just as easygoing and soft on the kids. Neither parent disciplined the kids or laid down ground rules. The children, especially Gerald, loved to tease Kate, who was too young for most farm chores. Gerald often pulled his baby sister uphill in her carriage, then let her go crashing down by herself.

Once, when Kate was five, Gerald tickled her mercilessly in the car where her parents had left the children while they called at a sick relative's house. That same night, the Sullivans rushed their youngest child to a hospital, and Kate underwent emergency surgery for an intestinal obstruction. When Kate came home a few days later, she told her brother, "You can't tickle me anymore!"

Although her brother knew his tickling hadn't caused her bowel obstruction, he never dreamed how fateful that childhood operation would turn out to be.

When Kate was seven, Leonard Sullivan gave up farming and moved his family into town. He bought a restaurant in the old stucco bank building on Highway 30, the main road through Dunlap, renamed the place Sullivan's Café, and made it a twenty-four hour operation to serve truckers rumbling through town on their way to and from Omaha. Working the night shift, Leonard went to bed at six every morning in the modest living quarters above the restaurant. All four kids pitched in and worked after school behind the horseshoe-shaped counter downstairs. On Christmas Day, when a town ordinance closed all of Dunlap, the Sullivans left their back door open and let it be known that anyone who had nowhere to eat could get a holiday meal at their café.

Like her older siblings, Kate attended St. Joseph's, a small Catholic school that lumped elementary and high school students under one roof. She earned perfect grades straight through school and stood number one in her graduating class. Not only did Kate have a knack for languages, turning out impressive papers and learning Spanish with ease, she also displayed artistic leanings. She and her mother painted watercolors of parrots and bullfighters and hung their work on the café's walls. Kate never developed her talent as a painter, though, and years later her husband would poke fun at her artwork.

When she finished high school in 1958, Kate moved clear across Iowa to Davenport to attend Marycrest College, a tiny women's teaching school run by a progressive order of nuns. Her classmates loved Kate and gave her a new nickname: Kitty. She threw herself into the newspaper and yearbook, the spiritual council and the Spanish club. She debated metaphysics with the nuns and took her studies seriously, even though she procrastinated on assignments.

"I always marveled because the night before a major paper was due, she would get out all her source material and then at the last minute bang out a final draft of her paper," recalled her friend Sally. "She would sit there with the typewriter, making her final copy directly from the books, with footnotes, the whole thing. Absolutely no draft. And get A's on it. And that was talent."

Kate partied, too. Although there was a small Catholic men's school nearby, neither she nor her friends dated much. They tended to run in gangs. One member of her group was Sally Hayes, whom she would eventually rejoin at the University of Maryland. Sally recalled that although Kate never drank much, she could be wild at parties. Without prompting, Kate would do the Irish jig or jump up on a table and go into a Mexican hat dance. "She just thoroughly enjoyed life," said Sally. "She never really cared what other people thought about her."

In 1962, Kate left Marycrest with a degree and began teaching high school in Davenport, where her parents had moved while she was in college.

Kate spent her first two summer breaks as a teacher living outside Mexico City. She served as a lay apostolate with a Catholic order, helping poor women learn the basics of sanitary living. By the end of her second summer, Kate spoke fluent Spanish.

Soon she moved to the suburbs of Denver, Colorado, to teach high school Spanish. She rented a small apartment on a ranch at the foot of the Rockies and welcomed visits from her nieces and nephews, most of whom had never seen the west. She drove an aging Volkswagen on which she never bothered to have maintenance work done. When the starter broke, she parked on hills so she could get a rolling start. If she couldn't find a hill, she left the engine running while she popped into stores on quick errands.

After several years in Denver, Kate decided she wanted to live on the East Coast and applied to graduate school at the University of Maryland.

A few days after she arrived there, Kate bumped into Sally on an elevator as they headed up to an orientation meeting for graduate residents.

"Kitty!" Sally blared.

"No," Kate said, smiling. "I'm Kate now, or Katie."

Sally had just arrived from St. Louis and hadn't seen her friend since college. Soon they were partying together again, taking the bus up to New York City and cramming in three or four Broadway shows in one weekend. Back at school, Kate occasionally stood in the bushes under Sally's dorm window and hollered, "Sally, 'ya wanna play volleyball?" At one-thirty in the morning, Sally knew what she meant: She'd slip out to meet her at a local pub.

Once Kate roped Sally and two other girls into crashing an upscale party at an exclusive hotel in downtown Washington. Since all but Sally spoke fluent Spanish, the girls waltzed in pretending to be foreigners. Kate instructed Sally to keep her mouth shut, which of course she did. Sally was thankful to get out that night without Kate jumping on a tabletop and doing her Mexican hat dance.

That was Kate Sullivan: having a grand time; playfully pulling the wool over other people's eyes; doing everything with panache. Years later, her brother, Gerald, to whom she stayed close even though he was a decade older, described his little sister this way: "She was one of those persons you'd notice the moment she'd walk in the room. She had a flair about her that would draw your attention. She didn't just step into your room, she'd come in twisting and turning. She probably would have been a good saleslady."

4.

For their wedding, Bob and Kate picked a Roman Catholic church in Bowie, fifteen minutes from Bob's apartment. While Kate was from a devout Catholic family, Bob and his relatives were Protestants. Yet Kate had introduced Bob to the ritualistic world of Catholicism and it was love at first sight. Sometimes Bob acted as though Kate had pushed him into converting. Once he asked Sally whether she was going to make her fiancé join the Catholic church, and Sally replied that she'd never force anyone to convert. "I know how important it is to Kate for me to become a Catholic," Bob said, "so I'm going to become a Catholic for her."

Truthfully, though, Bob joined the Church as much for himself as for Kate Sullivan. There was a void in his life, he later told friends, which he had long felt powerless to fill. Although he'd never really come close to becoming a preacher, he had flirted with the idea. He had flirted with doing lots of things, and had done lots of things, but he had yet to establish himself in a career, or to marry and have children. He had earned his undergraduate degree only two years earlier, after bouncing in and out of school for nearly two decades. Bob felt he was headed nowhere, accomplishing little more than spinning the wheels of his new motorcycle. He had squandered much of the emotional energy of his youth rebelling against his father over inconsequential things. He felt his life was vain, devoid of all meaning at the time he met Kate.

Kate and the Roman Catholic Church soon changed that.

Starting in January 1970, Bob drove one night a week into Baltimore to take religious instruction at the Catholic Information Center. He spent two hours a week listening to Father James F. McCabe, a Paulist priest, explore the mysteries of the church. McCabe later described Bob as a quiet student who attended class more faithfully than most. On May 23, a month before his wedding, Bob made his profession of faith and was received into the Church at the cathedral in Baltimore.

June 20 was a beautiful Saturday, clear and unusually hot. Forty or so wedding guests climbed the hill halfway between Washington and Annapolis and filed into the Sacred Heart Chapel, a frame building built by the Jesuits as a mission house in the eighteenth century.

Kate and Bob's relatives had flown in from the Midwest the night before and met one another for the first time at the rehearsal dinner. The bride and groom were so elated that both families shared their exuberance. All of Kate's relatives attended except her father, who had died the previous year, and Gerald, who was selling appliances for Sears Roebuck and didn't feel he could leave with air-conditioning season just getting under way.

To share special time on that special weekend, Kate and Bob

singled out two of their younger relatives. Since all three of Kate's siblings had married and had children, she had a legion of nieces and nephews. By contrast, Bob had only one of each— Joe's children, for his youngest brother hadn't married. Therefore, the bride and groom singled out Joe's children and invited them to share their rooms the night before their wedding. Kate took fifteen-year-old Barbara Swartz into her room at the Holiday Inn and Bob took Barbara's thirteen-year-old brother, Jeffrey, back to his small apartment in Beltsville. Both children were thrilled to be the chosen ones.

To marry them, Kate and Bob chose the University of Maryland's chaplain, Father William Kane, a dynamic young priest who knew Kate from her faithful attendance at campus mass. Kate wore a white lace top over a street-length white satin skirt that she had made herself. Sally wore a short yellow dress, which looked striking with her platinum-blond hair. At the end of the nuptial mass, Kate and Bob surprised their Protestant guests by turning to their wedding party, proclaiming "Peace be with you," and warmly embracing the people at the end of each pew as they retreated slowly and joyfully down the chapel's lone aisle.

After a reception in a shopping-center restaurant, the bride and groom climbed into Bob's soaped-up red car—HELP scrawled across the windshield and SCHWARTZ misspelled on the doors—and drove away with beer cans swinging from the bumpers, yellow streamers trailing in the wind.

5.

Shortly after their honeymoon, Bob and Kate started talking about moving. They had floated around, living out of boxes and suitcases for most of their adult lives. Now they wanted children and a home. They wanted a community that offered more peace and quiet than the Washington suburbs. They also wanted a house near the water. Bob had been spoiled by his father's cottage on the Choptank River. After exploring the river in his dad's speedboat, Bob had bought a sailboat and taught himself to sail on Chesapeake Bay. He and Kate agreed it would be impractical to move all the way to the Eastern Shore, for Bob worked at the Goddard Space Flight Center in Greenbelt. The commute would be too long. Still, they wanted to be close to the bay, so they began exploring Anne Arundel County on the bay's western banks. The county boasted seven rivers, an incredible 430 miles of shoreline, and the charming colonial town of Annapolis, which was undergoing an historical facelift and earning a reputation as a quaint little Georgetown on the Bay. Its sailing and tourism industries booming, Annapolis was becoming a playground for wealthy Washingtonians who were buying waterfront homes and commuting to work.

Kate quit her teaching job in New Jersey and applied for positions in Maryland. She soon found one at a business school in Annapolis, instructing high school students how to use computers. It was not exactly what she wanted, but she was confident that the local high schools would need an English teacher sooner or later.

Shortly before Christmas, Kate found a house just north of Annapolis in Cape St. Claire, a sprawling community of nearly two thousand homes on the Broadneck Peninsula. The peninsula jutted into the bay between the Magothy and Severn rivers, and seemed an ideal location, only thirty miles east of Washington and twenty-two miles south of Baltimore. The Cape sat on the north side of the peninsula, fronting not only on the wide Magothy but also on two smaller bodies of water that flowed into it: Deep Creek and the Little Magothy. In 1929, the land between those rivers had been targeted for development as an exclusive large-lot subdivision. However, that plan, as so many others had, fell victim to the Great Depression, and the Cape sat idle until a developer chopped it into modest parcels in 1949. During the fifties and sixties, homes of all kinds popped up, from beige stucco ranchers to white Cape Cods. Although many of the homes bordered the water, most sat inland, partitioned by a dizzying maze of streets named after saints. In the 1950s, the Cape became a popular summer resort. But by the 1960s, more and more people were building year-round residences and the Cape turned into a full-time residential community.

The house Kate found seemed as ideal as its location. Bob loved it, and when Kate took Sally to see it, Sally liked it, too. The three-bedroom house was only five years old and in a lovely wooded neighborhood bounded by four short streets that formed a rectangle. The Swartzes bought the house from a mailman for $29,900 and moved in during February 1971.

Now, more than ever, Bob and Kate wanted children. How could their home ever be cheery without them? Their first summer on the Cape, they invited their nephews to fly out from the midwest for a visit, and the next summer they invited their nieces. The children watched the Orioles at Memorial Stadium, went sightseeing in the nation's capital, sailed the Chesapeake Bay with Uncle Bob, and took home crabs for backyard feasts. "They treated us royally for a week," one nephew later recalled.

Bob and Kate spent long evenings talking about God and what He wanted from them. They both worried about the political climate that seemed to pervade the country: long-haired hippies marching against their own government, and women, many of them unmarried, freely taking the Pill and marching for "equal rights." Bob and Kate hoped Congress would show enough sense to reject the Equal Rights Amendment. They thought it degraded the very role that fulfilled women and made them special: motherhood. Undoubtedly, the ERA would wind up as a defense for such abominable practices as abortion.

Bob and Kate planned to make an example of their own lives, raising their family as a beacon against the spreading darkness of moral decay. They would soak their children in love, wrap them in the spirit of Christ, and send them forth into the world as living models of goodness.

Their family didn't turn out exactly as they had planned.

Kate's doctor delivered the first blow: In all probability, Kate would be unable to conceive children. Her fallopian tubes were damaged, and the doctor doubted they could be repaired. Apparently, her tubes had ruptured when she underwent the emergency bowel surgery at the age of five.

Disappointed, Bob and Kate refused to be deterred: They wanted children, and would have them. Even before the wedding, before they learned about Kate's problem, they had discussed the possibility of adoption. There were so many homeless children in the world, children who needed love as urgently and keenly as Bob and Kate wanted to give it—children born into this world unwanted; children who had been abused; children whose parents were ill or had been killed. "She thought probably it was God's calling for her not to have children, that she should take on some of the homeless children of the world," Kate's brother recalled.

When they contacted several adoption agencies, the Swartzes learned that the waiting period for infants could be months, even years. Most couples wanted infants, and there was an unbelievable waiting list for newborns. Most prospective parents did not want children over age two. Still fewer couples wanted to adopt children older than five or six. As children grow older, it becomes proportionately harder to bond, both for the parent and for the child. By the age of six or seven, many children have been in and out of several foster homes, their psyches scarred by the trauma of each move. Stung by rejection and neglect, most of these children are deeply troubled, even if they don't show it. Professionals agree that it takes extraordinary parents, more loving and giving than most, to adopt older children.

The Swartzes, of course, were extraordinary people. Everyone who knew them believed that. *They* believed it. Bob and Kate agreed that God wanted them to adopt older children, the kind who needed them most. After all, the Swartzes were older than many prospective parents. When they married, Bob had been a week shy of thirty-eight and Kate just under thirty. They were teachers, with patience and special skills that would enable them to help older children make up for what they had missed.

Bob and Kate filled out adoption applications and agreed to accept older children of any age, any ethnic background, either sex. They filled out questionnaires, sat through interviews, opened their home to social workers. One worker who interviewed the Swartzes described them as a "warm, outgoing" and "mature, sensitive" couple who "seem to have a secure and wholesome marriage." They appeared "highly motivated to adopt" and were interested in taking an older child.

What the Swartzes wanted most was a ready-made family, a group of brothers and sisters. In May 1973, they were thrilled to learn from the Maryland Children's Aid and Family Service Society that a family of four brothers was being offered for adoption. Eagerly, the Swartzes planned where each boy would sleep. Bob told his family he was making up for lost time. Why, he would have twice as many kids as his brother Joe.

But on the evening of June 7, a social worker called with bad news. "After talking it over," the worker told Bob, "we've had second thoughts about the brothers. We think four children might be too much for you. Your marriage is only going on three years, you know. We're not sure you're ready to take so many kids all at once. I'm sorry."

Although Bob sounded upset, all he said was, "Kate will be very disappointed."

The worker already had another child in mind for the Swartzes, a slender six-year-old in urgent need of a new home. The agency wanted to remove the boy from his foster home as soon as school let out the following week. But, sensing Bob's frustration, the worker kept quiet.

The next afternoon, the worker phoned Kate, who had been out the previous night, and gently explained why the Swartzes couldn't have the four brothers. "We do have a boy who really needs a home," the worker said. "His name is Larry and I met him yesterday. I liked him a lot. He's small and dark-skinned and very good-looking. He'll be seven in August. We've got to find him a new home as soon as we can."

"Where is he now?" Kate asked.

"With a family that was going to adopt him, but it just didn't work out. It wasn't his fault. They had their own biological children; I don't think they were able to accept an adopted child. It's been hard on the boy. He knows he's not wanted, and he's asked us to find new parents for him."

"Is he in school?"

"First grade, but he's being held back. He couldn't concentrate. His teacher said he comes to school upset a lot. He does things like eat other kids' lunches in the cafeteria. The boy's adorable, though. We think all he needs is a massive dose of love and attention."

"When can we see him?"

The worker was pleased; Kate sounded genuinely excited.

"Why don't you and your husband come up to the Baltimore office next Friday?" He said the agency would have custody of Larry for the weekend, and suggested that she and her husband take him home for a tryout. "If it works out, you could take him home for good the next weekend."

After Kate told Bob, they talked of nothing else all week.

Finally, they would have a child.

THREE

January 17, 1984

1.

Riding to the police station in the rear seat of a police cruiser, Larry Swartz let his head droop. Officer Randy Derrossett, watching in his rearview mirror, saw the boy shut his eyes, then take a deep breath. Suddenly, Derrossett got a whiff of booze. Could the boy have been drinking? he wondered.

Perking up, Larry inquired where they were going. The police investigative offices, Derrossett replied, located on the grounds of the state hospital in Crownsville. The police station and the hospital were side by side. Glancing again in his mirror, Derrossett noticed that Larry looked agitated, as though this piece of news disturbed him.

The man in charge at the station was Lieutenant William Donoho, a twenty-year cop who had headed the criminal investigative division for the last three years. Donoho had visited the Swartz house that morning to see everything firsthand and had talked to Mock immediately after the detectives questioned Larry and Annie. Right off, Mock had told Donoho he suspected the boy was lying. As his colleagues often said, Mock's nose was twitching.

"You think he did it?" asked Donoho, startled.

"Either he did it," replied Mock, "or he was there."

"What makes you think that?"

"He's way too calm. All he's telling us about is his crazed brother at Crownsville. He wants us to think it was his brother. Something's not right."

While Mock and the rest of the homicide team stayed to search the house, Donoho decided that Larry and Annie should give formal witness statements at the station. Donoho would supervise that himself. Over the next couple of hours, the lieutenant repeatedly conferred with his investigators by telephone, quibbling over how the statements should be taken.

Neither Mock nor Barr felt comfortable with Larry's story, especially his heavy finger-pointing at Michael, but they could not spare the time to interrogate the children in depth. They would do that later, armed with evidence from the scene. "Don't let anybody pressure the kid or question him. Just take his statement," Barr told the lieutenant. "The kid will get spooked if anybody starts reading him his rights."

On orders from Donoho, Detective Roland Mitchell took Larry into a private office to get his witness statement. The questioning began at 11:13 A.M. and lasted a little more than an hour.

Mitchell sat behind a typewriter and recorded Larry's answers to his questions. Larry told the cop he'd taken no drugs or alcohol in the last twenty-four hours and that no one had visited or phoned his house the night before. Asked what had happened, Larry repeated his version of Monday afternoon's events and said he had returned home at five and studied until he went to bed around nine o'clock. Just before he went to bed, he went downstairs to put his laundry in the washer and noticed that his mother was watching TV in the family room.

Later he awoke to hear Annie walking around, and went to join her. When Annie said she'd heard a scream, Larry told her she could sleep with him, and she did. "I was tired," Larry said, "and usually if she gets scared, I let her sleep with me."

In the morning, he added, when he looked over the railing on the carport to see whether the dogs were in their pen, he saw his mother and immediately phoned the police.

"The night before," the cop asked, "when Annie came out and was talking to you, did you come out of your room, and did she come into your room?"

"I came out and into the kitchen. She was outside the kitchen door, standing on the porch. Just standing out there, I guess."

"What was she saying or doing that had awoken you?"

"I don't know. I just woke up. I don't know what woke me up. I told her then to come in and go to bed and sleep with me."

"Did you look around to see what made her go outside?"

"Not really. She usually gets up and goes to the bathroom a lot."

"Why didn't you check about your dad after you saw your mom?"

"Once I saw her, I was just too afraid to look."

"Did you ever go down and see where your dad was?"

"No."

"Do you know what happened to your dad?"

"Nobody has told me anything about my dad."

"Has anyone been mad or angry at your parents, either family or neighbors?"

"Not that I know of."

"You have another brother. Who is he and where is he at?"

"He is Michael Swartz, age seventeen years. He's in the Crownsville institution."

"Were your parents concerned about him, or having problems with him?"

"They weren't really concerned with him. They were . . . well, not really concerned with him."

A few minutes later, the detective asked him again, "Do you know of anybody who might want to hurt your mother or your father?"

"No," Larry replied. "Not that I know of, except for my brother."

Mitchell didn't follow up that comment. Instead he asked, "How is your relationship with your parents and your sister?"

"I guess average, you could say. Nothing serious."

"How were your mom and dad getting along?"

"They were doing all right. They would argue, but nothing really serious."

"Is this statement the truth as you have told it?"

"Yes."

"Can you think of anything that you may know that may help us to locate the person who assaulted your mother?"

"I have no idea."

The detective finished typing the statement and asked Larry to read and sign all five pages, top and bottom. Larry signed his name all over the document in a childish scrawl.

While one detective questioned Larry, a female detective questioned his sister and typed up her responses in a separate room. The female detective began by asking Annie to relate everything she'd seen and heard the previous night.

When she had gone to bed at eight, Annie recalled, her brother had been studying in his room and her parents were "playing" with the computer downstairs.

"I woke up at about eleven or eleven-thirty when I heard my father screaming 'Help! Help!' I knew what time it was because I had looked at my watch. It sounded like he was outside. I left my bedroom and I ran downstairs and I saw the sliding glass door in the family room was wide open. I saw my father laying in the snow on his back. I ran back upstairs because I was frightened, and I tripped on the step. I'll show you my knee where I hurt myself."

Then Annie repeated her earlier story: She went out to the carport and saw a man leaving her yard, walking down the steps outside the fence and carrying a bloody shovel.

"Anne, would you describe the man for me?"

Reiterating what she'd told Mock and Barr, she added a few details about his hair and face: "He was pretty tall and skinny. His hair was black and straight and shoulder-length. His hair looked clean, but it looked funny because just one part on the top was curled. I think he might have had a beard-face."

"Did you know this man, or had you ever seen him before?"

"It looked like my brother Michael, who doesn't live with us."

"Do you know for sure if it was Michael?"

"No, because I only saw him from the side, and he was walking away from me."

"Did this man with the shovel see you?"

"No."

"What did you do after you saw the man leave?"

"My brother Larry called me in. He was in the kitchen. My brother told me to just go back to bed. I told him that I saw Daddy's body, and he told me that I was just dreaming. I went up and laid down on the bed and I heard Larry go back in his bedroom. Then I heard him throw up, so I went in his bedroom and I saw all this saliva coming out. I told him that he was throwing up. And he told me that I was just dreaming again. Then I asked him where my mother was and he said, 'I don't know.' He told me to just go back to bed. I guess it was three or three-thirty in the morning before I went back to sleep."

"When you heard your father screaming for help, did you hear any other voices?"

"No."

"Do you know of anyone who would want to hurt your mom and dad."

"Probably Michael, my oldest brother." Both boys were seventeen, but Michael was six months older.

"Why would Michael want to hurt your mom and dad?"

"My mom and dad adopted me when I was three, and I guess Michael was sixteen or so," said Annie, with a nine year old's distorted sense of time. "He used to drop me on my head. He stole stuff from other people and us. My parents said they couldn't handle Michael. Michael used drugs. He has been gone since I was six, but I don't know where he stays."

"Did you ever see Michael hurt any member of your family or anyone else?"

"No."

"When you saw something outside in the snow, are your sure it was your dad?"

"It was my father with his clothes off."

"Do you know why your brother Larry vomited? Had he been sick?"

"No. He had been sick a long time ago."

"Did you get frightened and go into your brother Larry's bedroom?"

"I don't know when, but I did go into my brother's room and slept in his bean-bag chair. I had forgotten about that."

"Is this statement the truth as you have told it?"

"Yep."

"Do you want to add or change anything you have told me?"

"I didn't hear a car, and there are paths in the woods behind my house that lead to the school, Broadneck High School. I could see the man walking out from the yard because the carport light was on."

"Is there anything else?"

"No."

The little girl scrawled her name, Anne Lee Swartz, at the end of the three-page statement after the detective pulled the third page out of the typewriter. Following the detective's instructions, Annie carefully scrawled her initials on the bottom of each page.

Shortly after they questioned Larry and Annie separately, the two detectives went into the lieutenant's office to compare their statements. It was immediately obvious that Annie had volunteered more about the night's events than Larry. He claimed he couldn't even remember what had awakened him, and he conveniently forgot to mention that he threw up. He said nothing about Annie seeing a body, or a man leaving their yard.

"I think you'd better talk to Larry again," Donoho said.

After the detectives took Larry back into the interrogation room, Mock—who was still at the murder scene—called Donoho. Mock and Barr were growing increasingly skittish about leaving the children at the station while they searched the house. Mock thought he stood an excellent chance of getting a confession from Larry if nobody scared the boy into silence before he got there. "I don't want anybody talking to him," Mock told Donoho.

"Somebody's already talking to him," the lieutenant replied.

On instructions from Donoho, Detective Roland Mitchell was solemnly informing Larry that he had the right to remain silent, that anything he said could and would be used against him in a court of law. He had the right to talk to a lawyer, and even if he chose to talk to police without one, the questioning would stop as soon as he requested one.

Larry initialed a form stating that he agreed to talk without a lawyer, then suddenly announced that he had forgotten to mention something earlier: He had thrown up in the bathroom the night before.

"Anything else different in your statement?" Mitchell asked.

"Not that I know of."

Mitchell led Larry back through his statement and Annie's, and Larry insisted he didn't remember Annie mentioning that she saw her father's body in the snow. He remembered her mentioning a man walking back to the woods, but she had said that to the police that morning, not to him the previous night.

"Anybody by this description?" asked Mitchell, reading aloud the description from Annie's statement.

"Only Michael," Larry replied. "But I don't see how he could have been there since he is here in Crownsville."

"Any neighbors look like this, or any of your friends?"

"No."

"Do you know kids at Broadneck?" Mitchell mentioned the name of a student suspected in some burglaries. Larry said he knew the boy and gave a brief description of him.

Shortly after 1 P.M., Mrs. Smithmyer, who had accompanied Annie to the station, put her head in the door and asked whether she could have a word with Larry. He stepped into the hall, and a moment later, she returned and asked permission to take both children to lunch.

Aware that they lacked sufficient evidence to hold Larry, the detectives assented.

2.

For several hours after they arrived at the Swartz house, detectives Mock and Barr both operated under the assumption that they had the case. Both were on it, but only Barr had the lead. The county's four homicide men worked in pairs and usually rotated the lead. Their boss assigned this case to Barr moments after he arrived and forgot to mention that fact to Mock. When

Barr set his partner straight, it proved to be no problem; Mock was an affable partner who enjoyed nosing around but hated the paperwork that fell to the lead man.

People who knew Mock and Barr thought they were as dissimilar as hot and cold showers. Brimming with energy, Mock came on warm and friendly. He could sit on a bar stool, puffing on a Benson & Hedges, and knock back half a dozen Seven and Sevens in no time. A more diffident man, Barr never smoked and almost never drank.

Some of their contrasts sprang from their different backgrounds. Mock grew up in Orchard Beach, a rough suburb south of Baltimore. He left school in the tenth grade to help his ailing father run a gas station. While some of his schoolmates carved careers inside the walls of the Maryland Penitentiary, Mock enlisted in the Marines, then came home and worked for a few years as a clerk and a fireman before joining the Anne Arundel County police force.

After twelve years in uniform, Mock was tapped for the plainclothes division, where he earned a reputation for tenacity, cunning, and imagination. In his most notorious display of trickery, Mock conned a young Catholic murderer into confessing by reminding him during interrogation that he was in mortal sin and would go straight to hell if anything happened to him before he had a chance to confess. When Mock suggested the boy make an act of contrition, the terrified youth said he had forgotten the words. Grateful that he'd been raised a Catholic, Mock provided the words and obtained a confession.

Unlike Mock, Barr had led an extraordinarily sheltered childhood. He traced his rigid self-control at least partly back to his early separation from his parents in Pennsylvania, a traumatic event that shaped his personality and altered the course of his life. Eventually, it would cause him to feel a powerful empathy for the Swartz children.

For reasons Barr never understood, his mother and his father, a career army officer, left him intermittently in the care of relatives in Pine Grove, Pennsylvania, when he was a child. At the age of five, Barr was forced to choose where he wanted to live: with his mother, who was going to join his father in North Carolina; or with his mother's uncle and aunt, who had kept him for long stretches in Pine Grove, a small town surrounded by mountains in eastern Pennsylvania. Barr would never forget his mother screaming at him in front of her brother's house: "Are you going or are you staying?" The choice was excruciating, but Barr felt most secure in his hometown, so he stayed in Pennsylvania with his great aunt and uncle.

His new "parents" had no children of their own and were well past forty when they adopted Barr. A disabled veteran who had lost both his legs during World War II, Barr's uncle spent nearly all his days at home. Both he and his wife, a garment-factory worker, severely disciplined Barr. They occasionally beat him with a belt and rarely let him leave his yard. Barr had no friends and few chances to make any.

He never forgot the clothes his parents gave him for school: baggy pants and bargain shirts that his adoptive mother made him wear for three days consecutively. Naturally, the other boys taunted him at school, and he got into a string of fights. He formed a chip on his shoulder that he would carry into adulthood. When he was seventeen and approaching six feet tall, he threatened to hit his crippled uncle one day, but he held himself back. He knew he'd be off to college within a year.

At his adoptive parents' urging, he went to Pennsylvania State University but quickly grew disaffected. Trying to break from his parents and prove that he could stand on his own, Barr enlisted in the Marine Corps. He spent most of his tour processing court-martials at Fort George G. Meade in Maryland, where he excelled in paperwork and spit-and-polish but made himself unpopular with some of his colleagues by snitching on a roommate for using marijuana.

Barr left the Marines in 1974 to join the Anne Arundel County police force. Displaying more ambition than his peers, he tied with another man for number one in his training academy class. Using veterans' benefits, he enrolled in college and obtained an associate degree, a bachelor's degree, and finally, to the wonderment of his peers, a master's degree in forensic science. He attended school and patrolled the streets all week, then scaled the Reserve ranks on weekends. In 1982, he attained the rank of captain. The old-time cops couldn't fathom his relentless drive, and many younger ones were jealous. One colleague summed him up this way: "I don't see too much comedy in Gary's life. In other words, he's old before his time."

In 1981, Barr wormed his way into homicide as an evidence technician. Two years later, when he was barely thirty, he won a promotion to investigator. By the time of the Swartz murders in January 1984, he and Mock had worked a few murders together as partners, but none were nearly as big as this one.

Largely due to public reaction, the Swartz murders would become the most publicized case the county's small homicide unit had handled in years. Over the next five days, the department's public-relations man would do thirty-nine interviews with television stations in Baltimore and Washington, most of them live.

At 9:30 A.M., more than an hour after Barr and Mock arrived at 1242 Mount Pleasant Drive, they entered the picture-window rancher accompanied by two supervisors and two evidence collectors. As the firemen had earlier, the cops found the mess appalling. The threadbare furnishings also took them by surprise. Although Cape St. Claire was a working-class neighborhood, these did not appear to be poor people. Larry had said both his parents worked, and the family had enough money to install a swimming pool in their backyard. Why, then, would they furnish their kitchen with a cheap redwood picnic table and benches, and their living room with shabby green armchairs?

Searching for clues, the caravan of cops moved slowly from room to room on the main floor. A parakeet peered out from its dining room cage. The beds in all three bedrooms were unmade and clothes were strewn across beds and floors. On the master bed, one pillow was missing its case. A few feet away, investigators noticed jewelry, a pile of silver coins, and Mrs. Swartz's purse lying in plain view on a dresser.

Barr thought it odd that amid all the rubble, virtually no family photos were on display. The only photo frame anyone saw was a small silver one beside the master bed.

Barr also thought it odd when he wandered back into the dining room and looked out the window that he couldn't see the body in the snow out back. Didn't Larry say he'd seen his mother's body through the dining room window? The detective decided to check the kitchen. He went in, pulled over a chair, and climbed up on the kitchen countertop; he leaned as far right as he could and raised his head as high as he could. No way could he see that body from the kitchen, either.

The legal documents dealing with Michael Swartz, which the investigators found near the front door, were puzzling, too. One announced a court hearing two days away on Michael's placement in the Crownsville Hospital. Reading them, Barr wondered who had put the papers there, and why. Had someone laid them out deliberately to cast suspicion on Michael? Barr didn't like the way they smacked him in the face when he walked in the door. "This is like a trail of crumbs," he told Mock. "I get the feeling these were put here for our benefit."

Some of the papers were on a table in the entrance foyer, stuffed inside an open manila envelope marked with Michael's name on it. They included documents pertaining to his placement in reform school and his arrest for breaking and entering, correspondence between his parents and their lawyer, and a couple of Michael's old school report cards. Other papers lay on a glass-topped end table in the living room, beside some book-shelves. Two papers there had just arrived from circuit court: a summons for Bob and Kay to appear at Michael's review hearing on Thursday and an order directing them to continue support payments for Michael.

Barr sensed that the scene was staged. Yet the evidence technician who collected the documents thought it appeared the result of a hurried rifling, perhaps by someone who was searching for a document in the chaotic-looking bookshelves. "Someone made a mess there," said the technician. "They pulled off papers and books, took mail and letters and strewed them around the floor, like they were looking for something."

Downstairs, the men entered the tiny study where Bob Swartz lay in a pool of blood. Scanning the study, the detectives instantly concluded that a violent struggle had occurred. Blood splatters covered the walls. A Commodore 64 computer, attached to a printer and a thirteen-inch television set, was a shambles. The computer was upside down, flipped by the cord to a gooseneck lamp that had fallen to the floor. A typing stand had tipped over beside the computer, dumping a pile of papers on the carpet. The detectives wondered if Bob Swartz had been working on his computer when his assailant surprised him.

The officers noticed dried blood—left by someone's bloody hand, no doubt—on the doorknobs leading into and out of the study. They dismantled both knobs and took them as evidence.

The man's head lay beneath an ironing board, in front of a weight-lifting bench. The detectives studied the bloodstains in his salt-and-pepper beard and the holes in his short-sleeved shirt. At first, it was hard to tell whether he'd been stabbed or shot, but closer inspection of the wounds revealed that he'd been stabbed at least a dozen times.

In his pants pocket was a wallet containing $150 in cash and several credit cards. Stuffed into his shirt pocket was a tiny New Testament inscribed, "From Mother, 1952." And under his shirt, a large silver crucifix with a sculpted Jesus welded to it dangled from a black cord.

None of the detectives had any theories on why the man's legs were spread-eagled. Obviously, if he'd been dragged—and it looked that way, judging by the bunching of the carpet at his feet—his legs would not be spread so unnaturally far apart. Someone must have pushed them apart.

The detectives began to sense that the killer or killers had been emotionally close to the victims. None of the detectives rejected the possibility of an outsider; they thought it quite possible that an intruder or intruders had slipped in downstairs, killed the couple, and fled. After viewing the grisly scene out back, however, they concluded that if it was an intruder, it had to be one who knew the Swartzes. The attacks seemed so savage, so full of overkill, that Barr and Mock believed they were acts of hatred, not the random work of a burglar. Nowhere in the house were there any signs of forced entry, ransacking, or theft.

Moving to the main basement room, the cops found a puzzling pattern of bloodstains. Two black vinyl chairs faced a television set near the stairway landing. One chair, a recliner, was heavily stained with blood. The blood had seeped under the cushions, forming a stain on the carpet more than a foot wide. Barr immediately suspected that the mother had been attacked in this chair. He noticed a pair of brown-rimmed eyeglasses lying upside down on the floor by the chair. The right lens of the glasses, which belonged to Mrs. Swartz, had popped out. A Schmidt's Light beer can lay on the floor, empty.

Barr inspected a coffee table across from the chairs. It held a nineteen-inch portable TV set, several crumpled candy wrappers, and a small bowl with a spoon in it. He wondered, Had Mrs. Swartz been sitting here, perhaps watching TV and eating from this bowl, when she was attacked?

Barr saw red streaks on the carpet across the room, directly in front of the sliding glass door. He immediately thought they were bloodstains made when someone dragged the mother from the chair over to the patio door. Oddly enough, there were no stains on the carpet between the chair and the door—a distance of fifteen feet. There were just four thin streaks, two feet long, in front of the door. How could someone have dragged the woman all the way across the room without leaving bloodstains anywhere else on the carpet?

The basement also housed a small laundry room behind the staircase, where the cops found a washing machine with clothes inside: a pair of Levi's blue jeans, gray sweat pants, and a gray T-shirt with BROADNECK & BRUINS printed in small burgundy letters across the front. The clothes were still wet and clinging to the perimeter, as though the spin cycle had just stopped. In the dryer, they found five additional items, all dry: three shirts, a pair of gray corduroy Levi's, and a burgundy T-shirt with BROAD-NECK printed in block letters across the front.

When they went outside to reexamine the female corpse, Barr cursed inwardly at whoever had placed the blanket over her, potentially contaminating fiber evidence—those revealing little threads that killers often leave behind.

An evidence technician carefully removed the blanket. In addition to a massive head wound, the woman's throat had multiple puncture wounds, several of them large, apparently from a knife or sharp object. The cops also noticed a short gnarled stick, curved like a boomerang, lying on the snow near her knees. It was bloodstained.

"Christ. You don't suppose somebody assaulted her with this stick?" asked Barr, instantly suspecting just that.

"Could be," replied Tankersley, who was starting to get a measure of the rage that lay behind these murders. The position of her legs particularly troubled him, reminding him of things he'd seen working sexual assaults. He thought it was bizarre to see both husband and wife spread-eagled.

Carefully, an evidence technician retrieved the woman's blue sleep suit from the snow. Barr and Mock walked over to examine it. It zipped up the front and was made of super-heavy flannel all the way down to padded footies. Blood coated the upper half, front and back, but there were only a few red smears from the waist down.

"See how the blood stops there?" Mock said, pointing at the waistline. "I bet she was sitting down when she got attacked."

Barr agreed. He found a green sock inside the left footie of her pajama suit, apparently the mate to the green sock that still clung to her right foot. One sock must have stayed on when her killer stripped her, while the other sock was pulled off with her pajamas. He observed bloodstains on the backs of both heels of the pajama suit, suggesting that someone had dragged her while she was still clothed.

Barr went back into the house to compare the heel stains with the blood streaks on the carpet in the family room. The streaks inside were too skinny; they didn't match the pattern on the pajamas. He guessed, then, that the heels of her pajamas became stained when the killer dragged her through the snow outside. Her body lay a distance of twelve feet from the large pool of blood in the snow. Obviously, someone had moved her after she bled in the snow.

Barr remained stumped, though, about the parallel streaks on the carpet inside.

An evidence technician looking for fingerprints made the most significant find of the day: a bloody smear on the sliding glass door frame. Extraordinarily distinct, it appeared to be a right palm print outlined in blood. It was on the inside white frame, inches above the door handle. Several other bloody smears were visible above and below it. A few were clearly fingerprints, although they were less distinct than the palm print. "This guy must have been covered in blood," said Barr. "Looks like he was in a hurry, frantic almost, and grabbed the door frame instead of the handle when he slid the door open."

The evidence technicians decided not to remove the door frame. Instead, they lifted the handprint by sprinkling it with powder, then lifted it with a tapelike adhesive. Once the print was transferred onto the adhesive, a technician pressed it down onto a white paper square.

Barr formulated his first theory, based on blood patterns and the position of the corpses. First, the killer could have stabbed Kay with a knife while she sat in the black chair watching TV. Then maybe the killer dragged her across the room, through the sliding glass door, and dumped her outside in the snow. Or perhaps before the killer took her outside, Bob—working in his little office—heard his wife screaming and opened the office door. Spinning around, the assailant could have plunged the knife into Bob's chest. The door to the study was only two or three body lengths from the black chair. After pushing Bob into the study and finishing him off, the killer might have returned to the family room and carted the mother's body outside.

Mock thought Barr's theory sounded plausible, but there were still chunks missing. Neither he nor Barr discounted the possibility of a domestic dispute. Barr's theory played just as well with the son Larry as the killer as it did with an intruder. Obviously, the Swartzes had been caught by surprise, and Mock wondered how an intruder could have entered the house undetected.

"This guy kills two people in two different rooms downstairs and doesn't wake the kids upstairs—don't you think that's fishy?" asked Mock.

Barr certainly did. Neither was it lost on Barr that the killer had gotten past the family's two dogs. The big rambunctious one had bitten a fireman that morning and almost gotten a hunk of Barr, too. What would that mutt have done if a stranger had broken in at night, wielding a knife?

3.

After they completed their search of the house, the cops fanned out in the backyard and inspected everything from the rabbit hutch to the footprints that were spreading through the snow, obliterating potential evidence.

A neighbor, Steven Speargas, arrived and announced, "I found some blood in the snow in front of my house."

Since he lived a block away, the cops eyed him skeptically. What could blood so far away have to do with the Swartzes? Yet, mindful that the murderer could have dropped blood while escaping, Barr, Mock, and Tankersley decided to see what Speargas had found. They went around front and began trudging over to Speargas's house when Mock, still cursing himself for having worn slippery new shoes, turned around and let the others go without him.

The red marks did appear to be blood. Several droplets were visible along Pine Hill Lane, the street that ran parallel to Mount Pleasant Drive. Near the droplets, Barr and Tankersley found footprints and pawprints in the soft two-inch snow blanket. They followed the trail of prints and blood, which led to the end of Pine Hill Lane, turned sharply right, and headed back toward Mount Pleasant Drive. A few doors down from the Swartzes', the trail veered off the street into a neighbor's yard and led back into the dense woods that ran behind the homes on Mount Pleasant Drive. The woods formed a barrier between the neighborhood and Broadneck High School. In the woods—a low swampy area full of sticker bushes and pine trees soaring seventy to eighty feet high—the tracks ran along a fairly narrow footpath. The snow was uneven and soggy along this path. Barr soon noticed what appeared to be two different sets of footprints, running in line with each other. As it neared the rear of the Swartz house, the footpath forked, and the tracks became difficult to follow. The path here was apparently well traveled; myriad tracks were visible in the day-old snow.

After wandering in the woods for fifteen minutes, the men abandoned their search and rejoined Mock in the Swartz backyard. Soon the detectives noticed more footprints to one side of the yard, along the steps outside the gate—where Annie had told them she'd seen a man walking last night. These footprints suggested that someone had walked up from the woods along the wooden steps parallel to the fence, and entered the backyard through the side gate. Again, there were two different sets of footprints.

Determined to find more clues, the detectives went back down into the marshy woods. At the top of a gentle embankment, Mock, unsteady on the soggy snow, stopped and looked down at a log spanning a stream covered by icy lacework. Suddenly, he lost his footing and slid down the embankment. Barr, standing at the bottom, chuckled as Mock, still in his three-piece suit, rolled over on his knees.

"Hey," Mock cried, pausing on all fours. "Look here. It's a bare foot in the snow."

Barr peered at where Mock was pointing. "Bare foot, my ass. It's your hand print from where you fell."

"Bullshit! My hand don't have a big toe on it, Gary."

Barr bent over for a closer look. Mock was right. An unmistakable outline of toes had been mashed into the snow. A left footprint. Not made by a shoe, but by a bare foot. It had left ridges, distinct toe outlines, across the top.

Barr and Mock stared at each other incredulously. Who would walk outside barefoot in January? And with snow on the ground?

"Hey," Barr suddenly cried. "That woman's got one bare foot. She's got a sock on the other." Barr paused, picturing the corpse and the sock he'd found stuck inside in the sleep suit. "Her left foot's bare."

Mock struggled to his feet and followed the bare left footprint a short distance, looking for the matching right print. He found it. Sure enough, its toes appeared less distinct than the bare print, yet more distinct than a shoe print. Had someone wearing one sock made this trail?

Mrs. Swartz?

A few minutes later, Tankersley found a wood-splitting maul deep in the woods, a hundred and fifty yards behind the Swartz house, lying in a pristine snowbank with no footprints around it. He summoned an evidence technician to photograph and retrieve it.

Gathering around, the detectives inspected the maul closely. It was a massive instrument, weighing about ten pounds and measuring nearly three feet long. A cross between an ax and a sledgehammer, the maul had a short blunt end and a longer sharper end for splitting logs. It had been wiped clean of fingerprints, but the cops saw dried blood and hair—three gossamer strands that the FBI later would match with hairs pulled from Kay Swartz's head—stuck to the dull metal blade. There was little doubt in the cops' minds that the killer had used this log-splitter on Mrs. Swartz's skull.

Barr and Mock spent the next few hours reexamining the tracks that wound along the streets and through the woods. They developed a new theory. They surmised that Kay's attacker stabbed her inside the house, injuring but not killing her. Then he took her outside and stripped her in the snow. Then— maybe after the subfreezing air revived her, or maybe after she broke away—he chased her around the neighborhood. At some point, he caught her in the woods, walked her back to the yard, and killed her with the maul.

It was a horrible theory, which neither detective found very credible. How does a naked injured woman run three-quarters of a mile through the snow, past ten or twelve houses, without someone hearing her scream? No one in the neighborhood had heard a peep, according to the detective who had canvassed the neighborhood. Adrenaline might have kept her going, the detectives surmised, while raw fear might have prevented her from screaming. The wounds in her neck also might have silenced her.

Barr and Mock believed the evidence supporting their theory was strong. They were convinced that one of the two sets of tracks along the trail belonged to Kay's assailant. These were shoe prints with a distinct rectangular marking in the middle of the sole. In many places along the trail, the detectives spotted tracks beside the shoe prints that appeared to be the same bare and stockinged feet that they had first noticed in the marsh. The bizarre trail of double tracks began in the woods across from the front of the Swartz house, cut through a neighbor's yard one street over, circled around the block, and finally cut through another neighbor's yard into the woods *behind* the Swartz house. It was the same trail Barr had followed earlier without realizing that some of the tracks were bare footprints. Now he ordered a police photographer to take pictures of the bare footprints. Unfortunately, the snow was too powdery to make a plaster cast of them.

In the woods behind the house, Barr and Mock discovered an area where the snow was disturbed, as though some sort of struggle had occurred. Blood droplets were scattered in the snow, and a chunk of bark had fallen or perhaps been scraped from a tree trunk.

At several points along the footpath, the detectives noticed the tracks were farther apart than at other points. In some places, they appeared to be skid marks, as if the people had been running and sliding in the snow. Closer to the house—near where the apparent struggle took place—the footprints became more distinct and closer together, as though the people were walking again. Those clues convinced the detectives that the assailant had chased Mrs. Swartz through the woods, caught and scuffled with her in the snow, and walked her back to the yard.

Along the footpath in the woods, the detectives retrieved a flimsy piece of white plastic emblazoned with a green and red Christmas holly design. The seven-inch square was ragged at the edges, as if it had been torn from something, and had big red smears in the middle. The smears appeared to be blood.

Returning to the backyard, the detectives reexamined the pool of blood near Kay's body. They saw scads of shoe prints, some quite distinct in the red mush. Soon they noticed three identical shoe prints, each with a tiny rectangular imprint in the middle and wavy horizontal lines above and below it. These prints strongly resembled the shoe prints in the woods.

When the detectives made another sweep of the recreation room, they noticed a pair of well-worn Docksides placed neatly side by side on the floor by the couch. The shoes were still damp and had mud caked in the seams. Although the soles looked as if they'd been wiped, the leather trim bore reddish stains. Inspecting the soles closely, Barr saw the same rectangular imprint and sea of choppy lines he'd seen in the bloody shoe prints outside.

You didn't have to be Sherlock Holmes to realize that these shoes probably belonged to the killer.

A few hours later, Barr took the shoes to police headquarters and performed a quick chemical test. The test confirmed that the stains were blood.

Right away, Barr took Annie—who had spent all afternoon at the station—into a private room. He held up the Docksides and asked if Annie recognized them.

Indeed she did.

"Whose are they?" he demanded.

"Larry's," she replied.

4.

While Larry and his sister left the police station to eat lunch, detectives Moore and Mitchell were dispatched to the Crownsville Hospital again, this time to look at the soles of Michael Swartz's shoes. Barr and Mock wanted to know whether his shoes had a rectangular imprint and wavy lines across their soles.

Greeting the investigators personally, the hospital administrator demanded to know what their visits were about. After leveling with him, the cops asked the administrator whether they could see Michael first, then the staff could inform him of his parents' murder. The administrator acquiesced.

Michael was in the hospital dayroom, listening to music again, when he was summoned to another room to talk to the detectives. Lying to him a second time, they said he was still a suspect in a motorcycle theft and they wanted to determine whether he had left the hospital last night.

When they asked him to take off one of his tennis shoes, Michael obliged. Turning the shoe over, the detectives saw little circles all over the rubber soles—no horizontal lines and no little rectangle. Clearly, these did not match the shoe prints Barr had described at the scene.

The detectives asked Michael a few more questions and then left. The second session with police lasted maybe ten minutes. Within a matter of hours, Michael would have his own criminal lawyer, who would advise him to say nothing further to the police.

Immediately after the police left, Michael later recalled, a doctor came in and fumbled around, telling him that "something" had happened to his family. His parents were "ill," the doctor said. Finally his social worker arrived and told him the truth: His parents had been killed.

"I said, 'How?'" Michael recalled. "They said they didn't know. I said, 'Do they know who did it?' They said, 'No.' That was pretty much it."

Michael's reaction to the news?

"I don't know," he said, adding that he'd lost many sets of parents before the Swartzes. "I pretty much brushed it off at first. I mean it's hard to take, but . . . I was shocked. You could say that."

5.

The Office of Maryland's chief medical examiner occupied a three-story glass-and-brick building one block from Babe Ruth's birthplace in Baltimore. As a joke, a framed photograph of TV's Quincy hung in the gallery of former chief medical examiners in the lobby. One floor below sat the basement morgue, a big cold room filled with stainless-steel sinks and body trays.

At 1 P.M. on January 17, undertaker James Barranco pulled up outside the morgue. An attendant helped him wheel the corpses inside, then logged in Bob Swartz as No. 84–87, and Kay Swartz as No. 84–88. Each number went on a manila tab, which the assistant tied around the big toes before starting the routine of photographing each corpse.

Two hours later, Dr. Merle E. Reyes, a training pathologist, entered the autopsy room to begin the work on Kay Swartz. At the same time, Dr. William Gormley, another training pathologist, began the examination of Bob Swartz a few feet away.

Standing in between the two steel body trays, looming over everyone at six foot five, was Deputy Chief Medical Examiner Dr. Thomas Duvall Smith. A veteran of the morgue at age thirty-nine, Smith had performed more than nine hundred autopsies. His hazel-green eyes watched intently, for as the supervising pathologist he would be called to testify when and if these homicides came to trial.

Also watching intently was a sergeant from the Anne Arundel County police department, whose job it would be to carry back blood and hair samples, and to give the detectives a quick report on the doctors' findings.

The findings:

Kay Swartz had been stabbed seven times in the neck, mostly on the front and right side. Five wounds were fairly shallow, nonfatal cuts. Two, however, had punctured her upper esophagus. Her stab wounds ranged in depth from one and a quarter to two and a quarter inches. Dr. Reyes noted several areas of abrasion on the front neck, near the bottom of the throat, yet she saw no slashes on the woman's arms, or anywhere other than her neck, that might have indicated she had put up a struggle.

The only other injury was by far the most devastating: Someone had crushed her skull with an object much heavier and more blunt than a knife. Without a doubt, Reyes concluded, the massive wound on top of her head would have killed her almost at once. The blow had cracked open her skull, leaving a hole four and a half inches long, two and a half inches deep, a half-inch wide. The wound ran diagonally, from the left front toward the right rear of her head. The blow had fractured her skull and injured her brain. Dr. Reyes found a large bone chip pushed down under the skull, toward the rear of her head.

Kay's blood alcohol tested at .01 percent, consistent with her drinking perhaps one beer the night before. Vaginal swabs revealed no semen traces.

Bob Swartz was a different story. Dr. Gormley counted seventeen stab wounds all over his upper body, from his chin to his abdomen. He had been stabbed repeatedly on the right arm, shoulder, and neck. Two neck wounds had punctured his right and left carotid arteries, the major arteries that carry blood to the brain. Both were potentially fatal wounds. Another wound had slashed four inches into his chest, severing a vein that carried blood to his heart. That, too, was potentially fatal, for it had caused bleeding inside his chest cavity. Other wounds perforated his lungs and stomach. One slash on his arm appeared to be a classic defensive wound, as if he had raised his arms to shield himself.

Most of his neck and shoulder wounds were directed downward, and from right to left; but one cut on the back of his neck was forward and to the right, and one stomach wound was upward. Based on the diverse trajectories, Dr. Gormley concluded that Bob Swartz and his assailant had been moving during at least part of the attack.

The autopsy also revealed that Bob's stab wounds ran deeper than his wife's. While only two of his wife's cuts reached two inches, ten of Bob's went that deep, and four were four inches deep.

Still, the wounds on both victims were similar enough that Dr. Smith concluded the knife used to attack them could have been the same. Some of the wounds appeared to have a flat side, causing the doctors to believe the knife was single-edged. Judging by the wound dimensions, Dr. Smith guessed that the blade was at least three and a half to four inches long, an inch or more wide. Dr. Gormley later would describe the weapon as a "strong sturdy knife . . . more typical of a hunting knife than a steak knife."

6.

Despite repeated telephone entreaties from Barr and Mock to leave Larry alone, the detectives at the station took another crack at Larry when he returned from lunch with Annie and Mrs. Smithmyer. They had reread Larry's signed statement and decided it was riddled with dubious assertions.

The cops thought it bogus, for instance, that Larry claimed he couldn't remember what had awakened him or what Annie had said about their father's body. "Wait a minute," Detective Moore drawled, looking back and forth from the typed statement to Larry. "How can you be so accurate at this point in the evening, and yet at the next, you're saying, 'I'm really confused. I don't remember'?"

"Well . . ." Larry hesitated, then told the officers that in truth he had been drunk last night. He had stolen a bottle of rum from a friend's house several days earlier. Because he didn't want his parents to find the rum, he drank it. "I got very high," Larry claimed, "and that's why I'm not as clear about the details later in the evening as I am earlier."

Bull, thought Moore. What a convenient excuse for all the gaps and errors in his story. Moore excused himself and went into the lieutenant's office. "Hey, this little son of a bitch is now saying he got drunk last night," he told the lieutenant.

The questioning, though low-key, had moved into the danger zone that Mock and Barr had feared. Larry had been advised of his rights and was undergoing the kind of probing that the lead detectives wanted to do themselves later.

Before Moore hurried into Donoho's office, he casually asked Larry if he would take a polygraph examination. Moore could hardly believe his ears when Larry unhesitatingly replied, "Sure."

But Eileen Smithmyer's husband, Jack, had just arrived at the station and had misgivings about letting Larry take a lie-detector test without an attorney present. Larry was still a minor, only seventeen. "I want to call an attorney for him," said Smithmyer.

While Smithmyer went to place the call, Moore conferred again with Donoho, and Donoho reluctantly decided to delay the polygraph.

Detective Mock took exception to this decision when he telephoned from the Swartz house. "The neighbor hasn't got any rights with those kids," Mock said. "*We* are looking out for their rights now. They're *our* responsibility."

"They're already calling an attorney," said Donoho.

"Has the boy asked for an attorney?"

"Well, the boy didn't, but the Smithmyers are calling one."

Mock was getting hot. "The attorney isn't entitled to get to the boy until the boy says *he* wants an attorney."

"No," Donoho replied. "I don't see it that way."

7.

When Jack Smithmyer called, Ronald A. Baradel listened attentively and reacted instantly. "Stop everything," he said. "Tell the police not to talk to Larry. I'm going to represent him. Wait until I get there."

A partner in the prestigious Annapolis law firm of Hartman & Crain, Baradel had a rumpled vulnerable face that at the moment looked dazed. At forty, he had a receding brown hairline and bushy brows over sad hazel eyes. There was a large gap in the middle of his crooked front teeth and a tension to his demeanor that was hard to diagnose. He let his six-foot frame slump in chairs and talked so softly that associates sometimes asked him to speak up, yet his controlled presence bespoke strength and power. His manner was drawing room formal, yet his personality was warm as a country kitchen. Often quiet and brooding, he could be loquacious once he opened his mouth. That was a trait he traced to his boyhood in Brooklyn—a pitiful boyhood that he preferred to forget but that never seemed far from his mind. The sorrow of his boyhood, more than anything else, eventually would create a deep emotional bond between him and Larry Swartz. Although he had known Bob and Kay Swartz for six years, Baradel knew their children only in passing, and wasn't sure Larry knew him at all.

Ron Baradel's parents were native New Yorkers who married after a summer romance at Rockaway Point, a colony of bungalows on Long Island's southern fingertip. Richard Baradel was a lifeguard, trim and handsome at thirty. Helen Collins, seven years his junior, was the pretty queen of the colony's Mardi Gras festival. They had polar personalities. Although Richard charmed listeners by strumming his ukulele, he was cool and crisp as the bow tie he clipped on his shirt. She was the warm, sociable one, always smiling and enjoying life. They married in 1930 and had a daughter, Marie, three years later. Ron was born a decade later, in May 1943, in St. Louis, Missouri. Richard was forty-three when his son was born and was in army training in St. Louis. He was shipped off to the war in Europe later that year while his family went home to Brooklyn.

It would be another four or five years before Ron's father returned home; he extended his tour in Europe when the war ended. That didn't go over well with Helen, who was struggling to raise two children on her own. When Richard finally returned, he took a modest job in the city's purchasing department. "He was an intelligent man who kind of got stuck in a city job with a pension at end of it," Marie would say later.

Richard was severe with his young son, often demanding silence, sometimes confining him to a chair. As a small boy, Ron was an incurable chatterbox. He loved to talk and couldn't control himself at the supper table, where his father demanded silence. You gotta be quiet, you gotta be quiet, Ron told himself each time he sat down. Inevitably, thoughts formed in his head that he felt powerless to contain, even though he knew the next stop was exile.

"Out to the hallway!" his father hollered when Ron began babbling.

Ron's mother bit her lip as the boy took his plate and trooped out to the dark entrance hallway to their two-bedroom apartment. Ron ate a lot of meals out there alone at a tiny table, listening to tenants stirring in the other apartments.

Later, when they became adults, Ron's sister teased him, "Watch your step, or you'll be out in the hallway!" But deep inside, Marie knew the joke wasn't funny. Those solitary meals had so scarred her brother that she could never figure out why their mother had tolerated them.

Their mother doted on Ron, who was her favorite, as Marie was their father's. Throughout childhood, Ron was blessed with what his sister called an "innate appropriateness," which helped him stay out of trouble. As a young boy, Ron developed a severe stutter. He managed to conquer it after a few years, but for the rest of his life he spoke in a soft and tightly controlled voice—almost as though he feared his stutter might return.

Although he regarded his father with apprehension, Ron treasured his mother. When he was ten, he came home from grammar school every day for months to fix lunch and tea for her while she was bedridden with a hip injury. She had slipped one rainy Sunday getting off a bus on her way to visit her mother in Queens. Actually, Helen had been sick even before her injury. A heavy smoker who hacked and coughed all the time, Helen at forty-six looked prematurely old and was undergoing treatment for pleurisy.

On May 10, 1954, one day after Mother's Day, Helen went into the hospital for what she told her son was a routine examination. "I have to have one more checkup so we can go out to Long Island for the summer," she told Ron. He was looking forward to their annual summer vacation, which they'd missed the year before because of his mother's illness. Ron accompanied his father to the hospital the next day, but the boy had to wait outside her room in the corridor. "I don't want him to see me like this," Ron overheard his mother saying.

On Friday afternoon, with his mother still hospitalized, Ron decided to go by himself to a neighborhood church bazaar. His sister told him to come home promptly after the bazaar, but when he arrived, he discovered the bazaar hadn't even started yet, so he ran all the way home for permission to stay later.

Weeping in the living room, Marie groped for words to tell her little brother what had happened. When she couldn't find the words, her boyfriend, Jim, told the boy that his mother had died of advanced lung cancer. It had invaded her aorta, and when they opened her up, she bled to death on the operating table. After he broke the news to Ron, Jim walked over to the liquor cabinet and poured the boy his first drink. Then Marie took Ron into her arms and lay with him on the couch; but he couldn't be comforted. It was beyond his comprehension. How could he lose the person he loved most in the world?

At the funeral home, Ron stared at the closed casket. They said it held his mother's body, but he didn't believe it. What a scam. He was a smart fellow and they couldn't fool him. He had figured out that she'd gone on a secret mission. She was working for the government. They were just *telling* him she was dead because they weren't allowed to tell him the truth, that she was on an important mission. For months, he truly believed that his mother was alive and would come back to him one day. "I can remember for a year, seeing people on the street, running up to them, essentially expecting them to be her," he would recall. "It probably took a year to sink in."

By then, Ron was living alone with his father. His sister had married Jim Tully, a medical student, and moved out. Ron spent the remainder of his boyhood pretty much on his own, yearning for the family intimacy he had lost when his mother died. It was a yearning so strong that his friends in college and law school later would notice it and feel sorry for him.

After Helen died, the chief mode of communication in the Baradel household became notes. Richard wrote a meal schedule and elaborate instructions for chores and left them out for his son. Because father and son almost never talked, Ron went over to a friend's house after supper almost every night. His friend's family encouraged him to try staying home and talking more to his own father. Ron tried but got nowhere. His father always watched TV after they ate and resented intrusions. Whenever Ron started a conversation, his father barked, "Can't you see I'm watching this program?" Ron would wait until a commercial, only to watch his father bury his nose in the newspaper.

It wasn't that Richard made no effort to raise his son properly. He didn't attend church ("I graduated from church," he was fond of saying), but insisted that Ron should go every Sunday, as he had with his mother, a devout Catholic. Richard also signed Ron up for Boy Scouts and became a troop leader. At first, Ron enjoyed scouting, but like many boys, by his mid-teens he wanted out. Yet his father insisted on his staying in until he was sixteen, even after he begged for permission to quit due to conflicts with basketball practice. "We are doing this together whether you want to or not!" his father said.

Despite his rigidity, Richard gave his son more freedom than most kids his age, chiefly by leaving him alone. Ron had no curfew and often roamed his neighborhood at night for no particular reason. He stayed out some nights until nearly dawn. Sometimes he wandered alone, peering in neighbors' windows, wishing he had a real family.

Before he reached high school, Ron was a stellar student. He stood number one in his class when he left his Catholic grammar school in 1957. He won acceptance to Catholic high schools all across the city and was crushed when his father announced that he had to attend public high school because he had no more money for tuition.

Watching his friends go off to Catholic schools, wanting desperately to join them, Ron instead went to Brooklyn Tech, a large public high school with six thousand boys. A football and basketball player, he selected the school for its first-rate sports teams. Rather than becoming a high school superjock, however, he became a disciplinary problem. One day he dumped a milk container on a boy in the cafeteria, initiating a fight that spread through the vast dining hall like fire through a wheat field. After

Ron exchanged punches with a classmate on another occasion, the powers that be summoned his father to a school conference. Part of the problem was that Ron, a freshman, was hanging around with juniors and seniors and saw himself as a big deal. Not everyone agreed, especially not school officials. "We don't think your son has a future here," they told his father.

In addition to his behavioral problems, his once-perfect grades took a free-fall. When his first report card arrived home—a pale green document with the courses he was flunking circled in red—Ron's father grew furious. "What the hell is this?" he demanded.

"An early Christmas card," Ron replied dryly.

Secretly, Ron was still angry at his father for not finding the money to send him to Catholic school. He felt left out and missed his friends terribly.

In the tenth grade, Ron switched to Erasmus High School but did no better there. He cut classes and was indifferent toward his homework. The following year he enrolled in Midwood, a predominantly Jewish school, where he felt even more like an outsider. Eager to finish, Ron finally buckled down, accelerated his studies, took summer classes, and earned his diploma.

Throughout high school, Ron exasperated his father with his poor grades and irresponsible behavior. Alternately, Richard would wring his hands and tell his son, "It's your life," then proclaim him uncontrollable and threaten to send him to reform school.

At age fifteen, Ron landed his first summer job, as a truck loader working nights for Wonder Bread. Excited about his good pay, Ron told his father he had to hit the sack early because he was starting work at midnight.

"You're not old enough for that job," protested Richard, who didn't like the neighborhood or the hours Ron would be working.

"Well, they think I am!"

Richard took care of that. He called Wonder Bread and revealed that his son had lied about his age. You had to be sixteen to load Wonder Bread's trucks.

Furious, Ron stormed out of the house, slamming the door in his father's face.

By graduation, Ron was despairing about his future. He'd blown it in high school, earning a diploma but otherwise making a mess of his life. Unless he could get out of Brooklyn, Ron felt he was headed down the drain with a future the same as, or even bleaker than, his father's—some boring job with a pension at the end.

His brother-in-law finally yanked him out of Brooklyn by driving him down to Emmitsburg, Maryland, to visit Jim's alma mater, Mount St. Mary's College. Ron felt an instant affinity for the small Catholic men's school. Isolated in the foothills of the Blue Ridge Mountains, it had fewer than one thousand students. Aware that he lacked self-discipline, Ron felt he might thrive in such a small, controlled environment.

He did. He excelled academically, edited *The Mountain Echo*, the college newspaper, and did everything so slowly and effortlessly that his buddies nicknamed him Blaze. They regarded him as brilliant and envied his ability to earn top grades without seeming to lift a finger.

After his graduation, Ron enrolled as a law student at Georgetown University Law Center, where he earned room and board by living with undergraduates and serving as a prefect. He worked at odd jobs and bartending to pay his tuition, with modest financial assistance from his father.

Most of Ron's close friends realized that his relationship with his father was troubled. Thomas O'Hara, a law school roommate, recalled, "It was a funny relationship. He would write Ron these long letters and not send him much money. I always had the feeling his father could have sent Ron more money so he didn't have to worry about where his next dollar was going to come from. It was a cold relationship, and it kind of bothered Ron. He used to read his letters to me, and they were ridiculous. It was not a normal father-son relationship."

The relationship worsened as Ron moved through college and law school on his way to becoming a successful attorney. Ron rarely saw his father after they had an hellacious fight at his college graduation. Richard had gone north from Florida, where he had moved two years earlier, to watch his son receive his diploma. It was a bleak day for Ron, who was suffering from girlfriend woes and fancied himself to be the only dateless senior at graduation. They went out to eat after the ceremony, and Ron stormed out of the Holiday Inn restaurant when his father suggested what he should order for lunch.

He didn't see his father again for two more years, when he went to visit a girlfriend in Fort Lauderdale and stopped in Miami Beach. That short visit ended in another fight, and Ron grabbed his girlfriend and marched out of his father's home. Ron and his father didn't see each other again for five more years. By that time, Ron was married and the father of a two-year-old son. They remained estranged like that for decades, with only a casual encounter every five or six years.

After Ron finished law school, he surprised his classmates by joining the FBI, which was not regarded as a terribly promising career for a young lawyer with the kind of brainpower Ron had. A few months after he was sworn in as a special agent, Ron married, and he wasn't surprised when his father didn't attend the wedding on Long Island.

"It's too cold up north in December," Richard complained.

"Well, we'd love to have you, but we're not going to wait until August," Ron said.

A few months earlier, Richard had remarried in Florida without notifying or inviting his son.

Ron spent only a few years in the FBI before he sought a new career. He made the decision abruptly after the agency transferred him to New York City, the very place he had struggled so hard to leave. Casting about for a new career in New York in 1969, he went to La Guardia airport one night to meet a former college roommate and close friend, Thomas B. Finan, Jr., who was en route back from a Peace Corps stint in Bolivia. Ron told Finan he was planning to quit the FBI and asked, "Do you think your father might have a job for me?"

"I'll check," said Finan.

Indeed, the old man did. In 1970, Ron quit the agency and moved to Maryland to clerk for Judge Thomas B. Finan on the Maryland Court of Appeals—a prestigious clerkship on the state's highest court, which assured him a foothold in the state's legal community. The job also gave him time to pass the Maryland bar exam and decide where he wanted to practice law. He chose Annapolis and joined Hartman & Crain, one of the town's leading firms.

Ron steadily built a reputation as one of the brighter and better prepared trial lawyers in the state capital. He consistently earned A ratings from the *Martindale-Hubbell Law Directory*. Although he specialized in banking and insurance cases, and never handled high-profile cases, in 1981 the Baltimore *Sun* named him among the few Annapolis attorneys deemed by their peers to be "the local legal all-stars." Ron had been in private practice barely a decade and was pleased. He was not pleased, however, when the newspaper quoted local lawyers as saying his "solid, thorough arguments" compensated for his "dry and unimaginative" courtroom style. Dry and unimaginative? What about his junkyard foray to find the front end of a 1957 Chevy for a jury demonstration? Not sexy stuff, but innovative. Ron thought most lawyers would have settled for a diagram and would not have bothered hauling in the real Chevy. Ron prided himself on going that extra mile in trial preparations—indexing and cross-indexing depositions, placing every statement and fact at his fingertips. He had a compulsive personality and streak of perfectionism that showed in court. "I've always lived in fear that there's going to be some young guy or girl who is going to kick my butt because I'm not prepared," he said, "so I probably still overprepare. They may beat me because they're better, but they're not going to beat me because I'm not prepared."

The morning Smithmyer called him, Baradel had been working on one of his bread and butter cases—a particularly messy divorce. He'd just gotten off the phone with his client and was in a lousy mood when his secretary handed him a phone message from Dick Maio marked "urgent." Doubting that it really was urgent, Baradel nevertheless returned the call to Maio, a fellow parishioner at St. Mary's Church. Maio delivered the dreadful news about the Swartzes, and Baradel spent the rest of the morning in a fog.

He knew the Swartzes through St. Mary's, where both families were active members. For nearly two years, Baradel had spent an hour every Saturday with Bob and two other men in the lower sacristy of the church, developing their spirituality through a movement called Cursillo. Last Saturday, their group had gone to a seminar in Baltimore together, and Baradel had driven Bob home afterward. Just three days later, Bob was not only dead but apparently murdered. Baradel worried about Larry and Annie, but Maio assured him the children were safe with friends.

Now Jack Smithmyer's call started Baradel worrying again— and with good cause. The cops wanted to polygraph Larry. As a former FBI agent, Baradel knew that polygraphs were bad news. You don't polygraph your witnesses unless you suspect they are lying. It was crazy; Larry was the mildest-mannered boy in the world, but obviously the cops thought they had something on him.

Baradel hurried down the hall and barged into the office of his partner Jim Nolan, a burly ex-football player who had some experience in criminal law. Baradel had done no criminal work since his FBI days more than a decade earlier; He was strictly a civil lawyer. He needed help to deal with something as serious as murder. Nolan was tied up with a client and recommended Charles Bagley IV, a young lawyer who had recently come to the firm from the state's attorney's office.

8.

At four o'clock, Baradel and Bagley entered the homicide offices together and were ushered into the lieutenant's office, where they encountered half a dozen cops, including Mock and Barr. The cops said they wanted to give Larry a polygraph merely to verify his story.

Baradel was doubtful. "Why don't you fill me in on the circumstances?" he said.

Mock sketched the evidence, then told the lawyers that "inconsistencies" between the children's statements were the main reason for the polygraph. Mock—they didn't call him the Fox for nothing—declared that their prime suspect wasn't Larry at all, but another Broadneck student who was a suspect in an unrelated rape case. The student was suspected of attacking a woman at knife point. "We checked the kid out, and guess what he was wearing in school yesterday?" asked Mock.

Baradel knew the detective was bluffing as soon as he said the kid's clothes matched those Annie had seen on the man leaving her yard the previous night. That was too much.

The lawyer pointed to a plaque on the wall embossed with the emblem of the FBI's National Academy. "See that?" he retorted. "I used to be in the FBI. Now don't tell me you're suspecting someone else. This is crazy. If you've got this suspect, what the hell are you all doing in *here*? Why aren't you out there getting him?"

Calming himself, Baradel looked at Mock. "I don't want to tell you how to do your job," he said quietly. "Just let me talk to Larry, will you?"

The lawyers took Larry into a private room, where he related the same story he had told the cops. Baradel thought Larry looked tired and drained, almost to the point of shock. The boy spoke softly, and Baradel believed his story. Baradel had known Larry only casually as the son of a friend. Now Baradel made a point of telling the stunned youth his name, that he was an attorney who was there to help him. "Do you have a problem with that?" Baradel asked.

"No," Larry said simply.

Next the lawyers talked privately with Annie, who seemed antsy but not as upset as they had expected. Baradel thought she seemed surprisingly unaffected. Annie, too, narrated the same tale she'd told police. Baradel took solace from one point that seemed to him highly significant: Annie said that while she was standing on the carport, watching a man walk away with a shovel over his shoulder, Larry had called her back inside the house. If that was true, the killer couldn't have been Larry. How could he be walking away from the house and, at *the same time, be standing in the kitchen*?

Baradel and Bagley rejoined the detectives. "We don't see any discrepancies," Baradel told them. "What are you talking about?" The detectives ticked off three or four conflicts between the children's statements, but Baradel thought they amounted to nonsense, and said so.

Mock had had little use for lawyers ever since one had called him a "Hollywood Glib" in front of a jury. Now he challenged Baradel's right even to be at the station by reminding him that

Larry had not requested an attorney. The debate escalated into a disagreement over who had custody of the children, with Mock contending that once children were orphaned, the state automatically took custody of them. At least for tonight, however, the police were willing to let the children go home with the Smithmyers, who had been Bob and Kay's closest friends.

Meanwhile, Baradel was emphatic about the polygraph: Larry was too tired; any results would be suspect. He would not take the test tonight.

The detectives knew their evidence was too flimsy to arrest Larry, yet they didn't want to let him go without at least rolling his fingerprints and seizing his clothes for blood and fiber tests. They also wanted combings from his pubic hair, to see whether any of his mother's hair was on him. Earlier, when the legal wrangling over evidence had first begun, Barr had summoned an assistant state's attorney, who was now quietly dispensing legal advice from a back room at the station. The assistant state's attorney, George Lantzas, told the detectives that their requests for nail and hair evidence were valid, but he was unsure about the fingerprints. The police desperately wanted to compare the boy's hand with the bloody palm print they had found on the sliding glass door frame. Lantzas made several phone calls before he found the deputy state's attorney at the Elks Club. The deputy urged caution: Unless the boy was arrested, they would need a grand-jury summons for his prints.

In the midst of this skirmishing, a lawyer from the public defender's office called and asked to speak to Larry's lawyer. Timothy D. Murnane, an assistant public defender, informed Baradel that he was representing Michael Swartz and had advised Michael not to talk to police further. The police wanted to polygraph Michael, but Murnane had blocked it. Murnane told Baradel that he should pack up Larry and Annie at once and leave the station. "Get out of there!" he said.

Baradel was getting ready to do just that, but first he had little choice but to yield to the detectives' demands for physical evidence. In a private room, on the lawyers' advice, Larry dropped his jeans to allow a technician to comb his pubic hair. Barr, who was watching, spotted an inflamed scratch on Larry's thigh and ran to get a camera.

"What are you doing?" Bagley protested as Barr held up his Polaroid and snapped the shutter.

"Taking a picture."

"No, you're not," the young lawyer retorted, placing himself in between Larry and the camera.

After a few seconds of jostling, Bagley ordered Larry to pull up his pants. The youth did, but not before Barr had managed to snap two quick shots. Barr then grabbed a notebook and sketched the three-inch scratch, thinking it would bolster his testimony if Larry was ever tried for the crime.

When that hassle ended, the lawyers announced it was time to leave. Aware that this could be their final shot at the boy, the police made one last try: Why not make everything easy and get the polygraph over with now? They could eliminate Larry as a suspect and be done with him.

"No," Baradel insisted wearily. "Maybe tomorrow, but not tonight."

Lantzas emerged from the back room, showing his face to the lawyers for the first time. He, too, urged the lawyers to reconsider. "Let's do it the easy way, guys," the assistant prosecutor pleaded.

Baradel was firm: "No. Our client needs rest."

Finally, at 9:30 P.M., nearly twelve hours after they had arrived at the station, Larry and Annie, bone-tired and hungry, went home with the Smithmyers.

Their lawyers, also hungry, went into downtown Annapolis to eat at the Maryland Inn, an eighteenth-century flat-iron building barely a cobblestone's throw from the State House. Waiting for their food in the inn's subterranean dining room, the lawyers talked in low voices about the legal worries facing Larry. Obviously the cops had something on him; the question was what. Baradel longed to believe in the boy's innocence, yet the realist in him acknowledged the possibility of guilt. Though he was a brilliant civil lawyer, Baradel felt emotionally drained and not quite up to the legal challenge confronting his dead friends' son.

"We need a good criminal lawyer," Baradel declared.

"I know one who's the best there is," replied Bagley.

"Who's that?"

"Joe Murphy."

The name meant nothing to Baradel, but he trusted Bagley's judgment. They would call him in the morning.

While the lawyers dined in the historic district, the cops grabbed chow at the Blue Channel Inn, a shopping-center restaurant near Cape St. Claire.

Barr told his boss he'd received an emotional telephone call from a neighbor—a call that offered the first clue to a motive for the violence that had erupted at 1242 Mount Pleasant Drive. Identifying herself as Susan Barker, the woman had wept into the telephone. "You don't know what that family was all about," she cried. "It was so terrible how they treated poor Larry and Michael." When she insisted it was "too involved" to explain over the telephone, Barr had agreed to visit her later.

The three cops talked at length about their failure to polygraph Larry or obtain a confession. Larry was their number one suspect, although they still had not discounted his brother, Michael. Barr grew more suspicious of Larry—and even more disappointed that he hadn't been able to question him—when he went back to the radio room and replayed the tape recording of Larry's call to police. "I think my parents are dead," the boy had told the dispatcher. How could he have known both his parents were dead, when he claimed he had no idea where his father's body was?

As they picked Larry's story apart, it dawned on the cops that they should return to the house. For one thing, they had left the wet clothes in the washer. Those were probably Larry's clothes. They should be tested for blood. And there was the matter of the knife. The sergeant had phoned in the autopsy results, confirming that both husband and wife had been stabbed, not shot. Both probably had been stabbed with the same knife. Could the knife still be hidden in the house?

"We'll need a warrant," said Tankersley.

Barr agreed to draft an affidavit for a search warrant the first thing in the morning.

After their food came, the cops talked at length about the absurd trail of footprints—the bare and socked prints that wound nearly a mile through the snow. Who was going to believe that? Barr was convinced a chase had occurred, but Mock wasn't so sure. Cranking up his imagination, Mock wondered whether the boy could have *walked* his naked mother around the neighborhood in some sort of sadistic ritual—perhaps to humiliate her? Could he have held her hair at the back? That would explain the hanks of hair in the snow. Barr listened intently, but didn't think Mock's walking theory made sense. No, the more he contemplated the evidence, the deeper Barr's conviction grew: The killer—whoever he was—had chased Mrs. Swartz through the snow. Tankersley, too, bought the chase one hundred percent. Mock didn't dispute it, he just wondered about alternate explanations for the footprints.

On one thing, though, all three cops agreed: The injured mother had somehow, for whatever strange reason, traveled barefoot around the neighborhood last night, her assailant either right at her side or chasing close behind. And once they had made up their minds, *nothing* would convince the detectives otherwise.

A chase had taken place.

And that was that.

FOUR

June 16, 1973

1.

The little boy held the glass in his hands and stared at the chalky liquid inside. It didn't look very appetizing. Glancing up at the tall woman who had poured it for him, he asked, "What is it?"

"Why, milk," replied Kay Swartz, startled. She studied the boy's puzzled face, wondering what was wrong with his foster parents. Could he really be six years old and not recognize milk?

Larry took a sip and it was like nothing he had tasted before—not sweet like the Kool-Aid and iced tea he usually drank.

It was Larry's first day with the Swartzes, and Kay had given him milk and cookies. He was a magnificent child, with deep dark eyes that could swallow you right up, surrounded by thick curly lashes. He was tiny for his age and had dark skin. That surely came from his father, who was from East India, a social worker had said. Larry was healthy despite a mild growth deficiency from an apparent lack of calcium.

The Swartzes took Larry on a picnic in the park that first Saturday, and everyone had a glorious time. Larry seemed shy and nervous but obviously enjoyed being the center of attention. When Kay put him to bed that night, she thought about his chronic bed-wetting. His social worker had warned her that it would be natural for him to wet the bed his first night there. Kay and Bob had told the worker they weren't worried about that, or his overeating, or failing in school. They would help him overcome all those problems.

On Sunday morning, Kay was surprised to discover that Larry had not wet his bed. On Monday, the bed was dry again. Although he was nervous, Larry was on his best behavior, anxious to please. An old hand at tryouts, Larry knew he was reading for the part of son—a role he desperately wanted but had failed to get many times before.

When Bob and Kay took Larry back to the agency in Baltimore on Monday, Larry informed his caseworker that he did not want to go home to his foster parents; he wanted to move in with the Swartzes. Pleased, Bob and Kay agreed to scrap the agency's plan for Larry to go home with them the following weekend. The Swartzes signed all the agency's placement papers, agreeing to take custody of Larry that day, with the goal of adopting him after a supervisory period of one year.

Meanwhile, caseworker Sylvia Rumer drove Larry to his foster home north of Baltimore to pick up his few clothes and say good-bye to the Miltons, his foster family of the last three years. Even though Larry didn't want to live with the Miltons anymore, he told Rumer he wanted to keep visiting them.

"I know how you feel, but I'm afraid you won't be able to see Mr. and Mrs. Milton again," Rumer explained gently. "You're going to tell them good-bye today."

Playing with hand puppets in the car, Larry appeared hyperactive, anxious. He told his puppets, "You're in trouble. You're going to a new home."

At his foster home, Mr. Milton took Larry aside and talked to him while Mrs. Milton packed his things. Then, with her own two daughters watching, Mrs. Milton tearfully kissed Larry good-bye.

Her tears touched Larry, who had powerful feelings for this foster mother who had spurned him as her son.

"I have a sad face and a happy face," Larry told Rumer as they climbed into the car.

During his first month in his new home, Kay took Larry swimming at the Cape St. Claire beach almost every day, and one Saturday she and Bob took him to the Baltimore zoo. The neighborhood boys initiated Larry into their games in the swampy woodland behind his house.

When Rumer visited in July, Larry took her into the woods and showed her the secret place where he and his new friends played. He introduced her to his new puppy, Hercules, whom he called "Whoook-you-lees" because he couldn't say his *R*'s yet. Kay reported that Larry seemed happy and hadn't wet his bed once. He was an energetic tyke who ran everywhere, climbed on everything, tumbled around like a bale of hay in a tornado.

Years later, Larry would describe those earliest times with the Swartzes as his happiest ones. Kay stayed at home for the first few months, doting on her new son. In August, they met Bob's brother, Joe, and his family for a seashore vacation in Ocean City, Maryland. Then, before school started, Bob and Kay put the icing on Larry's cake: They took him to Disney World in Florida.

Rumer visited again at the end of September, arriving while Larry was at school. He was repeating the first grade at Cape St. Claire Elementary School, four blocks from his house. "He's wet the bed a few times," Kay told Rumer, "but I think that was just because of school. He was nervous about going." Describing his progress as excellent, Kay said she already felt close to her son. He rarely talked about his former foster home but had confided to his new mom that his foster mother had been mean.

When Larry came home from school, he told Rumer, "I'm glad you found my pah-wents foh me."

For the remainder of his first year with the Swartzes, Rumer got good reports whenever she phoned: Larry wet his bed only occasionally. He was thrilled to inherit two rabbits when neighbors moved away. Also, he managed to bring up most of his grades to "satisfactory."

Larry drafted a list of what he wanted from Santa in December, and when he got up Christmas morning, he found every item on his list wrapped up under the tree.

"Why did Santa bring me all this?" he asked, astonished.

"Santa thought you wanted it," his mother replied anxiously. "You did, didn't you?"

"Yes, but I thought I was getting only one thing!"

His mother laughed, relieved that Larry liked his new toys.

In the spring, Rumer drew a series of sanguine conclusions in her final adoption report, conclusions that years later would be disputed in a protracted probe of the Swartz family life. "We feel the Swartzes are especially well suited to be Larry's parents," she wrote. "They are flexible, loving people who will not be pressuring him to conform to their set of standards."

The Swartzes were anxious to sign Larry's final adoption papers, for they had applied to adopt a second child. They weren't the only ones who wanted another child. From the beginning, Larry pestered his parents for a brother—a younger one. He was emphatic about that. Larry would be the big brother and would show his little brother around.

In July 1974, the Swartzes received Larry's final adoption decree from the circuit court for Baltimore City. From now on, in the eyes of the law, Larry was as much their son as if he had been born to them. They were fully responsible for his support and care, and he was entitled "to all the rights and privileges of, and . . . subject to all the obligations of a child born to the petitioner in wedlock." The decree was almost as irrevocable as childbirth. Because adoptions were intended to be final and binding, surrounded by "a high degree of certainty," Maryland law made no provision for revoking them unless someone proved that they had been obtained improperly.

Within a matter of months, the same agency that handled Larry's adoption sent Larry a brother. Like Larry, the new boy was eight years old. But Michael had been born in March 1966, making him six months older than Larry.

Michael, not Larry, would be the big brother.

2.

Clutching one of his prized Indian arrowheads, Michael, a tall gangly lad with a wide handsome face, stood beside an orange Datsun pickup truck and waited impatiently for Mr. Swartz, the stocky bald man who wanted to adopt him. Michael's social worker had brought him to the agency to meet the Swartzes, and the adults were still talking inside.

Michael was agitated. His biological father had shown up unexpectedly and wanted Michael to go home with him. Michael hadn't lived with his father since he was three or four and didn't want to go home now. His memories of his father were unpleasant: He used to beat Michael with a board. Michael hardly remembered his mother. She had vanished one day, abandoning him and his sister and brothers.

Growing impatient, Michael took his arrowhead and began scratching the orange paint off the roof of the Datsun. Mr. Swartz came outside and yelled at him. "What do you think you're doing?" he cried, his face reddening.

The first eight years of Michael's life had been like that—a blur of angry faces, for as a child, he had tumbled into more than his share of trouble. He also had had more than his share of parents. He had stayed, on the average, less than one year in each foster home. The Swartzes would be the seventh family to take him in, not counting his natural family. Each home had rejected him for one reason or another. One parent had died. Another couple found him unmanageable. Yet another accused him of stealing money from the pocketbook of a visitor in his foster home.

Like Larry's, Michael's first weekend at the Swartzes was billed as a visit, "a weekend retreat kind of thing," he later recalled. "I was just there to check it out. And I met Larry. It was fun. I had a good time. Larry said, 'Hey, man, we're going to Disney World next week. If you come, you can go.' So naturally I went."

For the second year in a row, the Swartzes took a Florida vacation. At the amusement park, Michael and Larry angered their father by rubbing off the mark that had been stamped on their hands at the admission gate, requiring their parents to pay twice for their admission.

It didn't take Michael long to realize that his new dad was not exactly slow to anger. Neither he nor Larry would forget what a big deal their father made over the flowers a few days after Michael moved in. The boys were sitting on a wall near their driveway when they decided to pick the beautiful flowers from the honeysuckle bushes lining both sides of the driveway. As soon as Bob and Kay noticed that the flowers were missing, they asked who had picked them.

"I don't know," Larry lied.

"We did," Michael confessed.

Furious, Bob chewed out both boys and sent them to their bedroom with orders to "think things over."

Another incident during Michael's first week with the Swartzes made an impression on Kay. The family was eating dinner, she later told friends, when Michael's table manners provoked an outburst from Bob. Stung by the criticism, Michael, still edgy and insecure about his new home, jumped up from the table and ran outside to the carport, sobbing. As the family listened to him crying, Larry pushed back his chair and ran after his new brother. Outside, Larry put his arm around Michael and hugged him, while Kay stood at the kitchen door and watched.

"Don't worry," Larry said softly. "It's not such a bad place once you get used to it."

Although not exactly with flying colors, Michael passed his tryout. Bob and Kay decided to make him their legal son.

Only four years into their marriage, Bob and Kay were bursting with pride over their two handsome sons. No sooner had each boy arrived than the Swartzes sent pictures off to all the relatives. Then they called everyone long distance and put the boys on the phone. By the end of Michael's first summer there, both boys had met most members of their new extended family.

Although he was not as dark as Larry—who told his new parents that he thought his natural parents must have been black—Michael also had dark skin. Michael had the build and coloring of his father, an American Indian. He stood a head taller than Larry, and his dark brown hair was a shade lighter than Larry's thick black mop. Michael also had larger eyes that weren't as deep-set or mysterious as Larry's. Still, strangers took one glance at the boys, with their wide faces and toothy smiles, and assumed they were brothers.

Michael and Larry shared a bedroom across from their parents, leaving the third bedroom free for guests. Bob and Kay laid down strict ground rules: No leaving the neighborhood, bounded by one block in all directions; no television except on weekends; no soda pop or candy. Lights were to be out at eight o'clock on school nights. Both boys had to help their mother with housework. Michael, the stronger one, had to mow the lawn and take out the garbage. Each drew a weekly allowance of one dollar, which they could spend as they pleased, and Kay gave them extra money for such chores as raking the yard.

When Michael showed an interest in music, Kay signed him up for piano lessons and made sure he practiced an hour each night. Michael laughed at his dad's musical endeavors, especially when Bob retired to his green armchair in the living room after supper and played the mandolin he had brought back from Europe. However, the mandolin sounded better than his singing: When Dad sang, the whole family snickered.

Michael and Larry became buddies and ice-skated on the pond in the woods out back with the same neighborhood boys. They rarely talked about one thing they had in common: the procession of families each had left behind. When the Swartzes adopted them, their records were sealed and along with them, their troubled pasts—a subject the whole family preferred to forget. "He doesn't know where I came from, and I don't know where he came from," Michael would say.

In time, a natural rivalry sprang up as the boys vied for their parents' approval. Michael thought the edge belonged to Larry, who had arrived first and already was close to his mother by the time Michael moved in. Relatives noticed the bond between Larry and his mother at family get-togethers. "Larry would hang around Kay and try to do things for her," one aunt recalled. "I would see her, for no reason at all, go up and hug Larry and hold his hands."

Kay's brother, Gerald, liked both boys but felt sorry for Michael. He seemed so awkward and unsure of himself, maybe because of his extraordinary height or maybe because of his Johnny-come-lately status in the family. Uncle Gerald, who had four daughters and no sons of his own, singled out Michael for special attention when the two families visited, and he felt honored when his sister named him and his wife Michael's godparents at Thanksgiving in 1975. The Sullivans drove to Annapolis from their suburban Chicago home to watch the baptism.

Although Michael and Larry remained friends, they bickered and clashed like all siblings. Shorter and slighter of build, Larry was no match for Michael. With Kay watching one day, he and Michael scuffled in the yard and fell to the ground. Larry broke away, leapt to his feet, started running, and promptly collided with a tree. He collapsed, unconscious. After he came to, a doctor diagnosed his injury as a mild concussion.

Blaming Michael, Kay exchanged angry words with him. When he talked back to her, she slapped him.

"You bitch!" Michael bellowed.

"Go to your room," she shrieked.

He did.

But when Bob got home from work, Michael caught hell. Bob never tolerated such language from his sons, especially not toward their mother. Bob yelled at Michael and struck him four or five times with his fists, hard punishing blows the boy would never forget.

3.

Every Sunday morning, the Swartzes drove into Annapolis for services at St. Mary's Roman Catholic Church, a grand red brick building that loomed behind a brick wall on a large waterfront tract. A green knoll sloped down behind the church to the Annapolis harbor, where developers cruising Spa Creek in yachts or driving over it in Mercedes-Benzes couldn't help breaking the Tenth Commandment.

"One developer said, 'You name your price,' said Father Ted Heyburn, vice-pastor of St. Mary's. "We said, 'Forget it. We don't want to give up any of the land.'"

The land had been donated to the church more than a century earlier by heirs of an illustrious Marylander, Charles Carroll of Carrollton. The fortresslike church today adjoins the mansion where Carroll was born. The only Catholic signer of the Declaration of Independence, son of the richest man in the colonies when the Revolution began, Carroll earned fame by championing the cause of religious liberty, a cause deeply and painfully rooted in Maryland. Indeed, many historians trace the history of American Catholicism to the founding of Maryland, whose patriarch, George Calvert, the first Lord Baltimore, was a Catholic convert, like Bob Swartz. Bob enjoyed the story of the Calverts. It struck him as ironic that a Catholic family founded Maryland as a refuge from religious persecution, only to see Catholic settlers engaging in deadly river battles with Puritans.

Hoping to minimize religious strife in their New World colony, the founding Calverts established a then-unheard-of policy of religious tolerance. Despite the much ballyhooed "An Act Concerning Religion" passed by the new legislature in 1649, however, tolerance never got much of a foothold in Maryland. Certainly the Puritans who fled persecution in Virginia and started a new town on the Broadneck Peninsula—a few miles from where the Swartzes were to settle—didn't turn out to be tolerant of Catholics. The Puritans seized control of Maryland's government, repealed the Toleration Act, and passed laws restricting Catholics from observing their religion in public.

Charles Carroll of Carrollton—whose father worked for a grandson of the first Lord Baltimore—knew firsthand about Maryland's promise of religious liberty: He lived in Annapolis at a time when citizens were offered one hundred pounds for information leading to the conviction of Catholic priests for saying mass in public. Since Catholics were allowed to hold services only in private chapels, the Carrolls opened the top floor of their Annapolis mansion to brethren for miles around for baptisms, marriages, and holy mass. After serving Catholics in that fashion for more than a century, the Carroll estate fittingly wound up as home to an order of Catholic fathers and brothers in the mid-1800s, when Charles Carroll's heirs donated the mansion and grounds to the Redemptorists, an order of missionaries, for use as a novitiate. A parish sprang up around the novitiate, leading to construction of a majestic brick church with a lofty spire.

By the time the Swartzes moved to the area in 1971, the

novitiate had been converted to a rectory and was home to nearly two dozen clergymen. Adjoining the rectory was St. Mary's Church, the only Catholic church in Annapolis. Despite its congregation of more than one thousand families, St. Mary's was a sleepy parish when the Swartzes arrived. Soon it woke up as its congregation doubled, its ministry underwent revitalization, and lay participation boomed under the Second Vatican Council.

The Swartzes, especially Bob, took an active part in the revitalization. Not one to disprove the adage "Converts make the best Catholics," Bob hurled himself into parish life with the vigor of Richard the Lionhearted and his army of crusaders. The Swartzes took their sons to Sunday school, or "Con-fraternity of Christian Doctrine," every Sunday morning. After class, the whole family attended mass. In the evening, they sometimes returned, for Bob regularly volunteered to read Scriptures. The priests often called on him for evening duty because, unlike many lectors, he didn't mind attending more than one Sunday service.

Bob and Kay befriended a fiery young priest at St. Mary's, Father Patrick Lynch, who introduced them to Marriage Encounter, a weekend retreat that was becoming popular with Catholic couples around the country. Marriage Encounter blended old-fashioned prayer and letter writing with new-era jargon and sensitivity training. Hoping to improve their communication, couples spent hours writing missives to each other, then exchanged papers and talked about what they had written. It was a highly structured program, which the Swartzes loved. After their first retreat, Bob and Kay volunteered to return to the Manresa-on-Severn, a palatial Jesuit retreat house overlooking the Severn River, to serve as a "presenting couple" for other weekends and talk about what they found meaningful in their marriage.

Within a few years, St. Mary's became the social center of the Swartz family life. Most of their friends belonged to the church. Whatever the church event—picnic, costume party, volleyball game—the priests could count on the Swartzes to attend. Each summer, Bob and Kay dispatched Larry and Michael to Camp Wabanna, a Catholic camp south of Annapolis, where children drew pictures of Jesus and swam in the South River. When the boys were old enough, they spent months training to become altar boys, for their father believed the whole family should serve the Lord.

In the mid-seventies, before Larry and Michael became altar boys, Bob and Kay decided their sons were ready for First Holy Communion, an event so special that it called for a special party. They arranged for a priest to hold a First Communion ceremony in their home instead of at the church. Michael either wasn't ready or didn't want to participate, so Larry took center stage alone. For the elaborate ceremony in the family's basement recreation room, the Swartzes invited forty to fifty friends. "It was mobbed," one parishioner recalled. "You could hardly get down the stairs."

Quiet, polite Larry made quite an impression on the adults, some of whom saw him as a model son, almost too good to be true. "Larry would do *anything* to be good," recalled one woman who attended. "I thought, how wonderful to be able to adopt a child at that age and have him be so wonderful. Here was this beautiful, gorgeous kid who was *good,* too! He was just what everybody wanted to have."

As Bob and Kay struggled to adjust to parenthood, they found themselves growing outraged at the increasing number of Americans who heaped disdain on what they regarded as a sacred gift. To the Swartzes, parenthood was the heart and soul of marriage. They could not understand how thousands of women could so casually, so cruelly, so *immorally* kill their own unborn children through abortion. To them, it was murder, pure and simple. The Swartzes would never get over that fateful Monday in 1973, while they were still waiting for the adoption agency to send them their first child, when the Supreme Court issued its decision that women had the right to have an abortion during the first three months of pregnancy. A right to kill! And the justices declared that "reasonable people" did not agree on whether an embryo was a person. The Swartzes could hardly believe the decision. Those perfectly formed and helpless babies curled up inside the womb, not really alive? Who did the justices think they were kidding?

Roe v. *Wade* galvanized antiabortionists all over the country.

Within six months, the National Right to Life Committee was publishing a national newsletter. Although its local chapters cooperated closely with priests and parishes, the new group established itself as an organization independent of the Catholic Church. In Annapolis, the new Right to Life chapter met in the lower sacristy at St. Mary's. Bob and Kay Swartz were involved almost from the start. They also joined the new March for Life group and took the whole family to Washington every January 22, the anniversary of *Roe* v. *Wade,* to protest the abortion laws.

4.

Unfortunately, at school, Larry and Michael found themselves in the same leaky boat, taking water without having the foggiest idea how to bail themselves out.

Both boys had to repeat the first grade; Larry, because his performance lagged, and Michael, because he switched homes during the year and fell behind.

The year Michael moved in with the Swartzes, both he and Larry went to second grade at Cape St. Claire Elementary School. Although Michael's performance was adequate, Larry's was not—at least not in the eyes of his parents, who as teachers wanted to see both their sons reach their full potential. Larry's first two report cards in the second grade were punctuated with "unsatisfactories." His few "very goods" were mostly for effort. Larry had managed to pull up his grades the year before, and Bob and Kay expected him to do as well again this year. The last thing they wanted was for either son to be held back another year.

Larry's teacher sent home several notes. One advised his parents that Larry was stumbling over the basic sounds essential to reading and writing. She suggested a meeting, which apparently helped. Larry soon had a reading tutor and by June had pulled all his grades up to "satisfactory."

Neither boy's standing at school was fully satisfactory to his parents, however.

Kay and Bob thought Michael belonged one grade higher, where he would have been had he not had the misfortune of being bumped around so many foster homes. They thought it unfair to hold Michael back. When he had started first grade, he was six years old and already taller than most boys his age. Now that he'd been held back, he was freakishly taller than the younger boys in his class. Michael's intelligence was not lacking: He had an I.Q. of 108, according to one school report. His parents felt he should be able to catch up with his peers, so they pushed school officials to skip him from the second to the fourth grade. In the fall of 1975, Michael—now nine years old—was accelerated.

Despite his fourth-grade placement, Michael continued to do third-grade work, and his grades sank.

Larry, meanwhile, plodded through the third grade. Even at that level, his work was so poor that his teacher felt he needed special help. Kay was teaching English at Severna Park High School, fifteen minutes from the boys' elementary school, and she agreed to do whatever she could to help. At the suggestion of school officials, she made an appointment for Larry at the John F. Kennedy Institute, a private facility in Baltimore and a leading national center for testing learning-disabled children.

"Larry is a delightful person with a sense of humor who loves life and gets along well with everybody," Kay announced to the first doctor who evaluated her son at the institute.

She said it was puzzling that Larry seemed "bright conversationally" yet couldn't learn to read. She had tried to help him the year he moved in, but when he grew frustrated, she backed off. "I thought it was more important to help him adjust to his new family," Kay told the doctor. In most areas, Larry had adjusted quite happily, she added, except for occasional bed-wetting. She attributed that problem to his worries about school.

In October, Larry underwent a battery of physical, psychological, and academic tests. "I hate taking tests," he confided to a psychologist. Admitting that he was afraid of failing, he covered his answer sheet with his head and hands.

The tests showed that even though he'd repeated a grade,

Larry was still performing a grade or two below the third grade in most subjects. And his most recent intelligence tests suggested a decline in his functioning. Always before, Larry had ranked in the low–average intelligence range on I.Q. tests. Yet the Kennedy Institute tests placed him in the low–normal to borderline range, with a full-scale I.Q. of 78. That was near the bottom of the 75-to-90 zone, where students often are referred to as "marginal" or "slow learners."

Stating that Larry had learning disabilities and mild visual –motor perceptual problems, Kennedy's experts recommended special help in reading and math. A psychologist wrote that his lack of confidence was "probably secondary" to his primary learning disabilities.

"However," the psychologist concluded, in an analysis that would prove to be prophetic, "these limitations may make the school years difficult for Lawrence and his family to handle. His parents will need to put much energy into monitoring Lawrence's educational progress and in helping him with his feelings of inadequacy over his school performance. Therefore, the family might benefit from supportive counseling."

The psychologist was aware that Larry had suffered emotional problems before the Swartzes adopted him. Partly for that reason, he recommended Larry for a follow-up evaluation in two years. "Given Lawrence's sensitivity and past history," he wrote, "the possibility of earlier conflicts reemerging under stress cannot be ruled out."

For reasons that would remain unclear, Larry would never go back to the Kennedy Institute; nor would he or his family get the recommended counseling.

As the boys progressed through the lower grades, the Swartzes were not at all happy about their continued poor showing at school. Applying some homespun B. F. Skinner, they tried to motivate the boys, but the goal they set—straight A's—seemed absurdly out of reach to Michael. "They were always saying, Hey, you get straight A's, we'll buy you a ten-speed bike'," he recalled bitterly.

The Swartzes avoided scolding Larry about his grades after the Kennedy Institute tagged him as learning disabled. As the result of that evaluation, Larry entered the county's special-education program and received special help in his school's "resource room" during third and fourth grades. Although his teacher complained that he was a chatterbox, his grades improved.

Michael had none of Larry's armor to protect him from his parents' expectations. Every time Michael took home a report card littered with D's and E's, Bob lectured him: "You don't have any excuse for this. You're capable of doing more. You're not trying."

Yet Michael felt he was working his butt off and getting nowhere. He couldn't understand why his parents never said anything to Larry, whose grades were hardly scholarship material. Sometimes Michael went to his mother and complained: "What about Larry? Why are you always picking on me?"

"Larry's got a learning disability. He can't help it," replied his mother. She agreed with Bob that Michael could do better.

In addition to his learning disabilities, Larry suffered from chronic clumsiness. He was always hurting himself and dropping things. Dinner could be an ordeal, with Bob and Kay scolding him for turning his fork upside down. "You've got to be more careful," Bob would admonish when Larry's elbow knocked over his milk glass. In the third grade, Larry fractured his ankle when he fell into a hole in his yard where workers were installing a well. A month later, he tumbled and got a gash in his forehead that required stitches. Six months later, he injured his thumb playing baseball and went back to the emergency room, this time for a splint. Next, a toy gun lacerated his forehead, requiring more stitches. His injuries were never-ending. He also had a chronic stomach ailment, apparently stress-related, which prompted even more trips to the hospital emergency room and family doctor.

Although Larry's athletic abilities were marginal, Bob and Kay encouraged him at sports. Uncle Gerald was amused when the Swartzes took him to one of Larry's Little League baseball games. "He had to be the biggest liability on the team," Gerald recalled. "He was just a horror. He couldn't function at all. They'd put him in the outfield, and they'd hit it toward Larry, and he didn't catch any of them. And Bob and Kay would say, 'Oh my goodness, how great he is!' And Bob would say, 'You see that ball? It was hit hard right at him and he didn't flinch.' Well, he never caught it, either, you know. They were so proud of him, the fact that he was out there. They hollered and cheered like wild people."

Michael, in contrast, was healthy and generally well coordinated. Yet within a year after he moved in, Kay became convinced that her eldest son had deep emotional scars, apparently from the upheaval of his past family life, or lack of past family life. He was unhappy and angry most of the time. Kay quickly realized, from his comments and actions, that he was bitter and bruised about his repeated removal from foster homes throughout childhood.

For two years after he moved in, Michael's custody status remained foggy. His biological father refused to sign away his parental rights, so Michael arrived at the Swartzes' as a foster child, with no guarantee that he'd ever be available for adoption. Caseworkers called such children "legal risk placements" because, as a matter of law, the state had limited custody rights over them, not full guardianship "with the right to consent to adoption." Children such as Michael were at risk of being removed from the foster parents who wanted to adopt them.

Teaming with state workers, Bob and Kay went to court and fought for the right to adopt Michael. They feared the judge might side with the boy's biological father, who wanted his son back, and they were relieved when Michael told the judge he preferred his new family. The judge, after protracted legal wrangling, sided with the Swartzes and granted them the right to adopt Michael. The adoption decree took effect in April 1977, more than two years after Michael had arrived in their home.

Finally, Michael joined Larry in becoming the Swartzes' legal son.

Although they worried about Michael, Bob and Kay vowed to point him in the right direction and give him the warm, stable home he had never had. His rebellious streak would make that difficult; he was nothing like Larry, whose sweet, tame nature made him so malleable. Michael was a whirlwind, volatile as a tropical cyclone, every bit as uncontrollable. His propensity for lying particularly disturbed his new parents. He fabricated stories about things he hadn't done, then denied things he obviously had done. "He'd rather lie than tell the truth, even when the truth would be easier on him," Kay told her relatives.

Michael's defiant nature worked against him with his father. If there was one thing Bob Swartz hated more than disobedience, it was back talk. And Michael cursed a lot, sometimes to his parents' faces. Even as a child of eight or nine, Michael occasionally tried to stand up to his father, who literally knocked him down. It was not uncommon for Bob to march Michael back to his room and wallop him.

Larry never stood up to Bob, and almost never got walloped. Soon Michael took the heat for everything, no matter who actually had done it. "Michael was always getting into trouble over little things," Larry would write years later in a summary of his life. "We would get into fights and he would seem to be the one to blame. My parents seemed to always take sides with me, and I wondered why they took my side instead of his sometimes, even when he was right."

Relatives spotted the favoritism straightaway. "I remember feeling sorry for Michael because it seemed that Larry was the favorite child," said Lynn Sullivan, one of the boys' cousins. "Larry was very small and used to play a game with Aunt Kathryn. He would climb up one side of her legs, over her shoulders, and back down the other side, both of them laughing. Michael was a very tall boy, too big to play that game."

Uncle Gerald tried to make Michael feel good about his size through horseplay. He picked the boy up by his ankles and swung him wildly in circles. Larry would go over and beg to be swung too, but Uncle Gerald would tell him, "You're too little." Uncle Gerald figured that might even things out a bit.

The boys' cousins noticed something else about Larry that seemed to escape his parents. "Often Larry was very sneaky, doing something he wasn't supposed to do and blaming it on Michael," Lynn Sullivan recalled. "Larry would act innocent as Michael got in trouble."

Often, though, Michael brought the trouble on himself by calling Kay a bitch and using foul language in front of Bob. Once when he cursed at his mother, she washed out his mouth with soap and locked him in the bathroom for the rest of the day.

Another time, Michael and Larry were horsing around behind the altar at St. Mary's Church with a small glass decanter that the altar boys cleaned after mass. Someone knocked it over and shattered it. Furious that the boys could be so careless with holy objects, Kay exploded. She made both boys drop their pants when they got home and she beat their bare buttocks with a coat hanger. Kay and Bob could not be certain which boy was the culprit, but Larry insisted that Michael had done it. As usual, Michael took the blame. Telling him he would have to reimburse St. Mary's one hundred dollars, his parents deducted that amount from the education fund they had started with the monthly support payments the state gave them while he was still a foster child.

5.

By the mid-seventies, Bob was unhappy with his job. He still worked at what many considered to be *the* training center for the Apollo program, the Goddard Space Flight Center. He had gone to work there two months after Neil Armstrong implanted his footprint on the surface of the moon, a heady time for all the men and women involved in the space race. Many of Goddard's engineers and technicians were utterly absorbed by the space race and talked of little else, but not Bob, an instructor for the Bendix Corporation under contract to NASA.

"Bob never seemed to talk much about it," recalled John J. J. Jobes, the man in charge of the Bendix space training program. "There were other people you would see caught up in it, but he never struck me as one. His comments were somewhat reserved."

Bob was one of thirty-five instructors who trained technicians to operate the NASA tracking stations that sent and received data to and from satellites. Although he taught several different courses, he specialized in the high-powered equipment that transmitted computer commands from Ground Control at Houston to the Apollo spacecraft. Occasionally, NASA dispatched Bob to teach a course at a foreign tracking station, for it was more economical to send one instructor abroad than to fly a team of technicians home.

Bob's coworkers saw him as a competent and serious-minded instructor who kept to himself. They noticed he was touchy about his lack of hair and would redden whenever his colleagues—some of whom were bald themselves—bantered about it.

Bob befriended his boss, Hank O'Neill, a devout Catholic and his company's chief instructor at the Apollo Network Training and Testing Facility. When Bob took O'Neill sailing in his pride and joy, a twenty-two-foot Pearson sloop that he had bought shortly after he adopted his first son, his landlubber boss was impressed. "He was the most knowledgeable guy," recalled O'Neill. "He understood winds, currents, water movements. He could maneuver the boat across the bay, go into the wind and with the wind." After Bob became a Marriage Encounter fan, he tried to recruit his boss to that, too. With a brood of seven kids at home, however, O'Neill never had the time. Bob prodded him, saying over and over, "One of these days we're gonna get you there."

Bob tried repeatedly to get a supervisory job like O'Neill's, something with more pay and responsibility, but for reasons he never understood, Bendix always passed him over. He left Bendix in 1976 for a job at the RCA Service Corporation, another NASA contractor. RCA hired him to compile training manuals for space-communications equipment, the same equipment he had been training people to use at Bendix. His new office was in Riverdale, not far from his old office in Greenbelt, and he still commuted two hours a day.

At home, Bob became a tinkerer, pouring his energy into one project after another. He built cabinets and bookshelves, planted bushes and flowers. He went bird-watching. He bought a sixteen-millimeter movie camera and recorded family events. He bought an old motorcycle and all sorts of gadgets and took them apart. Every now and then, his family joked, he'd put something back together, but they got used to disassembled electronic gear collecting dust in the basement. When Bob recruited his boys into helping with his projects, neither one displayed much interest in things mechanical, nor much aptitude. That disappointed Bob.

Still, the boys provided cheap labor when Bob decided to re-fashion his homestead on the Cape. His backyard appeared so empty, he thought how much nicer it would be with a swimming pool, maybe some tennis courts. "Dad was a person that I think wanted to build the world," Michael later recalled. "Always doing something. I think he wanted to turn that place into a mansion or something, 'cause he wanted tennis courts in the backyard. He wanted the works. He had big dreams."

One of Bob's projects during Michael's first summer there was digging out a storage area underneath the carport and building a new walkway alongside the carport. Bob supervised a massive dig and paid his sons by the wheelbarrow. The more enterprising son proved to be Michael, who dug for hours and lugged away incredible amounts of dirt. After they finished digging, Michael helped his father lug railroad ties from the Datsun pickup and lay them in the ground as stepping-stones. "I don't think Larry dug out more than two wheelbarrelfuls," Kay later laughingly told a friend. "Michael spent all summer digging." Bob also corralled the boys into helping him lay bricks for a patio in the backyard, just outside the new sliding glass door that he installed in the downstairs recreation room.

When Michael got into mischief, Bob made him do manual labor as punishment, for he thought labor was a good outlet for Michael's aggression and a fitting lesson in the hard realities of life. When Michael was suspended from school for swearing at a teacher, Bob gave him a bicycle pump and said, "Go pump up the tires on the Datsun. And when you finish that, go see if Mr. Richard has some work for you."

Bob told neighbors Michael had let the air out of the truck's tires because he was angry that he'd been locked out of his house all day. Michael claimed he hadn't touched his father's tires. "The air just went out by itself," he insisted. Regardless, Michael took the hand pump and pumped them up, then reported to Richard Folderauer, who lived across the street and ran a tree-trimming and removal business. Folderauer put Michael to work and paid him for his efforts.

As the boys grew older, Folderauer employed both Michael

and Larry for weekend and summer help. He felt sorry for the boys because their parents never gave them lunch money, so he bought them lunch and deducted it from their wages. "The kids were ill-clad, without buttons, and no ironing," he recalled. "Both boys were unhappy."

Michael, in particular, was forever getting grounded. For days, even weeks, his parents forbade him to leave his yard. Bob and Kay felt they had no choice because Michael was so impossible, cursing all the time, never doing his homework. Although he could work hard when he put his mind to it, Michael always had to be told to do his chores. As often as not, he put up a fight, just as Bob had done when he was growing up in Pittsburgh decades earlier.

In 1976, the Barker family moved into a house on Mount Pleasant Drive and befriended the Swartz family. While Paul, the son, played with Michael and Larry, his parents socialized with Bob and Kay. Because Susan Barker was one of the few neighborhood women who was home during the day, neighborhood kids often stopped by to visit her. Michael became a regular, even though he had to sneak down the street because his parents forbade him to visit her. Michael liked Mrs. Barker and often confided in her. The closer she grew to Michael, the farther apart Mrs. Barker found herself drifting from his parents.

Although she liked Kay, Susan Barker had little use for Bob. He was so obnoxious in public, it wasn't hard to imagine what he might be like in the privacy of his home. When Susan and her husband played doubles with the Swartzes, she didn't like how Bob treated his wife on the tennis court, constantly yelling things, such as, "You *fool,* why can't you get the ball over the net?" And when they went out on Bob's sailboat, he was a little tyrant, assigning seats, barking orders, all but forbidding his passengers to breathe.

Bob's tyrannical streak didn't go unnoticed in his own family. Joe Swartz later speculated that Bob never stopped feeling jealous of him, the older brother who outperformed him. Joe thought Bob carried a chip on his shoulder—a resentment at being the family troublemaker, the son who never pleased his father—straight through to adulthood. It was the only explanation Joe could come up with for his brother's abrasive personality. "If he knew something, he always liked to tell everybody that he did know it, the facts that he knew, that *he* was *right*," Joe recalled. "He always liked to be right. He disliked very intensely being shown that he was wrong. I think he found it difficult to admit that he was wrong."

Mild-mannered Joe, in many ways the opposite of his brother, dealt with Bob by ignoring him. That infuriated Bob. When Joe made a mistake, or admitted ignorance of some obscure fact, Bob would taunt him. "You mean you didn't know that?" Bob would say with mock incredulity, then burst into loud raucous laughter. While Joe's wife considered Bob a little sadistic and extremely conceited ("Bob was the number one person in Bob's fan club," she said), Joe just thought he was jealous, still trapped in the sibling rivalry of their youth.

Bob's iron hand and rigid intolerance made him a sharp counterpoint to his wife, who often showed sympathy for the children—especially for Larry. Although her sarcasm sometimes rubbed people the wrong way and her temper occasionally flared without warning, Kay had a resilience about her and a sensitivity to other people that her husband lacked.

Kay's pliant personality was especially evident in the classroom. She always made time for students who stayed after class to chat or ask questions. When she began teaching tenth-grade English, some of her brighter students considered her class a breeze, an easy A. She tolerated an unusually high level of "learning noise" in her classroom. Partly for that reason, some students considered her lax. A lively nonconformist, she shared humorous tales about herself in class and let ordinary teenage mischief slide by. She wasn't one to send kids to the principal's office for uttering snide comments about her horn-rimmed glasses or aiming paper airplanes at her gawky frame; and her students did both.

Oblivious to superficial matters, she found her students amusing, especially their expensive look-alike fashions. Kay Swartz was anything but fashionable. She thought nothing of venturing out in clothes that clashed or bore old stubborn stains. She favored oversized coarse sweaters in winter and polyester stretch pants with flared legs in spring and fall. She often arrived at school in clunky old shoes or boots, then changed into a dressier pair. Even her dressy shoes weren't always in the best condition. One day, she glanced around her classroom and noticed that most of her students were wearing identical new shoes. When she looked down at her own feet, she chuckled. There was a hole in the scuffed leather over her big toe!

If she was unusually tolerant in class, Kay Swartz nevertheless expected her pupils to read "The Hollow Men" and to pay attention while she walked them line by line through the T. S. Eliot poem. Literature, especially poetry, was one great joy in her life that she wanted to share with young people.

6.

Early in 1978, spirits brightened in the Swartz family when Kay and Bob took Michael and Larry out of school one day and drove to New York City. The boys had been dying for a sister and they were finally getting one. For weeks, Kay and Bob had been acting so excited that Mrs. Barker thought it seemed as though Kay actually was pregnant.

The Swartzes had tried for several years to get a daughter before Kay's brother suggested they should try to adopt a Korean orphan. During the Korean War, Gerald and his buddies had taken in a sick Korean boy who had wandered into their navy corpsmen tent. Kay always enjoyed her brother's tale of little Tommy Tucker; now she couldn't wait to get her own Korean orphan. She and Bob were thrilled that their new daughter was going to be foreign-born, different from the boys. What a challenge to teach her English, to introduce her to American culture.

Anne was a dainty doll-like girl with chubby cheeks who alighted from the airplane in tears. Despite her distress, it was a joyous occasion for the Swartzes; Bob and Kay were completing their family. Bob was determined to record the moment for posterity, so Kay took one of Anne's tiny hands, Larry took the other, and they all walked toward Bob's whirring movie camera.

Exhausted, Anne fell asleep the moment she got into the car and slept most of the way home to Maryland. The next day, her brothers spent hours playing with her in the basement, rocking her in a white wicker swing. The boys taught her all sorts of English words and learned the Korean equivalents from her. When they held up an orange and pronounced the English word, she came back with the Korean word. Then the boys ran around chanting, Oh-ren-zy, Oh-ren-zy. Over the next few months, they played that game with a zillion words, for their little sister spoke no English at all. The boys also teased her a lot, pretending they were karate experts slicing the air around her, chanting, in singsong, Yung Wung Sook, their Americanized version of her Korean name.

Anne was four years old when she arrived, according to adoption records that listed her birth date as October 1973. Yet she seemed too tiny to be four, and Kay and Bob suspected that her birth date was erroneous. They therefore decided she was three and gave her a new birth date of October 1974. They figured the extra year would give her more time to break the language barrier before she started school. Anne, of course, didn't know her age when she arrived. She would grow up believing that she was a year younger than she really was.

The Swartzes knew little about Anne's background, except that she had been found abandoned and alone at a police call box in Seoul. The Korean police took her to an orphanage, where she was offered for adoption.

Her new family called her Annie and loved her dearly. Her father treated her as Daddy's little treasure. He surprised everyone by spoiling her, taking her everywhere and spending hours playing with her on his lap.

At first, she had trouble sleeping, so her new parents took her into their bed at night. After her arrival, the Swartzes moved Michael to the small basement study downstairs and left Larry in the ground-floor bedroom beside Annie's new room. When she couldn't sleep, she often went into Larry's room and slept with him. She was accustomed to sleeping on floor mats in Korea, and—although Larry later denied that he ever slept on the floor—Bob and Kay told neighbors that Larry slept with his sister on the floor to help her adjust.

Michael came to view Annie as the center of family life. "Everything was directed toward Annie. She got everything nice," he would recall. Kay told friends it was obvious from Annie's reaction to gifts that she'd never had many toys or clothes of her own. One of the first words they taught her was *mine* and she pranced around, touching her toys, gaily saying, "Mine. Mine. Mine."

"It's so much fun to spoil Annie because she gets so excited about everything she gets," Kay told a friend.

Most of Bob's family got their first glimpse of Annie in August 1978, when a cousin of Bob's got married near Harrisonburg, Virginia. The whole Swartz family gathered for a reunion in the Shenandoah Valley on Sunday, the day after the wedding. It was a glorious day, marred only by the radio announcement that Pope Paul VI had died. The news meant little to most members of the largely Protestant family.

Yet the Swartzes knew it would sadden Bob, who had become something of a fanatical Catholic. A few of his relatives thought Bob had gone overboard since his conversion. They resented his holier-than-thou attitude, the sanctimonious air he displayed as prominently as the oversized crucifix he wore on his chest. "Bob would sorta sneer at us because we were going to a Protestant church," one relative recalled. "He thought Catholic was *right.* He was very impressed with being a reader in his church."

Bob skipped the wedding on Saturday so he could attend services at St. Mary's early Sunday morning. With his family in tow, he finally arrived at the reunion on Sunday afternoon just as the Swartz clan was finishing lunch. Although Annie still didn't speak English, she delighted everyone by giggling and laughing as she was introduced. Bob's stepmother, Jean, scooped her up and took her into the fold, calling her "Grandma's little posy."

Kay's side of the family met Annie that same summer in Tennessee. Her sisters and brother rented a row of lakeside houses at Fairfield Glade, a resort near Nashville, and cheerful, adorable Annie stole everyone's heart. When they went to a restaurant, she spent the entire meal on her father's shoulders; All the relatives laughed.

For the most part, both families readily accepted the adopted children and viewed them as part of their extended family. They thought it wonderful what Bob and Kay had done, giving a home to children who obviously needed one. Some of the relatives, however, felt sorry for Michael, whose acceptance by Bob and Kay seemed tenuous.

Although Bob was closedmouthed about his problems, Kay shared with Bob's parents some of the heartaches Michael was causing them. Michael had no respect for other people's property. He had been accused of taking things at school, and Kay suspected he stole money from her purse. "You'll wind up in jail," she warned him.

When Bob took everyone to visit his folks in Youngstown for Christmas, Michael went wandering in the bedrooms. Bob yelled at him in front of everybody, and Kay quietly warned Bob's family, "Don't trust him."

When the Swartzes went to Illinois in the summer, Kay's nieces and nephews played with Larry and Michael and noticed that Michael was hot-tempered. He exploded over little things, indignantly shouting "That isn't fair! That isn't fair!" He also got into trouble over the oddest things. While the Swartzes were visiting Kay's sister in Minonk, Illinois, Michael watched his cousin Jim mow the lawn of neighbors who were away on vacation. Jim put the neighbors' lawn mower back in their garage, then went home and put their automatic garage-door opener on top of the refrigerator. Later, when no one was looking, Michael sneaked into the kitchen and snatched the opener, then went down the street and played with the garage door, opening and closing it until it stuck open.

Yet his relatives never really saw Michael act like the ogre his parents made him out to be. Bob's family, in particular, thought Michael wasn't that bad. Oh, he sulked a lot, and you could tell he was an angry, rebellious kid, but he didn't run around swearing or doing anything disgraceful in front of his relatives. Some of them had a hard time understanding why his father came down so hard on him.

Joe Swartz couldn't bear how his brother treated Michael on the soccer field. Bob was coaching a soccer league at home, and his sons were still learning the game. When the family gathered at Grandpa Swartz's in Ohio, they kicked the soccer ball around on the field behind Grandpa's house. Joe noticed that Bob was always showing Larry how to improve his game, yet he yelled and found fault with Michael without giving him a word of advice. Then Michael would walk off the field and sulk, further inciting his father.

Joe sensed that Michael had the same compulsion to win that Bob always had shown, which intensified the father-son conflict. "I always said that Bob did not like to lose, card games, Ping Pong—anything," Joe recalled, "and I was usually better. And I don't say that in a boastful way; I just beat him. He would get so angry sometimes because he couldn't win. Well, Michael was even *more* like that. He did *not* like to lose."

7.

When he entered the seventh grade in the fall of 1978, Michael's behavior problems fully erupted. Sadly, Kay and Bob began to wonder whether they'd made a mistake adopting him.

Kay had a terrible time getting Michael out of bed every morning, and often he missed the bus. At night he had insomnia, then in the morning couldn't wake up. At first when Michael missed the bus, Kay dropped him at Severn River Junior High on her way to work, for she passed his school on the way to hers. After a while, she got fed up: Michael obviously wouldn't make the effort to get up on time if he knew he could hop a ride with her. So she made him walk all five miles.

Michael, now twelve, routinely misbehaved at school, cursing at teachers and fighting with classmates. When his teachers placed him on detention, keeping him after hours, he discovered it was no use calling his mother for a ride home; she wouldn't pick him up. He walked home from detention, too.

One day he got into a fistfight on the bus and the driver kicked him off the bus for a month. Bob and Kay were furious. They refused to drive him to or from school.

Stewing, Michael walked back and forth from school for thirty days. Neighbors who saw him walking along College Parkway were appalled; their hearts ached for him.

Bob's heart did not ache for Michael. It pumped blood to his brain, triggering fits of fury. He lectured Michael, and Michael talked back, prompting Bob to punch him with his fists. Although his mother occasionally slapped Michael's face, she never slugged him as Bob did. Once or twice she even intervened, pleading with her husband, "That's enough."

Michael later would say that Bob never beat Larry or Annie, only him—except once or twice when Larry "got cracked" at the dinner table for holding his fork improperly.

Larry also confirmed that Michael bore the brunt of their father's fury. During 1978 and 1979, Larry later told authorities, Bob beat Michael twenty or thirty times. Most of the beatings took place downstairs in Michael's bedroom. Often Annie was sent over to a neighbor's house beforehand. Larry could hear Michael's screams—loud piercing cries that frightened him.

At first Larry ran to his mother, panic-stricken. "Isn't that enough?" he pleaded.

"Stay out of it," she admonished.

After a while, Larry ran out back and hid in the swampy woods to wait until he thought it was over. He could not bear to watch. Sometimes, though, it was unavoidable. Bob occasionally swung at Michael in front of Larry and Larry ran to a corner of the room and cowered, terrified that his father would hit him, too. Once his father threw his mandolin at Michael in the backyard and narrowly missed him. Another time, he lost his temper and knocked Michael to the ground on the walkway beside the house. Bob kicked Michael again and again. With each kick, Michael rolled from one railroad tie to the next, crashing down the steps he had helped his father build. For weeks, Michael complained to Larry about pain in his ribs.

As Michael's hostility toward his father grew more intense, he was not shy about expressing it. He told his mother in a matter-of-fact voice one day, "You know, I could kill Dad."

"What?" She was shocked.

"I could kill him if I wanted to," he repeated. "Dad would come home one day and I would be standing behind the door with a knife. He would open the door, and I could kill him because he wouldn't know I was behind the door."

Kay stared at her son in disbelief. She did not for a minute believe he was serious. But his remark upset her tremendously, and she told Bob about it. They told their relatives, some of whom wondered whether Michael was mentally disturbed. Gerald Sullivan later said he thought his nephew must have fried his brain in a microwave oven. "I don't think she was nearly as concerned as I was," Gerald recalled. "I thought it was really weird."

Midway through the school year, Michael was suspended from school again for fighting. Bob decided to teach him a lesson, and at the same time get rid of a dead tree stump in the front yard. Retrieving the heavy maul he used to split firewood from the storage room, Bob handed it to Michael.

"You're going to learn how people work in the real world," his father announced. "Go out front and chop up that tree stump. You're not leaving the yard until it's done."

It wasn't the first time Michael had split wood, for he was big for his age and occasionally had helped Bob in the wintertime. He'd also done work for the tree man who lived across the street. But this was the first major project that Michael had tackled on his own. He slammed the log splitter, which was nearly three feet long and weighed about ten pounds, into the stump. Then he removed it and swung again. He did this over and over until his arms ached. After a few days, Michael returned to school, but the fat stump stubbornly remained in the ground. Though Michael protested the job was too much for him, Bob was adamant: "You *will* get it out. You're going to chop for three hours every day after school. Until you finish, you're grounded." Michael came home after school every day for weeks and pounded on the stump. He worked until his hands blistered. He went over to Susan Barker's house in tears one day and told her he didn't think he would ever finish. Finally, Bob acknowledged the task was too much for Michael and called Richard Folderauer to finish the job.

Michael's grades dropped steadily as the school year progressed. In the first quarter, he failed one subject. The second quarter, two. By the third quarter, he was failing three subjects and Bob was furious.

That was 1979, the year the Barkers moved to Italy. A few months before they moved, Michael went to their house in tears.

"Please take me with you," he begged Mrs. Barker.

"Why? What's the matter?"

"They don't care about me, Larry, or Annie. They don't care about any of us." Michael was sobbing.

Mrs. Barker tried to soothe him and find out what had provoked his outburst. Michael said his parents were threatening to send him to reform school, and he didn't want to be sent anywhere. He wanted to stay home with Larry and Annie, the only real family he'd known. He was so convinced his parents were going to send him away that he wanted to go to Europe with the Barkers. Only he couldn't ask permission, he explained, because if he did, his parents would beat him.

Mrs. Barker assumed that Michael was exaggerating. She could not believe his parents would beat him for wanting to go to Europe with her, nor that they would banish their son to reform school. Michael may have been a troublemaker—so was Larry, for that matter, he was just sneakier about it—but he was no juvenile delinquent. Michael's story was probably full of half-truths, she decided. Besides, it wasn't her place to interfere.

By June, Michael had managed to pull his grades up a little. He squeaked out D's in almost every subject except math, which he failed.

When he started eighth grade in the fall, his troubles started all over again. He missed the bus, got into fights, and stole from Kay's purse. The Swartzes told relatives they were worried that Michael was developing a drug problem; they were convinced he was smoking pot and feared he would graduate to other drugs.

Bob's father gently lectured Michael about drugs while they played chess during a visit to Youngstown. Grandpa Swartz told Michael that his father, Bob, also had strayed as a young man, experimenting with drugs and a wild lifestyle before he settled down, married, and became a responsible citizen. Grandpa told Michael he hoped he would straighten out, as his father had.

Although the thought of his father "experimenting" with drugs amused Michael, Grandpa's gentle lectures had little effect on him. His belligerence at home intensified. If he was trying to get Bob and Kay to reject him, to do as his other parents had done, throw up their hands and admit that their noble experiment had failed, then he was doing a terrific job.

After threatening repeatedly to send Michael to reform school, the Swartzes called the state Department of Social Services to request assistance: Michael was becoming a delinquent; they were losing control. The state assigned a new caseworker to supervise him and arranged special counseling sessions. Bob and Kay warned Michael one last time: Pull yourself together, or you're gone.

Kay was driving home from an errand in the family's Plymouth station wagon one day, with Annie in the front seat and the boys in the back. They were on the other side of town, the west side of Annapolis, a largely undeveloped area where the county had built its detention center.

Rounding a bend, they came in view of the drab brick complex enclosed by tall fences topped by razor wire, glinting menacingly in the sun. Apprehension suddenly gripped Michael and Larry. They peered intently out the car windows, sizing up the jail. It looked spooky and grim.

As the jail faded from view, Michael turned to Larry and whispered, "Not me, I'm not gonna end up there."

"Me neither," Larry quickly agreed.

For Kay, it was Annie who finally made her acknowledge they might have to get rid of Michael. Her first inkling came with the baths. Michael wanted to give his little sister baths. He was too old for that, and Annie was, too. Michael was entering puberty; there was no mistaking his sex drive. It frightened Kay. Although she never gave her relatives specifics, she told them that something about Michael wanting to give Annie baths set her off. Kay became increasingly fearful of incest between her children. "She was afraid that Michael would attack Annie," Kay's sister, Maureen Riely, later recalled. "She just never trusted him with Annie. She would not leave Annie alone in the house with Michael. No way."

If Kay was frightened that Michael would molest his little sister, she and Bob were puzzled by his budding sexuality. They told relatives they were shocked to discover that Michael dressed up in his mother's clothes when they weren't home. Larry snitched on Michael after he caught his brother putting on their mother's clothes one evening.

In the end, none of the relatives were sure exactly what prompted the Swartzes to give up on their eldest son; but Bob and Kay's attitude toward Michael clearly changed. Optimism gave way to pessimism, and they grew fearful of their own son. Stories of Michael threatening bodily harm against both parents filtered back to relatives. Kay told her family that Michael thought because he was a minor, he could literally get away with murder. One day he astonished her by declaring, "I could walk up and put a knife in Dad's back, and nobody could do anything to me because I'm a juvenile. I wouldn't be eighteen. They couldn't touch me." When Kay repeated Michael's remark to her family, they were stunned. They knew Michael was a big talker; they hoped his threat was as hollow as the fibs and exaggerations that tumbled so freely from his mouth. None of the relatives, however, liked the sound of his knife-in-the-back remark. It was creepy and odd. Why would a child threaten to kill the one man who had given him the only real home he'd known?

One night in January 1980, Michael asked his parents for permission to go out after supper. They said no: It was Monday night, and neither boy was allowed to wander outside on school nights, especially not with the derelict-looking characters who had come by the house earlier, knocking on the door and wanting Michael to go out.

Michael wasn't the kind of kid to take no for an answer. He went into his room, opened the window, and hopped out. Joining his buddies, Michael roamed the neighborhood for several hours, then returned at midnight, to find his house locked—every door, every window.

Michael knocked on the front door.

No answer.

He knocked again. "Let me in!"

Kay came to the front window and looked right at him, her brown eyes narrowing in anger. Silently, calmly, she shot him the finger. *Fuck you, Michael. You want out, you can stay out.*

Stunned, Michael realized they were not going to let him in, even though it was freezing outside. He walked to a buddy's house and asked to spend the night.

In the morning, Michael got up and rode the bus to school as if nothing had happened. His parents called his social worker and reported that Michael had run away. Michael would later see irony in that: "I'm a runaway kid, and I'm going to school, right?"

At the end of the day, when the announcements came over the loudspeaker, Michael heard himself being summoned to the principal's office. His social worker greeted Michael at the office and told him his parents had turned him in.

The social worker drove Michael home, where Kay stood waiting.

She gave him a choice: Either leave the Swartzes now and move to a foster home, or stay and the juvenile authorities would take legal action against him for running away. Either way, there would be court proceedings. His parents were at the end of what they considered to be a very long rope.

"What do you want?" asked Kay, tears streaking her gaunt face.

Confused, hurt, and more than a little frightened, Michael was crying, too. But after five and a half years with the Swartzes, Michael knew what he would face if he chose to stay.

"I want out of here," he declared.

Michael went down to his bedroom to pack his clothes. As he finished, Larry arrived home from school.

"What's going on?" Larry asked when he saw Kay's puffy eyes and Michael standing there, suitcase in hand. Neither his mother nor Michael would answer.

Weeping, Kay watched Michael climb into the caseworker's car and ride away. Then she turned and went inside the house.

Later that night, Larry asked his mother what had happened, but she gave him no explanation. All she said was, "Now we're going to have to crack down on *you*, just like we did on Michael!"

Bewildered, Larry didn't know what she meant, but he had enough of an idea to be afraid.

FIVE

Wednesday, January 18, 1984

1.

By Wednesday, the cold snap was beginning to annoy just about everyone. Snow and ice had glazed the roads for eight straight days, and the mercury seemed stuck around twenty-five degrees. For the second time in a week, Annapolitans had unclogged their driveways and sidewalks. They were ready for a reprieve, but instead they got snow, lots of it, dry fluffy stuff that began to fall at sunup.

At noon, snow-shy local officials shut down the county courthouse, where a hapless young man and woman soon arrived with their wedding party, only to find their wedding license locked inside.

Detective Gary Barr also wanted to get into the courthouse, but he knew better than the young lovers how to get around the locked doors. After typing an affidavit to justify a second search of the Swartz house, Barr drove into the Annapolis historic district, crossed the icy drawbridge over Spa Creek, and tracked down circuit court judge Robert S. Heise at his home.

A few hours later, armed with a search and seizure warrant, Barr and four other cops paid another visit to 1242 Mount Pleasant Drive. Their search of the crime scene the day before had focused on the basement rooms. This time, they were looking for evidence to prove that Larry was the killer. They expected to detect blood in the upstairs rooms, where no one was killed, where no intruder presumably would have ventured. They also expected to find the clothes that Larry had worn during the murders, with telltale traces of blood still present. They were also still hunting for the knife, which they figured could have been stashed in any number of hideaways.

Baltimore television crews greeted the detectives at the driveway and advanced with them to the house. Snooping through dirty windowpanes, a news crew filmed cops collecting knives in the kitchen, which soon triggered erroneous news reports that investigators had recovered the knife believed to have been the murder weapon. Police took several table knives, but the FBI lab found no blood on them. The only other knife police recovered—a sheathed hunting knife stored in Larry's bedroom closet—was also blood-free.

Convinced that Larry had tracked blood around the house in his boat shoes, the detectives asked the evidence technicians to bring a special blood-detecting chemical called luminol. It is supposed to make blood—even minute traces invisible to the naked eye—glow in the dark. Investigators often use it to recreate a killer's movements, hoping to find additional evidence as they retrace the murderer's path. The Anne Arundel County technicians didn't have a supply of luminol, so they requested a batch from the Maryland State Police Crime Laboratory.

The detectives saved the blood hunt until late in their search, shortly after dusk. Luminol glows faintly when it is mixed with sodium perborate. When the two compounds are mixed in distilled water, a barely visible bluish light appears. The glow intensifies when the solution comes in contact with iron, which speeds up the chemical reaction. Since blood contains iron, luminol glows especially brightly when it is sprayed on blood particles. A light spray of luminol will make the tiniest blood particles light up like fireflies.

The cops started in the bathroom across from Larry's bedroom on the main floor. Before they sprayed, a technician looked closely and saw a faint reddish palm print on the Formica counter beside the sink. The cops were excited. Who but Larry would have washed his bloody hands in here? They photographed the print, dusted it, and lifted it with adhesive tape.

A few minutes later, an evidence man sprayed luminol in the sink and hit the lights. Instantly, Barr was pleased: All around the sink trap, the rim glowed a bluish white. Blood had collected at the bottom of the sink.

Eager to reconstruct Larry's movements throughout the house, the cops left the bathroom and headed toward the basement steps. A technician sprayed the light switch at the head of the stairs. It glowed. Next, he sprayed the floor at the top of the stairwell, and particles glowed there, too.

Descending backward, the evidence man sprayed a step above him, then backed down a step and sprayed again. A footprint suddenly gleamed on one of the top steps. Watching from the top of the stairs, Barr felt elated. He watched intently as the evidence man moved down the staircase. The more he sprayed, the more blood seemed to shine all over the staircase. Obviously, thought Barr, Larry had walked upstairs with blood on the bottom of his shoes. Not only were shoe prints gleaming up at them, all the stairs glowed wildly. By the time the evidence man reached the landing at the bottom, the stairwell looked like a firefly convention, with millions of luminous creatures flashing in the dark.

"Christ, there can't be *that* much blood," Mock cried suspiciously. "These two people ain't got that much blood in 'em!"

Starting to worry, the cops carried the luminol into the basement laundry room for a test. They aimed the spray gun up at the ceiling above an old refrigerator and sprayed—a most unlikely spot for the killer to have deposited blood.

The ceiling glowed.

Crestfallen, the cops suspected their chemical wasn't working. "It was unbelievable," Tankersley said later. All the cops concurred with him, and also with Mock's dour assessment that "in court it isn't gonna be worth a damn, because we're seeing blood where blood isn't."

The cops never would figure out what, if anything, contaminated their luminol. One believed their mistake was mixing the chemical with iron-laden well water out of the faucet. Another thought the error was mixing up too large a batch and not using it fast enough. A chemist theorized it might not have been contaminated; any number of possible ingredients in the house paint or the carpeting could have made the luminol glow. Because iron is only one of many compounds that makes luminol glow, interpreting the results is a tricky art indeed.

Whatever the reason, their blood hunt had flopped. The cops figured there wasn't much sense in trying again, for they had contaminated much of the house with the spray.

Despite that setback, the detectives left the Swartz house satisfied that the evidence they did recover ultimately would prove Larry's guilt. They lifted more than half a dozen latent finger and palm prints, several in blood. They retrieved clothes from the washer and dryer. They took blood-smeared Clorox and Downey bottles. In the bathroom, after taking two towels, they attacked the fixtures with frenzied determination. They ripped out the ceramic towel holder, cut out a chunk of wallboard, pried off a section of the wooden doorjamb, and took away the sink trap.

The next day, they hand-carried all the items to the FBI laboratory in Washington, D.C., for analysis.

Before the cops left the house, Ron Baradel telephoned, looking for phone numbers of relatives that the Swartz children said were tacked on their refrigerator. The cops grudgingly gave him the numbers.

Then Detective Barr got on the phone. "There's a bird out here. What do you want me to do with him?"

"I don't know." The lawyer sighed. Baradel hadn't even managed to notify the relatives yet. Now, on top of making funeral arrangements and tracking down relatives, he guessed he'd better make plans to feed the parakeet.

2.

At eleven o'clock Wednesday night, John Riely had been on the phone to his fiancée in Rhode Island for an hour when suddenly an operator broke into the call and announced, "I have an emergency phone call for John Riely from Perine Riely."

Riely froze. He had a mother named Maureen, a sister named Jeaneen. Who was trying to call him? As he hung up, he tried to steel himself for bad news. Within seconds, his phone rang.

"Something terrible has happened," cried his near-hysterical mother in Illinois. "Bob and Kay have been murdered."

A third-year law student at Catholic University of America, Riely, who was twenty-five, pumped his mother for facts: When? Where? How? She knew almost nothing except that an Annapolis lawyer had called her sister, Helen Rodden, in Indianapolis with the news.

"Who did it? Do they have any clues?" Riely asked.

"No. They don't know yet."

"Do you think it's Michael?"

"Well, Helen thinks it was either Michael or Michael had somebody do it."

Riely was quiet. He agreed with his Aunt Helen, of course. Almost all the relatives would. It was perfectly plausible that Michael had killed his parents, for he had threatened to do it many times. The Swartzes had lived in fear that their incorrigible son would sneak back into the house one day and knife them in the back. All their relatives knew that. Yet it was so incredible to think that Michael had actually made good on his threats.

Normally an undemonstrative woman, John's mother sobbed throughout the call. At one point, she wasn't going to attend the funeral. Then she was going to climb into her car at midnight and start the fourteen-hour drive to Annapolis in a blast of arctic cold that had driven the windchill factor in the midwest to fifty below zero. Riely hung up and called his uncle Gerald in Morton Grove, Illinois, who telephoned a neighbor in Minonk, who ran next door to make sure that Riely's mother was all right.

Meanwhile, Riely dashed downstairs in the house he shared with several other students and rummaged for *The Washington Post.* There in the Metro section, he found confirmation of what he had not quite believed. COUPLE FOUND SLAIN AT HOME, the headline read. Scanning the brief story, Riely realized his mother was right. Nobody knew much yet. His stomach turned when he read that his aunt's "nude" body had been found in her backyard. This could get ugly. He ran back upstairs to make a series of phone calls that would keep him up half the night. It was overwhelming, but for Riely, whose house would become "command central" for his family, it was just the beginning.

3.

On Thursday, the Annapolis *Capital* headlined the cops' theory in a front-page banner: WOMAN RAN FROM SLAYER. Word of the chase leaked to the media almost immediately after Police Chief William S. Lindsey and another officer met privately Wednesday night with nervous Cape St. Claire residents. Fearful that a homicidal maniac was roaming their streets, more than fifty neighbors attended the meetings in two different homes. Said Lindsey: "We told them we were increasing our patrols and presence. We were trying not to seem insensitive, even though we were pretty sure the Swartz boy was responsible."

Lindsey and the other officer tried to assure neighbors that they had suspects and would break the case soon. But, they explained, they needed the neighbors' help. After explaining their theory that the killer had chased Mrs. Swartz around the block, the officers asked the neighbors what they'd seen and heard Monday night.

A few neighbors said they had heard dogs barking between eleven and eleven-thirty. That squared with what Maria Briggman, who lived down the street from the Swartzes, had phoned police to say. She had been out walking her dog when she heard a shrill noise at eleven-fifteen. At first, she thought it was tires squealing. Then she realized it might be a scream. Suddenly, all the dogs were barking.

Beyond that, no one had heard or seen anything.

Although it was pure conjecture, the chase was so sensational that newspapers and television stations splashed it all over Baltimore and Washington. Speaking to reporters in hushed tones, neighbors questioned why Mrs. Swartz hadn't banged on their doors for help. And why hadn't anyone heard a commotion? Surely Mrs. Swartz must have screamed in terror as she fled.

The news accounts did little to boost Ron Baradel's spirits. He realized he was in trouble five minutes after he entered the Swartz house. Accompanied by Jack Smithmyer and Frank Napfel, a former Baltimore County cop turned private eye, Baradel had driven out to the house early Thursday afternoon. Like the police, Baradel was searching for clues but, unlike them, he was hoping to prove Larry's innocence.

As they walked into the kitchen, the defense trio saw on the table a search warrant and list of items seized by the police. Reading it, Baradel shook his head. The weak story Larry had told him suddenly seemed weaker. Surely police had a reason for tearing the house apart, for taking sink traps and doorknobs. Undoubtedly, they had found blood on these items.

Venturing into the basement, Baradel paused halfway down the stairwell. Oh my God, he thought. Not only was the family room in disarray, it was flooded from one end to the other. Water squished under their shoes as the men walked around, studying the evidence police had left behind. They soon discovered what they thought was the flooding source: The cops had cut away the sink trap under the laundry tub. It wasn't clear, though, why the water had been turned on.

Baradel and Napfel examined the small office where Bob's body had been found. They were surprised to see that police had left on the floor a gooseneck lamp that still had blood splatters inside its shade. Based on the pattern of blood in the room, the defense team deduced that Bob had been attacked while he was seated behind his desk, that he had risen to his feet, then fallen against the wall and collapsed to the floor near the middle of the room.

"Indications are that Mr. Swartz was not surprised by the presence of his assailant, but in all probability knew the attacker," the private eye concluded in his report.

The scene in the family room was less clear-cut. Water had soaked into the bloodstained carpet, making it difficult to judge the blood volume beneath the black chair. It was substantial, though. The police had cut away pieces of the bloodstained chair and swatches of carpet below it. Across the room, smeared blood was still visible on the tracks and jamb of the sliding glass door. Apart from the doorway and the area around the chair, though, virtually no bloodstains were visible in the room.

Everything in the room looked jumbled. That jumble, along with the pattern of blood—especially the blood on the door— prompted Napfel to conclude: "The family room bore certain characteristics of a violent attack, struggle, flee situation where the victim was in a panic. It is apparent she knew she was being assaulted, and was attempting to defend her person by fleeing."

Baradel rejected that conclusion. He believed that Mrs. Swartz had put up even less of a struggle than her husband. Baradel thought, as did the detectives, that the debris-strewn room reflected sloppy housekeeping, not a struggle. And there was no way of telling whether the bloodstains on the sliding glass door had come from the fleeing Mrs. Swartz or from her attacker, perhaps as he dragged her through the doorway.

Baradel stayed behind when Smithmyer and the investigator left. He had a morbid task, which he dreaded but knew somebody had to do. Rummaging through the closets, Baradel picked out a dark brown suit for Bob, and a high-necked red ruffled dress for Kay. The funeral on Saturday would be Bob and Kay's final trip to St. Mary's; hundreds of people would be there. His friends deserved to depart this world wearing their Sunday best.

Then Baradel fed the parakeet and left the house.

4.

Warren Bird Duckett, Jr., had little trouble playing devil's advocate. It was a role that fit the outspoken Anne Arundel County state's attorney better than some of his preppie blazers and duck-monogrammed shirts.

"Sorry, guys," he said, leaning forward, blue eyes peering through gold-rimmed glasses at the cops and lawyers assembled in his law library. "We just don't have sufficient evidence for a conviction. Not yet, anyway. You gotta remember Larry lived in that house: He had full and total access to every room. There are alternate explanations for all this evidence."

The powwow had dragged on for an hour, with the cops wanting to arrest Larry, and Duckett telling them to slow down and do it "by the numbers." The prosecutor had summoned everyone to take stock of a case that was consuming their attention like a nuclear bomb in a chicken coop. Although Duckett hadn't personally taken charge yet, he eventually would. The forty-four-year-old prosecutor, whose thin-lipped, sober face sat atop a wide neck and medium build, enjoyed courtroom dramas. He usually tried twenty or thirty cases a year, more than most state prosecutors—not just publicity-rich cases but a lot of nickel-and-dime things that he happened to find intriguing.

That, however, was not why Duckett would take over the Swartz case from the assistant prosecutor, George Lantzas. The real reason was a boy named Stuart Kreiner who had hanged himself in a state prison a year and a half earlier. Kreiner was the defendant in a messy and sensational murder case that gave Duckett's office a black eye. The prosecutor wasn't about to let it happen again. In retrospect, the bad publicity over Kreiner seemed so avoidable.

Kreiner, sixteen at the time, was convicted in 1978 of murdering three young neighborhood girls in the woods behind their homes. Although his motive remained unclear, Kreiner under the influence of a truth serum told a psychiatrist that he stabbed the girls when one of them refused to play along with a game. He agreed to plead guilty after Duckett agreed to recommend a sentence of life-plus in the Patuxent Institution, an unusual Maryland prison that offered psychological treatment to violent prisoners who were deemed good candidates for rehabilitation. The plea bargain sparked no immediate public reaction, but within a few weeks the national media was spotlighting the case and the families of the victims were marching in front of the courthouse, waving placards that demanded, DUCKETT, QUIT!

The target of everyone's wrath—something Duckett and his assistant who handled the case claimed they hadn't known—was the matter of parole eligibility. At Patuxent, Kreiner could be paroled whenever Patuxent's psychiatrists deemed him ready to reenter society. Although it was a maximum-security prison, Patuxent functioned more like a hospital for the criminally insane. Its eight-member parole board gave every inmate a hearing each year and could release anyone at any time. Relatives and friends of Kreiner's victims were outraged to think that he could be on the street—theoretically, at least—almost immediately. They feared he would be released, only to kill again. Led by one of the girls' fathers, a group of neighbors collected more than two thousand signatures on petitions requesting a delay in Kreiner's commitment to Patuxent. The judge allowed the protesters to have their say in court, then denied their request.

Kreiner went to Patuxent, and Duckett, stung by the public furor, went to the General Assembly in 1979 to make a half-hearted attempt to change Patuxent's parole law. Dubbed "the Kreiner bill," the measure he proposed would have required that Patuxent inmates who were under life sentences serve at least eleven years before they could be paroled. The bill failed and the brouhaha over Kreiner faded. Yet Patuxent's critics continued trying to impose new restraints on the prison's extraordinary parole powers and finally scored a victory in 1982, when the state legislature enacted a law requiring the governor to approve the paroles of all inmates serving life terms in the institution.

Less than two weeks after the new law took effect, Kreiner—a lifer who had been well on his way to winning parole from Patuxent—was found hanging from a bed sheet in his cell. No clear motive was established for the suicide.

Duckett was deeply disturbed by the furor over Kreiner's suicide and the furor over his plea bargain. In hindsight, the prosecutor believed that the plea was perfectly appropriate and that his only mistake was failing to inform the victims' families about the terms of parole before reporters did. "I said to the guys in the office," Duckett recalled, "if a case like that ever was to reappear, I would make sure that I assigned it to myself."

Now here was such a case. If the cops were correct and either Swartz youth was guilty, Duckett felt there had to be some deep emotional scar in him. Nobody cracks open his mother's head and stabs his father seventeen times unless something is profoundly, horribly, wrong with him. And whatever it was, it didn't seem farfetched to think that the Swartz youth might wind up at Patuxent. So Duckett decided to butt into the case and take charge personally when and if an arrest was made.

Politically ambitious since his youth, Duckett didn't like people to think politics influenced his prosecutorial decisions, not in this or any case. Yet the Swartz murders, because of their high profile, were politically sensitive for him. His long-standing desire for a congressional seat was no secret, even though that ambition had lessened. Many people thought Duckett's political career was paramount in his life, and critics had long questioned his ability to make nonpolitical prosecutorial decisions. Even he would have conceded that the last thing his political career needed right now was a megaton screw-up like the Kreiner case.

Duckett had never been a stranger to controversy. He'd drawn accusations that he'd milked cases for publicity, protected political cronies, and granted special treatment to prominent people. Critics charged that he was an empire builder, an old-fashioned, ward-healing pol. One TV commentator said he ran the prosecutor's office "like a country club."

He seemed to relish scrapes, to rush headlong into trouble, often with the same perverseness he displayed in 1972 when he threw off his shirt and shoes on an Ocean City beach and ran into the Atlantic Ocean in a hurricane. For most of his adult life, he had been like that—combative professionally, risqué socially.

Maybe it had something to do with the security of deep family roots, knowing his place in the world from the very beginning. Or maybe it was the legacy of being descended from two Maryland governors: Robert Bowie, who governed the state twice in the early 1800s, and Oden Bowie, who governed from 1869 to 1872. "My family was in Annapolis before Annapolis was Annapolis," Duckett liked to tell people. Politics ran through his lineage like red hair and color blindness in other families. His paternal grandfather, Oden Bowie Duckett, Sr., was a state delegate and register of wills. His maternal grandmother, Kate Linthicum, was the Annapolis city clerk. Her husband, Thomas Linthicum, was postmaster of Annapolis and a city alderman.

Young Warren made his political debut at the University of Maryland, rising through the student legislature to become speaker and vice-president. He worked his way through law school as a Chinese linguist for the National Security Agency. The supersecret listening post hired him to help track the movement of Chinese ships after he wrote on his job application that he had taken Chinese in college. He didn't reveal that he couldn't speak much Chinese and had studied mostly Chinese culture.

The ambitious young lawyer left NSA the moment he passed the Maryland bar exam—a feat that, to his chagrin, took two tries. He then went into private practice and worked part-time as an assistant state prosecutor. Soon he won a seat on the county council. In 1973, at the age of thirty-three, he made a grab for the state's attorney's post, whose occupant was appointed to the district court bench. Campaigning adroitly behind the scenes, Duckett won the appointment but ruffled a flock of feathers that he spent years smoothing back down. After more than a decade as state's attorney, he had amassed kudos for reducing the criminal backlog and creating a Victim—Witness Assistance Center.

Although he stayed politically active, he blew a chance to become lieutenant governor in 1978 by declining an invitation to join the ticket of a long-shot gubernatorial candidate. The long shot, Harry R. Hughes, won. Duckett repeatedly vowed to run for Congress but never did. "He likes to run the show," said his wife, Judy.

She knew his wild streak, and his dark side, better than anyone. He almost drove her into divorce court with his drunken carousing, but eventually he swore off booze and dedicated himself to what he termed an "internal renaissance" of jogging, working, dieting, and marital fidelity.

By the time of the Swartz murders, he had bowed out of the 1984 congressional race, claiming he lacked the "fire in the stomach" needed to win. Some political observers believed he was chicken, unwilling to risk the kind of beating congressional contenders sometimes must suffer a few times before they win. Regardless, he insisted that he was out of the race. So he didn't think anyone could justly accuse him of milking the Swartz case for publicity, or of moving too cautiously for purely political concerns.

Duckett certainly was moving cautiously in making an arrest, though. Barr found his performance in the law library frustrating. Like an accomplished counterpuncher, Duckett was blocking every blow the investigator tried to land on Larry.

Wet clothes in the washer?

"Good Lord, the kid *lived* there: He had a *right* to wash his clothes. At least wait for the FBI to determine if there's blood on the clothes."

Bloody fingerprints on liquid-cleaner bottles?

"Well, all right, let's wait until there's an I.D. on the prints. Don't jump to conclusions. You've got to make absolutely sure they're Larry's."

The kid said he never went down to look for his father? And he got confused about where he was when he saw his mother?

"Listen, you're talking about murder, remember? That's traumatic. The boy's brain could have been denser than a London fog. He might not have remembered what day it was, much less which window he looked through. He could have run around the house in a panic, maybe even run outside, getting his hands and shoes bloody when he looked at his mother—then blocked it all out. Let's face it, it's all circumstantial. Much of this can be explained away."

"Give me a break," replied Detective Barr. He realized that Duckett had a point, but, nevertheless, he believed the prosecutor was grossly overstating the defense. "The boy can't explain away everything. There are too many inconsistencies. He's obviously lying."

Duckett countered with his main concern, over and over: How could they be so sure it was Larry and not his brother, Michael? What if Larry knew Michael did it and lied to cover for him? Relatives said Michael disliked his parents. And he was in Crownsville because he had pulled a knife and threatened a counselor at an emergency shelter in Baltimore just three weeks ago. Here was a kid with motive, maybe even means.

"But Michael was in Crownsville," Barr protested. "He's got an alibi."

"Everyone in this room knows patients escape from Crownsville," Duckett retorted. "How can you be sure Michael didn't break out, make the trip home—it's not that far, you know, maybe ten or twelve miles—and murder his parents, then sneak back in before bed check the next morning?"

Reluctantly, Barr and the other cops agreed it wouldn't hurt to delay the arrest until after the FBI reports came back. The key, everyone agreed, would be that bloody palm print on the sliding glass door. If that matched Larry's hand, even Duckett conceded it would be damning for the boy. That would give them probable cause for an arrest.

George Lantzas had spent much of the day researching their authority to use the grand jury to subpoena a suspect's fingerprints. He told Duckett that Larry would receive a summons the next day to appear before the grand jury and submit to fingerprinting on Monday. Larry's lawyers undoubtedly would put up a fight, but they inevitably would lose, Lantzas said.

5.

Joseph F. Murphy, Jr., hardly looked like a distinguished criminal defense lawyer. When he appeared at Baradel's office Friday morning, Baradel was taken aback. This was Maryland's premiere defense lawyer, the one that Baradel's associate Charlie Bagley had raved about? He looked like an owl in a three-piece suit.

Murphy was indeed owlish, with a cherubic face atop his short stout frame. He wore bulky black-rimmed glasses over sky-blue eyes. When he pondered legal questions, he furrowed his forehead into a deep vertical crease, giving him an intense bookish look. Despite his stodgy appearance, Murphy had a breezy air about him and peppered his talk with slang, chopped for effect: "He got an extra five thousand for being a *moe*-ron," or "I could *bull*-shit you, but. . . ."

Murphy's twangy vowels instantly revealed to strangers his New England roots. Born in Fitchburg, Massachusetts, he attended Catholic schools straight through to Boston College. His first employer transferred him to Baltimore, where he attended law school at night and eventually became an assistant state's attorney. Five years later, he rose to become the top deputy. From there, the lure of private practice called.

At heart, Murphy was a slob. Anyone could tell that from entering his office: books open here, folders strewn there, as though he'd been interrupted from a dozen tasks and had never gotten back to any of them. Yet in the courtroom, it was always clear that he had finished his homework. Many attorneys believed there wasn't a keener legal mind in Maryland. Though he was barely forty, Murphy was one of the most sought-after attorneys in the state by his peers. Lawyers, even judges, ran to him when they found themselves on the wrong side of the law.

Murphy's reputation got its biggest boost at the 1979 trial of a Baltimore nurse charged with murder for disconnecting the respirator of a critically ill patient in a mercy killing. Prosecutors argued that Mary Rose Kaisler Robaczynski had pulled the plug on several patients. Murphy's defense was ingenious: The patients were already dead, he told the jury. A mistrial ensued after twenty hours of deliberation failed to produce a verdict. Jurors revealed their final vote was ten to two in favor of acquittal, and the state declined to retry Murphy's client.

Given his reputation, it was no wonder Murphy's name popped into Charlie Bagley's mind when Baradel said Larry Swartz needed a good criminal lawyer. It was more of a wonder that Murphy took the case. Actually, Murphy couldn't quite place Bagley when he phoned Wednesday morning and identified himself as a former prosecutor who had tried a few cases against Murphy. But Murphy knew Bagley's firm: a nice classy outfit. One of the partners was a friend of Murphy. The least he could do was drive down from Towson, north of Baltimore, and help these guys figure out their next move.

Murphy liked Larry right away. When they met briefly at Baradel's office Friday morning, the youth's doelike eyes reminded him of Larry Brown, coach of the Kansas Jayhawks.

After a brief meeting, the defense team headed for the courthouse—Murphy, Baradel, Bagley, and the Smithmyers, with Larry and Annie in tow. The defense lawyers had petitioned for custody of Larry and Annie on behalf of the Smithmyers, and Judge James Cawood had signed a temporary custody order and set a full hearing.

Duckett's team turned out in force—Duckett, Lantzas, and half the homicide unit. Judge Cawood was tied up on the bench, so they all waited, the lawyers in Cawood's chambers at one end of the second-floor corridor, and the cops in the hallway, where a pack of reporters had gathered.

Annie, wearing a plaid skirt and white leotards, sat on Eileen Smithmyer's lap in the judge's waiting room, giggling, playing, and innocently watching the somber-faced adults. Larry sat beside her in beige cords, pink shirt, tan corduroy jacket, and brown cowboy boots. He alternately looked awed and jittery.

Duckett settled on a strategy of divide and conquer. Larry's extraordinary defense team had drawn the wagons so tightly that the cops couldn't get near the children. Duckett believed that if the police could just question Annie again, they could crack the case. The custody petition seemed a perfect opportunity: Why not use it to separate the children?

When the judge came off the bench, Duckett and Lantzas suggested it could be dangerous for Larry and Annie to continue sleeping under the same roof. After all, Annie might be the sole witness to the murder, and right now her brother was the prime suspect.

Alarmed, Larry's lawyers disagreed: There was no need to separate Larry and Annie, they insisted. Police had no evidence to implicate their client, and even if they did, they had no reason to believe that Larry would harm his sister. "Had he wanted to, your honor, he's already had plenty of opportunity," Murphy argued.

Cawood sided with Duckett on the sleeping arrangements, and recognized that Annie's legal interests were distinct from her brother's: He decided to appoint another attorney to represent the girl. Hoping to get a sympathetic lawyer, Lantzas recommended Gill Cochran, a free-spirited Annapolis alderman who wore a goatee and puttered around town on a moped. Cochran was known as the lawyer people called in the middle of the night when they got stopped for drunken driving. He'd rush out and give them a Breathalyzer on the roadside to help them decide whether to take the official Breathalyzer. Understandably, cops weren't crazy about him, but the prosecutors believed he was the kind of lawyer who'd let them question Annie. Cawood summoned Cochran to the courthouse.

For the next hour, the prosecutors and defense lawyers waited in chambers for Cochran and yet another lawyer—the woman who represented the county Department of Social Services. She was at a hearing next door in the courthouse annex, with Timothy D. Murnane, the public defender who represented Michael Swartz.

Crownsville's psychiatrists had completed Michael's thirty-day mental evaluation, and his confinement was due for review in juvenile court. Michael had been sent to Crownsville for evaluation two days before Christmas, after Michael pulled a knife on a social worker. The shrinks unanimously concluded that Michael suffered no mental illness and that further hospitalization was unwarranted. By law, Crownsville couldn't hold him any longer. But who would take in a kid suspected of murder? None of the group homes would. Reluctantly, Juvenile Master James Dryden ordered Michael to stay at Crownsville for ten more days, pending "a more appropriate placement." Michael's lawyer left the hearing disgusted and later that afternoon complained to a reporter, "We've got a kid who's staying in the mental institution because he's had the misfortune of having his parents murdered."

Michael, meanwhile, returned to Crownsville. As his caseworker led the tall gangly youth out a courthouse door—maybe fifty yards from where his brother sat awaiting word on his fate—the two brothers did not see each other. None of the dozen or so reporters standing around saw Michael, either.

By now, all eyes were focused on Larry.

Shortly after noon, two cousins of Larry and Annie arrived at the courthouse and waded through the mob of reporters and court-watchers in the hallway. It had been three days since the bodies were discovered, and John Riely and Gregory Rodden were the first relatives to go and see the Swartz children.

Annie, who seemed pleased to see them, blithely talked about her new lawyer, whom she had just met. "My lawyer looks funny," she said, pointing at Cochran's bow tie.

Welcoming the comic relief, John Riely and Greg Rodden laughed and hugged her.

As the custody hearing dragged on, Bagley and the Smithmyers took the children and their cousins across the street to the Maryland Inn for lunch. They took different tables on opposite sides of the small dining room.

Sitting with Larry, Annie, and Eileen Smithmyer, John Riely noticed that Larry seemed distracted. John assumed he was grief-stricken. Eileen leaned over, clasped Larry's hand, and said in a soft voice, "Everything is going to turn out all right. Have faith, Larry. God will provide."

John Riely had realized that Eileen Smithmyer and her husband, Jack, probably were the Swartzes' best friends when he had met them at his uncle and aunt's house last Thanksgiving. John also realized that Eileen and Jack were basic, born-again, "love and faith conquer all" people. Jack was some kind of engineer; Eileen, a homemaker raising six children. Before they started their family, Jack and Eileen had been missionaries in New Guinea.

When the cream of crab soup arrived, thick and spicy hot, John noticed that Larry hardly touched his. Clearly he was in no mood to be interrogated, but John couldn't help himself.

"Didn't you hear something going on that night?" John asked.

"No, I didn't hear anything," Larry said.

"Were you sleeping?"

"Yeah. I sleep real soundly and I had my door shut."

Eileen seemed edgy, as though John's questions disturbed her. "Isn't this delicious?" she asked brightly.

Larry idly moved the spoon around in his bowl. "You should eat, Larry," Eileen urged. "Get a good meal. You need to be strong to get through this. Trust in God. Everything is going to be all right."

Annie looked at her brother and asked, "What's going to happen to you, Larry?"

He hesitated before saying, "Annie, they may want us to be separated for a while."

"Where will you go?" She looked at him anxiously.

"I don't know."

John could not comprehend why anyone would separate his

cousins. Apparently, the children had picked up on something that he had missed.

Then, slowly, the picture came into focus. "Why?" John almost gasped, not believing that anyone would really suspect his gentle cousin. "Why do they want to separate you and Annie?"

"Well," Larry said haltingly, "they think I'm a suspect."

"They think you did it," Annie blurted.

"Hush, Annie," Eileen said sharply. "Be quiet."

John could not understand why police would suspect Larry instead of Michael. "What about Michael?" he asked. "Do you think Michael could have done it?"

"Yeah," Larry replied. "I think he could have."

"Have you had any contact with Michael since this happened?"

"No."

Tears welled in Eileen's eyes and she leaned over and clasped Larry's arm. She gripped Larry so tightly that John saw veins bulging in her arm.

John suddenly saw his cousin in a new light. When John had talked to Detective Barr on the phone the day before, Barr had hinted that Larry was a suspect. Now it was confirmed. John realized how unlikely it was that Larry had slept through everything with his bedroom door conveniently shut. Still, John could not fathom Larry blowing up and killing Aunt Kathryn. Larry was *close* to his mother; John had seen that.

When they all returned to the courthouse, John filled in cousin Greg on the lunch conversation and the police suspicions about Larry.

"It's not possible," Greg said flatly. He had lived with the Swartzes one summer and had grown especially close to Larry. He was adamant: Never in a million lifetimes could Larry do anything so brutal to Aunt Kathryn and Uncle Bob.

Greg and John cornered detectives Barr and Mock at the other end of the long hallway and John demanded, "Who are your suspects?"

The detectives eyed each other. "Larry, for one," Mock replied.

"That's crazy," said John. "Why?"

"Presence, for one thing. He was there."

"All right. So Annie's a suspect, too. Right?"

"Well . . ." Since he considered it a false corner, Mock went right in. "Yes."

"Then you're nowhere," John shot back.

"There is no way Larry could do this," Greg repeated. "I know him. It's not possible."

After a few minutes, John mentioned Michael again. He could not understand why Michael wasn't the prime suspect. Didn't police know about the threats he'd made against his parents?

"Listen, Michael was not there," Mock said emphatically.

"How do you know?"

"We checked. He was at Crownsville. The nurses saw him there Monday night. He was locked up."

As the hearing continued in chambers, Jack Smithmyer emerged and asked to have a word with John. In a low voice, Smithmyer inquired whether John would be available to help supervise Larry over the next two weeks. Judge Cawood wanted to separate the children, and it was up in the air where Larry would go. Regardless of where he went, an adult was to supervise him at all times.

"Of course I'll help," said John. "But why are they so intent on separating Larry and Annie?"

Smithmyer hesitated, then led John into a private room. Closing the door, Smithmyer turned to face him with a somber expression, the kind John thought a father might have as he uttered the most serious thing he ever told his son.

"I guess if you're going to volunteer to watch Larry, you'd better be filled in," Smithmyer said. "It's starting to look like Larry may have done this."

"What?"

"All the evidence points to Larry. He may have snapped that night."

Although Smithmyer was calm, John felt, he said later, "as though I'd been hit in a face with a ton of bricks." For the first time he began to consider that maybe Michael was innocent; maybe Larry was guilty. So this is why people are innocent until proven guilty, he thought. This is why we have constitutional rights. Clearly, if we judged people by their reputations, we would have hung Michael from a tree two days ago.

*   *   *

The closed-door hearing had turned into an ordeal. The Department of Social Services considered Larry's position similar to his brother's: No foster or group home would take him while he was under suspicion of murder. The lawyers went around and around: place Annie in a foster home, leave Larry with the Smithmyers. Nobody thought it was fair to move the girl from the Smithmyers', but what else could they do?

Baradel finally said he would try to find a friend to take in Larry, or perhaps consult his wife about opening their own home to the boy.

Judge Cawood was stern. Larry could sleep at the Smithmyers' that night, but Baradel had until six o'clock tomorrow—Saturday, the day of the funeral—to find Larry a new home. If Baradel didn't call the judge by six o'clock, Annie would go to a foster home.

6.

The custody hearing ended shortly after four o'clock, and everyone was due at Taylor Funeral Chapel at seven. Although Eileen was worried about making it to the viewing on time, she acceded to the advice of Annie's new lawyer and took the girl to Gill Cochran's office, two blocks away on West Street, so the detectives could question her again—this time with a tape rolling.

"We're on the air," Annie's lawyer said, switching on his tape recorder. As everyone laughed nervously, Cochran turned to his young client. "Anne, will you answer Detective Mock's questions?"

"Maybe."

"Maybe?" Mock pretended to be hurt. "Are we still buddies?" Annie was silent. "Take it or leave it, huh? We got along pretty good the other day, didn't we?"

"Uh-huh."

"How are you feeling?"

"I couldn't go to sleep last night."

"Was anything bothering you?" Mock asked. "Anything on your mind that you couldn't go to sleep?"

"No, not really. I was just thinking about my parents."

"What were you thinking? Would you share that with me?"

"I just don't remember."

"I'm really interested in your parents, and I'd be very interested in what was bothering you and kept you from sleeping, because we're concerned about you, too. Maybe if you talked about it, then maybe you wouldn't have any trouble when you want to go to sleep tonight."

"I was going to talk about it, but . . ."

"But what?"

"Just tell my mom about it when I got home."

Annie's lawyer leaned toward her. "You mean talk to your mom, or to—what will we call her?"

"Sometimes I call her Mom and sometimes I call her Mrs. Smithmyer."

"Why don't you talk to her now?" suggested Mock.

"Yeah," Eileen agreed. "We'll just pretend we're by ourselves, okay? You sit up and talk so we can hear you." Eileen helped Annie move closer to the microphone. "I can hear you real good. Okay, that's better."

Annie continued: "I was just thinking, what if Michael did it? . . . If my brother did it, okay . . . I was just thinking about last night and, um, about the police, um, says that my brother did it."

"Which brother are you talking about?" Mock asked.

"Larry."

"What makes you think he—"

"I don't know. I just, he threw up and everything."

"He what?"

"Threw up."

"Well, try to think about it for a couple of minutes so you can get it off your mind, and think real carefully about exactly when and where different things happened when you woke up that night."

"I don't want to talk about that."

Her lawyer tried to reassure her. "I don't blame you, Anne."

"We know that," agreed Mock.

"Yeah," added Eileen. "We understand that, but maybe this will be the last time we have to."

"At least for a little while," said Cochran.

With prodding, Annie repeated her earlier story of Monday night's events: She awoke, went downstairs, and saw her father lying outside, groaning. She ran back upstairs and walked onto the carport, where she saw a man leaving her backyard.

"Now," Mock asked, "how long was it from then—go ahead, tell me the next thing you did."

"My brother told me to come back in, so I came back in and called Sandy." Sandy was one of her family's two dogs.

"Did you tell your brother anything then?"

"Yeah. I told my brother that, um, that Daddy was lying outside in the snow, and he told me that I was dreaming."

Asked to describe the man she saw, Annie repeated her earlier description. He wore a long-sleeved sweat shirt with BROAD-NECK printed on the front and back and it resembled one her brother Larry owned. When she said the man was carrying a shovel, Mock asked her what it looked like.

"Like our shovel," she said.

"Do you know how to draw? Are you an artist?"

"Somewhat."

"A little bit? Could you draw me a picture of the shovel that you saw?"

Mock, who never carried paper, grabbed Barr's notebook and handed it to Annie. She took a pen from the detective and made two attempts to duplicate what she had seen. Both drawings looked more like shovels than the wood-splitting maul the cops had found in the woods.

"We have two shovels like it," she told Mock.

"What do you use it for?" he asked.

"Once we used it to put our gate up around our pool, and we use it for digging stuff out."

"You ever use it on wood?"

"No."

"You didn't say anything to your brother about seeing somebody outside, did you? Or did you?"

Annie shook her head no. "I totally forgot to say that."

"You forgot to say that. Okay. So what did you do then, did you go back to sleep?"

Annie paused, thinking. "I don't remember that."

"Well, anywhere you went? . . . Okay, what did you do next?"

"I think I went back there to bed."

"Okay, and then what happened?"

"Like an hour and a half later . . . um . . . my brother threw up."

"OK. Where were you when your brother threw up?"

"On his bean-bag chair."

"Okay, and was he in bed, or was he in the bathroom, or where was he when he threw up?"

"In his . . . um . . . in his . . . um . . . bedroom."

"Okay, and what did he say when you told him he was throwing up?"

"You're just dreaming."

"Did he tell you to do anything?"

"He just told me to go back to sleep."

"When did he ask you for your pillow?"

"Um, I don't know when."

"Did he ask you for your pillow?" Cochran asked.

"Uh-huh."

"Why?"

"I don't remember."

Mock resumed his questioning. "Did you go get it for him?"

"No, I had it with me."

"Oh. And you just handed it up to him?"

"Uh-huh."

"Did he talk to you when you were trying to go back to sleep?"

"I don't think so."

"Did he talk to you about what you had seen?"

"I don't think so."

"And you didn't talk to him at all about seeing the guy outside?"

She shook her head no.

"Did he tell you not to talk about it?"

"No."

"Did he tell you not to talk about anything?"

"No. We can talk whenever we feel like it at home."

After Mock asked a few more questions, Barr—who had been silent, hoping to let his partner build a rapport with the girl—spoke up. Barr wanted to know whether Larry had gone downstairs or into the backyard at any time Tuesday morning, perhaps before the paramedics arrived. That, as Duckett had pointed out, could give Larry a defense for much of the circumstantial evidence against him.

But Annie said Larry did not go downstairs Tuesday morning.

"Did he stay with you?" Barr asked.

"Uh-huh," she nodded. "We stick together."

Another litany of questions followed. Then, as Annie began squirming, her lawyer promised, "Almost done."

"I want to go home," she begged.

"You're about to, Annie," he assured her.

"Oh, now we can go home?"

"Almost," Cochran said.

"Almost," Eileen agreed.

"Yayyy!!" Annie cheered.

"Your father's on the way, coming over right now," Cochran said.

"My father?"

Cochran instantly regretted his slip. "Excuse me."

"My father's up there," said Annie, pointing toward the ceiling.

"In heaven," Cochran agreed.

Mock wanted Annie to elaborate on what she had said at the beginning of the interview. "Why did you say a few minutes ago that you thought your brother did it?" he asked.

Actually, Annie hadn't said she thought Larry did it. She had said that the *police* thought he did, and she was wondering "what if Michael did it," and "what if" Larry did it.

"I don't know," Annie replied. "That's what I was thinking about, um, when I was trying to go to sleep."

"Was it your brother you saw out in the yard?"

"I don't know."

"You don't know whether it was Larry out in the backyard?"

"No. I don't know."

"Could it have been?"

"Probably, and probably not."

Her lawyer was exasperated. "What's that mean?" Cochran asked.

"Maybe."

Mock and Cochran looked at each other and at the same time echoed "Maybe."

Mock thought this might be his last crack at Annie, and he wanted to plug the one big hole in her story—how Larry could have been walking away from the backyard at the same time that he was calling her back inside the house from the kitchen. In order to do both, Larry would have had to turn around and walk back into the yard—in plain view of Annie—or go around the block and sneak in the front door, which obviously would take some time.

"So, when you looked out there, it may be him . . ." Mock echoed. "Then he must not have been in the kitchen right away? Was it a couple of minutes, a little bit of time between the time that you saw that guy and you saw your brother in the kitchen?"

"Uh-huh," Annie agreed.

"There was a time lapse there, huh?"

"Uh-huh."

"Would he have had enough time to get back in the house before you saw him, if it was him?"

But Annie refused to close the hole all the way. "If he ran," she said.

"If he ran, he could have got back in the house," Mock repeated. Obviously, that was the best he was going to do.

"You did real well," he told her, "and I bet you the next time I get a chance to see you, I'll have to get you something, a little gift. Okay?"

"All done," her lawyer announced cheerily. "Want to hear what you sounded like?"

SIX

Wednesday, January 30, 1980

1.

Michael's expulsion from the Swartz home marked the beginning of a long cold exile. As he moved through adolescence, cut off from what little security his adoptive family had offered, Michael grew more bitter and belligerent each year. The Swartzes turned out to be less than forgiving parents, their love of Christ notwithstanding.

When he left the Swartzes, Michael moved in with a foster family fifteen miles north of Cape St. Claire. It was his ninth home in thirteen years.

Predictably, it didn't last.

He went on a looting spree with two buddies a month later. On February 27, 1980, the youths broke into a house and stole a radio and two log splitters, then entered another unoccupied house and did two thousand dollars' worth of property damage.

They broke windows, ripped electrical wiring, and bashed plumbing fixtures.

They broke into another house the next morning and returned in the afternoon to loot it. During their second visit, the owner's grandson drove by and noticed that a front windowpane was broken. When he went inside, the grandson caught Michael Swartz pocketing a Kodak camera.

Police arrested the youths. Michael's delinquency petition accused him of a string of offenses, from felony breaking and entering to theft and malicious destruction of property. While he awaited a court hearing, Michael moved into the Palmer Family Boys' Home, a state-licensed emergency shelter in Crownsville.

Delinquency was one of only three charges minors could face in Maryland juvenile court. The others were being a child in need of "supervision" and "assistance." Michael stood charged with one of those, too. After he left the Swartz home in January, state workers asked the juvenile court to declare him a child in need of assistance because:

> Michael's parents are unable or unwilling to give proper care and attention to him; To Wit: Michael's behavioral problems in school and at home have made it impossible for his parents to deal with his problems.

In March, a few weeks after Michael's fourteenth birthday, a juvenile master agreed that he was a child in need of assistance and placed him indefinitely in the custody of the Anne Arundel County Department of Social Services. Pending his delinquency hearing, Michael shipped out to a state-licensed juvenile center 140 miles to the west, high in that mountainous sliver of Maryland that pokes into West Virginia.

Bob and Kay were horrified, outraged, and, most of all, ashamed of what their son had done. It confirmed their belief that he was incorrigible and belonged in reform school.

The Swartzes also feared what Michael's crimes might cost them. Would they be responsible for the thousands of dollars in damage that he and his friends had done? "He wasn't even living

with us," fumed Bob. "Why should we have to pay for something we had no control over? We warned his worker that he
would get in trouble if they didn't watch him."

Social workers told the Swartzes they would have to contrib-
ute to Michael's support while he was in state custody. To protect themselves on these prickly money issues, the Swartzes
decided to take a lawyer to Michael's hearing.

When Bob casually broached the subject with Ron Baradel at
St. Mary's, Baradel agreed to accompany them even though he
lacked expertise in juvenile law. Baradel hand-delivered a three-
page memorandum to the juvenile master the day before the
hearing. He argued that it would be inappropriate to require the
Swartzes to make restitution for their son's crime spree because
they hadn't even known where Michael was living when he
broke into the houses.

Michael and his young cohorts admitted their guilt at the May
6 hearing and were adjudged delinquent. The juvenile master
ordered Michael to pay $143.33 restitution out of the trust fund
that his parents had created for him, and postponed the question of child-support payments until another hearing two
months later.

Michael, meanwhile, returned to his new home in the Ap-
palachian Mountains.

Larry and Annie were kept in the dark about their brother's disappearance. When Larry asked his parents what Michael had
done wrong and where he was living, they gave terse cryptic
replies. Soon Larry stopped asking.

Annie seemed even more bewildered. "When's Michael coming back? When's Michael coming back?" she asked repeatedly.

"I don't know," Kay always replied. Neither she nor Bob
wanted to suggest to Annie or Larry that Michael might *not*
come back, but the thought hung heavy on their minds.

Relieved to have Michael out of the house, Kay no longer felt
compelled to keep her eyes glued to her baby girl; neither did
she feel compelled to find a baby-sitter every time she and Bob
went out. In the past, they had called on a teenage boy in the
neighborhood to baby-sit. Now that the family's chief troublemaker was gone, and Larry was thirteen, they didn't need a
sitter.

That summer of 1980 was the first time Michael didn't appear at the annual seashore vacation that Bob Swartz and his brother always took together with their kids. Joe wondered where Michael was but didn't dare ask. Although the boy's absence was conspicuous, Bob and Kay didn't mention it, and Joe didn't want to pry, for he knew how sensitive his brother was about his family.

Curiosity got the better of Joe's wife. Standing alone with Kay on the boardwalk, looking out toward the Atlantic, she said, "Kay, can I ask you a question?"

"I know what you're going to ask me," Kay replied. "Where's Michael?"

"Yeah."

So Kay told Joe's wife the whole story: Michael had gotten out of hand. She and Bob reluctantly had turned custody of him back to the state. Now he was living at a boys' home in western Maryland.

Although Kay told her relatives about Michael, Bob was close-mouthed to both family and friends. The financial implications of Michael's disappearance didn't make the subject any easier to discuss. Nervous about getting stuck with sizable support payments, Bob and Kay drafted a financial statement to submit to the judge at Michael's support hearing on July 7, 1980. The Swartzes painted themselves as a middle-income family with little money to spare for their adopted son. Their salaries barely matched expenses: Bob earned $18,013 a year; Kay, $14,074. They had $9,500 in cash savings, no life insurance, a $196-a-month mortgage payment, and a paid-in-full vacation cottage in Cambridge, which they regarded as their kids' college education fund.   ·

After reviewing their finances, the judge ordered the Swartzes to make monthly payments of fifty dollars to the state. The payments would continue until Michael turned eighteen or returned home, whichever occurred first.

A few months after Michael left home, his old neighbor Susan Barker received a letter at her new home in Italy. A friend back in Cape St. Claire wrote to inform her that Michael Swartz had been sent to a reform school.

More than four thousand miles away, where she felt

powerless to do anything about it, Mrs. Barker was crushed by this news. Michael had not been lying after all; his parents' threats had been real. She had let him down when he had needed help. Guilt burrowed its way into Susan Barker's conscience, where it would nibble at her for years.

2.

Sprawled across hundreds of acres atop Maryland's Big Savage Mountain (elevation: 2,900 feet), Long Stretch Youth Home was unlike any place Michael had lived. It boasted horses, a schoolhouse, a dairy farm, and boundless rural solitude. Its name derived not from the boys' worst fears—doing a "long stretch" at reform school—but from the gently sloping plateau between the two hills that flanked the youth center. Local legend ascribed the name to a settler who stood on the eastern hill, looked west across the plateau, and said with a sigh, "Long stretch over to the next hill!"

For Michael, who had spent his earliest years in Baltimore before bouncing around the city's suburbs, life on the brink of Appalachia was a turn for the dreary. Even if he wanted to run away, there was no place to go. Except for a sprinkling of residences, one tavern, a country store, and a lunch counter, the youth home had few neighbors. It was surrounded by forests and farmland dotted with billboarded barns urging occasional passersby to CHEW MAIL POUCH TOBACCO.

The nearest outpost of civilization was six miles east in Frostburg (pop. 7,715), a college town with white clapboard and brick Victorian buildings lining its main street. The nearest big town was Cumberland (pop. 29,724), a tired old industrial center eleven miles east of Frostburg, where spires and crucifixes sprouted from peaks and humps all over town. On Saturday nights, Cumberland and Frostburg were meccas for the Long Stretch boys, who were stuck on Big Savage Mountain the rest of the week.

There were worse places in the world to be stuck. Licensed

to hold up to seventy troubled youths, the center had a dairy where youngsters learned to milk cows and run tractors, a gas station where they learned auto mechanics, and a riding academy with wild horses and access to 520 acres of wooded trails. It also offered downhill skiing, a ceramic shop, and a balloon barn with a plywood floor where the boys played basketball and learned to roller-skate, away from the critical gaze of town girls. The center ran a school for youths expelled from public schools, offering not only the three Rs, but training in electronics and building trades, as well.

A cluster of cabins reserved for the older and better-behaved boys surrounded the schoolhouse. Independent living, they called the program. Boys who weren't headed home to their families aspired to it because it allowed them to live with minimal supervision while they went out to trade school, college, or work. To attain such freedom, the boys had to work their way up through a half-dozen houses scattered across the grounds, each with live-in dorm counselors and strict rules. It usually took years for a boy to attain independent living. Michael started at the bottom.

To those who ran Long Stretch, Michael seemed a sullen, rebellious youth. "He was one of those boys who would stand right up to you and say, 'I don't give a damn about you,'" recalled Bill Platter, the center's founder and director. Embarrassed about his height (he hit six one at fourteen and was as skinny as a licorice stick), Michael slouched constantly. Platter rode him: "You're belittling yourself, because when you leave here you're going be in a group of men who are going be your size. If you want to look nice, straighten up your shoulders."

Mischievous and perverse, Michael loved to do the opposite of what he was told. A sign in the state park that said KEEP OFF THE ROCKS translated to Michael, WALK ON THE ROCKS. So he did, and the counselor who had taken the boys to the park piled everyone in the van and drove them right back to Long Stretch. Michael caught hell from the other boys, but that was how Long Stretch worked: Everyone obeyed the rules or everyone got punished. Platter, a white-haired man with a kindly face and clear blue eyes, believed in turning peer pressure to his advantage.

The boys were allowed to go home one weekend a month provided that they had an approved home to visit. Parents were encouraged to visit their sons. Michael's parents never visited, even though they often passed through the area on their way to see Bob's family in Youngstown. It would have been a short detour to stop and see Michael, but they never did. Neither did they open their home in Cape St. Claire to Michael on weekends or holidays. After Michael left home, Bob and Kay didn't want him to set foot in their house. He seemed so angry that they felt they couldn't trust him.

Unlike most of his new friends, Michael had nowhere to go on his monthly pass. After a few months of watching everyone else get furloughs, he grew resentful and complained to his social worker, "Look, you gotta get me outta here for some weekends. I can't take this shit." His worker found alternate places for Michael to visit, starting with the emergency shelter in Crownsville that had housed him before he went to Long Stretch.

Eight months into his stay at the youth home, Michael's progress report stated that he visited the Palmer Family Home on weekends and occasionally came back "in a negative mood." The report described the fourteen-year-old as a follower in his peer group and said he had problems with authority. Although intelligence tests suggested he was capable of doing grade-level work in school, he had fallen behind his peers. Teachers at the center's school were preparing him to take the high school equivalency test, but he rarely finished his assigned work and wouldn't stay put in class. "Mike's work habits have been on the decline," the report said. "He accomplishes no work."

In May 1980, a few months after he moved to the youth center, Michael wrote a short sad letter home. The Swartzes filed it away with his court papers.

During the murder investigation nearly four years later, police found the letter in the puzzling pile of papers in the front hallway of the Swartz home. It said:

Dear Anne, Larry, Kay, Bob

Hello. I imagine you are all mad at me. But I would still like to keep in touch. I have graduated from high

school and I am going to Frostburg State college. I am
going to have a lot of fun there. How is Anne and you
all. how is Anne. I have a broken arm and wrist. I hope
you all are having a good time. I am. I am in independent living where we live with no supervision.

Michael Swartz

PS Write Back and send a picture of the Family and one
of Anne.

To his parents, it was vintage Michael, ridiculous as ever. He
expected them to believe that a fourteen-year-old who never
kept up with his grade level, already had graduated from high
school and was attending college? After being away only a few
months? And that he was living on his own without adult supervision? Michael's extravagant boasts were pathetic. And his obvious attachment to his six-year-old sister especially troubled
Kay. If he ever came home again, what would they do with Annie?

3.

After Michael left, Bob's fuse grew steadily shorter. He threw
himself into religion with a maniacal zeal. The fifty dollars he
placed in the collection basket at St. Mary's each month was
nothing compared to the time and effort he invested in church
activities. At least twice a month, he read from the pulpit or
helped with the Eucharist. He also taught ninth grade Sunday
school and served on the parish council.

Always gung ho about matters of faith, Bob became more so
after getting involved in Cursillo, a method of spiritual renewal
that originated in Spain in 1949. Sam and Dolores Price, a black
couple who attended St. Mary's, brought Bob and Kay into the
movement a few months after Michael left home. "Let's make a
deal," Sam Price suggested. "You do a Cursillo weekend with us,
and we'll do Marriage Encounter with you."

"You're on," Bob replied.

True to their word, Bob and Kay became "Cursillistas" in July 1980 at the Mission Helpers of the Sacred Heart, a retreat house north of Baltimore. They went on separate weekends because that's the Cursillo rule: Men go one weekend and their wives follow several weeks later. Bob and Kay enjoyed their three-day introductions to Cursillo. Bob took his mandolin and sang. Kay cowrote a humorous ditty called "What is a weekend with only two men?" about spending an entire weekend with no male companionship except for two priests, and sang it for the group.

Bob, more than Kay, was galvanized by Cursillo's central goal of remaking the world: "Make a friend, be a friend, and bring your friend to Christ." The idea was action, apostolic action, personal apostolic action. Live your life in Christ, then influence your environment for Christ.

After making their Cursillo weekend, Bob and Kay explored group reunions and other methods for keeping the movement's fires burning in their lives. Each method offered a format to share their experiences with Christ, to exchange battle plans for Christ. Cursillistas were free to wage the apostolic war on the battleground of their own choosing. It could be the peace movement, the war against hunger, even the simple act of loving family and friends.

For Bob, it was the fight against abortion. He did plenty of other good works—visiting senior citizens and sponsoring Naval Academy midshipmen were but two—and he preached about Christ incessantly at his office in Riverdale, where some of his coworkers regarded him as a religious fanatic. But none of Bob's causes stirred the same fiery passions in him as the war against abortion. He viewed abortion as the greatest American tragedy since slavery. Among local Right to Lifers, he was the most adamant, the most certain about the inevitability of victory. "We will win," he told friends. "I *know* we will."

Within a year after Planned Parenthood opened a clinic in Annapolis in 1978 and began offering abortions on Saturdays, protesters gathered outside. The picketing was sporadic at first, but by 1980, it was a mainstay of the city's Right to Life chapter. Bob Swartz was always in the forefront. He arrived shortly before 8 A.M. every Saturday, parked his Chevette across from the clinic, and opened his trunk to hand out placards. Some bore the toll-free pregnancy hotline number; others bannered the sobering abortion statistics; while still others—HITLER IS ALIVE AND WELL AND RUNS PLANNED PARENTHOOD—made clear their view that abortion was legalized murder.

Bob viewed his mission as "sidewalk counseling," not picketing. That was what he went down there to do: counsel women from the sidewalk. "Excuse me," he called out to them as they hurried down the sidewalk toward the clinic entrance. "We're from the Annapolis Right to Life. Can we give you some literature?"

Clutching a pile of pamphlets featuring a blow-by-blow account of how fetuses were killed, he would hand the woman a pamphlet or, if she ignored him, he moved to phase two and cried out, "Hey, have you thought about adoption?" or, "Do you realize your baby is *alive*?" He always tried to make that point before they disappeared inside the clinic. "Your baby is alive! Please don't kill your baby!"

Bob was the most aggressive of the sidewalk counselors. He never let a woman pass without making contact. If someone yelled profanity at him, he didn't turn the other cheek; he yelled right back. He grew enraged when a social worker tugged at the arm of a woman he was trying to talk to one day and said, "C'mon. Hurry up."

"You can't pull her in there!" he shouted. "Her baby is alive! Let her talk to me!"

Clinic workers occasionally called police, who required the Right to Lifers to obtain a weekly permit. The protesters only bothered filling out the permit paperwork for a couple of months, however. Then different patrolmen came by to question them: Who were they? What did they think they were doing? Bob viewed the interrogation as an infringement on his First Amendment right to free speech. "Let's go down to the station and tell the chief he's full of it. They can't do this to us," he fumed.

His colleagues urged a more moderate approach. At Father Heyburn's request, a lawyer from the parish mediated the group's differences with the police chief, and peace prevailed for a while. Eventually, complaints cropped up again, and Bob was a frequent target. Either he was "harassing" women or trespassing on private property by doing his "counseling" too close to the clinic door.

While Bob took his battle to the streets, his wife waged hers at home, using as weapons a typewriter and list of pseudonyms. Sitting at her round dining room table, Kay wrote dozens of letters to the editor. Her letters were clever, sometimes acerbic messages that reflected the keen edges of her personality. One year the targets of her wrath were little apple pies with *A*'s carved in the crust that prochoice lobbyists gave state legislators, along with notes stating, "Freedom of choice is American as apple pie." The pies grabbed a few headlines, irritating Kay. She conceded that freedom was as American as apple pie but added that when government sanctioned the elimination of the unwanted and powerless, "Wiener Schnitzel and Kraut are more appropriate." She was delighted when her letter appeared under the pen name Myra Weiss on the editorial page of the *The Capital.*

She wrote a longer letter in response to a newspaper article that quoted a local citizen urging state lawmakers to loosen eligibility rules for Medicaid abortions. The woman argued that the rules prevented poor women from getting abortions and led to the birth of thousands of unwanted babies. "If you could just see the babies of the poor, you might change your mind," she said.

"Not only have I seen the children of the poor, I've actually been one," Kay wrote in response. After recounting her childhood spent in a house without a telephone, electricity, or indoor plumbing, Kay noted that by the citizen's logic, she and her siblings "would be better off dead rather than have to suffer such deprivations." She said she doubted that the woman truly had seen the children of the poor, and added, "We children of the poor have as much right to this planet and to this country as you do, my dear middle class lady."

In addition to picketing and writing letters to the editor, the Swartzes joined other antiabortionists in lobbying legislators to tighten eligibility rules for state-funded abortions. In the liberal-leaning Maryland State House, no other issue more bitterly or narrowly divided lawmakers. Citizen crusaders on both sides of the issue packed the State House nearly every Monday night during the three-month legislative session.

Bob's prime target was Delegate Gerald Winegrad, an intense young attorney who belonged to St. Mary's Church. Bob could not understand how a good Catholic could vote for state-funded abortions, as Winegrad consistently did. "Poor people should have the same opportunities as rich people," Winegrad tried to explain when Bob visited his office.

At church social events, Bob needled Winegrad with an undercurrent of nastiness that the delegate felt didn't belong anywhere, much less in church. When Winegrad strolled down the hallway of St. Mary's school at the annual church bazaar one year, beer in hand, Bob happened by and said, "Hi, how 'ya doin'?" Then, dropping his voice, he added snidely, "I guess we have to be nice, even to our enemies."

Winegrad grew contemptuous of Bob and treated him like poison ivy, giving him the widest possible berth whenever he saw him. Winegrad viewed him as an unhappy man filled with frustration and rage. He thought Bob, like so many Right to Lifers, funneled too much feeling into a single issue. The Right to Lifers seemed to think that if they won the abortion war, the world would suddenly become a sunny place. "What about starvation?" Winegrad asked them. "What about all the other problems in the world? Don't you care about children *after* they are born?"

4.

After Michael moved to Long Stretch, Larry sensed that his parents' attitude toward him changed. He didn't know why, but for the first time they seemed unhappy with him. When Michael had lived there, Larry had been aware that he was the favorite son. It secretly had made him proud when his parents said to Michael, "Why can't you be like Larry?" Suddenly, those strokes stopped, and the tension in the house—which everyone always had blamed on Michael—did not evaporate. Michael was no longer there to be a lightning rod for Bob's anger, and Bob seemed more uptight than ever. He and Kay acted suspicious of Larry, for no discernible reason.

"No, we don't want you to stay out overnight," they said when Larry asked to spend the night with a buddy. "We know you've been drinking, and you'll get into trouble."

Larry was astonished, because he *hadn't* started drinking; and he was hurt when his parents, their voices full of worry and mistrust, told friends, "We hope Larry doesn't start experimenting with drugs." They said it in front of him, as if it wouldn't bother him. It did bother him because it wasn't true. Michael messed around with drugs, but not Larry. He'd never even been high. With all this talk about drugs, however, Larry was growing curious: What did it feel like to get high? Why did Michael like to smoke the stuff so much? At age thirteen, shortly after Michael left, Larry found out. He became an occasional pot smoker over the next couple of years, getting high whenever a friend offered him a joint.

Larry's grades drifted steadily lower. He finished seventh grade in June 1980 with five D's in his academic subjects and a sprinkling of C's in other courses. The year before, he had taken home two D's and his parents had seemed satisfied—at least they hadn't complained. Michael had been there then to soak up their worry like a sponge. "Then when he left they started yelling at me for low grades," Larry later recalled in a written summary of his life. "I never understood why their [*sic*] was such a change."

When Larry entered the eighth grade at Magothy Middle School, his grades drifted even lower. Each report card he took home eroded his father's dream of sending his sons to the Naval Academy, located so conveniently right there in Annapolis. "Don't you understand how important this is?" Bob shouted. "You'll never get anywhere if you don't do better. You *know* you can do better! If you don't pull yourself together, you'll turn out just like your brother!"

Mindful that the Roman Catholic Church had rescued his own lost soul a decade earlier, Bob saw a tantalizing glimmer of hope for Larry when he showed an interest in the priesthood in the spring of 1981. Bob did everything he could to nudge him along, proudly announcing to relatives, "Larry wants to be a priest!" while Larry stood at his father's side, smiling shyly.

Near the end of Larry's eighth-grade school year, a priest at St.

Mary's took a group of parish boys on an eight-hour drive to visit a high school seminary in the tiny town of North East, Pennsylvania—near where Bob had attended high school. Larry came back from the recruiting weekend enthused; he delighted his parents by announcing that he would apply to St. Mary's Seminary.

To friends, Larry confided that although he was curious about the priesthood, he primarily viewed it as an escape valve: "I'm going to get away from home! Besides, it might be something nice to try."

When Larry left for seminary in the fall of 1981, Bob's attitude toward him changed. Friends detected a new pride in his voice when he talked about his son studying to be a priest. The change was a relief to Sam Price, who often jogged with Bob and joined him on the picket line. It had disturbed Price to hear Bob say things such as, "Larry is so unbelievably stupid!" Now it pleased Price to hear his friend boasting about his son, saying, "Larry is finally on the right track."

If Larry was on track, his progress was wobbly at best. The small monasticlike seminary placed a great deal of emphasis on academics; and Latin, in particular, eluded Larry's grasp. He failed Latin his first semester and received D's in English and algebra.

Thinking Larry was lonely and needed encouragement, Kay asked her brother and sisters to urge their children to write him. Maureen Riely was especially concerned, for she believed her nephew would make a wonderful priest. "You don't need to be a scholar to be a priest," Maureen told her son, John. "Larry is such a gentle, sincere person, I'm sure he could help people in some parish somewhere." She asked John to write Larry and showed him a letter that Larry had sent her. Reading that letter, scrawled in childish big block letters, John shuddered. It was full of half-sentences and misused words. A letter Larry later sent John confirmed his suspicions: Although his cousin was in the ninth grade, he was a borderline illiterate.

Viewing seminary as Larry's last possible salvation, Bob prayed that his son would find a way to survive there and make the priesthood his vocation. When his final report card arrived in the mail in the summer of 1982, Bob was crushed: Larry's grades were unchanged, except that his C˙in religion had slipped to a D. Despite his best efforts, he failed Latin again.

The letter accompanying the report card, written by the seminary director, was even more shattering: It invited Larry not to return.

Several years later, when Ron Baradel went to North East and poked around the seminary as part of his pretrial investigation, the director said he was surprised that Larry's parents never responded to his letter. Most parents responded, said the director, either wanting to know more about their son's problems or hoping to reinstate him. Yet Bob and Kay never wrote back or phoned.

After Larry left the seminary, two stories circulated in his family as to why he was booted out. First, his lackluster grades were common knowledge among his relatives. Kay told a relative that another reason Larry couldn't return was that he'd been caught in a homosexual tryst with a seminarian.

In his trial research, Baradel also would hear rumors of a sexual scandal at the seminary—something about a whole group of boys being caught in a sexual assault—but the lawyer was unable to confirm that story during his visit to North East. One priest succinctly explained Larry's short seminary career to Baradel: "Larry would have been here until he was 103 years old and never passed Latin."

Baradel asked Larry about the rumored sexual escapade, but Larry denied it. "Nothing like that happened," Larry insisted. He contended his departure from seminary was due partly to grades and partly to his own attitude. "I decided I didn't want to become a priest. I learned I liked girls too much."

The summer Larry returned from seminary, his parents granted him more freedom than they had the previous summer. Larry soon noticed, however, that his freedom was selective and depended on who was with him. If, for instance, Larry was going to Tom Kenny's house, then he could stay out indefinitely because his mother and father liked the Kenny family. If he was with John Smithmyer, whose family his parents also liked, he had no curfew. Larry also had tremendous freedom to go crabbing and wind-surfing with his twenty-one-year-old cousin Greg

Rodden, who came for a long visit that summer. Kay thought Larry's cousins were wonderful role models for him.

However, when Larry went to see Eric Armstrong, a school-mate and neighbor, he always had to be home by six o'clock sharp. Eric was among that crew of neighborhood boys who didn't meet with Kay's approval. Frustrated, Larry challenged his mother one day when she forbade him to go out with some neighborhood boys.

"Why can't I go? It's not fair," Larry said.

"I don't trust those boys," she said. "You'll get in trouble."

"It's not fair to make me stay home when nothing has even *happened*! If anything happens, then make me stay home. C'mon."

"Young man, watch out or you'll stay home until you're eigh-teen!"

Larry occasionally drank beer with his friends, which got him into trouble. He went to party one afternoon in the palatial tree fort that Eric Armstrong had built behind his parents' house in Ulmstead Estates. The three-story fort was a boy's dream. Pyra-mid-shaped, it had three rooms on the first floor, two on the second, and one at the top, with decks all around. It had elec-tricity, heat, stereo, television, and carpeting on the floors, walls, and ceilings.

After downing several beers with Eric and their friends, Larry wandered home slightly smashed around six-thirty. He fixed a sandwich, went to his room, and crashed on his top bunk. He awoke to find his parents standing beside him.

"Get out there and clean up the living room!" Mom screeched.

Larry immediately hopped down from the bunk. When he staggered, Mom pounced on him. "You've been drinking, haven't you? I can't believe it!"

"No, I haven't."

"Yes, you have. Don't lie to me."

Larry hesitated, then admitted that he had consumed a couple of beers.

Dad jumped in. "How could you do this when your mother just had her operation?"

His mind still fuzzy, Larry wondered what Dad was talking

about. Operation? His parents had said they were going out shopping that morning. Why hadn't anyone told him that his mother was having an operation?

"What operation?" Larry asked.

"None of your business!" Bob snapped.

Larry never found out what kind of operation his mother had had, but his father was so angry that he put Larry on restriction—not as before, either. In the past, Larry had been grounded for a weekend here, a couple of weeks there. It certainly wasn't new for him to be confined to the house. But this restriction was indefinite: He couldn't go out again until his parents decided he was ready.

There was no telling when that might be.

5.

The year Larry spent struggling at seminary, Michael spent struggling at Long Stretch. Counselors at the youth center encouraged him to work on his "stealing problem" in group therapy after he got caught stealing candy from a country store. His behavior problems went beyond his nimble fingers, though. In a report during his second year there, his house parents wrote that Michael lacked goals, seemed depressed, and had an "aggravating" attitude in school.

He knew his stay was indefinite because the Swartzes didn't want him back. He'd been assigned a new foster family in Anne Arundel County, and he visited there once a month. Without an adoptive family willing to take him in, however, his prospects for leaving Long Stretch were bleak. Though he never talked about it, Michael very much wanted to rejoin the Swartz family. Each year he spent away from Bob, Kay, Larry, and Annie, he felt more unwanted, more of an outcast.

His dorm had the kind of telephone hookups they have in prison, where the boys could place collect long-distance calls but couldn't dial direct. Although they weren't thrilled to hear from him, the Swartzes accepted their son's collect calls.

Michael also called and wrote his Uncle Gerald in Illinois, whom he viewed as an ally in his struggle to get home. Secretly, he hoped his uncle might take him into his own home and provide the bridge he needed to rejoin the family.

Feeling sorry for Michael, Uncle Gerald usually accepted his nephew's collect calls and listened to the braggadocio that poured from his mouth like water from a faucet. He liked his nephew but found his bragging aggravating.

"I'm going to be a computer technologist and make fifty thousand a year," Michael said during one call.

"Oh?" replied Uncle Gerald. "You know, you have to work real hard to make fifty thousand dollars a year."

"Oh, no," Michael said. "It's easy making fifty thousand. Real easy."

"Easy?" Uncle Gerald said, exasperated. "Here you are, you can't even pay for your own phone calls, and you think it's easy earning fifty thousand a year?"

In another call, Michael announced that he wanted to live with his uncle. "They'll let me out of here if I have a place to go. Can I come there?"

Although he was surprised, Gerald thought it might not be a bad idea. He'd always wanted a son and was genuinely fond of his nephew. Perhaps he could straighten the boy out, succeed where his sister and her husband had failed. "I'll have to talk it over with your Mom and Dad," Gerald said cautiously.

Gerald's family soon doused his enthusiasm with a pool of objections. The thought of having Michael live with them terrified Gerald's wife. Although Gerald argued with her initially, he yielded after he called Kay for advice.

"You wouldn't want to bring Michael into a home with four little girls," Kay said ominously.

"What do you mean?"

"Believe me. Just don't bring him into a home with four girls. And don't feel guilty about turning him down. You should feel guilty if you *do* take him in."

If Kay was afraid of her own son, Gerald thought there had to be valid reasons. She wouldn't elaborate and seemed protective of him, but the warning she gave her brother was unmistakable: There's a chance he'll molest your daughters.

"I'm afraid it's out of the question," Gerald told Michael the next time he called. "I'll study it further, though, and get back to you. In the meantime, please don't call me. I'll call you."

Crushed, Michael stopped phoning Uncle Gerald.

At Christmas 1981, a girl named Phyllis caught Michael's eye when he went home to Cumberland with a counselor from Long Stretch. Holidays were bleak for Michael, especially Christmas, when he had no place special to go. His parents never once asked him home for Christmas. That Christmas in Cumberland was fun, though, for Michael met Phyllis and rode around town in her car.

He liked her right away. Two years older than Michael, Phyllis began meeting him in Cumberland on Saturday nights. Most of the Long Stretch boys rode into Frostburg or Cumberland in their house vans every Saturday evening. Free for a few hours to go skating, take in a movie, or wander around, they reconvened at the van late in the evening and went home together. Michael's house parents usually parked their van at the Cumberland Mall. The boys often hung around the parking lot to take turns at the privacy offered by the van. A few boys climbed in the van to smoke pot or huff gas. Michael usually climbed in to be alone with Phyllis while somebody stood guard outside in case their house parents returned early.

In the spring of 1982, more than two years after he left home, Michael's prospects for a homecoming brightened: The new citizen board charged with monitoring foster children in Maryland recommended his return to the Swartzes after another year if he continued to do well at the training school. Returning children to their parents was supposed to be the top priority of Maryland's foster-care program. If a return wasn't possible, priority number two was finding the child another permanent home. Institutions were not regarded as acceptable permanent homes except in extraordinary cases. Michael's long history of bouncing from foster home to foster home made it even more imperative for him to be reunited with his adoptive family.

Bob and Kay were ambivalent about a reunion, though. They worried about the influence he would have on family life. Yet they didn't want to close the door on him completely, for he was their son. "We can't just *disown* him," Bob said. Believing it would be tantamount to unadopting him, Bob refused to surrender guardianship to the state—a move that would have freed Michael for permanent placement with another family.

Kay attended Michael's review hearing in April 1982 and told the foster-care review board that she and Bob would take Michael home if he stayed out of trouble during the next year. The board forwarded its recommendation of an eventual homecoming to his caseworker and the juvenile court that had declared him delinquent.

The homecoming, however, was not meant to be. A few months later, Michael shattered his already-cracked relationship with his parents beyond repair. Bob and Kay had caught Larry drinking that summer and were worried that Larry, too, might be on his way to reform school. They knew Larry was easily influenced, highly suggestible, and they blamed Michael for many of Larry's problems. Fearful that their experimental family was on the verge of collapse, Kay and Bob were increasingly on edge. When Kay burst into tears following a heated telephone call from Michael, Bob promptly declared, "That's it, we're cutting him off."

The problem was Phyllis.

"Hi, how's it going?" Michael said when his mother accepted his collect call. "I got a favor to ask. I want to get married. The chick's name is Phyllis. She's old enough, man, but I need your permission to get married."

Kay laughed, suspecting that Michael was pulling her leg. Get married? How was he going to support a wife when he couldn't take care of himself? At sixteen, he was way behind in school. She doubted he ever would get his high school diploma. "Oh, come on, Michael. You're too young to get married. You can't be serious."

"Oh yeah, man. I love this chick and we want to get married."

He kept after her, but Kay was firm: She and Bob would never sanction his marriage. In Maryland, anyone under eighteen needed written permission from their parents to obtain a marriage license, unless the girl was pregnant.

Michael called again shortly after his first call. He renewed his request for permission to marry and said Phyllis was pregnant.

Neither he nor Phyllis approved of abortion, and they didn't want to place the baby for adoption; they wanted to marry. "Please sign for me," he pleaded. "I love her, and I'm gonna get a job and help her out. Her parents are gonna help her, too. All you have to do is sign."

"I don't believe you," Kay answered. Why hadn't he said that before? And did he really think they would let him marry at his age? While he was still in reform school? How convenient that his little girlfriend suddenly was pregnant. "No, Michael, we're not going to sign for you," Kay said. "You got yourself into this jam and you can get yourself out." She didn't really think he was in any jam except the huge mess he'd made of his life.

Kay doubted that Phyllis existed, and was convinced that if she did, she wasn't pregnant. Another Long Stretch boy, however, later would confirm that Michael did indeed have a girlfriend named Phyllis. As to what ultimately became of her and the baby, Michael later said in an offhand tone, "I got out of it, not meaning to get out of it. We were walking across this street and a drunk hit her. She was killed. Baby, too."

No one at Long Stretch, however, could recall the traffic accident. Cumberland authorities didn't recall it, either.

When Kay remained steadfast in her refusal to let Michael marry, he cursed at her on the phone, and Kay answered sharply. Their voices grew louder, their conflict, more intense.

"You fucking bitch!" Michael finally screamed in her ear.

Incensed but quick-witted as always, she retorted, "No, Michael. Your *girlfriend* is the fucking bitch!"

"Fuck you, bitch!" Michael shouted and slammed down the receiver.

Later, Kay told relatives the story in a droll, amused tone. They were shocked by her language but amused by her reply to Michael. How spunky she was to dish it right back!

Kay wasn't really amused, though, and neither was Bob. The next time Michael called home, Bob got on the line and solemnly announced, "Michael, you disturbed your mother too much the last time you called. Stop calling us, all right?"

So Michael stopped calling for a while.

At the end of August 1982, Kay and Bob took a step toward permanently ousting him from the family. They rewrote their

wills and asked three neighbors to witness them. The new wills
left all their worldly belongings to the other spouse if either one
died. In the event that the other spouse also died, the wills
named Larry and Annie as coheirs. The key change from their
prior wills was the fourth clause:

> I direct that no portion of my estate should go to
> Michael Swartz, a child whom I adopted but who has
> since returned to foster care, and the guardians named
> below for Lawrence and Anne are not responsible for
> Michael's care or support.

A lawyer might have regarded the wills as overkill, since under
Maryland inheritance law, children automatically were disinherited if their parents failed to mention them in their wills.

The Swartzes were taking no chances.

6.

Larry sighed. His mother was getting more like his father every
day, jumping on him for every piddling thing. "Why didn't you
take out the garbage? Can't you even wash the dishes right?
Look at this frying pan! It's covered with spots!" Once she had
been his ally; now she was Bob's enforcer, keeping Larry on the
longest running restriction they had ever imposed. Time
dragged so slowly. By Thanksgiving 1982, Larry wondered
whether he'd ever be free. Since they had grounded him the
previous summer, his parents let him go hardly anywhere except school, church, and soccer practice. He was playing on
Broadneck's new junior-varsity soccer team, which was racking
up an impressive first-year record. When Saturday night rolled
around, however, Larry had to stay home while everyone else
headed out to the Super Skate on Route 50 or to the Annapolis
Mall to hang out.

"His parents would never let him go out, but he would never

come out and say 'My parents won't let me go out,'" recalled Eric Armstrong, who played on the soccer team with Larry. "He would say 'I have to go pick up my sister,' or 'I have to clean the pool,' or 'I have to do this.' It was kind of a code of honor not to say anything."

When Larry started tenth grade at Broadneck Senior High that fall, Bob told him he expected straight C's on his report card. Without Latin to contend with, Larry surely could earn C's if he applied himself. Larry did make mostly C's the first quarter, but his one D riled Bob. "Well, maybe there's a little hope for you still," he said in a cutting tone.

Hope for him still? Larry had done what they asked and earned a C average. What did his father expect? Straight A's? Larry wanted to punch him in the face, but as always he steeled himself and walked away.

It made Larry even madder that he couldn't sign up for driver's education. He had turned sixteen the previous August; all he needed to get his driver's license was driver's education. Most of his friends were taking the course. At first, his parents said, "Fine, take it second semester," but when Larry took home the permission slip at the end of the semester, they changed their tune. "I told you I wanted all C's," Bob said. Larry made a couple of D's, and his father wouldn't budge.

"You have your whole life ahead of you," Bob said. "You can afford to wait until next summer to learn to drive."

Kay agreed. She didn't like the idea of Larry driving the family cars. He was so sneaky, she had to watch him closely. It terrified her to think of him drinking and driving. Every day, she read about more carnage on the highways caused by drunken drivers. Maryland recently had joined those states that were serious about curbing the death rate on their highways and it had raised its drinking age from eighteen to twenty-one, but teen drinking remained a problem.

Personally, Kay and Bob never drank and drove. They were casual beer drinkers who rarely kept hard liquor in the house. Perhaps even more than Bob, Kay was sensitive to the problems of teenage drinking and drug abuse, for she now confronted them firsthand at school. Nine students at Severna Park High, where she'd taught for nearly a decade, had been killed or seriously injured in alcohol-related car accidents during the last two years.

Although Kay and Bob never got tipsy in public or around their friends, Larry told his friends that his mother sometimes got drunk around the house. Then she underwent a metamorphosis and was "lenient" on him, he said.

During 1982, Bob withdrew increasingly from his family. His work consumed much of his time, for he still commuted to the Washington suburbs. He had switched jobs again and was working for a General Electric subsidiary under contract to the federal government, teaching people to maintain and operate computers that processed satellite weather data. What little free time he had, he spent on church-related activities.

In the summer of 1982, Bob began leaving the house even earlier than usual every Saturday to meet a group of men in the lower sacristy at St. Mary's. Ron Baradel had discovered that Bob wasn't "grouping" with any Cursillistas and he invited him to join his group. To accommodate Bob, who always picketed Planned Parenthood at 8 A.M., the group switched its weekly sessions from 8 to 7:15 A.M.

In addition to Bob and Ron Baradel, the group consisted of Scott Chapman, a communications consultant for Westinghouse, and Pat Donohoe, a retired army colonel. At thirty-seven, the tall, ruggedly handsome Chapman was the youngest of the group. At fifty-five, Donohoe was the group's senior citizen. A huge, gruff-looking man, he wore a heavy metal crucifix around his neck and had attended mass nearly every day for two decades.

Like most Cursillo reunions, theirs followed a rigid format. They started by hugging one another and saying "De colores!"— a Spanish greeting that referred to the beautiful colors of life. Bob always carried his eight-point agenda around in his wallet. The tiny pamphlet pictured Jesus on the cover above the words *I Am Counting on You!* Inside were questions the men took turns answering each week, such as "What was the moment in which you felt closest to Christ?" The questions probed what they had done that week in the areas of piety, study, and action. Group members were supposed to listen "prayerfully" to each other, rather than debate or voice their reactions. More than the others, Bob had a tendency to respond, offering little tidbits of advice, asking "Have you tried this?"

The reunions were supposed to bring the men together as

they explored their spirituality through the filter of everyday experience. They talked not just about the Scriptures or how many Hail Marys they'd said but also about their ups and downs at home and work. The other men soon noticed that Bob was more reserved than most new members. He rarely shared personal experiences or mentioned his family, except for an occasional reference to Annie. She often accompanied him and listened respectfully as the grown-ups talked.

To his credit, Bob was a good listener during the entire year and a half that he met with the group. He listened so intensely that Chapman felt he was living vicariously through them. In fact, Bob seemed so much in awe of the other men's devotional lives that Chapman wondered whether he had a spiritual inferiority complex. When Chapman would say he was sticking to a certain daily prayer time, Bob would say apologetically, "I just didn't have much time this week to pray," or, "I'd like to do more of what you're doing."

Donohoe detected no spiritual inferiority complex in Bob, but he noticed a rigid view of the world and attributed Bob's black and white vision to his fundamentalist upbringing. Donohoe always tried to follow Christ's example and not judge his fellow man, but he expected his fellow man to look him in the eye when they talked; and it bothered Donohoe that Bob never did.

"Bob had a beautiful, beautiful smile, a kind of charismatic smile," Chapman later recalled. "But if you looked into his eyes, you saw a mask of intimacy, because he always would have the most pained look in his eyes. I always looked at him and saw a man in great, great pain. It was almost like he was crying. His smile and the look in his eyes did not match."

7.

"Larry is certainly not watching *that*," Kay huffed into the telephone. "I don't care what the other boys are doing."

Standing beside Larry in her kitchen down the street from the Swartzes', Susan Barker—whose family had moved back from

Italy to Cape St. Claire—was taken aback. "What are you talking about?" she asked.

"You know."

"I have no idea."

Of course, Susan Barker didn't. Kay Swartz was so angry, she wasn't making much sense on the phone. It was a week night, but everyone expected school to be called off tomorrow because of a pending snowstorm. Larry had called home for permission to spend the night at the Barkers' along with a group of the Barker boy's friends. The boys planned to watch *Superman II* on a videocassette recorder. One by one, the youths had called their parents and gotten permission. Larry, the last to call, was having trouble getting his mother's consent. Susan had heard Kay shouting over the phone and poor Larry responding softly, "I am *not* lying. She asked me to stay."

Kay had demanded to speak to Susan, and when Susan got on the phone, Kay barked, "What's this going on? What are the boys going to do tonight?"

"They're going out sledding for a while, then coming in to watch a movie," Susan said.

"Larry's not to be trusted," Kay said. "I don't want him spending the night there."

"They'll be supervised, don't worry," Susan assured her. "All the other boys already have permission."

When Susan revealed what movie she had rented, Kay instantly objected. She knew all about that nasty sequel in which the Man of Steel sacrificed his superhuman powers for the earthy pleasures of Lois Lane's love. She assumed that Susan, too, would consider the film inappropriate for youths. "That movie shows Lois Lane *in bed* with Superman," Kay said. "Everyone knows they just had sex, and the movie doesn't say one word about preventing pregnancy. The last thing this world needs is another abortion or unwanted baby. The movie doesn't bother showing that when a baby is born, it may be adopted one day and some fool will have to take care of it!"

"But it's rated PG, and the boys are sixteen and seventeen years old." Susan tried to keep her voice down as Kay raised hers. She felt embarrassed for Larry, having to go through this in front of his peers. "There's no nudity anywhere in it. There's not even a mention of sex."

Susan winced when Kay responded with a sarcastic remark about her neighbor's poor taste in films and lack of concern about influencing children's attitudes. "That movie should be banned!" Kay cried. "You'll burn in hell for what you let go on in your house!"

Kay was just as hot about Larry sledding. She ranted so wildly about sex and hell that Susan could hardly believe her ears. There would be girls out there in the snow, Kay said, and boys couldn't be trusted around girls. Kay did not allow her son to date and Susan would surely burn for letting hers.

Burn in hell for letting her son date? Was Kay Swartz for real? Susan wondered. Susan tried to calm her neighbor down, to whittle away at her irrational complaints. After Susan promised that she and her husband personally would supervise the sledding, and that she would substitute a less offensive movie for *Superman II,* Kay finally relented. Larry could spend the night.

Relieved, Susan hung up.

For Susan Barker, that was it: She wanted nothing more to do with Kay Swartz. She was angry with Kay already for lecturing her son about sex and abortion. The boy had told his mother that Mrs. Swartz had preached to him about how sinful premarital sex was, how it led to abortion, a terrible, terrible thing. To underscore just how terrible it was, Mrs. Swartz had described the mechanics of the operation in gory detail.

There had to be something wrong with that woman, Susan thought. She seemed so *obsessed.*

8.

"I have a collect call to anyone from Michael Swartz. Will you accept the charges?"

"Yes," Larry said softly, picking up the phone in the basement.

"Hey, how 'ya doin'?" Michael was relieved that Larry had made it to the phone first. He was a good buddy, a helluva

brother. Mom and Dad refused to accept Michael's calls nowa-
days and even forbade Larry to talk to him. But Michael knew
Larry wasn't going listen to that bullshit. They were *brothers,*
man. It wasn't right not to let brothers talk.

"How's the bitch?" Michael asked—meaning Kay, of course.

"Still a bitch," Larry muttered.

Michael told Larry about his life in Western Maryland and his
visits to a foster family who lived fifteen minutes from the
Swartzes. Larry, in turn, told Michael about his dismal home life.
He had all but stopped talking to Bob, saying nothing to him
except when it was unavoidable.

For Michael, the surreptitious calls were special. He idolized
Larry and still dreamed of going home to live with him as a
brother, even though he probably had destroyed his prospects
for realizing that dream when he had cursed at his mother on
the phone. At Michael's review hearing in October, the Swartzes
had made clear they didn't want him home, and his caseworker
had recommended that he stay at Long Stretch indefinitely. Now
the Long Stretch staff was preparing Michael for independent
living. No longer was there even a plan for him to return home.

Michael's calls affected Larry just as deeply, for Larry felt his
brother's loneliness and pain each time he called. Larry could
not understand why his parents hated Michael so much that
they wouldn't even let him visit. He was *family.*

Larry couldn't help wondering, If they discarded Michael so
readily, what might lie around the corner for him?

SEVEN

Friday, January 20, 1984

1.

"Well, we'd better get started," Ron Baradel said.

Kay's relatives eyed each other nervously, agreeing but not really wanting to move. For fifteen minutes, they had been standing quietly in the entrance foyer of Taylor Funeral Chapel, waiting for Kay's brother to return from Dulles International Airport. Gerald Sullivan had gone to pick up his daughters, who were flying in from Arizona. His family was loathe to enter the funeral parlor without him, but it was twenty past seven, and the wake started at eight. They couldn't postpone the viewing any longer. Slowly, the family filed into the small chapel.

Larry was already there, sitting to the right of the caskets, doubled over with his head buried in his knees. Jack Smithmyer sat beside him, one arm draped across his back. None of the relatives approached Larry, and Larry approached none of them. On the few occasions when he lifted his head, Larry averted his eyes from theirs.

Nobody in the room talked except Annie, who ran eagerly from cousin to cousin, giggling and laughing as she greeted them all. An eerie, deathly silence fell over the room.

Suddenly, a towering man strode in wearing floppy galoshes and a ski parka over his dark suit. Gerald Sullivan marched straight to the center of the crowd and froze when he saw his sister in the open casket.

"Oh, my God!" he screamed, reeling away from the casket and slapping his forehead with his hand. Then, anger deepening his voice, he looked wildly around the room and shouted, "Who did this? Who did this?"

His nephew John Riely shot a quick glance at Larry, but Larry didn't flinch or even raise his head.

Sobbing, Sullivan's two daughters rushed to embrace their father. As they hugged him, he shouted, "What kind of animals do they have around here?"

John Riely approached and spoke briefly to his uncle, who then charged across the room to Ron Baradel. Sullivan addressed the lawyer in a voice more controlled than before but loud enough for others to hear.

"Are you Ron Baradel?"

"Yes I am," Baradel said, his voice a whisper next to Sullivan's.

"I just want to know one thing. Why are you impeding the police investigation?"

"I'm not."

"Well, why won't you let Larry be polygraphed?"

"There are a lot of good reasons for it. I'm not ruling it out entirely, but I wouldn't let him do it the other day because he was in no shape to take a polygraph."

"Why does Larry need a lawyer, anyway?"

"There are a lot of good reasons."

"Oh, yeah? Well, does Annie need one, too?" Sullivan's tone was facetious.

Thank God for Judge Cawood, Baradel thought. "Don't you know Annie *does* have her own lawyer?" he replied.

Sullivan seemed taken aback, and Baradel felt a little sorry for him. "Look," Baradel added, "I know you're upset, and I don't expect you to understand everything, but there are good reasons why both children have their own lawyers."

That seemed to chasten Sullivan. After a minute, he drifted away from Baradel and rejoined his family.

People who had been standing near the rear began venturing up to the caskets to pay their last respects.

Kneeling next to Bob, Ron George found himself picturing the lively, jovial man he had so loved. He imagined a familiar grin beneath Bob's pale grim visage, and he half-expected Bob to burst into laughter. The Life pin that Bob always wore—the one with a painted red rose and green leaf on white enamel—was pinned to his collar. George had asked that Bob be buried with that pin and his Precious Feet pin, which showed the tiny, perfectly formed feet of a fetus. Now George noticed that the Precious Feet pin was missing, so he unfastened his own pin, leaned over the casket, and fastened it to his friend's collar.

Detectives Barr and Mock stood at one side of the small viewing room, trying to look inconspicuous without succeeding. It was standard procedure for them to attend homicide funerals, but they'd been invited to this one by John Riely, who had wanted security for his family. "I thought if somebody is crazy enough to do this to them, who knows what their next step might be, out of desperation or revenge," Riely explained. "Who knows, maybe we are all victims. Maybe there is somebody out to get the whole family."

As 8 P.M. approached, Jack Smithmyer led Larry up to the caskets with one hand firmly wrapped around his waist and the other gripping his arm, as though he feared Larry might faint.

Detective Mock edged closer. This is what he had come to see. John Riely, who had been about to leave, turned to watch, too.

Larry showed no reaction: no tears, no emotional outburst.

That, Mock believed, was because he didn't really look. Larry stared at the foot of each casket as though he was afraid to look his parents in the face. After Larry left, Mock walked over to

Barr and whispered, "Did you see? He won't look! He won't look!"

Barr, however, was feeling like an intruder and didn't want to look any more than Larry did. He hated attending strangers' funerals because he never knew what to say and he always felt out of place. In Barr's estimation, he paid dearly for the benefits of his being there. As the family left the funeral parlor for the wake at St. Mary's Church, located a short walk down Duke of Gloucester Street, Barr lingered behind. "I really don't see why we need to go to the wake," he told his partner. "I think we've seen enough."

Reluctantly, Mock agreed.

Ron Baradel also stayed behind. In disbelief, he watched the relatives file out ahead of Larry and Annie, not waiting to escort the children to the church, not even stopping to talk to them, leaving them entirely to the care of the Smithmyers, who were not, after all, family. Neither of Kay's two sisters nor her brother had spoken a word to Larry; and this was their first encounter with him since the relatives had arrived in town. Baradel could not understand it. Later that night, after returning home from the wake, he would turn to his wife and shake his head. "Did you see how they treated those kids? They didn't even talk to them. I couldn't believe they didn't show more attention and concern to those kids. They're *relatives,* for Chrissakes."

Louise Baradel was not surprised. "They probably think of them as family pets," she said. "They probably look at them as Bob and Kay's children, not part of their family."

The Swartz family entered the church late, after the nearly six hundred mourners already had crammed into the pews and jammed the outside aisles. The relatives marched silently down the center aisle while a band of TV reporters filmed their entry from the choir loft in the balcony. Although the Friday-evening service was but a prelude for the Saturday-morning funeral, it drew a capacity crowd.

"Look around you in this church tonight," Father Heyburn said, his voice booming from the pulpit. "There are so many people we do not know. So many people we have not seen before. Yet each one was known and loved by Bob and Kay. Each one of us was touched by the gift of their lives."

At the reception afterward in the rectory, Ron George noticed that Larry seemed more relaxed. Gone were the tension and strain that had been so evident at the funeral parlor. Now Larry seemed carefree, as though he'd undergone a release. The implications bothered George, who was aware that police considered Larry a suspect.

Larry's transformation caught his cousin John's eye, too. Larry had slipped off his coat and tie and slung them over one shoulder as he stood casually in the rectory, laughing and talking to his high school buddies. John watched a pretty young girl approach, stand beside Larry, hold his hand. After a while, Larry wandered down the corridor with her and disappeared into one of the tiny rooms where mourners had left their coats.

One of Larry's female cousins went looking for her coat a few minutes later and found Larry kissing his girlfriend. She promptly told the rest of her relatives, who were stunned by Larry's nonchalance.

"It was Friday night, and he was making out with his girl," John Riely said caustically.

After the wake, Kay Swartz's relatives drove back to Bethesda, stopping first at a Roy Rogers restaurant to pick up several buckets of chicken. They took the chicken to one of their rooms at the Marriott Hotel, where they sprawled on the beds and chairs to eat and debate who the killer was.

John Riely later described the scene:

"There were two names being bantered about: Michael and Larry. Without being specific about who was saying what, the general consensus was . . . 'Michael did it.' And the rest were saying, 'Michael did it, but we're not going to let Larry off, either.' In other words, Larry is a suspect until it's proven.

"The great majority were saying, 'It's Michael, Michael.' Even Greg Rodden, who knows what I've told him from the Smithmyers. The only person who is acknowledging it might be Larry is Helen Rodden, and she's saying, 'It's Michael, but I think

Larry may be implicated somehow, too.' All the Sullivans were saying, 'There is no way it's Larry,' except for Gerry Sullivan, who is saying, 'They are both guilty.' So nobody was saying it was Larry by himself.

"Finally I said, 'Listen, we've got to acknowledge the possibility it may have been Larry acting alone, that he may have just snapped that night. Larry may have made a big mistake that night'—I remember using that word and regretting it, calling it a mistake—'One of those "I hate my parents" type things. He took it a step further, a mistake in that he went one step beyond "I hate my parents," "I wish you were dead." He acted on it.'

"Some of the Sullivan girls now, when I say this, two of them left the room in tears. They couldn't believe Larry would do this. That was their response. They just completely broke down, left the room and went to another room, sobbing immensely."

2.

Saturday morning brought stark skies and icy cold to Annapolis, a cold so stubborn it refused to thaw as the day wore on. Four inches of dirty snow still smothered the town, which would make a mess of the funeral procession down West Street, the town's perpetually clogged main artery.

Before the pallbearers carried the caskets out to the hearses for the procession to St. Mary's, a social worker escorted Michael Swartz into the funeral home. He had not been allowed to leave the Crownsville Hospital to attend the viewing or the wake the night before. He wanted to view his parents privately before their caskets were closed for the funeral.

Nobody had to tell Michael that he, too, would be on view today. He was a prime suspect in the murders. Michael knew that, and knew all his relatives knew, too. Michael also realized that most of these people hadn't seen him in years and would be straining for a glimpse, peering at him as though he were some near-extinct wild animal about whom they had only heard tales.

Ron Baradel, one of the pallbearers, saw Michael right away and fixed his attention on his height. The last time Baradel had seen Michael, nearly four years ago, he'd been tall, but nothing like this. Michael's thin, elevated frame, bushy hair, and scraggly goatee made him look wild. Even in his dark conservative suit, he looked wild. Baradel stared at Michael's goatee, that hint of hair on his chin. The man Annie had seen fleeing her backyard Monday night had a "beard-face," she had said.

Would Annie consider Michael's goatee a "beard-face?" Baradel wondered.

The funeral started at ten. Fifteen minutes beforehand, Michael and his social worker left the funeral home and walked down Duke of Gloucester Street to the church.

There, Michael saw Larry for the first time since the murders. As they looked at each other, tears welled in their eyes. Neither had much to say. The entire Smithmyer family was there, also Annie and a crowd of people milling behind them. The boys had no privacy and no time to talk before the service.

Michael, Larry, and Annie sat with Jack and Eileen Smithmyer in the front left pew. Again, St. Mary's overflowed with more than five hundred mourners and television crews who filmed the pageantry from the balcony.

Detectives Barr and Mock joined the crowd early. Bent on watching the boys' faces, Mock elbowed his way down the aisle on the left to get as close to the front as he could. Moments before the funeral ended, he would hustle back down the aisle and position himself near the exit, where Larry and Michael could see him on their way out. Mock wanted maximum eye contact; he was determined to psych the boys.

Ten robed priests and three deacons stood at the altar, an extraordinary number for a funeral, though not so extraordinary given the role that Bob Swartz had played in their parish. Excruciating care went into planning this funeral. Everyone who knew the Swartzes wanted to participate, which called for innovations, such as the roses. Before mass, Right to Life members walked down the center aisle and laid a lone red rose, the symbol of life, on the white cloth draped over each coffin. The roses later would be lowered into the frozen earth with Bob and Kay.

Father Heyburn gave the homily and spoke at length of the Resurrection: how Bob and Kay had believed so deeply in the Christian message of life everlasting, and how they still lived in Christ Jesus.

Heyburn looked at the children in the front pew. "Michael, Larry, Annie," he said slowly, softly. "You are the young, broken ones. Much of what has happened will take time to understand, and to heal. Perhaps it will never make complete sense to you. But you are the chosen ones . . . Bob and Kay chose you for their sons and daughter. Through their death, may you grow in their light.

"God love you."

For family members, the service was so tense that when a member of the folk choir fainted during a reading, falling with a *thud* to the chancel floor, a few relatives jumped in their pews.

One dropped his head. "I ducked," explained John Riely. "I thought for sure somebody was up in the choir loft with a rifle and took out somebody in the choir. I thought the thud was a gun. The thought lasted one second, but sometimes you can have a hundred thoughts in three seconds."

Other thoughts flashed through their minds as the relatives sat looking at Michael, whom John described as "looking like he just got off the starship from planet Zeon." One of John's sisters noticed red marks—bruises or scratches, it was hard to tell which—on Michael's neck and pointed them out to her relatives. There was a mark on his cheek, too. Soon the relatives were all staring at Michael's long thin neck. Crying softly, one girl whispered, "Look, those are Aunt Kathryn's finger marks!" It wasn't hard to imagine those reddish marks as the claw marks of a dying woman. Especially a spunky woman like Kay Swartz.

Several relatives remembered the time Kay was vacationing in Puerto Rico and a mugger stole her handbag as she walked down the street. It contained only forty or fifty dollars, but it also held her passport. Kay was not the kind of woman who would let her handbag get away that easily. She ran after the mugger. She didn't catch him, but she managed to reach out with her fingernails and scratch him all the way down his fleeing back. When Puerto Rican police caught the mugger the next day, Kay identified him by the scratches on his back. No, it was not difficult to imagine Aunt Kathryn scraping her killer's neck.

During the funeral mass, Kay's relatives paid close attention to Larry and Michael. They wanted to see whether the boys took communion. Most of them realized it was illogical to believe that a person would murder two people—commit two mortal sins—and then heed the Catholic injunction against taking communion while still in mortal sin. Still, Kay's family had been raised Catholic, and it made good Catholic sense to believe that the killer would not take communion. After all, the boys were Catholic, too.

Larry took communion. Michael did not.

"I'm a person that won't take it unless I feel I'm worthy of it" was the explanation Michael later offered for his abstinence.

Now, more than ever, his relatives were convinced of Michael's guilt.

When the funeral service ended, the family and close friends returned to their cars and drove two miles down West Street to St. Mary's cemetery. They trudged through the snow-covered graveyard. John Riely spotted Detective Mock and approached to tell him about the marks on Michael's neck.

Partly to inspect those marks, but more to monitor him during the service, Mock followed Michael to his parents' open graves. He wanted to zoom in on Michael like a video camera, to see everything—facial expression, eyes, every little nuance of body language.

While the priests said a few quick prayers, Michael, Larry, and Annie stood with the Smithmyers in a row directly in front of the graves. Larry wore a tan leather coat; Annie, a short ski jacket. Michael wore no overcoat and shivered. Michael was acutely aware of the detective standing across from him, glaring at him through dark glasses. Both boys kept their eyes downcast. Michael stared at the thin green mats laid out on the snow beside the graves; he noticed that the mats were frozen solid.

After the prayers, Father Kevin Milton held a chalice over each coffin and shook holy water from it, blessing the bodies, then handed the chalice first to Larry, next to Michael. Each son was expected to sprinkle holy water over the bodies, blessing his parents for their journey to everlasting life. Jack and Eileen helped the boys, gripping each one in a kind of bear hug when his turn came to lean forward and sprinkle the water. Michael was nervous, as stiff as the icy green mats beside the graves. He shook it and thought, Oh man, ain't nothing coming out! He shook it again and a sprinkling of water fell.

Watching Michael intently, Mock saw nothing he could interpret as a sign of guilt. Of course, Mock wasn't sure what he was looking for. The neck marks did not look like scratches to Mock; they looked like hickeys. After talking to the hospital staff at Crownsville later, Mock decided that's exactly what they were. Crownsville staff members told Mock that male and female patients had access to one another in the hallways, and Mock speculated that Michael had found himself a little lady.

At first, though, neither detective took the marks so lightly. As John Riely was leaving the cemetery, Barr walked over to him and said, "Why don't you go up and ask Michael what those marks are?"

Riely looked at the cop as though he'd lost his mind. Go up and ask him? What the hell are you getting paid to do? Riely wondered.

After the burial, the mourners returned to St. Mary's for a luncheon reception in the school gymnasium beside the church. Like the funeral, the atmosphere was strained, uncomfortable. People ate at long tables and stood in small groups, talking quietly.

Larry took his tie off again and stood with his teenaged friends, but he didn't look as relaxed as the night before. His eyes danced around the room as a circle of girls quickly formed around him.

Joe Swartz, Bob's brother, approached Larry and was puzzled when his nephew made a strange face at him. "I don't know how to describe it," Joe would say later. "It was sort of like, uh, *I may have done something to hurt you.*"

As they chatted, Larry asked his uncle, "Have you talked to Michael?"

"Not yet, but we will," Joe assured him.

Joe had the impression that Larry felt sorry for Michael, who was standing twenty feet away from Larry and slightly apart from everyone, exuding the air of an outsider. Fewer people were approaching Michael than Larry. You could almost see the barrier that fear had built around Michael. Joe, one of the few relatives who did not fear Michael, approached and hugged him. They chatted about Michael's life and plans for the future.

Most of the relatives stayed away from Michael. Watching from across the room, Joe's stepmother, Jean Swartz, told relatives she wanted nothing to do with that "scary-looking young man." John Riely watched Michael from afar without once approaching him. It had been at least four years since he had last seen Michael; Riely hoped his gangly cousin wouldn't recognize him.

Near the end of the reception, Sullivan approached Ron Baradel. "I want to apologize for last night," he said. "I'm sure the last thing you needed was some crazy guy coming at you."

"That's all right," Baradel replied. "I know you were upset."

Conscious of his approaching deadline, Baradel wandered around the room, talking to a small coterie of friends about what to do with Larry. Who would take him in? It was past one o'clock, and Baradel had to make his decision by six. Otherwise, the judge would hand Annie over to the state. Larry had asked Ron George, his Sunday school teacher, if he could stay at his house. George had agreed, but Baradel thought it wasn't fair to involve Ron George and his unsuspecting family without informing them that Larry was, quite probably, a murderer. On the other hand, Baradel didn't feel that ethically he could be so frank. After talking it over with Louise, Baradel decided to open his own third-floor guest room to Larry. Larry and Jack Smithmyer could sleep up there, then return to Jack's home during the day, because the judge had ordered the children to be separated only at night. Baradel asked Jack to take Larry over to the Baradel's town house in the Annapolis historic district that evening.

As the reception wound down, Michael left and returned to Crownsville. Larry approached Maureen Rodden. "How about going out for some lunch? I know this great place, Phineas Fogg's. You and some of the cousins can go. We can talk."

Soon, Larry, John Smithmyer, and a small group of Larry's cousins were seated at a table, waiting for hamburgers at the teenage hangout across town. Riely went along eagerly, hopeful that Larry wanted to confide in his cousins, to confess what really had happened Monday night.

Instead, Larry babbled about his favorite hamburgers, his girlfriends, what fun times he'd had here. The cousins knew it wasn't uncommon for people to react to overwhelming trauma by denying it, blocking it out, escaping into fantasies of happier days—anything to avoid the painful truth. Yet the absence of anything even resembling grief in Larry struck the cousins as bizarre.

As all the cousins had done with Michael earlier, Riely studied Larry, looking for abrasions or signs of injury. Riely couldn't believe that Uncle Bob would have gone down without a fight. Noticing a mark on the back of Larry's right hand, Riely pointed and asked, "What's that?"

"Oh, I burned myself fryin' hamburgers," Larry said.

Riely nodded, thinking Larry was probably telling the truth. The mark was brown and looked more like a burn than a scratch.

The cousins kept nudging the conversation back to the murders. One asked Larry pointedly, "Do you have any idea who did this?"

"Naw," Larry said. "I really don't."

"Who do you think might want to kill them?" Riely asked.

"Well," Larry said, "my mom had a run-in with a student at school."

"What, over grades?"

"Yeah. He's kind of a troublemaker. Mom was mad at him about something he'd done. The police are checking on him."

"Do you think Michael did it?" Maureen asked Larry.

"He could have."

"How likely do you think it is that Michael did it?"

Larry shrugged, but Maureen wouldn't let it go. "Do you think there's a fifty percent chance?"

"Oh, probably more," said Larry.

"Sixty percent chance?"

"More."

"Eighty?"

Larry paused. "Yeah, I'd say eighty," he said.

That was pretty lame, Riely thought. A minute ago, Larry was suggesting some kid at school was the murderer. Now he was saying it was probably Michael.

Riely didn't believe it was either one.

3.

Ron Baradel spent what remained of Saturday afternoon working in his law office. At exactly ten minutes to six, he phoned Judge Cawood and told him that Larry would be sleeping with the Baradels. Then, before he headed home, he drove to Cape St. Claire to feed the Swartzes' parakeet.

At home, Baradel's actions before Larry arrived belied the lawyer's outward calm. Methodically, he searched all the rooms in his house and hid every sharp object he could find.

"God forbid, if the boy wants a peanut butter sandwich, he's going to have to put on the peanut butter with a spoon," he told Louise.

Jack took Larry over after dinner, and they both slept in the Baradel's third-floor guest room.

Shortly after Larry and Jack went to bed, Baradel, fearing for the safety of his wife and three children, carried a beige wing chair into the second-floor hallway and placed it ten feet from the foot of the stairs leading up to the guest room. If Larry had any ideas about escaping, or hurting anyone, Baradel planned to stop him. Fitfully, he dozed all night in the chair.

The next day was Super Bowl Sunday. In the morning, Jack and Larry returned to the Eastern Shore. Baradel, meanwhile, went to the Swartz house to root around for the wills that relatives had said Bob and Kay drafted. Everyone was wondering to whose care had Bob and Kay had entrusted Larry and Annie. Who were the children's legal guardians? When Baradel found the wills, he phoned the Smithmyers', where all the Swartzes' relatives had been invited for brunch.

Most of Kay's out-of-town relatives were there. So was Larry, who was wrestling bare-chested in the living room with John Smithmyer. John's father, Jack, took the call, talked briefly, then walked into the living room and somberly announced, "They found the wills."

Larry stopped wrestling and sat upright on the floor.

"In the wills, the guardians are James and Helen Rodden," Jack said. He looked right at Helen—Kay's sister—and her husband.

"Oh, my God!" Helen cried involuntarily.

"We're happy to keep Larry and Annie for as long as you want," Jack added softly. "If you want to let this lie for a while, that's fine with us."

"I think that would be a good idea," Helen said quickly.

Larry was looking at Aunt Helen, watching her. She refused to look at her nephew.

"Am I in the will?" Larry asked suddenly.

His relatives were aghast. At a time like this, how could Larry ask about his inheritance?

"I don't know," Jack said. "All Ron said was who the guardians are."

After talking it over, the Roddens agreed to postpone a decision on custody of the children. For now at least, they were safe with the Smithmyers. Telling the Smithmyers they'd be in touch later, the relatives headed back to Washington to catch flights home.

That afternoon, Ron Baradel took time out at home to watch the Washington Redskins clobber the Los Angeles Raiders, 38 to 9. Then he went to his office and worked until 3 A.M. researching and drafting a motion to quash the grand jury subpoena for Larry's fingerprints. Even though he spent hours polishing it, he gave his motion little chance of success—so little that he took time to draft an appeal.

At nine o'clock the next morning, bleary-eyed from another night in his beige wing chair, Baradel went to the courthouse and filed his motion to bar police from fingerprinting Larry. Circuit court judge Bruce C. Williams set a hearing on the motion for the next day.

While Baradel was talking to the judge, detectives Barr and Mock met with prosecutors in the courthouse annex. Afterward, the detectives drove back to the Crownsville Hospital to make yet another check on Michael's alibi.

After interviewing family friends and neighbors over the weekend, the cops still felt uneasy about Michael. People kept saying the kid had been sighted in the neighborhood while he was supposed to have been in Crownsville. Larry, of course, was still saying that Michael could get in and out with ease. Barr and Mock were completely sold on Larry. Yet "just to cover our butt," said Mock, "just to make sure there isn't a back door that maybe we might be missing," they paid a final visit to Crownsville.

Barr remembered the Crownsville patient who had fallen to her death during an escape attempt four months earlier. He had heard the allegations of a hospital cover-up. The woman, who had just returned from an escape and was placed in isolation, jumped through an upstairs window that supposedly was locked. After she died, state police investigated charges that hospital employees had altered records and lied to investigators. Several hospital employees were summoned before a grand jury, but no criminal charges were filed. The case added to the hospital's notorious reputation for lax security; Barr knew that the hospital workers would be especially sensitive about this murder case.

When the detectives arrived, Michael was out with his social worker. The cops talked to the nursing director, who showed them Michael's bed and personal belongings. The cops found no gray sweat shirt or any sweat shirt with BROADNECK printed on it amid his meager possessions.

The nursing supervisor introduced the cops to an attendant named Clarence Taylor, who told the cops he'd grown friendly with Michael during his four-week stay.

"Do you remember seeing Michael here last Monday night?" Barr asked.

"Yeah," said Taylor. He had worked the shift ending at eleven o'clock that night. "I remember I said good night to him when I left around 11:15."

Barr eyed Mock. If Taylor was correct, the timing was significant. By now, based on Annie's statement and neighbors who had heard the Swartz dogs barking, the cops were pretty sure the murders had occurred at approximately 11:30.

The supervisor volunteered that another nurse had seen Michael on the ward last Monday night. The nurse, who was off duty at the moment, had mentioned it to the supervisor after the murders made the news.

Finally, the cops asked the supervisor to lock them in Michael's ward and leave them alone. They wanted to see how secure it really was. It was a large open room with long rows of beds, similar to the squad bays where Barr had slept when he was in the Marine Corps. Methodically, they checked the windows: Each had a locked heavy metal screen. Standing beside Michael's bed, the cops saw that it was visible from the nursing station at the end of the hallway outside the ward, where the night attendant usually sat. Unless Michael had escaped through a window, he would have had to sneak past the attendant at the nursing station and get through several more locked doors farther down the corridor.

"No way," was Mock's appraisal of Michael's chances of escape.

"Only if he had a master key," said Barr.

"He'd have to have a cape with an *S* on it," Mock joked, "to get over there, do his dastardly deed, and get back in the time frame he had to work in."

Now, more than ever, they were convinced of Larry's guilt.

Late Monday night, Larry wandered into the Baradels' kitchen and poured a glass of water. Ron Baradel, standing by the sink, noticed the youth barely touched his water. He suspected Larry wanted to talk. Eileen Smithmyer had phoned earlier in the day to say that Larry wanted to talk to her, but she had urged him not to. Now, when Larry looked like he was fumbling for words, the lawyer encouraged him to open up.

"You have to trust me," Baradel said. "I know what happened, and I want you to know it doesn't make any difference to me."

Larry looked confused, so Baradel walked over and hugged him. Just when it seemed Larry might confess, Baradel's eight-year-old son, Brice, walked into the kitchen and poured a glass of orange juice. Larry clammed up.

The next morning, while Jack Smithmyer took Larry to eat breakfast with Father Milton at St. Mary's, Baradel headed for the courthouse to meet Joe Murphy. Behind the closed doors of his chambers, Judge Williams heard the attorneys' arguments on whether Larry would have to surrender his fingerprints. As Baradel expected, the judge ruled in favor of the prosecutors.

Baradel immediately called Jack Smithmyer and asked him to bring Larry to his law office. He and Murphy wanted to sit down with their client before they drove him to the police station. Depending on how things went, this might be their last chance for any real privacy.

When Larry arrived, Baradel ushered him into his first-floor library, a large room with leather-bound legal tomes lining all four walls. Wearing blue jeans and a T-shirt with a colorful wind-surfer scene emblazoned across his chest, Larry took a chair at one end of the oblong table. Murphy sat facing him at the other end, while Baradel sat casually on the table next to Larry.

Murphy opened with what must have struck Larry as an interrogation: "Look, the police don't believe your story. They think you're lying and here's why." Sternly, methodically, Murphy recited the holes in Larry's story. How could he have known his father was dead if he never went downstairs? Did he really expect anyone to believe he slept through everything? That he told Annie she was "dreaming"? As lawyers often tell juries, "false exculpatory statements are evidence of guilt," and Murphy thought Larry had told police some whoppers. Those statements could hang him in front of a jury.

Larry sat on the edge of his chair and avoided Murphy's

eyes. Baradel leaned forward, took his hand, squeezed it, and in a soft low voice reassured him: "It's okay. I know. The Smithmyers know. We're going to get it worked out. We aren't going to leave you. We're going to take care of you and Annie."

Murphy kept urging Larry to come clean, confess, let go of the truth. "This is why the police are going to arrest you, Larry," he was saying.

Realizing he and Murphy were slipping into the old good guy-bad guy routine, Baradel squeezed Larry's hand again. "Let it go," he said. "It's over. We love you. It's not going to change that. You've got to let it go."

Then, barely five minutes after they had started, Larry broke, collapsing like a mud dam under floodwater, unleashing a torrent of emotion so strong that it threatened to swamp his lawyers. "Yes, I did it!" Larry cried. Sobbing uncontrollably, he dropped his head and his whole body began to shake. He wept without restraint, as if to vent a lifetime of sorrow. Unable to help himself, Baradel broke into tears, too. Even Murphy's eyes were wet.

"He wouldn't stop hitting me!" Larry cried. "He wouldn't stop hitting me!"

The lawyers didn't ask Larry what he meant. They didn't ask him to explain anything. His body went into dry heaves, jerking as though he were trying to expel something, some twisted thought or vile feeling that had driven him to kill his parents. His lawyers had no idea what that was, for Larry hardly spoke during the rest of the half-hour session. He was in no condition to answer questions. Baradel had never seen anyone dissolve so suddenly and so completely. He worried that the youth was in the throes of a nervous breakdown. Fearing that he might turn suicidal, Baradel suggested they take him to a psychiatrist as soon as possible.

Murphy agreed. Based on the barbaric nature of these killings, Murphy already was contemplating an insanity plea; and he figured the sooner they got started with psychiatric examinations, the better. They could decide later whether insanity was the best defense; first, they needed psychiatric opinions. Murphy called Dr. Michael Spodak, a psychiatrist who worked part-time for the state and who was well known for his frequent testimony on behalf of prosecutors. Spodak agreed to see Larry immediately after the police fingerprinted him.

Although Murphy was late for a trial in Towson, he told Baradel, "I'm going to go see Warren. It's important for him to know we found something out."

"What the hell are you going to tell him?"

"I don't know. I'll figure something out."

Although Murphy couldn't reveal that Larry had confessed, he wanted the prosecutor to know that something dramatic had happened. He wanted Duckett to suspect they were contemplating an insanity plea now, before Larry was arrested. Otherwise, Duckett might later tell a jury that, after first proclaiming his innocence, Larry lamely raised insanity as a last-minute ploy. "Naturally, when a defense is interposed late in the game, or after the charge is made, the question is raised as to its sincerity," Murphy would later explain.

Murphy called Duckett, then drove across the Spa Creek Bridge to the courthouse annex and climbed the staircase to Duckett's private office, where he found Duckett conferring with an assistant, George Lantzas. Declining Duckett's invitation to sit down, Murphy paced the small elegantly furnished room. Although Murphy said little, Duckett and Lantzas quickly inferred that Larry had confessed. Lantzas thought Murphy was doing a masterful job of not telling the prosecutors anything but emoting a great deal.

"There may be something happening," Murphy announced. "Maybe in a few days we'll have some information for you."

"What kind of information?" Duckett asked.

"I can't tell you now. There'll come a time when I will be able to, but I can't now."

Murphy made a few more mysterious statements, then, just as suddenly as he had come, he was gone. No good-bye, just a few paces around the room and whoosh, out the door.

Lantzas and Duckett stared at each other. They were convinced now that they had the right boy—Larry had to be the killer—but what was Murphy up to? Lantzas thought he might be making preliminary moves for a plea bargain. Duckett thought perhaps he was so emotionally overcome by the confession that he rushed right over to tell them about it, then realized he couldn't. They were both wrong: Murphy just wanted to hint that Larry had made a confession, one so dramatic that it might later figure into the trial as the starting point of a possible insanity defense.

While Murphy met with the prosecutors, Larry rode to police headquarters with Baradel, Charlie Bagley, and Jack Smithmyer. They arrived at the brick building at ten minutes to one. Police Chief Lindsey watched through his first-floor office window as television news crews filmed Larry walking up the wide front steps and entering through the glass doors. A half-dozen reporters rushed to the rear of the building and peered through a peephole in a back door, where they soon saw a police officer roll black ink impressions of Larry's fingers and palms.

Within half an hour, the defense team was back on the road, heading north to see Dr. Spodak. After talking to Larry for an hour or so, the psychiatrist told Baradel he thought Larry might be suicidal and should be admitted to a hospital right away. But before they could find a suitable hospital or resolve the problem of cost, word came from Duckett: Police were seeking a warrant for Larry's arrest.

An evidence technician had carried Larry's handprint cards to the FBI lab in Washington, where, at Barr's request, a latents man stood waiting to make a quick comparison. Within hours after Larry surrendered his fingerprints, the evidence technician called the results in to homicide: The FBI had identified the bloody handprint from the patio door. It was Larry's.

"Swear out two first-degree warrants," Duckett told Barr.

While Barr typed an affidavit to take to the courthouse, Duckett called Murphy's office to track down Larry. When the prosecutor reached Baradel at the psychiatrist's office, Baradel immediately agreed to surrender Larry. Duckett suggested that Larry should come to his office rather than police headquarters, and Baradel assented. Baradel wasn't admitting anything by turning the youth in: Duckett had a warrant and Baradel had no choice but to surrender him. The defense lawyer said nothing to Duckett about Larry's confession, which was privileged information and which couldn't be used against Larry in court. So far as the lawyers knew, Larry had confessed to no one else.

Baradel took Larry aside. "We're going to turn you in."

Larry nodded, as though he'd expected this all along.

"This isn't the end of things," Baradel added. "It's just the beginning. Above all, remember, you can trust me. It won't be easy, but you can."

Larry's face hid his emotions. "I understand," he said calmly.

So collected, so composed was his demeanor that Baradel found it hard to believe that Larry had fallen apart in the law library only a few hours ago. Baradel told Larry that he and Murphy would provide him with the best defense possible, even if that meant a plea of not guilty by reason of insanity. "But there is no way you are going to walk out of the courtroom a free man," he added. "If that happens, I want your promise that you and I will walk out, and we will go right away to a hospital."

"Okay," Larry said meekly.

Dodging television cameras, the defense team arrived at Duckett's office a few minutes past seven o'clock, before the paperwork did, and went straight upstairs. Duckett greeted them in the foyer outside his office. After politely shaking Duckett's hand, Larry sat on one of two apricot leather armchairs in the prosecutor's inner sanctum. Duckett was struck at once by the youth's handsome face and mild manners. He looked and moved a lot like a boy who lived in Duckett's neighborhood. The resemblance was extraordinary.

"Would anyone like coffee?"

Larry nodded, and Duckett poured it out for him. Larry stirred in sugar, then set down his cup on an English Provincial butler's table and began making small talk with the man who would prosecute him. As they chatted, Duckett asked Larry a pointed question about his home life, and Baradel leaned forward and said sharply, "Don't answer that."

Realizing he'd gotten carried away with geniality, Duckett stopped asking questions.

At nine minutes to eight, Detective Barr arrived with the arrest warrant and summoned Larry to the outer reception area. "Empty your pockets," he commanded.

Reaching into his jeans, Larry drew out his rosary beads and a holy card with a picture of Jesus Christ. Barr kept the beads but handed the holy card back to Larry.

As Barr read aloud the statement of charges and probable cause, Larry listened with the same blank face that he had displayed to the TV cameras all week. Lantzas watched in amazement, thinking the kid was either in shock or remarkably self-controlled, for he didn't even blink when Barr alleged that he "did kill and murder his parents."

After Mock read the Miranda rights to Larry, Baradel asked the detectives if he could drive Larry to the station in his car. He didn't want the detectives questioning Larry.

"No," Mock said irritably. They'd waited long enough while the lawyers had coddled this boy. Larry was *their* prisoner now.

"Well then, I don't want you asking him any questions," said Baradel. His voice was choked, and it seemed as though he were surrendering his own son. He watched Barr and Mock shackle Larry's hands and lead him downstairs to the squad car.

After everyone left, Duckett found himself sitting alone on his sofa, intense pain pulsating in his head. He hadn't eaten all day, and he felt sad. The sadness intensified as he stared across his office at a framed color photograph perched on a bookshelf below hundreds of red-bound *Maryland Digests.* In the frame was a studio portrait of the three Warren Bird Ducketts: his father, himself, and his son.

Duckett pictured Larry being led out of his office in handcuffs. He strained to imagine what could have driven such a polite, graceful boy to murder his mother and father. It could have been his neighbor's son, Duckett thought. It could have been his *own* son, for Larry seemed no different from either of them. As Duckett gazed across the room, the long-haired youth in the photograph stared blankly back at him.

Suddenly, Duckett realized that his own son looked like a stranger.

For the first time in as long as he could remember, Warren Bird Duckett, Jr., broke into tears. He wept for his failings as a father, which he knew were substantial and he feared were irreparable. He was to blame for the strained distance, the constant bickering between himself and Bud, as he liked to call his son and namesake. Guilt gnawed at Duckett. He had pushed Bud too hard to emulate him, to be the school politico and super-jock he thought Bud ought to be. He had pushed Bud even when it had grown painfully obvious that the boy did not share his father's love of politics or team sports. Now Bud hardly talked to him anymore. They weren't communicating any better than Larry had communicated with his father, and the pros-ecutor felt it was all his fault. He hoped it wasn't too late to change.

After crying for five minutes, he stood up, collected his coat, and locked his office door.

When he arrived home, he walked straight over to Bud, who was watching TV, pulled him to his feet, and gave him a bear hug.

Bud drew back, his large brown eyes widening. "Dad, what's wrong?"

EIGHT

Summer 1983

1.

"Aw Mom, where am I gonna get that kind of money? You *know* I don't have it," Larry pleaded.

"Well, then, just wait until school starts and you can take it for *free,*" she said.

"But you *said* I could take it this summer."

"Why should we pay for you to take it now, when it's free in the fall?"

Larry was fighting a losing battle to get his mother to pay the fee for driver's ed in summer school. He was sixteen, and she still didn't want him to drive. Neither parent had offered to give him driving lessons, and Bob had forbidden him to start his 1981 Honda motorcycle or either family car, even though Larry regularly washed the cars. Now his parents had announced that he couldn't take driver's ed this summer unless he paid for it himself.

They knew he didn't have the money. Although he made a few dollars mowing lawns and doing odd jobs for neighbors, he spent most of his money on clothes. His mother made him buy his own because he tossed the ones she bought all over the floor of his room, which was a pigsty. "If you can't treat your clothes responsibly, then I'm certainly not going to buy them for you!" she huffed.

Summer had been a long time coming for Larry. He had spent the winter on restriction, looking forward to summer so he could get his driver's license, which he viewed as his ticket to freedom. Now he had no money to buy that ticket. He would turn seventeen in August—be a junior in high school—and still couldn't drive. It seemed so unfair.

When he finished his sophomore year in June, his parents finally let him go out with friends. As everything else they did, it came out of the blue. They didn't announce that his restrictions had ended; Larry had to find out for himself. When he asked whether he could go with a friend to the mall, or the Super Skate, his mother surprised him by saying, "Yes." His freedom remained limited, though, and he could never stay out as late as his friends. He wasn't allowed to go out as he pleased; he needed permission, which wasn't always forthcoming. By now, though, Larry had devised ways to get around his parents, which included sneaking out after they went to bed.

"Hey, there's a killer party tonight," Eric Armstrong said one Friday. "Let's go." Because Larry's parents never allowed him to attend those big bashes, he waited until his parents were sleeping, left his bedroom door ajar so it wouldn't creak when he crept back in, and walked down to a neighborhood boat dock shortly after midnight. Eric picked him up in a friend's speedboat and they roared off to the party. Other nights, they just cruised in the boat, drinking beer.

By now, Larry had won permission from his mother to start dating girls, although she admonished him not to take out the same girl twice. Dating a girl only once would reduce the likelihood that Larry would be seduced, Kay reasoned. She thought the temptation of sex would be greater for Larry than most boys. He was filling out in the chest and losing his wiry, skinny look. He was so handsome that girls already were chasing him at school. His extraordinary looks drew glances from men, too. That worried his parents, especially Bob, who feared that after the mysterious incident at seminary, his son might become a homosexual.

Larry felt increasingly confused by the way his mother treated him. She smothered him sometimes, then acted totally indifferent. In the blink of an eye, she could switch from tenderness and affection to sarcasm and spite. Although he grew accustomed to his father's ranting, his mother's sharp belittling was more than his brittle ego could bear. She used to take his side when his father was being harsh. Larry couldn't understand why she didn't stick up for him one night in July when he came home late from a double date to the movies.

His parents had instructed him to be home by midnight, his standard curfew. At 11:30, Larry called and told his mother, "The movie just got out, and I'm not going to be able to make it by midnight 'cause we still have to take the girls home. Is it okay if I'm half an hour late?"

She said okay, so Larry and his buddy took their dates home. His buddy dropped Larry off at 12:30 and Larry went to bed.

In the morning, Bob announced that Larry could no longer go anywhere with the young man he'd gone out with the night before.

"Why not?" Larry asked.

"You didn't have a good enough reason for being late last night. Besides, he obviously has more freedom than you. You shouldn't be going around with him."

Larry didn't expect his father to be fair, but he couldn't understand why his mother didn't step in anymore when his father yelled at him. Larry would look down until his father paused for breath, then ask quietly, "Are you finished? May I go to my room now?" While he listened to his father, Larry drained himself of thoughts and feelings and became inert. His face sometimes appeared so lifeless that it stunned his best friend's father one afternoon.

Roughhousing inside the Smithmyers' house, Larry and John Smithmyer knocked over a lamp, prompting John's father, Jack, to enter the room and chew them out. Jack saw Larry staring back at him with a zombielike expression, which alarmed Jack:

He had six children of his own and had never seen an expression like that before.

When Jack broached the subject later, Larry explained he'd had trouble expressing emotion since he was small. He always made an effort to hold things inside because he feared the consequences of letting anything out. "Before I came to live with the Swartzes," Larry said, "it seemed every time I gave my opinion, or showed any emotion, I got moved to a new home."

Jack felt sorry for Larry; his relationship with his father obviously was going downhill. Jack wasn't the only one who noticed the growing enmity between Bob and his son. Dick Maio, Bob's right-hand man on the picket line, got a glimpse of it that summer when Bob opened his pool for the annual Right to Life picnic. The picnic started in midafternoon and lasted all evening.

Bob hopped in the water at first and swam with the kids. Larry dunked his father a couple of times with help from a buddy. Climbing out, Bob dried off and began making his rounds as host. Moments after he sat down in a lounge chair and began regaling a group of friends with a funny tale from the office, Annie yelled at Larry to stop splashing her. Bob looked over, yelled "Stop splashing, Larry!" and returned to his story.

A while later, Larry took a running leap from poolside and did a cannonball, splashing water everywhere. The spray came within inches of Bob and his crowd.

Getting up from his chair, Bob walked over and screamed "I *told* you not to splash! If you're going to splash you can go inside the house!" Bob walked back to his friends, muttering what a pain his son was.

Later in the party, Dick Maio glanced across the pool and saw Larry sitting silently, glaring across the water at his father. Maio was taken aback by the cold, terrible look in Larry's eyes. He instantly sensed that something much more intense than the splashing scene had triggered that stare.

Although Larry felt his mother had abandoned him, had crossed an invisible line to side with his father, Kay's family had no inkling of trouble when Kay took her children to the midwest that summer of 1983.

The second week of August, Kay packed Larry and Annie into her Plymouth station wagon and drove northwest to Detroit to attend a nephew's wedding. Although Bob claimed he couldn't spare time to attend, Kay wouldn't have missed it for the world. It was a gay affair and everyone danced, even Larry, who had never set foot on a dance floor. While Kay did the soft shoe with her brother, Larry led his female cousins out one by one and learned to dance by watching everyone else.

The night before the wedding, when most of Larry's cousins were heading out to party, Kay pulled John Riely aside and asked him to keep an eye on Larry. "Don't let him drink, will you? He's got a tendency to drink, and he's too young."

Her nephew nodded. "I'll keep an eye on him."

At the wedding on Saturday, Kay let Larry drink champagne. It was a special occasion.

On Sunday, in Kay's car Gerald drove Kay, Larry, and Annie back to his home outside Chicago. During the drive, Gerald noticed how exceptionally close Larry seemed to be to his mother. Kay sat in the front seat, while Larry sat in the back and leaned forward, draping his arms around his mother's neck. He rubbed her shoulders and fooled with a gold chain necklace around her neck. Gerald couldn't get over what a loving son Larry was—so tender and solicitous to Kay. Gerald thought his nephew would turn out all right, despite the school problems about which his mother often complained.

Later in the week, Kay drove southwest to see her sister, Maureen Riely, in the tiny town of Minonk, Illinois. Maureen hosted a backyard barbecue that was largely uneventful except for a minor incident that she later looked back on as an example of how spoiled her nephew was. Maureen never understood why Kay *indulged* Larry so. At the barbecue, Larry twirled his glass endlessly around on a paper tablecloth, seemingly mesmerized, until a hole widened and the entire tablecloth fell apart. Kay watched without saying a word, then a few weeks later mailed her sister a new tablecloth with a note: "I noticed that one of my kids tore up your tablecloth, so here's a new one."

Kay also had indulged Larry six months earlier, when Maureen and her daughter went to Annapolis for a visit. Although it was a weekday, the whole Swartz family played hooky and went to Baltimore's Harborplace. Late in the afternoon, when they stopped at a city market to get fresh fish to grill at home, Larry complained that he didn't want fish; he wanted ravioli and was too hungry to wait.

"All right. Go ahead," Kay said.

Larry ordered Italian food at one of the market's counters, and everyone waited while he ate.

Maureen disapproved. Never in a million years would she cater to one of her children in that way.

Maureen's son John came to spend two weeks with the Swartzes at the end of August and noticed nothing terribly amiss between Larry and his parents.

While Riely visited, Larry bickered with his parents over a party he wanted to attend with his friends. Riely considered the bickering normal, especially in a family headed by a man like Uncle Bob. "Bob could be a real horse's petunia," Riely explained.

Bob and Kay wouldn't let Larry attend the party because they knew liquor would be served. They had caught Larry drinking several times and were worried that he was developing an alcohol problem. Although Kay felt a little sorry for her son, realizing that he had considerably less freedom than most of his friends, she wouldn't yield to peer pressure. It wasn't her fault if other parents were ignorant about the wild drunken bashes the kids threw.

"I'll tell you what," Kay finally told Larry. "Why don't you have a party of your own here? Invite your friends over to swim in the pool, and we can keep tabs on whether there's drinking."

"All right," said Larry. He loved having friends over to his pool. He picked a date and invited his friends.

On August 25, Larry's birthday, Riely stopped at a local bakery on his way home and bought his cousin a cake. Kay broke out the cake and ice cream after supper and organized a family party in the dining room. Larry opened a handwritten card from Annie and three presents, including a bright Hawaiian flowered shirt from his father.

*   *   *

That summer Kay joined the faculty at Broadneck, the new school behind their house, where Larry had been a sophomore the previous year. Kay had applied at Broadneck when it opened the year before, but fewer English teaching positions had been open then.

One morning in late August, Larry helped his mother cart her files into her new classroom on the second floor of the large brick building. After they lugged several boxes upstairs, Kay and Larry wandered down to the English department office, where department chairwoman Linda Blackman was unpacking books. She and Kay had taught together one semester at Severna Park High.

"Can I do anything to help?" Larry asked Mrs. Blackman.

"Sure," she said, smiling. "I've got hundreds of books in here. They all have to come out of the boxes, then get stamped and numbered. We write in the numbers by hand. Here, I'll show you."

Mrs. Blackman showed him the stamp and explained her numbering system. Since he asked no questions, she left him alone while she went to sort supplies.

A few minutes later, Kay interrupted her friend and nodded toward the hallway. "Can we have a word out there?"

When they were out of Larry's earshot, Kay said softly, "What you asked Larry to do is going to be difficult for him. Is there some way you could get him out of it? Could he do something else for you?"

"Sure." Mrs. Blackman nodded. She considered the sequential numbering system complicated even for her bright students. So she returned to the office and told Larry that she had forgotten where to start the numbers. Why didn't he just skip the numbering and stamp the books?

"Okay," he said.

A few days later, Kay took Linda Blackman home for lunch. It was the week before classes started, and the cafeteria hadn't opened yet. All the teachers were busily preparing for classes to start the following week.

As they entered the house, Kay noticed water drops on her hardwood floors and heard girlish giggling down the hallway.

The sound seemed to be coming from Larry's bedroom. "Larry!" she called.

Her son, wearing his swimming trunks, appeared in the hall-way beside two bikini-clad teenaged girls.

Kay was perturbed but held her tongue. "May I see you for a minute?"

While the girls went outside to the pool, Larry looked sheep-ishly at his mother.

"I don't mind you having your friends over for a swim," she admonished, "but make sure you stay outside. And you know better than to take girls into your bedroom!"

Larry looked down. "But they had to use the bathroom."

"That's all right, but I don't want girls in your bedroom. If they have to come inside to use the bathroom, make sure they dry off first. I don't want water all over the floors."

Although Kay was calm and collected the day she disciplined Larry in front of her friend, she wasn't always that way. Eric Armstrong later recalled that Mrs. Swartz "freaked out" that fall when she came home one afternoon and discovered Larry and Eric watching television together. "She just started into him, saying, 'I told you never to have anybody over when we're not here!'" Eric recalled. "I said, 'See you later, man, I've got to go.'"

2.

The same month that Kay took Larry and Annie to the midwest, Michael received a weekend pass to leave Long Stretch and visit a new foster family fifteen miles north of Cape St. Claire. He wanted to visit his old neighborhood while he was back in the area, so he called Susan Barker, who had moved back from Italy the previous year, and asked whether he could spend Saturday night with her.

Of course, he could. Susan thought the Swartzes had treated Michael shabbily, and she was more than willing to help him in any way she could. She planned a barbecue and invited Larry, her son, and a boy who was visiting from Georgia.

At the afternoon cookout, Michael stood awkwardly, shifting from one long leg to the other, and he declined to join everyone else at the table when they sat down to eat.

"Sit down," Susan urged. "Go on."

Michael looked embarrassed. "Naw. I can't. I don't have any money to pay."

It was enough to make Susan cry. *"Of course you don't have to pay,"* she said quietly. "Go sit down and eat. Please."

Joining the other boys at the picnic table, Michael seemed especially happy to see Larry. They sat and talked for a long time. Michael talked about how nice it would be to have his brother and sister back, to move in with them again.

When Larry told his parents that Michael was back in the neighborhood, they invited him for dinner Saturday night. Pleased and nervous, he accepted.

After the Barkers' picnic ended, Michael walked down the street to his old house. Before he left, Susan noticed he seemed as skittish and eager as a boy going to pick up his date for the prom.

When Michael returned to the Barkers', he looked like a cool, mean shark, calculating his plan of attack. The change shocked Susan. What terrible blow had his parents inflicted on him? Barely an hour ago, he had seemed so excited, so happy. Now he was enraged.

"I'm going to kill them, that's what I'm going to do," he announced. He spoke with a hard mean edge to his voice that frightened Susan.

"What happened?" she asked.

Michael wept as his story tumbled out: His parents had rejected him; he wasn't their son anymore. After they had finished eating outside on the carport, he had volunteered to go inside and do the dishes, but they wouldn't let him. He wasn't part of the family; it was over. "All I wanted was for Mom and Dad to like me," he said, sobbing. "I wanted my brother and sister back. I wanted my family."

When Michael stopped crying, a cold look crossed his face. "I'm going to kill them. That will free Larry and Annie. And when Larry turns eighteen, he's gonna move away with me. We're gonna live together."

Susan stared at him, horrified. She had planned to keep him overnight at her house, but she couldn't possibly let him stay. In this condition he just might slip out in the middle of the night, creep over to the Swartz house, and stab Bob and Kay in their sleep.

"Come on, Michael. I'm taking you back tonight."

Michael later said that was the last time he saw his parents alive.

Allen Cheshire was a short youth from Romney, West Virginia with chunky cheeks and shifty blue eyes. Michael Swartz thought he was a country hick and couldn't stand the sight of him.

"Where the hell are my books, man?" Michael screamed.

"How should I know? I didn't touch 'em," Allen lied.

"I know you did. I'm gonna bust your ass if you don't give 'em back!"

Allen and Michael had been feuding for several days. The two youths lived together in a big white house atop Dead Man's Hill, a long steep bank where the Long Stretch boys went sledding every winter. Earlier that hot August day, Allen had slipped into Michael's basement bedroom and swiped some magazines and books from his dresser. After passing a couple of the books around the house, Allen still had one stashed in his room. One of the other boys in the house had snitched to Michael.

Now Allen, who wasn't even five six, looked up at Michael, who towered over him by a foot.

"I want my books!" Michael screamed.

Allen shifted gears. "I thought we were friends. I thought you wouldn't mind."

Michael sure did mind. "I'll break both your arms!"

Allen walked across his room and turned up the volume on his radio to drown out Michael's screams.

Michael marched over to Allen's dresser, yanked the radio out of the wall socket, and lifted it over his head, ready to hurl it to the floor.

"No, don't!" Allen pleaded. "Don't do it!"

It was too late. The radio left Michael's hands and shattered to the floor.

The next morning, Allen vowed revenge. When the other seven boys in the house left together, Allen stayed behind, telling his house parent that he had to finish making his bed. Instead of making his bed, Allen crept down the hall to Michael's room to hunt for Michael's prized possession—a small silver crucifix that he used alternately as an earring and a roach clip. Both were taboos at Long Stretch. Bill Platter didn't allow boys to walk around with ornaments dangling from their ears, and he certainly didn't permit them to smoke pot.

Allen approached Platter a while later, handed him the pronged sliver of metal, and told him it belonged to Michael Swartz.

That night, Allen would later recall, after he took a shower and was climbing into his bunk, he noticed a shadowy motion on the wall in front of him. Before he could turn around, he felt a sharp wallop that knocked the bejesus out of him. When he regained his senses, Allen recalled, Michael was standing beside the bed with an inch-thick slab of wood, laughing. According to Allen, as soon as Michael got a look at the blood running down Allen's stringy blond hair, he begged Allen, "Oh man, don't tell on me!"

According to Michael, he never hit Allen over the head with the board: Michael claimed he merely beat Allen with his fists. "I bloodied him up pretty bad," Michael recalled. "It was built-up anger. It was the only way I could get it out."

At first, Allen didn't tell on Michael. But when his head wouldn't stop bleeding, he went upstairs and told his house parents, who took Allen into Cumberland to see a doctor.

Another counselor, alerted by the house parents, went to talk to Michael. When Michael uttered wild threats at the counselor, the staff decided to remove him from the home for the night. They drove him into Cumberland and placed him in a psychiatric center.

Although Allen declined to press criminal assault charges, Michael's days at Long Stretch were over. He was beyond control; the center refused to take him back.

It was no small task for state workers to find Michael a new place to live. He was no longer welcome in the Swartz home;

his parents had all but disowned him. And who else would take in a surly boy with the height of a basketball player, the mouth of a truck driver, the slick hands of a thief?

Only six months away from his eighteenth birthday (after which, as Michael knew, he would lose the protective benefits of juvenile court if he ran afoul of the law again), Michael returned to the suburban area of Baltimore from whence he had come. While social workers waited for Michael to turn eighteen, they could do little more than find him spare beds in group homes and juvenile shelters. It was a waiting game, really, for Michael had tried out every cubbyhole that the Maryland child care system had to offer, and had outgrown them all. The only place left for him to go was out.

Even though social workers repeatedly told him that his parents didn't want him back, Michael still dreamed of a homecoming. Despite his bitter feelings for Mom and Dad, he continued to fantasize that they would take him home again and treat him as a son.

3.

Sarah Slaughter was eating in the noisy lunchroom near the entrance to Broadneck High School when out of the corner of her eye she saw a gorgeous male entering the cafeteria. What a doll, she thought. What beautiful cheekbones and shiny black hair. Her eyes followed him through the food line to a table. She *had* to find out who he was. It was her first day at Broadneck, however, and she didn't know anyone to ask.

A senior, Sarah had switched schools that fall because her family had moved into a new house. She was only two years back from Europe, where her father, an air force officer, had been stationed for six years. Sarah had long bouncy brown curls and a pretty face with a wide smile. She was more sophisticated than the average senior, perhaps because she'd grown up overseas, and was articulate and bright enough to earn straight A's, yet she earned mostly B's because she seldom bothered to study. Her classes bored her; occasionally she skipped them.

When she got home that night, Sarah called a girlfriend from her old school. "Ooohh, I wanna meet this guy," she squealed. "He's sooo beautiful!"

She saw the same boy around school several more times over the next week. Then one day, he strolled into the cafeteria while she was eating with a new girlfriend.

"Who *is* that?" Sarah gasped.

Sue Kindred glanced up. "Oh, that's Larry Swartz. He's a junior."

"My God! He's so cute."

Sue Kindred smiled. She knew Larry and thought him a nice quiet boy. Sarah obviously was smitten.

Sarah's crush on Larry intensified every time she saw him. He had big brown eyes and an adorable sunny smile. She was surprised when Sue mentioned that Larry was Mrs. Swartz's son. Sarah had Mrs. Swartz for speech, her first class of the day, but she hadn't connected her teacher's name with Larry.

Mrs. Swartz seemed so different from her son. Sarah thought her a dowdy, unpredictable teacher who could be a blast one day and a bitch the next. She exploded one morning when Sarah sauntered into speech class a couple minutes late, took her seat, and turned to say hi to the student behind her. "You always talk in my class!" Mrs. Swartz screeched. "Would you be quiet for once?"

Reddening, Sarah fell silent.

For Larry, school that year was a mixed bag. On the good side were the girls, who flirted with him like crazy, and the soccer team. He was still on JV, which wasn't so hot for a junior; but he was cocaptain and they were off to a terrific season. Driver's ed was another plus. His parents finally let him enroll and promised that if he passed, he could get his license second semester.

On the minus side were his classes—all of them, especially Spanish, which his mother had recommended but which Larry could not grasp. He had no ear for languages, and he didn't try to develop one.

"Where's your homework?" Anne Klyman, his gray-haired Spanish teacher, asked several times.

"Aw, I was too busy," he muttered. "I didn't have time."

Mrs. Klyman liked Larry, who was polite and occasionally raised his hand in class and tried to answer questions. She couldn't help noticing that girls regularly struck up conversations with him. Obviously shy, Larry rarely initiated conversations but seemed to enjoy it when girls flirted. His incredible laziness puzzled her, though. He made almost no effort to learn and acted indifferent to the prospect of flunking. At the end of the first marking period, she gave him an E.

Mrs. Klyman also had Larry for homeroom, the ten-minute period where teachers counted noses every morning, and Larry was always late. Sometimes just by a couple minutes, but other times he showed up a full ten minutes after the bell. "Larry, you're going to be late to your own funeral," she told him, but it did no good. When she mentioned it to his mother, Kay replied casually, as though she'd didn't care, "Oh, I just can't get Larry up in the morning. He has such a terrible time waking."

In October, Larry took a part-time job at the Chesapeake Sub Shoppe, a deli less than a mile from his home. One night, he took home a pizza that he'd made and, after wolfing down a couple pieces, left the remainder on the kitchen counter instead of wrapping it in foil and putting it in the refrigerator.

The next night, Larry gobbled more of the pizza, then woke up in the morning too sick to go to school. Kay thought it served him right for being stupid enough to eat leftovers that had sat out overnight.

When Larry asked for an excuse to take to homeroom the following day, Kay penned a short note to Mrs. Klyman: "Larry was absent because he got sick on his own cooking!" Kay thought her quip was funny; Larry did not. He didn't bother turning in the note during homeroom.

"Where's your excuse?" Mrs. Klyman asked.

"I don't have one," he muttered.

Before writing up an unexcused absence, Mrs. Klyman went down the hall to have a word with his mother. Mrs. Swartz's classroom, a doorless room on the second floor like Mrs. Klyman's, was across the hall and down fifteen or twenty yards.

Stepping into the hallway, Kay laughed and explained what had happened with the pizza. "Larry's so upset about it," she said. "He doesn't want anyone to know he got sick on his own cooking."

Shortly afterward, the Chesapeake Sub Shoppe fired Larry. "He didn't catch on quick," the deli manager later explained. "Food is not his line of work. When it gets busy in here, you have to do a lot of things at once."

One day in October, a friend of Larry's, Sue Kindred, finally introduced Larry to Sarah Slaughter in the school lunchroom. The threesome ate together, then walked into the hallway, where Sue—who knew Sarah had a crush on Larry—exclaimed, "Oh, look!" and shot off to talk to someone else.

Within a few days, Sarah and Larry were an item at school, flirting, seeking each other out in the hallways, eating lunch together. On days when Larry had wrestling practice, Sarah persuaded her parents to let her drive to school so she could stay late and see him. They talked a lot, sharing snippets about their families, and Sarah quickly realized how close Larry was to his little sister.

He would tell Sarah, "I'm gonna go take Annie to the park," or "I've gotta go pick up Annie," and he never seemed to resent being his sister's keeper. "Sometimes she has nightmares and comes into my room at night," he told Sarah. "I rock her to sleep."

Larry's exceptional closeness to his sister was something most people who knew the Swartzes noticed. Yet Larry later made a point of denying that Annie meant anything special to him. "By the way," he wrote in a biographical essay, "Annie came when Mike and I were about ten years old. Annie didn't have much significance, or you could say significance on my part in the family. I treated her as a normal sister and I loved her."

4.

Near the end of October, Bob and Kay went to juvenile court for a review hearing on Michael's custody. His caseworker reported that Michael had spent the last six weeks at the Muncaster Boys' Shelter, a state-licensed brick and wood rambler in a northwestern suburb of Washington. He was doing "fairly well" and was receiving help to prepare for his emancipation when he turned eighteen in March.

Offered an opportunity to speak, Bob and Kay said they continued to have contact with Michael and considered his present placement "appropriate."

Michael didn't have much to say, except that he was willing to cooperate with the Department of Social Services.

A month later, Michael's cooperation slipped when he lost his temper one morning. Like many of the state's privately run group homes, Muncaster had a sliding scale of privileges that youngsters worked their way up through good behavior. Michael was on his way to the top of the scale, on fairly good behavior, when he got exasperated with a boy who wanted to sleep in. Michael was convinced that everyone in the house would be restricted if the youth stayed in bed.

"Get up!" Michael yelled. "Get up!"

When the youth didn't budge, Michael grabbed the mattress to push it off the top bunk's frame. But he miscalculated, and when he flipped the bunk, somehow the whole contraption came crashing down on the youth's head, giving him a concussion.

"You're on twenty-four—fifteen—twenty-four," his counselor declared. Michael was grounded to his room for twenty-four hours, then had to put in fifteen hours of manual labor, then spend another twenty-four hours confined to the house. Just like that, all his privileges were gone. Whoooom, down he slid.

Never one to play by anyone else's rules, Michael refused to stay cooped up in his room. He nonchalantly sauntered out, lit up a Marlboro, and wandered around as if nothing was wrong. He shot baskets with friends, then went to the garage for a game of pool.

The next day, citing his refusal to obey rules, Muncaster kicked him out.

The next stop in Michael's game of musical homes was the Palmer Family Boys' Home, the same Crownsville shelter that took him in after he first left the Swartzes. Jayme Palmer, the founder and director, knew him well, for he'd been in and out of her home many times in the past five years. He came first as a twelve-year-old booted out of a foster home, and in the years that followed, he spent many a lonely holiday and vacation there. Now he was seventeen and still without a home.

Palmer felt sorry for him as he entered her transitional living center to prepare to make his own way in the world. She knew he had plenty of anger inside—who wouldn't if they grew up without any parents or relatives to care for them?—but rarely had she seen him this angry. When he arrived from Muncaster, Michael was cranky and uncooperative. He broke house rules, wouldn't listen to anyone, cursed and slammed doors, and sat around scowling.

Ironically, not long after Larry lost his job at the Cape St. Claire deli, Michael lost a restaurant job, too. Early in December, Michael landed employment in the kitchen of Popeye's, a fried-chicken joint along fast-food row in Annapolis. He was pleased to have a job but not pleased about how he was expected to get there. Without a car, and with strict house rules against hitchhiking, Michael was expected to walk the nearly five miles into town whenever he couldn't find somebody headed in his direction.

Michael slept through his work shift one afternoon nearly two weeks before Christmas. Later, he claimed he hadn't overslept; he just grew sick of hiking five miles to work in the freezing cold. Regardless, Michael didn't bother to call in. When he didn't show up for his shift, he was fired.

Depressed, Michael sat around the house sulking. He made no effort to look for work elsewhere and wouldn't talk to his counselor.

"Come on, Mike, you have to look," the counselor said. "We'll take you around."

"It's raining. I'm not goin'. anywhere."

Although house rules forbade the youths from staying out overnight, Michael left the center one night before Christmas and didn't return until the next day. After he returned, he continued to flaunt the rules, slamming in and out as he pleased, disturbing other youths and the staff.

Finally, on December 21, Palmer called the Department of

Social Services to request his immediate removal; she could no longer control him.

The following day, a social worker drove Michael to Baltimore to the Fellowship of Lights, an emergency shelter for homeless and runaway youths.

Michael's stays everywhere were getting shorter and shorter, and in Baltimore, he set a new record for getting kicked out— less than a day.

This time, Michael crossed a line that he hadn't crossed before: He pulled a knife on a female counselor and waved it near her throat.

The next day, December 23, Michael was hauled back into juvenile court. Juvenile Master James W. Dryden committed him to the Crownsville Hospital Center, a state psychiatric facility, for thirty days to undergo a full mental evaluation. A psychiatric report prepared at Crownsville explained his expulsion: "A counselor felt threatened by Michael when he opened a knife in her presence and held it in proximity to her throat."

Michael described it a little differently: "I was reading the rules of the program, and they said, 'No weapons.' So I took my knife and chucked it up on the table. The lady said I pointed it at her and all this bullshit. I didn't do nothing like that. I just took it and put it on the table."

During Christmas and the weeks that followed, Michael made the most of his telephone privileges at Crownsville and called Larry regularly.

When Larry complained how sick he was of Bob and Kay, Michael said he responded with faint sympathy: "I told him, 'You got your choice. Do what I did: Get the fuck out.' Larry didn't want to because of Anne. See, when I was there, it was me that caught everything. When I left, Larry started catching it. And he figured if he left, Anne would catch it. So he said, 'Fuck it.'"

5.

At the same time that Michael was caught in a tailspin, Larry was whirling downward at an equally alarming rate of speed. His free-fall started one day in late November when Annie handed some pink pills to her mother and said, "I found these in Larry's jacket."

Kay knew right away they weren't aspirin or any kind of ordinary pain-relieving medication. Each oblong tablet was covered with brown and red spots. On one side was stamped PKS; on the other, 20/20.

"What are these?" Kay demanded when Larry came home.

Staring at the tablets, fumbling for words, Larry hastily concocted an excuse. "Uh, they aren't mine. They belong to a friend of mine."

"Oh? What were they doing in your coat pocket?"

"I was carrying them for my friend. He asked me to give them to someone at school."

Kay didn't think Larry was stupid enough to believe she would really fall for that. "What are they?" she demanded.

After hemming and hawing, Larry disclosed that the pills were speed. *He* didn't use speed, of course; he claimed he was only delivering the pills to a friend. Actually, Larry had taken one and hadn't felt any different afterward. He couldn't figure out why.

"You're grounded," Kay announced.

Bob exploded when he got home and bellowed, "Don't you ever bring drugs into this house again!"

After talking it over, the Swartzes decided they should find out what kind of drugs their son was using. They took one of the pink tablets to a pharmacist and asked, "Can you tell us what this is?"

The pharmacist agreed to test it.

Several months later, after the pharmacist read in the newspaper that Bob and Kay Swartz had been murdered, he phoned Ron Baradel and turned the pill over to the lawyer. Baradel then had it tested at an independent laboratory. The lab tests revealed that the pill was not a controlled dangerous substance but a look-alike, some harmless substance that a drug dealer probably had sold as an illegal drug to naïve teenagers.

One night in late December, the police cruiser's headlights hit two figures on the side of the road. As he pulled closer, the officer saw two youths horsing around, as if they were kicking something along the roadside. It was the middle of the night, no time, the policeman thought, for boys their age to be wandering around outside.

The officer pulled over and climbed out. "What's going on?"

The boys identified themselves as Larry Swartz and John Smithmyer. They claimed they were walking home from Denny's, an all-night restaurant on Route 50. No, they had not been drinking, they said. They'd been eating pizza.

"Get in," ordered the officer, suspecting the youths were lying. They were acting goofy, nervous. They'd probably been boozing. He'd better drive them home.

Bob and Kay were dumbfounded when the uniformed police officer escorted Larry and John into the house. John was spending the night with Larry, and they never dreamed their son would get into trouble with a model youth like John. The officer told the Swartzes he had brought the youths home because he thought they'd been drinking.

After the cop left, however, Larry and John assured the Swartzes that the officer was wrong.

Bob and Kay were skeptical. What were the boys doing outside in the middle of the night? Larry had lied to his parents so many times that they couldn't believe he'd really gone out because he was "hungry." But Kay detected no odor of alcohol on their breath, and she and Bob were too tired and upset to deal with the problem at that hour, so they told the boys to go to bed.

Alerted the next morning by a phone call from Kay, Eileen Smithmyer went over early and found the boys eating cereal at the picnic table in the Swartzes' kitchen. Kay and Bob sat down in the living room and explained the whole story to Eileen. Kay obviously thought the boys were lying. "Larry is an alcoholic," she told Eileen. "I read someplace that a teenager can become an alcoholic in six months, and I think that's what has happened to Larry. He's become an alcoholic."

Eileen was surprised. A trained nurse, she had never heard anything about it taking six months for a teenager—or anyone else, for that matter—to become an alcoholic.

When John and Larry came into the living room, Kay looked her son in the eye and asked, "Are you an alcoholic?"

Larry looked startled. "No!"

"Well, if you're not an alcoholic," she replied, "then I think we need family counseling. Something is terribly wrong here."

Dropping to the floor and crossing his legs, John calmly told his mother the whole story about their late-night trip to Denny's. He insisted the cop was mistaken. "We weren't drinking, Mom, honest. Neither of us was."

Eileen believed her son, but Kay was convinced that hers was lying. She lambasted Larry in front of Eileen and John, telling him that he had ruined his life. "You're never going to amount to anything! You won't be able to go on to college, because no college will ever accept you. You just wait and see! John will go off to college and leave you in his dust. You have finally pulled John down to your level!"

Like Kay, Bob believed the boys were lying. Rage shook his voice as he shouted at Larry. "You should have been thrown in jail and vomited on and urinated on and given hard labor! Then you would learn what life's about like I did! What you need is labor, physical labor, back-breaking labor! Then you wouldn't be going out at night like this."

Bursting into tears, Kay leapt to her feet and ran out of the living room.

Eileen was stunned. Why were Bob and Kay so angry over a seemingly minor incident? She followed her friend down the hallway into the master bedroom and tried to comfort her. "I'd be glad to help take care of Larry," Eileen said gently. "I'll do anything to help."

"I just don't know what we can do about him," said Kay, still weeping. "He's beyond help."

"Kay, if things are that bad, why don't you have him do his next semester over on the Eastern Shore and live with us? It will take off some of the pressure."

Kay wiped her cheeks and looked at Eileen. "Would you do that, really? Wonderful!"

When Bob entered the room, Eileen repeated her offer. Kay suggested it might do Larry a world of good to get him out of the house, where the atmosphere was so strained, and subject him to the positive influence of John Smithmyer and his parents. Bob nixed the proposal, however, insisting that Larry had to stay home and finish his junior year at Broadneck. Perhaps next summer, Bob said, if Larry could find a job over on the Eastern Shore, he might consider Eileen's offer.

"There are plenty of construction jobs over there," Eileen suggested. "I'm sure Larry could find something next summer."

"I want to be sure that whatever he is doing, it's real work," Bob replied. "I don't want him just sitting on a lawn mower mowing lawns. But we'll talk about this later."

As the tension built at home, Larry fantasized about what it would be like to belong to a normal family, one that would love him no matter what—a family like the Smithmyers, or the Barkers. He thought about it especially after dinner sometimes, when he went out for a walk alone.

All around the small rectangle that formed his neighborhood was a string of lights: bright, cheerful, glowing house lights that danced and flickered behind the trees as Larry trudged up the street. Through windows lit up like big-screen TVs, he caught distant glimpses of families sitting down to eat, to watch television, to talk and laugh and carry on as he imagined normal families did.

Why couldn't his family be like that? he thought, digging his hands deeper into his coat pockets. Why couldn't he have a father like Mr. Smithmyer or Mr. Barker? Larry loved to wrestle with Mr. Barker. He was such a cool father, nothing like his own. Larry dreamed of what it might be like to horse around on the floor with his father the way he did with Mr. Barker. How wonderful it would be to have a real dad you could love, a dad you could talk to and feel comfortable with the way Larry always felt when he spent the night with John Smithmyer.

Larry stopped in front of the Barkers' house near the end of Mount Pleasant Drive. It was all lit up. He crept quietly across the lawn, approached the house, and peered through a window where no curtains blocked his view. Waiting silently, nervously, for a glimpse of any member of the Barker family, Larry hoped he could see for himself what a real family looked like. How did they act? What sort of things did they do together at night? Perhaps he could make himself a part of the Barker family by peeking in like this.

Later, when Larry returned home, he felt profoundly ashamed. He felt like some kind of Peeping Tom.

*   *   *

"Take off your shirt," Susan Barker commanded.

She usually charged three dollars for her haircuts, but Larry seldom had any money, so she let him earn his doing odd jobs around her house. He was a good kid, usually so high-spirited that it was impossible not to like him. As a small boy, Larry had been a sneaky prankster—the neighborhood Eddie Haskell, Susan used to call him. But he had changed so much. Back then, Larry had been the brightest star twinkling in the Swartz household; he could do no wrong and his parents worshiped him. Susan would never forget Kay Swartz dashing down to the Barkers' yard and lighting into Michael—without stopping to learn whether Larry had been the one behind their latest lark.

After the Barkers left for Italy, all that had changed. When Susan returned, she realized almost at once that a transformation had occurred. Poor Larry had stepped into Michael's shoes, and now he was catching it, just as Michael used to. Now the sun rose and set on Annie, and Larry could do no right.

Sitting quietly, with slumped shoulders and downcast eyes, waiting for his haircut, Larry was a pitiful sight—so obviously depressed. As she approached to drape a cloth around his shoulders, she saw an ugly purple welt on his back, up near his shoulder. She froze.

"My *God,* Larry, what *happened* to you?"

Larry sat perfectly still, saying nothing. Tears welled in his eyes. She knew at once this was no wrestling bruise. "Who did that to you, Larry?"

Crying softly, Larry confessed that his father had given him the bruise, but he insisted "It was an accident."

She pressed him, but Larry refused to discuss the incident. He wept openly, though, as he talked about his miserable family life.

"I thought people adopted you because they liked you," he said, crying. "But that's not the case. Mom and Dad don't love me at all. They never show any affection. They've threatened to send me away like Michael. Why can't they be like you?"

She tried to reassure Larry that his parents indeed loved all their children. "I'm sure they love you, Larry; they just don't know how to show their love."

"No, they don't care about me, and that's all I want, is for my parents to love me. But they don't."

He had stopped crying and spoke slowly, with a distant look on his face, as though he were in a faraway dream. Larry had always been such a wild pony, full of spirit and fun. Now, she thought sadly, he seemed like an old broken workhorse.

6.

Even though she was recovering from an eye operation, Kay Swartz decorated for Christmas with her usual good cheer. She had gone to Johns Hopkins Hospital in early December to have a detached retina in her left eye repaired. After she came home, she draped shiny red foil over the front door and hung a green wreath on the door knocker, making the entranceway look like a Christmas package.

Inside, the holiday mood was muted and cheerless. Larry was barely speaking to his parents. They were still distressed over his drinking and the pills Annie had found in his coat pocket; and he was furious with them for changing their minds about his driver's license.

Larry was taking driver's ed because they had promised he could get his license second semester. He wasn't doing so well—a D, if he was lucky—but all he had to do was pass the course to get his license. Now, out of nowhere, his parents had announced he couldn't get his license unless he passed every single course—even though they *knew* he couldn't pass Spanish: He had failed it last quarter and was well on his way to failing it again. So he figured, why bother studying for anything? Obviously Mom and Dad would never let him drive.

He was stuck at home until he could earn enough money to move away, and there was no telling when that might be. He'd been saving money to buy a lawn mower so he could mow lawns in the neighborhood, but he knew he could never support himself mowing lawns.

"You know what I'm afraid of most?" he confided to John

Smithmyer. "That when I turn eighteen, I won't have enough money to move out of this house."

On Christmas morning, a Sunday, the Swartzes gathered in the living room, and Larry opened his two presents from his parents: a black nylon windbreaker and a classy gray pinstriped suit.

When classes resumed in early January, Larry wore his new suit to school, and one of his teachers complimented him on how nice he looked in it. "Thanks," he said, beaming proudly. "Mom and Dad gave it to me."

Kay blew up when she learned about Larry's date with Sarah Slaughter.

It was three weeks after Christmas, and Larry had done his best to ease his way into it by telling Sarah when they made their plans, "I think my parents might feel better if it was a double date." So they had agreed to meet Sue Kindred and her boyfriend Barry at the mall and see a movie on Saturday, the fourteenth of January. Sarah was going to pick up Larry and take him home.

Although Larry hung around with Sarah at school—he even walked through the halls with his arm draped around her shoulder, and Sarah more than once had leaned up to kiss him before dashing off to class—this was their first real date. Sarah was a part-time sales clerk at Hecht's department store, and always before, it had seemed that either she had to work or Larry was on restriction. Even though their romance had been budding over the last few months, they had spent almost no time alone together.

Larry knew his mother was not crazy about him dating anyone and would be even less crazy about him dating Sarah. Still, the vehemence of her reaction caught him off guard.

"I can't *believe* you're going out with a girl like Sarah Slaughter!" she cried. "Why can't you go out with a *nice* girl? Why, that girl is a *slut*! She's nothing but a *whore*! She's got a *terrible* reputation!"

Larry steeled himself for his mother's tirade. But how humiliating it was to stand there and listen to this. How could he defend his girlfriend against her bitter outburst when it came out of nowhere? Where did she get these ideas? Why did she have to teach at his school, anyway? She not only knew everything he did, she knew everyone he *spoke* to. He couldn't *breathe* without her watching. He was determined to go out that night, though, so he heard her out: Larry was too good for a trashy girl like Sarah. Why couldn't he pick someone with *class*? A *nice* girl. *Nice* girls didn't kiss boys in public. Didn't Larry know what sort of girl Sarah was?

After promising to be in by midnight—his usual curfew—and assuring his mother that it was a double date and they were only going to the movies, Larry finally secured permission to go out with Sarah.

It was seven-thirty when Sarah pulled up in front of Larry's house in the Bomb, as her family called their copper-colored rust-eaten Pontiac station wagon. Sarah honked as Larry had instructed her. When he didn't come out, she walked down his snowy driveway in her tan suede boots and tight Jordache jeans and knocked on the shiny foil-covered door.

Larry appeared immediately and held up a hand, signaling her to stay outside. "I'll be right out. Let me get my coat."

When Sarah had passed by the front picture window, she had noticed her speech teacher sitting in the living room with a white patch over one eye. Waiting awkwardly at the front door, Sarah decided to be friendly. She stuck her head inside and called out brightly, "Hi, Mrs. Swartz! How'd your operation go?"

"Very well," Mrs. Swartz replied cordially.

Sarah noticed that Larry's father, who was sitting with his back to her, didn't even acknowledge her presence. Annie sat playing on the living room floor, and she didn't acknowledge her, either.

At the theater entrance, the line looped back so far inside the mall that Larry's group figured they'd never get seats, so they walked to the Friendly Ice Cream parlor. Larry and Barry ordered huge Reese's Pieces sundaes while their dates settled for more modest ice cream dishes.

Taking separate cars, the two couples headed north after they ate, for a beachfront parking spot at the end of a secluded dirt road in Pasadena. Along Ritchie Highway, they all laughed and waved through their car windows as Sarah and Barry tried to edge ahead of each other at stoplights.

Inside the Bomb, listening to Elton John, Sarah wondered why Larry seemed so quiet. He'd never been exactly talkative, but she'd never seen him this mute before. "What's wrong?" she prodded.

"Oh, it's stuff Mom said. It upset me, that's all." Larry buried his hands in his jacket pockets and looked out the window. "You know, she's got a really low opinion of you."

Sarah was surprised. She had no idea Mrs. Swartz didn't like her. She had always considered herself a pretty decent student and couldn't imagine what her speech teacher could have against her. "What did she say about me?"

Larry hesitated. "Well, now, don't take this to heart," he began. "Don't feel bad about this, because Mom says it about every single girl I go out with. You know she won't even let me go out with a girl twice."

"What did she say about me?"

"She said you were a slut."

"Your mom called me a *slut?*" Sarah was incredulous.

"Yeah, but don't worry about it. Mom says that about a lot of girls."

God! thought Sarah, and here I thought I got along great with Mrs. Swartz.

Both couples pulled into the parking lot of a liquor store, where the girls went inside for a six-pack of Heineken. Although Maryland had raised its drinking age to twenty-one, the store was notorious for rarely carding anyone, especially girls. If they got carded, Sarah wasn't worried; she had a fake I.D.

A while later, the foursome pulled their cars off at the end of a dirt road and discovered that they had a clear, private view of the water. Each couple sat inside their car, sipping Heineken and listening to music.

The beer seemed to relax Larry. After he opened his second bottle, he began chattering to Sarah about school, himself, his family. He talked about his exams and how poorly he was doing in school. He told her he hoped to be a model one day. As he talked, Larry touched Sarah lightly and smiled shyly, but he made no effort to kiss her. She figured he was too timid to make the first move.

Sarah wasn't. Snuggling against him in her darkened Bomb, relishing their sweet, long-awaited privacy, Sarah could feel how excited they both were. He probably only needed a sign; undoubtedly, he wanted something to happen as much as she did. Once she gave him the sign, Larry responded at once, kissing and caressing her, gently then hungrily, until passion overwhelmed them both.

Afterward, looking back on it, Sarah thought their lovemaking seemed so natural, so smooth, so *wonderful* that she never for a moment dreamt it could have been Larry's first time.

He certainly never let on that it was.

The next day, Larry called Sarah. He was supposed to be studying because semester exams started Monday, but his parents had gone out, or so it seemed to Sarah. She sensed that he was trying to sneak a quick call and was anxious to hang up.

"Did everything go okay last night?" she asked him. She had dropped him off ten minutes before curfew, but considering what Mrs. Swartz had said *before* their date, there was no telling how she might have reacted *afterward.*

"Sure," Larry said softly. "Everything went fine."

Their conversation was brief, and Sarah knew better than to phone him back later that night. Larry was forbidden to take calls after 9 P.M. on school nights. She would have to wait to talk to him at school tomorrow.

Moments before the first bell rang Monday, Larry suddenly appeared and gave Sarah a quick kiss as she was heading to homeroom. Larry had his worst exam—Spanish—and wasn't in the best mood that morning.

After the second exam period ended at noon, Larry walked Sarah to her bus. Snow fell lightly around them as they kissed. "I'll call you on my break from Hecht's tonight, okay?"

"Okay. Bye."

"Bye."

It was beautiful and barely twenty degrees outside as Larry trudged home through the dense woods behind the Broadneck football field. The snow had died down to a pretty white dusting after falling heavily for two hours. It would continue lightly like that all afternoon, creating soft powdery conditions perfect for sledding.

After lunch, Larry went over to Craig Casey's house and played chess, then walked with Craig a mile and a half to McDonald's on Route 50. "I hope my parents don't find out I came here," Larry told Craig nervously. "I'm not allowed to come out here."

"Why not?"

"Oh, they're afraid I'll get hurt crossing the highway."

From McDonald's, the boys hitched a ride back to Broadneck and went sledding with a group of friends on a hill beside the school's soccer field. Worried that his parents would punish him if he didn't start studying, Larry left around five o'clock and walked home.

After supper, without bothering to change out of his work clothes, Bob Swartz loosened his tie, retired downstairs to his study, and switched on his Commodore 64 computer. He had bought the computer that fall and spent almost every night closeted in his study, teaching himself to program it.

Both he and Kay left the kitchen a mess, with their dinner dishes piled all over the sink and countertop.

Kay went to her bedroom and changed into her blue flannel sleeper, then went downstairs and switched on the TV in the family room.

After ten or fifteen minutes, Bob emerged in a fit. Larry could hear him all the way upstairs in his bedroom. A computer disk was messed up; his tax program was ruined. Bob was shouting like a maniac.

Kay finally yelled back at him. "I don't know anything about it! Why don't you go ask Larry?"

When Bob began screaming for him, Larry quickly went to the top of the stairs. There was Bob, his face crimson and grotesque with rage, standing down on the landing.

Trembling with his own quiet fury, trying to head off yet another confrontation, Larry confessed that he probably was the culprit. He'd gone into the study yesterday with Tom Kenny and his brother. Larry took the Kenny boys in to show them his father's computer when they stopped by with their mother, who brought flowers for Kay. "We were foolin' around with your computer. Maybe we did mess it up. I'm sorry."

"You're *sorry*! Do you know how much this disk cost?"

"I'm sorry," Larry repeated. "I'll buy you a new one."

"That's not the *point*! With all the work that went into this disk, you *can't* replace it!"

Bob roared on about the untold hours he'd spent on the program, how thoughtlessly Larry had destroyed his work. "How can I trust you when you're always sneaking around behind my back?"

After he and Larry exchanged more heated words, Bob suddenly wheeled around and disappeared into his study, slamming the door behind him.

As the sound reverberated, Larry retreated to his bedroom, his body taut with rage. He was too worked up to study now. He was too worked up to do anything except think about how much he hated his father. He sat on the edge of his bunk, Bob's words still echoing in his head. He could hear his mother, too. *That girl is a slut!*

Why did they degrade him like this? His fury intensified as his mind swept back over all the mean and horrible things they had said and done to him and Michael. They had adopted him, yet they didn't love him any more than they loved Michael. All they cared about was how *they* felt, *their* rules, *their* games. And the rules were so unfair. They changed so fast it made him dizzy: "You can drive next summer. No, you can't drive until next year. You can't get your license until you pull all your grades up." Then after finding those pills, Kay had threatened to send Larry to reform school, just like Michael. Would they give *him* back to the state, too? Would he wind up, like his brother, in a mental hospital with a bunch of crazies?

Maybe he could put an end to it all. Maybe he could set himself and Annie free—just as Michael had said. Larry trembled at the thought. He fantasized about killing his father. He fantasized about killing his mother, too. But how could he? Where would he get the nerve?

Maybe a drink would help. He always felt looser with a buzz on. He had swiped some rum while he was baby-sitting for a neighbor a week or two ago; it was still stashed in his dresser drawer.

Quietly, he went to the kitchen, opened the refrigerator, poured some grapefruit juice in a glass, went back to his room, and walked over to his dresser. Opening a drawer, he reached under a pile of clothes and pulled out the Pepsi bottle where he'd hidden the rum. He mixed the rum and juice.

Sitting on his bunk, sipping the rum while his head pounded with tension and dread, he wondered, Could it really be that easy?

Could he just walk downstairs and *kill* Mom and Dad?

NINE

January 24, 1984

1.

From the night of his arrest, Larry Swartz was confined to the Anne Arundel County Detention Center, the same forbidding brick building he and his brother had passed as boys, and they had whispered "Not me!" Life inside the county jail required no minor adjustment for Larry. Although they stood only a few hundred yards apart, the cramped dingy jail was a world apart from the bright and bustling shopping mall where Larry and his friends used to hang out. Placed in solitary confinement, Larry cried for hours his first night there. Guards kept a watchful eye on him for the next several weeks because Ron Baradel had made it clear that he considered his client a suicide risk.

Baradel tried to get bail for Larry, even though he knew Larry was penniless and could never post it; that was one service Baradel didn't plan to offer his client. Larry would remain in jail for more than a year awaiting trial, unable to post the $200,000 cash bond set by a district court judge the morning following his arrest.

After a few days in isolation, Larry went briefly into a two-man cell, then into a four-man cell, where one of his new cellmates took an instant liking to him. John Kemmer, a convicted arsonist at age twenty-four, had a small build and a sly, ingratiating manner that helped him befriend Larry. It was a natural alignment for Larry, given his other choices: Nick Ess, a convicted thief who stood six four, wore his brown hair to his shoulders, had a long mustache that drooped at the ends, and had F-U-C-K tattooed across the knuckles of his right hand. Or Dean Prince, a dour wiseacre who let it be known that he had nothing but contempt for anyone who would murder his parents. "The murderer's on TV," Prince would say whenever a spot about Swartz came on the evening news.

Larry enjoyed watching himself on TV. The inmates had a thirteen-inch black and white set across the cell from their gray metal bunks, and Larry stayed glued to it during newscasts. When he appeared on the screen, Kemmer would counter Prince's sarcasm by teasing, "Larry, you're a TV star now."

Larry slept on the bunk over Kemmer, and the inmates showed him how to smear toothpaste on the back of pictures and paste them up on the yellow cinder-block walls. While other inmates hung *Playboy* centerfolds over their bunks, Larry pasted wallet photos of Annie and John Smithmyer over his.

It didn't take long for the other inmates to notice what a slob Larry was. They washed their clothes in a plastic bucket with county-issued soap, but Larry dropped his clothes all over the tile floor and let his laundry pile up. He was the only inmate in the cell who seldom made his bunk. He collected candy bar wrappers, empty cigarette packs, and old commissary bags under his bunk. That bugged Kemmer, a confirmed neatnik, who whined at him to pick up his trash.

"Oh, stop bitching," Larry would say. "You're always bitching at me."

At first, Larry let his personal appearance slide; he shaved infrequently and sometimes went a day or two without combing his long curly hair. He seemed depressed most of the time and confessed to friends that he had insomnia. He nibbled nervously on the inside of his lip and cheeks, a habit that would continue throughout his jail stay. His slovenly appearance did not continue, however. Larry seemed to right himself emotionally after four or five weeks. He began shaving regularly and paying attention to his hair, particularly when he was expecting visitors. Within a few months, friends noticed another change: a tougher veneer. He wore open-neck shirts with cutoff sleeves, leaned casually up against the bulletproof glass window in the visitor's room, and puffed on Marlboros as he talked to friends. Larry hadn't smoked before he went to jail. Now he lighted one Marlboro after another, a habit that he begged Kemmer not to reveal to John Smithmyer, a regular visitor. Larry also toyed with getting a tattoo like many inmates had, but when he mentioned the idea to Kemmer—to whom Larry had confided his ambition of becoming a model—Kemmer dryly remarked, "Not too many models have tattoos." Larry quickly dropped the idea.

While many inmates went weeks without receiving a visitor, Larry almost always had people lined up to see him when the detention center doors opened at eight o'clock Wednesday and Sunday mornings. The Smithmyers were regulars from the start. Priests and parishioners from St. Mary's came, too, as did a few of Larry's buddies from high school and a steady stream of neighbors from Cape St. Claire. Occasionally people Larry didn't know signed up to meet him. It wasn't unusual for the guards to turn people away because Larry had met his quota of three visitors for the day.

Then there were the letters, which began arriving a few weeks after Larry's arrest. He got four or five a day sometimes, mostly from girls and other people who had read about him or seen him on TV. Many of the writers felt sorry for him, believing he must have been horribly abused to have done something so heinous to his parents. They wrote not only to Larry but also to his lawyer and the prosecutor. Larry answered a few, but found the volume of his mail overwhelming. He often started to draft a reply, then put it down halfway through and left it lying in his cell until he finally threw it away.

2.

Larry already was enshrouded in a jailhouse celebrity aura because of the extraordinary publicity surrounding his case when the Annapolis newspaper, *The Capital*, focused even more attention on him two weeks after his arrest. Splashing an article across page one under the banner TRAGIC TALE and a subhead SWARTZ HOME RIFE WITH HATE, the newspaper concluded that Larry had murdered his parents in an "insane rage" because they had treated him with "cruelty, neglect and threats of abandonment." Quoting unnamed sources, reporter Effie Cottman portrayed the Swartzes as cold, cruel disciplinarians. Cottman wrote that Larry "masked the fear and anxiety brought on by unaffectionate parents who enforced an excessive disciplinary code and demanded an excellence he could not achieve."

Already aroused, community passion rose to a fevered pitch soon afterward. A torrent of letters to the editor appeared in *The Capital*. Some were sympathetic to Larry, but more defended Bob and Kay Swartz and berated the newspaper for exaggerating their failings as parents. The Swartzes were strict, not cruel, devout, not fanatical, the letter writers insisted. They were typical parents making typical mistakes as they struggled to cope with the problems of their son's adolescence. Many writers decried the public emphasis on adoption, which one said "leaves the impression that adoption is somehow shameful." Another letter, signed by two dozen parishioners and priests from St. Mary's, said simply: "The reporter who wrote the article . . . obviously never knew Bob and Kay Swartz. And it's tragic that *The Capital* published it." So many letters poured in that the newspaper printed a two-page spread of them, along with an editorial defending the story as "not a pretty picture of the Swartz family, but . . . a picture accurately told."

Not everybody sided with Larry's parents. One woman called Ron Baradel at his law office shortly after the story appeared, identified herself as "a concerned person," and said the article made her suspect that Larry was the victim of "big-time child abuse."

"I'm a veteran of that myself," the woman added. "I'd like to tell you about it."

"Why?" Instinctively, Baradel was suspicious.

"So you'll know what goes on inside a person's mind when something like that happens, and how it can affect you. I know sexual abuse can make you capable of doing something like that, because I almost did the same thing myself. The only reason I didn't kill my father was, he shot himself first."

"Well, I appreciate your offer, but I don't see a parallel." Baradel didn't want to seem rude, but he couldn't waste time meeting this woman. He didn't bother asking her name. "I don't think anything like that is involved here."

"I'm not so sure," the woman persisted. "Larry's parents were painted as such perfect people in the paper that I'll bet something is hidden in the bush. Somebody who's been in that situation can recognize the roadmarks; I'm definitely seeing roadmarks."

Baradel thanked her again and hung up.

The woman who phoned Baradel was only one of many strangers who identified strongly with Larry. Another woman recited her sad tale of abuse in a letter that appeared in *The Capital* March 5. Two days later, the letter prompted Larry to break his public silence.

Effie Cottman was sitting at her battered gray desk in the *The Capital*'s dingy newsroom shortly before her 7 A.M. deadline when the phone rang.

"I have a collect call for Effie Cottman from Larry Swartz. Will you accept the charges?"

"Yes," said Effie, a pretty twenty-seven-year-old reporter with sharp brown eyes that seldom strayed from her interview subjects.

A soft monotone came on the line. "This is Larry Swartz. I bet you didn't expect to hear from me."

The caller asked for the address of a woman who had written a letter to the editor about him. Then he rambled about his case, saying, "There are a lot of mistakes, a lot of rumors."

Cradling the receiver on her shoulder as she typed notes, Effie asked him to be more specific.

"This stuff about PCP," he replied. "A lot of people are saying I take PCP. I don't even know what the stuff is."

Effie had heard the PCP rumor and considered it a natural suspicion, given the brutality of the murders. She told him that although some people believed he had taken PCP on the night of the murders, it was strictly rumor and she had no plans to print it. She asked whether he would meet her and tell his version of what happened.

"I'd like to," he replied, "but my lawyers told me not to say anything. If I said anything, I'd probably slip. They explained that to me. It's like a game of chess. It's all strategy."

"Who's winning?"

"I don't know who's winning. It's all up in the air now."

Would he ever be able to tell his story?

"I don't know," he said softly. "That depends on how everything turns out. I promise you if I can, I will."

Everyone thought Larry would plead insanity, and Effie hoped to get that on the record; but he dodged her questions, saying, "I can't get into specifics."

He told her that the thought of standing trial frightened him and that he had "started shaking all over" when he read in the newspaper that he could draw two life sentences if he was convicted. It also had startled him, he said, to read that the prosecutor wasn't seeking the death penalty: "It never occurred to me that I could get the death chair. I'm really afraid of the death chair."

Maryland law required prosecutors to announce their intention to seek the death penalty at least thirty days before trial. Multiple killings generally qualified for the death penalty, but Duckett had announced that he wouldn't seek capital punishment because Larry was only seventeen and appeared to have mental problems. Maryland law considered youth and mental impairment among the factors to be weighed against imposition of the death penalty.

Realizing that Larry was nervous, Effie tried to relax him with questions about his friends and school life. He talked briefly about his jail life, and surprised her by saying, "A lot of the inmates are treating me like a celebrity and want to talk to me. It's not my way I want to be a celebrity."

Effie was aware that Larry was receiving an incredible out-pouring of public support through letters. She sensed that he regarded himself as some kind of folk hero, and she wondered whether he had called her with hopes of obtaining a favorable news story.

After forty minutes, Effie promised to track down the address of the woman whose letter had appeared in the newspaper, and Larry hung up.

Effie placed a quick call to Ron Baradel, fishing for confirmation that the caller indeed had been Larry Swartz. Indirectly, Baradel confirmed it by saying he had given Larry some science-fiction books, which Larry had mentioned during the call.

"I can't believe Larry called you. That's every lawyer's night-mare!" Baradel groaned. He worried that Effie had obtained some incriminating statements from Larry that would appear in print.

Larry soon called Baradel to own up to the call. First, Larry called Baradel's home, and Louise Baradel told him to call her husband at the office. Larry demurred: "I don't want to bother him at the office."

"*Bother* him, Larry," Louise said.

That was Baradel's first inkling that Larry was fearful of him, that he saw him as an authority figure and not a friend. Larry didn't seem to trust anyone, including his lawyers. He rarely called Baradel except for the few times—such as after his tele-phone interview with Effie—when he knew he'd screwed up and figured he'd better do something about it. It would be hard for Baradel to break through Larry's barriers and establish a rap-port, but Baradel knew he couldn't provide an effective defense unless he did.

3.

The extraordinary legal defense that Ron Baradel provided for Larry was an enigma to those who watched, and Baradel would not explain himself. If anyone asked what motivated him, he just shrugged and said, "Somebody had to do it."

Clearly, he was drawn to Larry by forces more powerful than a sense of duty, more complicated than a lawyer's desire to help the orphaned child of friends. True, he had been something of a family lawyer to the Swartzes. They had seemed to think so, anyway. Bob and Kay always referred to him as "our lawyer friend," and when they needed a lawyer to sort things out with Michael in 1980, he had been their choice. That was it, however. Bob and Kay never called on him again for legal advice, nor did they see him socially. They didn't invite him to their parties, maybe because they felt their "lawyer friend" dwelled in a different social world. His chief contact with the Swartzes had been at church on Sundays and at the Cursillo sessions on Saturdays. In a quirk of fate that seemed poignant to Baradel, the first occasion he had to set foot inside the Swartzes' darkened, wood-paneled home was their murders.

Although he didn't realize it at first, Baradel's defense of Larry was destined to become a cause, a crusade that would consume his professional and emotional energies for fifteen months. Not only did he take Larry under his own roof and give him free legal counsel, he also petitioned the court to appoint him as the youth's legal guardian—an unusual move that bewildered observers. Baradel filed the guardianship petition partly to lend a helping hand, but he later conceded there was no legal reason to do so. "Part of it, I think, was a statement," explained, "me wanting him to know I was going to be something else other than just his lawyer."

When it became obvious that Baradel was developing an obsession, some friends and legal associates looked at him askance. He put in such astonishing hours on Larry's defense that he had little time for new civil cases. He acquired a haggard appearance that made him look older than his forty-one years. A few senior partners in his firm grew annoyed at the publicity, for Hartman & Crain was a civil firm and a silk-stocking one at that. Its lawyers represented businessmen who were less than thrilled to see their law firm linked to a gory murder. Although the partners didn't acknowledge it publicly, rumors spread through the town's close-knit legal fraternity that the Swartz case contributed in some measure to the eventual breakup of Hartman & Crain. It was a messy breakup, too, complete with verbal volleys, a lawsuit and countersuit between the partners. The final split would occur late in 1984, at the height of preparations for Larry's trial.

In preparing for trial, Baradel logged more than a thousand hours, virtually all of them unbillable since Larry had no money and wouldn't inherit any if he was convicted of the murders. When the bills rolled in for the private detective, lab tests, and psychiatric evaluations, Baradel dug into his own pocket. He paid $18,000 in expenses for Larry, mostly fees for the psychiatric experts. With a wife and three children to support, Baradel was no wealthy man, his successful law practice notwithstanding. It puzzled everyone, including the other attorneys who helped Baradel defend Larry. Like Baradel, they worked with no promise of payment, but they didn't pay the bills or log the extraordinary hours Baradel did. "I've never seen anything like it," recalled Joe Murphy, who initially served as Larry's lead counsel because of his expertise in criminal law. "It is really a remarkable thing Ron did. I've seen a lot of lawyers put in time on matters and cut their bills, and I've asked people to cut their bills. But what Ron did was heroic, really." Although Murphy knew there was little chance he or Baradel would ever get paid for defending Larry, Baradel acted from the start as if *he* was going to pay Murphy, as if *Baradel* had hired Murphy. Baradel would say things such as, "Let me know how much your bill is going to be," and Murphy would ignore him. Many months into the case, after Baradel paid a pile of psychiatric bills and was making noises about Murphy's legal bill again, Murphy turned to him in frustration and said, "Look, Ron, you are not going to pay me out of your *own pocket.* You've already paid the doctors, and you can't pay anymore. Just forget it."

Another lawyer who joined the defense team six months later was shocked to discover how much legwork Baradel had done. "Initially, I was kind of suspect," Baltimore attorney Richard M. Karceski recalled. "I almost said, 'What is this? Why is this?' He put in so many hours, did so much, spent so much of his own money that I couldn't believe what I was seeing. There was *nothing* he wouldn't do. If I needed to call *Alaska,* he would call Alaska. And then as time goes by, you begin to understand that you have a guy who was genuinely, sincerely interested in

Larry Swartz and just wants to do the very best he can to help this kid, because he feels it's almost one of his missions in life. It's one of the things he has to do, like it's *preordained,* like God sent the Holy Ghost down to Ron Baradel and said, 'Look, Ron, you're going to have to do this.'"

Bob and Kay's relatives were equally perplexed, but more cynical, in assessing Baradel's motives. Kay's relatives believed he was using the case to his own advantage, basking in the media spotlight. "He always has time for the reporters," grumbled one.

After Larry's arrest, Kay's family grew increasingly angry, thinking that for years Larry had fooled them into believing he was a gentle, good-natured boy. A few of Kay's relatives hoped the "gentle boy" would get the gas chamber. Their hostility spilled over to his lawyer. They couldn't understand why anyone would want to defend such a despicable murderer. After all that his parents had done for him, Larry's vicious attack on them seemed so indefensible. The relatives wondered, Who was paying Baradel's legal fee? Who had hired him to probate the estate?

Eventually, Kay's sister, Maureen Riely—whose husband had been named executor of the estate—phoned Baradel and demanded to know, "Who hired you to do all these things?"

At first, no one in particular, Baradel replied. He had begun handling routine matters: funeral arrangements, shutting off utilities in the house, wiping blood off the walls—things that Bob and Kay's relatives never got around to doing. The relatives left town the day after the funeral without even stopping by 1242 Mount Pleasant Drive. They also left without making arrangements for headstones, and Bob and Kay's graves remained bare until someone noticed the oversight and ordered a grave marker a year later. So, Baradel told Maureen Riely, he had stepped into what he perceived to be a vacuum and phoned her estranged husband, James, the executor, shortly after the funeral. James Riely authorized Baradel to represent the estate, and Baradel dispatched a clerk to 1242 Mount Pleasant Drive to start compiling an estate inventory.

The Rielys' son, John, questioned the propriety of Baradel handling the estate while he was defending Larry on murder charges. Both wills named Larry and Annie as their parents' sole heirs, and under Maryland law, a murder conviction automatically would disqualify Larry from any inheritance. "Baradel is wearing two hats," John complained to his mother. "And that's a conflict of interest. He's representing a person who could be disinherited by his actions."

In April, three months after the murders, Maureen Riely phoned Baradel and fired him as the lawyer for the Swartz estate.

That virtually destroyed his chance of receiving a legal fee, but Baradel continued to defend Larry as vigorously as if he were his own son. As the months slipped by, even Baradel began to wonder what was driving him so hard. He eventually acknowledged that Larry had unlocked a room in his own past, one that Baradel had sealed off in his youth and tiptoed past for many, many years. Baradel couldn't remember when he had last spoken to his father, against whom he still harbored a bitter resentment. Baradel knew that deep inside himself he had buried much of the same pain and anger that must have driven Larry to kill. The more he learned about Larry's life, the more parallels he discovered between himself and his client.

More than anything, Baradel believed that his own deep childhood sorrow bound him to Larry. He identified with Larry's sense of isolation, the longing for the family life that his friends seemed to have. As Baradel and Larry talked, they were amazed to discover that both of them had peered through neighbors' windows at night as teenagers. When Baradel learned of Larry's experiments with drugs and booze, the lawyer saw the free-fall of his own adolescence, the rebelliousness that had exploded during those lonely teen years when he had lived with his father in uneasy silence. Why, he thought, he could have *been* Larry two decades ago!

"Somebody once said to me, 'Do you think you were an abused child?'" Baradel later recalled. "I said, 'No, I think I was an isolated child.' I was very much alone. I know what it is to grow up with a father who can't, won't, or doesn't speak—for whatever reason. The difference between me and Larry is that I had an escape. I told him, 'The only difference is that when I didn't like what was happening, I could go at any time. He couldn't. He was trapped.'"

Despite Baradel's identification with Larry, which grew during fifteen months of trial preparations, the lawyer found it nearly impossible to break through his client's emotional barrier. Withdrawn behind a cool facade, Larry was shy, secretive, introverted. Prying information out of him was as frustrating as cross-examining an opposing witness in court. He spoke in monosyllables and volunteered little. He gave clipped replies to questions: "Yes. No. I dunno." It took months of interviews before the defense attorneys began to understand what had driven him to kill his parents. It took months for them just to piece together what it was that he had done. Even then, the picture never came sharply into focus. Larry was reticent not only about the murders but about anything involving emotion: He buried his feelings so deeply that he had trouble expressing why he did anything. The whys meant a lot to his lawyers, who considered his motivation crucial to his defense. They wanted to learn everything they could about his personality and family life, including his early childhood.

Toward that end, soon after his arrest, his lawyers prepared a series of court orders seeking background data on him. They needed to know, Who *was* Larry Swartz? For the first six years of his life, Swartz hadn't even been his name. He'd had another name, another identity. Larry told them he had lived in several different foster homes; they had to find out how many, what each had been like. Those were his formative years, and Larry remembered almost nothing about them. Because psychiatrists deemed the early years crucial in determining personality, they offered clues to his emotional and mental development that might be pivotal to his defense.

Murphy, in particular, saw the significance of events that happened to Larry before he joined the Swartz family. Murphy did not want to put Larry's parents on trial; he wasn't going to stand before a jury and make monsters of two dead people. Undoubtedly, Bob and Kay Swartz had made mistakes as parents. Who hadn't? But Murphy would never forget—and neither would a jury—that the Swartzes had made room in their lives for three unwanted homeless children.

Early in March, determined to probe Larry's family background, the defense lawyers told Duckett they would seek a court order to gain access to the adoption records of all three Swartz children. Adoption records were sealed under Maryland law, closed even to the adopted child and his biological parents. The court could unseal the records only upon a showing of good cause. The defense lawyers said they needed the records of all three children in order "to learn as much as possible about the defendant's prior life history and treatment, the environments in which he was raised, and the backgrounds of his brother and sister."

Circuit court judge Raymond G. Thieme, Jr., agreed. He signed orders that opened the adoption records to the defense team.

TEN

August 24, 1966

1.

The Mississippi oozed out of its banks into the stagnant hot air hanging over New Orleans. It was August 24, 1966, and no rain had fallen in nearly a week. Sheila Paulson's condition made the heat seem worse. The petite bleached blonde with the large blue eyes was expecting her first child in October. A native Californian, she was not yet acclimated to the humidity that made New Orleans seem hotter than it was. Three bodies of water surrounded the city, forming a heat barrier—a kind of reverse windchill factor—that could drive people stark raving naked.

Only three days away from her twentieth birthday, Sheila could hardly believe she was going to be a mother. She didn't really want the baby, and her boyfriend wasn't wild about the idea, either. They had no plans to marry. Her boyfriend, Luther Singh, was several years older and incredibly handsome. He had curly black hair, round chocolate eyes, and smooth olive skin. Those wide-set eyes above strong cheekbones melted Sheila every time she looked into them. She had been drawn to him instantly when they met at Mardi Gras the previous year. Like the festivities, the dark flashy stranger, whose family was from East India, was exotic and exciting. She had picked him up during the two-week party preceding Fat Tuesday, and now they were living together.

Sheila had moved to New Orleans on a whim. The wild street carnivals appealed to the romantic in her, the adventuress, so she had left Chicago at the end of January 1965 and headed south to work as a waitress. Six months earlier, just after her eighteenth birthday, she had made a similar move in the middle of the night without telling anyone. She and a friend drove all the way to Chicago, where they landed jobs waiting tables.

Wherever she went, Sheila rarely had trouble finding work or a boyfriend. Her pretty face, fair complexion, and small-boned figure attracted plenty of suitors. She dyed her coarse brown hair blond and looked straight at men with innocent blue eyes. She stood nearly five feet seven and loved athletics. Although she could be sweet or sarcastic, her friends found her easygoing. She took business courses in high school, earning B's and C's with minimal effort. Sheila was no dummy, yet she was flaky, missing appointments, pretending not to know things. She candidly described herself to one social worker as "a spoiled rotten brat with everything."

Her father had adopted her at birth and clearly adored her. She adored him, too. He was permissive and gave her dance lessons, piano lessons, and unlimited attention. After high school in California, Sheila worked as a keypunch operator and talked her father into setting her up in an apartment of her own. She still loved her father, but their relationship had grown increasingly rocky during her teens.

When she was fifteen, she ran away after a fight with her stepmother. Sheila hated her stepmother, considered her a spiteful woman who was trying to replace Sheila's adoptive mother. A beautiful woman whom Sheila had loved, her adoptive mother had died of cancer and tuberculosis when Sheila was only ten. It broke her heart. When her adoptive father remarried three years later, Sheila got angry. Her father said she was jealous, and he probably was right. She had basked in her daddy's attention for several years and enjoyed having him to herself. Well, almost to herself; her parents had adopted a retarded girl two years younger than Sheila. Sheila didn't want to share her father with her new stepmother. It did no good to admit her jealousy; she still despised the woman. "I simply can't stand her and never could," she confided to a social worker.

Although she often told friends, "I've had three mothers," Sheila actually knew next to nothing about her first mother. The Paulsons had plucked Sheila from her true mother at birth and adopted her from the maternity ward.

Now here she was, nineteen and pregnant, carrying an illegitimate child, just like the first mother she had never known. Sheila had no idea how she would manage with a baby. She guessed she'd keep it, but she was fearful of Luther, who could be charming one minute and as mean as a sewer rat the next—especially when he got drunk. How would he treat a helpless baby?

She worried, too, about the outlandish characters who stopped by their apartment. Queens, Luther called them. Some of them strutted down Bourbon Street wearing dresses, multi-colored eye makeup, and come-fuck-me pumps. They were always bringing money to Luther. When she asked why, he laughed and whispered, "It's a con!" It didn't take her long to figure out that Luther was a pimp, and the queens, his paycheck. Sheila heard Luther promise them all manner of things when they dropped off the dough. He was something, promising them this or that. And when the queens left, he'd chortle and hiss at Sheila, "And they *believe* me!"

Luther wasn't tall, but Sheila thought he had a perfectly proportioned body, broad and sturdy through the chest. His strength frightened her when he erupted into a fiery rage, sometimes without warning, and revealed his ugly underside. Occasionally, he beat her after he'd been drinking. She feared and loathed his violence but found him irresistible when he turned those mysterious brown eyes toward her.

His eye-catching looks were the only legacy the New Orleans pimp left the son that Sheila bore him.

At 10 P.M. on August 24, more than a month before her due date, Sheila went into labor. Robustly healthy, she had a smooth, quick delivery three hours later. Her first son, weighing a scant four pounds, squeezed into the world at 1 A.M. on August 25.

She named him Lawrence Joseph and called him Larry, but left his last name open to debate. Although she sometimes called herself Sheila Singh and pretended to be Luther's wife, her legal surname was Paulson. Sheila used neither of those names when she checked into the hospital. She signed in as Sheila Dunn, using a name taken from a friend's drivers license that she had borrowed when she was sixteen and wanted a job in California. Her alias went on her son's birth certificate, a mistake that she would pay money to correct two years later.

A colicky baby, Larry cried night and day. He never seemed to stop. In a pattern that continued throughout childhood, he became undernourished and failed to gain weight. At four months, a pediatrician diagnosed a hernioplasty in Larry's right intestine, which was making his digestion difficult. So a surgeon sliced open his tiny abdomen and removed the blockage.

Life was not easy for Sheila in the months after Larry's birth. She had to contend with his endless wailing and her boyfriend's drinking. Luther's anger at home frightened Sheila even more than his wild street doings. One night in a drunken rage, he pulled out a revolver and shot at her, then burst into tears, begging for forgiveness, crying, "I didn't mean it, I didn't mean it."

Shaken, Sheila was unharmed and sought to reassure him. "I know you didn't mean to hurt me. I won't go telling anyone."

When Luther moved north to the Washington, D.C., area, Sheila and the baby moved with him. They took an apartment just outside the city in Maryland.

A social worker later asked Sheila why she continued living with Luther when he beat her. Sheila replied, "He was so handsome. I guess it was the physical attraction."

That attraction inevitably waned. After nearly three years of living with a man she described as "an awful person," Sheila decided one day that she was tired of him and packed her belongings. Hoping Luther wouldn't track her down, she took the baby and moved into an apartment with two girlfriends in Silver Spring.

Within a month, Sheila was waiting on tables again and living in a small, twenty-dollar-a-week walk-up apartment of her own. Money was tight, and it was a struggle to find baby-sitters. A woman who lived downstairs frequently cared for Larry while Sheila worked. When she dated on weekends, she resorted to a variety of sitters. They all seemed to love Larry, a tiny energetic toddler.

In late fall 1967, another man moved in with Sheila, but their affair was short-lived. By the end of January, he was gone.

When Larry came down with the chicken pox in February, life was growing bleak for Sheila. The baby tied her down, and her job didn't provide enough funds for child care, rent, medical bills, clothes, and everything else.

By April, her money problems were acute. In a fit of despondency one night, with the rent long overdue, her landlord increasingly irate, her baby hungry, and her pocketbook empty, Sheila took Larry to the police station and tried to give him away.

No chance, the police told her. They did *not* take custody of babies. If she was that desperate, she should apply for welfare.

Taking the advice, Sheila applied for emergency assistance at the Montgomery County Department of Social Services on Wednesday, April 24. The next day, she received a small emergency grant under the General Public Assistance program. By Friday afternoon, Sheila was gone.

A woman who lived downstairs from Sheila heard Larry crying for long uninterrupted periods that afternoon. He cried so long, the woman knew the poor thing had to be alone. Wondering where his sitter was, the neighbor went upstairs and knocked. Nobody came to the door. Still Larry wailed. Sheila had told the woman she was going out of town and had left a phone number where she could be reached, but when the woman tried calling, Sheila wasn't there. She had no key to Sheila's apartment, and by midafternoon, she was seriously worried. Larry was only twenty months old. He needed feeding and changing, not to mention supervision. His piercing cries were unbearable. Where was his sitter? She finally called the police.

An officer from the county's juvenile aid bureau entered Sheila's apartment late in the afternoon and found Larry alone, in dirty diapers, hungry and scared. Neighbors reported that welfare authorities were probably familiar with Sheila. It was 5:30 on Friday, however; most government offices were closed for the weekend. So the officer took Larry back to the station, where his sergeant phoned a social services supervisor at home to request an emergency placement.

That evening, Larry was placed at the home of a Montgomery County couple who had taken in many foster children before. The family was told that Larry had been abandoned and his stay with them would be indefinite.

On Saturday, Sheila, feeling scared, called the police to inquire into Larry's whereabouts.

She had left town on Friday for a beach party near Annapolis, nearly an hour's drive east of her apartment, and had spent the night with her new boyfriend there. She said she had arranged for a teenaged boy to baby-sit Larry, and that the sitter inexplicably had vanished. The woman who lived downstairs had reached Sheila by phone late Friday night and told her that the police had taken her son and issued a warrant for her arrest.

The police told Sheila there was no arrest warrant but that she should report to the social services office Monday to meet her new caseworker. Sheila did not show up Monday, however. She phoned the worker Tuesday and said she had no transportation but would try to get there later in the week.

Unbeknownst to the worker, Sheila was moving out of Montgomery County—where her rent was $118 in arrears—and into Anne Arundel County. Within a week, she was sharing an apartment near Annapolis with Dan Norris, the man she stayed with the night she abandoned Larry.

Unfortunately, Dan only had eyes for Sheila. "Icicles hang from his eyes when he looks at the baby," Larry's new foster mother told a social worker.

Sheila's first reunion with Larry occurred two and a half weeks after their separation, when Larry's foster mother took him to the Montgomery County social services office to see her. In phone conversations with her new caseworker, Sheila had expressed no strong desire to take Larry home; and after meeting Sheila, her caseworker concluded that she was in no position to do so. Sheila was job hunting in Anne Arundel County; she had no car, phone, or income.

Kathryn A. Swartz in 1958, when she was a seventeen-year-old high school senior.

Robert L. Swartz in 1952. He was a twenty-year-old seaman.

Bob and Kay Swartz eating lunch on an Ocean City, Maryland, beach in 1973.

The Swartz family, Christmas, 1974. From left to right: Michael, Larry, Kay, and Bob.

Larry Swartz, Ocean City, Maryland, 1973. (Joseph F. Swartz)

Kay Swartz with Anne, who was eight years old at the time of the picture. (Anne Maïo)

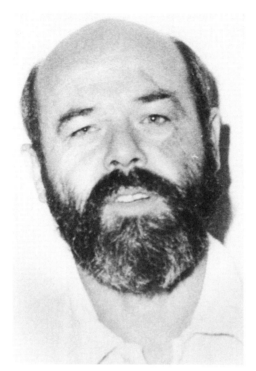

Bob Swartz (Robert Worden)

Kay Swartz (Robert Worden)

Michael leaving his parents' funeral. (Clarence B. Garrett/ *Baltimore Sun*)

Michael Swartz, August 1985.

Larry Swartz with Sarah Slaughter in the fall of 1983. (Kathy Duray)

Larry Swartz on his way to the courthouse, April 18, 1985.
(Bob Gilbert/*The Capital*)

The wood-splitting maul found in the woods behind the Swartz residence. (Anne Arundel County Police Department)

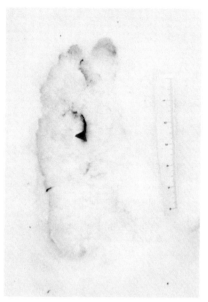

A left footprint in the snow, which police believed matched Kay Swartz's foot. (Anne Arundel County Police Department)

Larry Swartz outside his house on the morning his parents were found murdered, January 17, 1984. (Keith Harvey/*The Capital*)

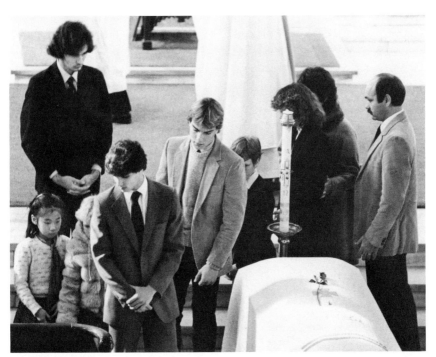

The Swartz children at their parents' funeral. From left to right: Anne, Michael, Larry, and John Smithmyer, Jr. At the far right is John Smithmyer, Sr. (Bob Gilbert/ *The Capital*)

The Swartz funeral at St. Mary's Church on January 21, 1984. (Bob Gilbert/*The Capital*)

Warren B. Duckett, Jr., State's Attorney for Anne Arundel County. (*Baltimore Sun*)

Joseph F. Murphy, Jr. (*left*) and Ronald A. Baradel, Larry Swartz's lawyers. (Bob Gilbert/*The Capital*)

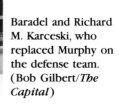

Baradel and Richard M. Karceski, who replaced Murphy on the defense team. (Bob Gilbert/*The Capital*)

Because social workers prefer to place children in the care of relatives, Sheila's worker called her home in California. Mrs. Paulson, her stepmother, said Sheila had left home four years earlier, and twice in the last year and a half had canceled plans to take her baby home to visit, even though Mr. Paulson had sent her plane tickets both times. Her parents only recently had learned that Sheila hadn't married. No, Mrs. Paulson said, she and her husband could not take custody of Larry. They were too old and had health problems. If Sheila would come home, however, and live with them, Sheila's father would be more than happy to help.

Once again, Mr. Paulson sent his daughter two plane tickets. Once again, Sheila said she'd go. But at the last minute, as in the past, she scuttled the homecoming. When her caseworker asked why, Sheila replied, "I was all packed and ready to go to the airport, when I suddenly realized I couldn't take all of Larry's things with me. I didn't know what to do. So I decided not to go."

After determining that Larry had no other relatives to care for him, the agency decided he should stay in foster care while Sheila filled the gaping potholes in her life. Her caseworker recommended moving Larry to a foster home in Anne Arundel County, where he'd be closer and more accessible to his mother.

Anticipating the move, the Montgomery County social services office turned Sheila's case over to the Anne Arundel County office. A new worker repeatedly made appointments to meet Sheila over the next three weeks, but each time Sheila canceled or failed to show.

She finally arrived at the Annapolis office on June 5, neatly clothed in a shirtwaist dress. Everything about Sheila struck Carol Luckhardt, her new worker, as petite, except for her bloated belly. Instantly, Luckhardt suspected that Sheila was four or five months pregnant. After a few preliminary questions, Luckhardt asked point-blank whether she was pregnant.

"No, I'm not." Sheila was emphatic. "I haven't had my period in five months, but I'm sure I'm not pregnant, because one can't get pregnant if they don't have their period."

Luckhardt stared at the pretty young woman. Did she really

believe that? Surely she realized she could have conceived *before* she stopped menstruating. "When was your last period?"

"December, I think, or January," said Sheila. "The last one went on so long I went to see a doctor. He gave me a hormone shot to stop the flow. At first, he thought I was pregnant, but then he gave me a blood test and I wasn't."

"The test was negative?"

"Yeah."

"Did you go back to the doctor?"

"No."

This girl was either a fibber or a world-class dingbat, the social worker thought. "You haven't had a period in five months and you haven't gone to a doctor?"

"No. Why should I? I don't want to have my period. It's such a nuisance."

After the interview, Luckhardt wrote in her case file that Sheila had a "shabby" personality and was "slightly flippant and flighty." Later, she dispatched a nurse from the county health department to visit Sheila's apartment and inquire about her apparent pregnancy.

After the visit, the nurse called Luckhardt and cheerfully announced, "She seems quite healthy, and not at all pregnant."

Surprised, Luckhardt asked whether the nurse had noticed the girl's protruding abdomen.

"No," the nurse replied, "and I felt her stomach with my hand. It was very flat. She had on tight shorts and a loose blouse. I didn't notice any enlargement."

Later, when she learned that Sheila had in fact been five months pregnant, the nurse told Luckhardt that she was "mystified" by the encounter and wondered whether Sheila had duped her. A colleague who had stayed in the car while the nurse climbed the stairs to Sheila's apartment later said she had seen a pregnant woman downstairs.

Had the nurse, Luckhardt wondered, examined the wrong girl?

2.

Social-service agencies, boxed in by a jumble of policies and regulations, all too often move with the lumbering speed of a giant land tortoise. The State of Maryland was no exception in its handling of Larry Paulson. Over the next five years, as it struggled to provide stability in little Larry's life, the state assigned a dozen different workers to help him and his mother, making stability all the more elusive. The workers jumped in one after another, like a team of slow runners in a relay race, getting off to a late start and falling farther and farther behind. Larry, meanwhile, shuffled from foster home to foster home, from caseworker to caseworker, his anxieties multiplying with each move.

During his brief stay in his first foster home in Montgomery County, Larry outwardly appeared to adjust well. He displayed no problems eating or sleeping. Sheila couldn't visit due to the fifty-minute drive from her new home in Anne Arundel County. Worried that a prolonged separation from his mother would inflict irreparable harm on him, Larry's caseworker and foster parents decided that Larry should be moved to a home closer to Sheila. The move took more than three months to accomplish.

On August 1, Larry's Montgomery County worker picked him up and drove him to Annapolis, where his new caseworker was waiting. When the car door opened, out stepped the tiny boy in bright red suit and hat, tears streaming down his little cheeks. Hesitating, he turned and looked back at his first worker before he climbed into his new worker's car.

By the time he arrived at the home of Harold and Betty Herron, Larry's eyes were dry. He appeared calm as he entered the house to meet his new foster parents and their three foster children.

Although the Herrons seemed happy to have Larry, their marriage was stretching at the seams. Soon it would pop open, creating yet another trauma for the foster children whose wounds they were trying to heal.

The day Larry switched homes, Sheila called the agency and demanded to see her son at once, so a supervisor in the Annapolis office drove her to the Herrons' late that afternoon. "Larry seemed to recognize her a little, but paid not much attention to her," the supervisor wrote in her case file.

Sheila was working as a waitress again but still hadn't seen a doctor about her obvious pregnancy. Although she told social workers that she wanted her son back, they were more convinced than ever that she wasn't ready for him.

Earlier in the summer, a social worker had visited Sheila's new apartment near Annapolis to determine its suitability for a child. The worker found the apartment in good condition, though sparsely furnished. In Sheila's bedroom, the worker saw two single beds pushed together as a double bed, and men's clothes strewn around the room. If the worker had any doubt that a man was living there, the jockey shorts stacked neatly on a shelf erased it.

"Your boyfriend lives here with you?" the worker asked.

"Oh no," Sheila insisted. "He comes over a lot. He's here most evenings, in fact. But he lives with his mother."

When the worker asked whether Sheila was planning to marry her boyfriend, Sheila said she had considered marrying Dan, but she wasn't willing to give up her son for his sake. Dan wasn't thrilled with the prospect of being a stepfather, she explained.

"Do you have any plans for day care for while you're at work?" the worker asked.

"I'm going to leave him with a woman who lives downstairs," Sheila replied.

"What's the woman's name?"

"I don't know."

"Does she have children?"

"Yes."

"Do you know their names?"

"No."

The worker was unimpressed with Sheila's plan and concluded that the home was unsuitable for Larry's return.

In mid-August, two weeks after Larry moved to Anne Arundel County, Sheila was assigned to yet another caseworker. The new worker came to visit late one Monday afternoon and found Sheila's boyfriend asleep on the living room couch. Sitting down with Sheila in the kitchen, the worker asked straightaway whether Sheila had seen a doctor.

"No," Sheila admitted.

Sheila's case file showed repeated references to her likely pregnancy, and the worker decided to make it clear that Larry's fate was linked to her health. "I've been assigned to help you get back on your feet so you and Larry can be together again," the worker began. "First, though, several things need to happen. We believe you are sincere in wanting Larry back, but we've got to level with each other. If you and I are to work together, then you've got to cooperate with me. And the thing that upsets me most is you still haven't had a checkup." She looked Sheila in the eye. "Don't you think you're pregnant?"

"No. I don't think so."

"Then you must have a very large tumor inside you, and you'd better see a doctor right away!" In a stern voice, the worker said Sheila could not see Larry again until she saw a doctor. After Sheila saw a doctor, the worker explained, she could visit her son every two weeks.

Sheila hadn't seen Larry since the day he had moved in with the Herrons, and she didn't want to miss his second birthday on August 25. Reluctantly, she agreed to make a doctor's appointment.

As the two women talked, Sheila repeated what she'd told her previous worker: that she hoped to marry Dan at some unspecified date.

"Well, if you're going to get married," her new worker replied, "I'm going to have to meet Dan a few times too, so I can evaluate his role as a stepfather."

As she was preparing to leave, the worker heard Dan stirring in the living room and asked Sheila to introduce them. When Sheila called Dan into the kitchen, he came grudgingly. The worker explained that she had come to help Sheila get her son back. Dan openly scoffed. "You're going help her get Larry back? It's probably just the opposite."

"That's not true," the worker retorted, but she decided not to risk stirring his hostility further. Rising to leave, she looked at Dan. "If you'll talk to Sheila," she suggested, "I'm sure she can explain it better."

A week later, Sheila went to the agency office for another interview. Her stomach appeared larger, and her worker remarked that it was a sure sign of her pregnancy.

Sheila then related one of the more ridiculous stories the worker had heard. A girlfriend of Sheila's had been in a similar predicament, appearing pregnant, and finally went to a doctor, who admitted her to the hospital. When she woke the next morning, her friend concluded that she must have had an abortion because her stomach was flat and there was no baby. "But the doctor said no, she hadn't been pregnant at all, she merely had an excess of fluid," Sheila told her incredulous caseworker. "After they withdrew the fluid through a needle, my friend was fine again."

"Do you *really* believe that's what wrong with you, Sheila?"

Sheila squirmed. "Well, I guess I could be pregnant. But I really don't think so."

The worker studied Sheila's face, which showed signs of distress. "How do you think Dan might react if you really are pregnant?"

"He thinks that's entirely up to me."

"Would it be Dan's child?"

"No. I didn't meet him until February."

"Who would be the father?"

"A boy I was living with before I started seeing Dan."

Now Sheila's denial was starting to make sense. Plain old wishful thinking—nothing too complicated about that—she just didn't *want* to be pregnant, especially not by another boyfriend.

"What will you do with the baby if you do have one?"

"Dan's mother said if I didn't want to keep it, she has a friend who wants to adopt it. She'd pay the hospital bills."

"Have you decided you don't want to keep the baby?"

"Well, no—but I'll give it up if I have to, to get Larry back."

The worker was startled. "We would never expect you to give up your baby in order to get Larry back."

When Sheila said she had a doctor's appointment the following evening, the worker told her to phone the agency right away with the results.

Two days later, the worker hadn't heard from Sheila, so she called the restaurant where Sheila worked. The man who answered the phone said Sheila hadn't been to work in two weeks. The worker then called Sheila's doctor's office, where a nurse said Sheila finally had kept her appointment after breaking three earlier ones. Sheila was eight months pregnant; her baby was due in mid-September.

Two weeks later, on September 5, Sheila gave birth to her

second child, a healthy girl. At the end of the month, realizing that her boyfriend had no interest in the baby and that she lacked the resources to care for her alone, Sheila signed documents freeing her for adoption.

During August and September, Sheila visited her son at the Herron foster home four times. Each time Larry acted cool toward his mother, even when she gave him a ball and a truck on his second birthday. A social worker noted in her case file that Sheila made no effort to break through her son's barrier. Although Sheila professed to want him back, her worker realized that she was torn between her feelings for her son and her boyfriend. As a result, she vacillated on whether to keep Larry or surrender him for adoption.

At the end of October, Sheila requested permission to visit Larry every week. Viewing that as a good sign, her worker granted the request, and Sheila soon had a standing appointment to visit Larry each Thursday.

On October 8, Sheila went to work for a firm next door to the company where Dan worked. It was an ideal location, for her hours allowed her to commute with him. Two weeks later, though, Sheila quit, explaining to her worker that her boss had failed to give her a promised pay raise.

In early November, she took yet another job as a secretary in Annapolis. It provided her with fifty-seven dollars a week in take-home pay and gave her an opportunity to learn bookkeeping and inventory skills. She and Dan soon moved into a new house, but she confided to her social worker that she was being careful not to push him to the altar even though their relationship was stabilizing.

"We are almost like an old married couple," she laughed. "I used to be after Dan all the time to take me out, and we were always on the go. Now we spend most of our time visiting friends or watching TV at home."

Pleased by Sheila's maturing attitude, the caseworker reminded her once again of the importance of birth control. Sheila replied that she had switched gynecologists because of a dispute over her bill and had gone on the Pill after her daughter was born.

Her worker reviewed Sheila's budget and determined that she

should be able to support Larry if she started saving a little money. "Try to put ten dollars a week into a savings account to cover emergencies for when Larry comes home," the worker urged.

When the worker proposed February 1 as a target date for Larry's return, Sheila readily assented. After months of wavering, Sheila finally seemed to have made up her mind that she wanted her son home.

As the date approached, the worker explained, Larry would go home with her for several overnight visits. In mid-January, he would spend an entire weekend with her to prepare for his permanent homecoming in February.

Little did Sheila's worker realize, though, that by the time February rolled around, Larry's world would be turned upside down not once but twice. Not only would his mother reject him; his new foster parents would, too.

By then, however, Sheila's worker would be long gone. As she explained to Sheila in November, she was switching jobs after Thanksgiving and turning her clients over to a new social worker.

From the start, it was obvious that Larry had problems adjusting at the Herrons. He displayed a willful, mischievous streak, which his caseworker blamed on his first foster parents, claiming they had "spoiled" him, even though they had kept him only three months. At the Herrons, he delighted in doing as he pleased and ignored his foster mother when she told him, "No-no."

Although he smiled and laughed a lot, Larry was not an affectionate child, nor was he sociable. Apparently unaccustomed to playing with other children, he stood in a corner and watched the Herrons' other young foster children play games. Rarely did he join in, even though his foster brothers were near him in age. He was slower to talk than the other children, and for a while *Mama* was his only word that anyone understood. Yet he was active and forever climbing on furniture. He took a hard tumble from the backyard swing in September and had his head stitched in the emergency room. "You little daredevil," Mrs. Herron said.

At bedtime, Larry grew restless and had trouble falling asleep.

He sucked his thumb night and day, and Mrs. Herron usually gave him a bottle at bedtime to calm him.

"He is an insecure child, and sometimes has a rather frightened look in his eyes," Larry's new caseworker wrote in his file after a home visit.

When Mrs. Herron tried to toilet train him shortly after his second birthday, he resisted her efforts, and the family pediatrician warned her not to push it. "He's rather nervous and highstrung," the doctor said. "I don't think he's ready to be toilet trained."

Sheila took Larry for a visit on most Thursdays, but occasionally she stood him up. Sometimes Larry came home from those visits distraught, and it took Mrs. Herron hours to calm him.

During November, Larry seemed to grow more devilish by the day. "Larry is so mischievous and stubborn. He doesn't listen to correction and doesn't mind," Mrs. Herron told his worker. "He is the instigator of mischief with the other children and he's always into something. He gets very mischievous smiles on his face and seems to take pleasure in doing the opposite of whatever I tell him to do."

While his worker was visiting one day, Larry got his hands on a can of baby powder and shook it all over the playroom floor, exasperating Mrs. Herron. "Maybe you should put things like that away where Larry can't get to them," the worker suggested.

In December, Larry awoke early almost every morning and ran to wake his foster brothers and sister. He also arose in the middle of the night, dashed out to the living room, and ran around in a disoriented state. He did the same thing during his afternoon naps. "It's as if he wants to make sure we're all still there," said Mrs. Herron, puzzled. "I pick him up and hold him, trying to comfort him. But he doesn't seem to respond."

On January 11, while he was recovering from an ear infection and the flu, Larry spent the night with his mother for the first time since his abandonment.

The next day, Sheila brought him home in dirty diapers and hurriedly dropped him off at the doorstep six hours early, without offering any explanation to his foster mother. Judging by the penicillin bottle, Mrs. Herron didn't think Sheila had bothered to give Larry his medicine.

For the next ten days, Mrs. Herron reported that Larry "cried constantly" and became "hysterical" whenever he couldn't find someone in his foster family. He broke his toys, refused to play with his siblings, and stood by himself in a corner, sucking his thumb. When another set of foster parents visited, Larry cried so hard he threw up.

Larry's new worker visited the Herrons once a week in January and noticed that Larry appeared increasingly withdrawn and moody. He refused to approach her or smile, and once he hid behind the living room draperies. Mrs. Herron grumbled endlessly about Larry's behavior, blaming it on his biological mother.

Yet when Larry's worker got together with Sheila's new worker to compare notes, they concluded that Larry's foster mother was probably as much to blame for his increasing emotional turmoil. The Herrons' marriage obviously was in trouble, and Mrs. Herron was showing signs of severe stress. "It is probable that much of Larry's distress was attributable to stress in the foster home rather than in his own," Sheila's new worker wrote.

The last week of January, the workers' suspicions were confirmed when Mrs. Herron, citing her marital difficulties, requested removal of all their foster children.

No sooner had workers began hunting new homes for the children than Mrs. Herron called the agency on Monday, February 3. Near tears, she begged her worker to take Larry off her hands—at once, by Friday at the latest.

"What's wrong?" asked the worker.

On Sunday, Larry had risen early, climbed on a kitchen stool, snatched a bottle of syrup from a cabinet, and poured it all over himself. Mrs. Herron spent an hour trying to rinse the gooey stuff out of his curly black hair. The next day, Larry got up early again and emptied two boxes of rice and a box of pancake mix on the kitchen floor.

It was ordinary two-year-old mischief, but Mrs. Herron declared, "I've reached the end of my patience."

"Okay," the worker said sadly. "We'll try to find him a home by Friday."

*   *   *

Larry's sudden ouster from the Herron home wouldn't have been so tragic if Larry's mother had been a safety net.

True to form, however, Sheila wasn't there. She had begun to waffle about Larry's homecoming shortly after she had been assigned a new social worker in December. After she initially assured the worker that she would reclaim Larry without marrying Dan, gradually she revealed that she desperately wanted marriage and feared Larry could jeopardize her prospects.

In January, Sheila called her new worker and said that her father had phoned from California and urged her to give up her son. Her father didn't believe she was capable of caring for him, and she reluctantly agreed. She had decided to surrender him for adoption.

When the worker phoned a few days later, however, Sheila had changed her mind again. Dan was worried that if she gave up Larry on his account, he might prove to be unworthy of the sacrifice. "Her feeling at this point was that if she gave Larry up and eventually lost Dan anyway, she would have given up Larry for nothing," the worker wrote in Sheila's still-growing file.

When the Herrons abruptly expelled Larry from their home in February, six months after his arrival, Sheila still was lukewarm to the idea of taking him home. In truth, she was leaning toward giving him up for adoption. At least for now, the agency had no choice but to cancel Larry's homecoming.

For the first time, social workers began hunting for a couple who wanted to adopt Larry. That way, they reasoned, if Sheila relinquished him, Larry would have a chance to get the permanent home he so desperately needed without having to switch homes again. Soon the agency found a set of parents who wanted to adopt a son and were willing to gamble with a foster child who wasn't legally free yet for adoption. Workers called such children "at-risk placements" because the would-be adoptive parents ran the risk of losing them to their biological parents.

Friday, February 7, 1969, was moving day again. This time, two social workers picked up Larry—now two and a half years old—and drove him to his third foster home. Unlike his last move, he did not cry. He did not utter a single word. Throughout the drive, he sat in the lap of his new caseworker, Sandy Shusta, who was assigned to his new foster family.

"He looked around with his big eyes, seemed very serious, as if in deep thought," one of the workers later wrote.

As the two social workers walked him up the sidewalk toward his new home, they held his little hand. It was trembling.

Inside, Larry behaved politely. The perfect little gentleman, he even smiled at one of his new brothers, Bobby, a toddler like Larry. "I hadn't seen him smile for a very long time," Larry's worker wrote.

His new parents, Paul and Susan Webb, had two sons of their own: Bobby, who was just a few months younger than Larry, and an infant. The Webbs were eager to round out their family by adopting a third son.

Mrs. Webb soon reported that Larry was adjusting well. Although he had resisted toilet training at the Herrons', within one day at the Webbs', Larry was using his new brother's little potty chair. Mrs. Webb dressed Bobby and Larry in identical outfits and took delight after a few months when Larry began calling only her and her husband Mommy and Daddy.

At first, Larry had called everyone he met Mommy and Daddy.

Sheila, meanwhile, continued to visit Larry, and several times she revealed what her caseworker considered to be gross immaturity. One day, for instance, she expressed pleasure at Larry's progress in toilet training and remarked, as if he was a puppy, "I'm waiting to take him home until after he's potty trained."

Dan finally proposed to Sheila in mid-February but refused to set a date. Sheila insisted on setting one so she could make a final decision on whether to surrender Larry for adoption.

"Both adults were using the child as a weapon," Sheila's worker wrote.

Dan and Sheila finally set their wedding date for April and moved in temporarily with a relative of Dan's. By March, they both had new jobs.

Determined to let nothing spoil the marriage she had sought for so long, Sheila signed a petition granting full legal custody of Larry to the State of Maryland. The guardianship petition would take effect June 26, freeing Larry at last for adoption.

In April, Sheila and Dan exchanged wedding vows at a Roman Catholic Church in Anne Arundel County.

Although Sheila couldn't have known it at the time, her fear of surrendering Larry for naught would turn out to be well founded.

After only four years of marriage, she and Dan separated and lived apart for three years, he in Anne Arundel County and she in Baltimore. Dan then filed for and received a divorce in 1977, after Sheila didn't answer his complaint or show up in court. Five years later, she left Maryland and moved to a western state.

By the time of Larry's arrest in 1984, Sheila had been gone from Maryland for two years and hadn't seen her son in nearly fifteen years. She lost contact with him after she surrendered him for adoption. If she ever tried to reestablish contact, Maryland's adoption law would have prevented her from learning the identity of his adoptive family.

Because she was out west at the time, and news accounts of the Swartz murders were concentrated in the Washington–Baltimore area, it seems unlikely that Sheila read about the murders. Even if she did, she probably would not have recognized the son she hadn't seen since he was two.

Larry, though, would have no way of knowing for sure what his mother knew about him. State law sealed his adoption records—including his birth name and that of his parents—from both him and his parents. Although his lawyers unsealed that information for his legal defense, they decided not to attempt to locate his natural parents. The lawyers considered it doubtful that after so many years either parent could offer any information helpful to Larry's defense.

3.

At his third foster home, Larry appeared determined to win the acceptance that he had failed to find in his other homes. He stayed on his best behavior throughout his early months with the Webbs, an affectionate couple who were firm yet gentle with children.

An extraordinarily athletic man, Paul Webb took delight in

Larry's boundless physical energy. He loved roughhousing with Larry and told his wife, Susan, that he hoped his new son might grow up to be an athlete. Within a few months, Paul began talking about Larry's college education. Although Susan was a little less enthusiastic about their new son, she, too, found Larry adorable. Both the Webbs were pleased to see Larry warm to their natural two-year-old son. Larry and Bobby played and squabbled, it seemed, as naturally as siblings.

Six months after Larry moved in, thrilled that he had been freed for adoption and that the adoption procedures were starting, Mrs. Webb reported to his caseworker that Larry was "adjusting beautifully." He slept soundly, never wet his bed, and had such a huge appetite that he would eat as much as her husband if she allowed him to, Mrs. Webb cheerfully reported. She attributed his near-flawless performance to the love she and her husband had immersed him in, which presumably soothed his insecurities. Mrs. Webb told the family's caseworker, Sandy Shusta, that all their relatives and friends already had accepted Larry as their real son.

Shusta seemed delighted by his smooth adjustment. "For the first time," she wrote in a glowing report, "Larry appears to be a permanent member of a family." That was the first week of August 1969.

The next entry in his agency record was October 1, when Shusta tried to telephone the Webbs and discovered their phone had been disconnected. She immediately drove out to their house and found another family living there.

Worried, Shusta went knocking on neighbors' doors. A woman who lived next door disclosed that the Webbs were strapped financially and had moved in with Mr. Webb's parents.

"What kind of financial problems were they having?" Shusta asked.

"Mr. Webb is attending classes at Johns Hopkins," the neighbor replied.

"I know, but that's only night school."

"Well, I suppose Mrs. Webb doesn't help," the neighbor said. "She doesn't know how to handle money, and she spends foolishly. I think that's the problem."

Months earlier, Shusta had noticed that Mrs. Webb didn't

seem evenhanded with the boys. She had seemed much stricter with Larry than her own sons, and Shusta had wondered whether the young mother would be capable of loving Larry as much as her own boys. Now, Shusta asked the neighbor whether she'd noticed Mrs. Webb showing any favoritism.

The neighbor said no, then added, "You know, my husband and I would be thrilled if we could adopt Larry. He's such a darling."

Two days later, Shusta tracked down the Webbs by telephone and asked Mrs. Webb to come to her office. When Mrs. Webb showed up that afternoon, Shusta—barely able to conceal her irritation—asked, "Why didn't you notify us that you were moving?"

"I did send you a note with our new address," Mrs. Webb said. "Didn't you get it?"

"No."

"We moved because my husband got a new job and his parents' house is closer to where he's working."

"Are you having money problems?"

"Somewhat. We're trying to buy a new house, and we're hoping to save the down payment while we live with his parents for a few months."

Shusta inquired about Larry, and Mrs. Webb confessed that he had become something of a problem. To be truthful, she didn't feel that she loved him yet.

"I'm worried about that," Shusta said. "When you said you wanted to adopt Larry, you accepted him as your own son."

Mrs. Webb appeared troubled. "I don't know what I'd do if I lost him."

"Why don't we talk about the problems you're having with Larry," Shusta suggested. "What seems to be wrong?"

"He's very stubborn. I have to spank him a lot because he doesn't listen to what I tell him."

"Do you feel differently about Larry than your own two boys?"

"Yes." Mrs. Webb looked away, as though she was embarrassed.

"And do you feel badly about that?"

"Yes, because my husband and all our relatives love Larry.

They want him as a permanent member of the family. They'd be upset if I don't go through with the adoption."

"Don't you think you should consider what's best for Larry, too?" After a thoughtful pause, Shusta advised gently, "I don't think you're ready for adoption yet."

"Well, it certainly is a relief to talk about it," Mrs. Webb confessed. "I've hardly been able to sleep, worrying about this."

Shusta was disappointed. Mrs. Webb's emotional rejection of Larry seemed all too clear. She told Mrs. Webb they would talk again after Larry underwent the medical examinations that were standard for children being placed for adoption.

On October 16, Dr. Julius Loebl, an Annapolis physician, examined Larry and found him to be "a normal child of small stature." Barely three years old, and an inch shy of three feet tall, Larry weighed twenty-four pounds—only one more than he had weighed fifteen months before. His foster mother told the doctor that Larry was a "restless child" with a "short attention span" who was toilet trained but still had accidents.

The same day, Larry went to see Dr. Robert L. White, a Severna Park psychologist, who administered the Stanford-Binet Intelligence Scale and the Vineland Social Maturity Scale tests. Larry's "social adjustment" quotient on the Vineland scale suggested he was functioning at a level about four-fifths the average for three-year-olds. His I.Q. tested at 85, placing him in the dull-normal range.

Dr. White noted that Larry was slightly overactive and demanded his full attention. "It is likely that this child has some tendency toward hyperactivity, and this needs to be further evaluated before a definite statement can be made about the possibility of some central nervous system dysfunction," White wrote. "It was of interest to note that the foster mother is probably covertly rejecting the child and has difficulty accepting it," he added. "This probably has had some effect on his maturation."

Two weeks later, armed with White's report, Mrs. Webb and Shusta took Larry to the Harriet Lane Clinic at Johns Hopkins Hospital. Dr. Kenton R. Holden, a pediatrician specializing in neurology, examined Larry and concluded that he showed no signs of central nervous system disease. Based on Larry's puny build and enormous appetite, Holden suggested that he may have been suffering from "post psychosocial syndrome," or symptoms triggered by the stress of his unstable home life. The doctor recommended a biannual check of his height and weight by a private pediatrician.

"What he really needs is a permanent home as soon as possible," Dr. Holden told Shusta.

The Webbs spent many hours debating whether they could fit Larry into their family and give him the love he seemed so desperately to need. Mrs. Webb finally told Shusta that she and her husband had decided not to adopt Larry. "We think he should be in a home where he'll be the only child," she said.

Shusta had to agree.

The Webbs had bought a new home and were planning to move into it the day after Thanksgiving. Hoping to spare Larry from an extra move, Shusta redoubled her efforts to find him a new home before then. One couple already had expressed interest in Larry and was waiting to meet him. If everything worked out, Shusta hoped he could move in with them for the holiday.

Shortly before the holiday, however, Larry's prospective father became ill and entered a hospital for a liver biopsy. The man's doctor diagnosed his condition as chronic hepatitis and recommended postponement of the adoption plans.

Larry, meanwhile, continued to live with a family that didn't want him while social workers continued to hunt for one that did.

One morning in January, Mrs. Webb phoned the agency and complained that Larry had been getting up in the middle of the night to scavenge for food and drink. The night before, she had found him sitting on the kitchen floor with a glass in his hand and an empty pint of gin lying beside him on the rug. Since the bottle had been half-full, and the rug was dry, she concluded that Larry had drunk the gin.

Shusta thought the story sounded phony. She discussed it with Mrs. Webb during a home visit three days later. "Did Larry act inebriated?" Shusta asked.

"No, he acted fine," Mrs. Webb replied.

"Then I don't believe he drank it. Any three-year-old who

could drink all that gin and not appear inebriated would be a most unusual child, wouldn't you think?"

Mrs. Webb grumbled that Larry had been scavenging for food almost every night. Shusta was well aware of Larry's abnormal appetite—a symptom often seen in emotionally traumatized or neglected children—and she couldn't understand why Mrs. Webb seemed so blind to Larry's emotional turmoil.

"Do you give him a snack before bedtime?" Shusta asked. "He's probably hungry."

"No." Mrs. Webb was unable to conceal her annoyance with Larry.

Shusta, irritated, shifted gears. "We've gotten another referral for an adoptive home and we hope to move Larry by the end of February. If that doesn't work out, I'm afraid we'll have to move him to a temporary foster home. He seems to be upsetting your household most of the time."

"He's welcome to stay here as long as he needs to."

"Larry needs to be in a home where he's loved, not tolerated. His behavior problems are due, I think, to a great need for attention."

4.

Larry's name was in the Maryland Adoption Resource Exchange, a statewide referral system that matched couples waiting to adopt to available children. In the file on Larry circulating through the exchange, Shusta wrote, "Larry needs a childless family where he can receive much attention and love."

At the end of January, the Maryland Children's Aid Society found a childless couple who seemed tailored to his sizable emotional needs. Workers presented Larry to the prospective parents by way of a color photograph and a background report.

The couple, Charles and Mary O'Hara, took one look at Larry's rich olive complexion, scanned his brief life summary, noted that he was "half East Indian," and declared they were not "interested in him because he was not one hundred percent Caucasian."

On February 2, 1970, Larry was presented to yet another couple, John and Mary Weaver. The Weavers had two little girls, both older than Larry, and were anxious to adopt a son. They had requested a boy exactly Larry's age: between three and four. John Weaver, a salesman who lived north of Baltimore, studied Larry's photograph and remarked happily, "He's got my dark coloring! I was hoping for a boy with some of my features, since both our girls have my wife's light coloring."

"Larry's natural father was from India," said the Weavers' social worker, Robert Short. "That's why he's so dark. Would that pose a problem for you or your wife?"

"Not at all," said John Weaver. His wife quickly agreed.

The social worker had suspected as much, since the Weavers had displayed no bias when they discussed mixed racial adoptions.

When the Weavers took Larry's picture home that night and showed it to their daughters, the girls were delighted by Larry's handsome heart-shaped face and dark eyes framed by long thick lashes.

"We'd like to meet him as soon as possible," John Weaver told his worker the next day.

The following week, Shusta took Larry to lunch at a McDonald's.

"You're going to meet your new mommy and daddy next week," she said.

"Okay," replied Larry, who was now three and a half.

"On the first visit, you'll visit with them in the playroom," Shusta explained. "The next day, you'll go home with them. And after you go home with them, you won't go home anymore to where you're living. You'll be staying at your new home for good."

"Okay," Larry said meekly.

Shusta wanted Larry to understand what was happening to him. She didn't want him to think that his new home was just another place he'd live for a year or two. It would be his fourth foster home in less than two years. What was he supposed to think?

All Larry said, over and over, was "okay." No matter what she said, he said "okay." She had no idea whether he understood a word of her explanation.

Two days later, Shusta returned to the Webbs' and found Larry sprawled on the living room floor, watching TV.

"I'm going to get a haircut today," he announced proudly.

"He's getting a new outfit, too," said Mrs. Webb, "to meet his new mommy and daddy."

Once again, Shusta walked Larry through the procedure: first the meeting, then the placement, then no more contact with the Webbs.

"Okay," Larry said.

On February 16, 1970, Shusta picked up Larry and drove him to the agency's main office in Baltimore. Brimming with excitement, he begged Shusta to buy him a chocolate bar from the vending machine.

"Your new mommy and daddy will probably want to buy you a treat, so let's wait. Okay?"

"Okay."

When the Weavers arrived, their worker ushered them into a room adjoining the one in which Larry and Shusta were playing so the Weavers could view Larry through a two-way mirror. After the Weavers peered at him for a few minutes, Larry was taken into another room. He was sitting quietly with Shusta when his new mother and father walked in. Larry regarded the Weavers shyly, saying nothing but not shrinking away from them. They smiled and handed him a metal airplane and a puzzle.

After the social workers left, Larry warmed to the Weavers and spent the next forty-five minutes getting acquainted with them in private. When the two social workers returned, Larry was eating peanut butter crackers. The Weavers reported he had eaten continuously for forty-five minutes.

Earlier, Robert Short had told the Weavers they would not be expected to make a decision on the spot; they should go home and think it over. Now the Weavers declared there was no need to think it over; they wanted to take Larry home today. "We know he's right for us!" said John Weaver.

Shusta replied that the Weavers could not, under agency policy, take Larry home after their first meeting, but she agreed with the Weavers' caseworker that Larry could move in with the Weavers the next day, when his first overnight visit was scheduled.

Late the next afternoon, Shusta drove out to the Webbs' and found Larry dressed in his new outfit, ready for his move. Mrs. Webb had packed his clothes and toys in a single shopping bag.

Mrs. Webb appeared distraught. "Everything seemed to happen at once," she told Shusta. "My mother has gone into the hospital for a hysterectomy, and now Larry is leaving. I'm sad to see him go."

Mr. Webb, who had been on the telephone in the kitchen, came into the living room, walked over to Larry, picked him up, and kissed him. As Mrs. Webb stood uttering a stream of last-minute instructions for Larry's care, her husband set Larry down, pulled on Larry's coat and hat, and kissed him again.

One year after he had moved in with the Webbs, "Larry walked happily out the door, not even turning around to wave good-bye," wrote Shusta.

At the main office, Larry gaily occupied himself with the agency's toys and bubbled with excitement when his new parents entered the playroom with their daughters. After introducing the children, Mr. Weaver lined the whole family up and took photographs. While the Weavers went to sign the placement papers, Larry played with his new sisters.

Mr. and Mrs. Weaver took Larry's hands, walked him out to their car, and drove off to their first family outing—a spaghetti dinner.

The next day, Robert Short phoned the Weavers. As their caseworker, Short would handle Larry's case after he moved into the Weaver home. Short, not Shusta, would monitor the family's progress during the one-year supervisory period that would lead to the adoption decree.

"He's been quiet and shy, but he hasn't cried," Mrs. Weaver said. "I think he's doing all right. He did have trouble falling asleep after I put him down last night, and by the time I went into his room this morning, he'd wet the bed."

"Is that a problem?"

"Oh no, I think it's normal, given the circumstances. I mean, the move and all. Don't you?"

"Absolutely," replied Short. "Bed-wetting is to be expected at times like these."

Short said he would stay in touch and visit after a month or so, and hung up.

He telephoned several times over the next few weeks. Each time Mrs. Weaver reported that Larry was still wetting his bed. At first she downplayed it, but by the time Short visited their home March 17, she conceded, "It's become a problem."

"How so?" Short asked.

"He wets so much, I have to wash all the bedclothes each day. We've tried to limit the amount of fluids he drinks after supper, but it hasn't helped. There hasn't been one night that he hasn't wet his bed."

"Well, maybe you shouldn't wash the sheets every single day," Short suggested. "Why not try pulling the sheets back and letting them air dry? I don't think it would hurt if you washed the sheets every other day."

But Mrs. Weaver resisted that idea. "I have the time and energy. I'd rather wash them."

"Well, don't get discouraged," Short said. "You should get your husband involved, too. Ask him to take Larry to the bathroom just before bedtime. You might even wake Larry up and take him to the bathroom again when you're getting ready for bed."

"All right."

"Whatever you do, don't show anger over the bed-wetting. Try to show Larry that it doesn't upset you. That's very important."

In addition to his bed-wetting, Mrs. Weaver said that Larry was displaying abnormal eating habits.

"Abnormal? How so?" inquired Short.

"He eats his regular meals, then in between meals, if he finds a box of cookies or any snack food, he'll eat the whole box."

Short smiled. "That might be normal, don't you think?"

"Our girls never do anything like that. They've taken cookies when they knew they weren't supposed to, but this is different.

He eats the *whole box!* And when I catch him, he reacts differently than the girls." Mrs. Weaver shook her head. "It's like
he's afraid he won't get enough to eat."

All in all, though, the Weavers said Larry seemed to be getting
along fairly well in his new home. He wasn't showing much
affection, and he didn't reciprocate when his new mother
hugged and kissed him. He often refused to go outside and play,
saying it was too cold. Yet he laughed and smiled a lot, and the
Weavers felt proud of their handsome new son.

"It's getting on my nerves," Mrs. Weaver confessed when she
and her husband visited Short's office two months later.

"Oh, it's not *that* bad," her husband interjected.

"You're not as close to it as I am," she rejoined. "He still does
it almost every single night, and it's been three months."

Short jumped in. "Has the bed-wetting been causing arguments between you two?"

"A few," Mary Weaver conceded.

"Has Larry overheard you?"

"We try not to let him, but I'm sure he's aware we were arguing about him," John Weaver said. He stated that his wife was
being "too strict" with Larry, fussing at him constantly about the
bed-wetting.

"Do you think this amount of bed-wetting is normal?" Mrs.
Weaver asked.

Short shrugged. "At Larry's age, it's neither normal nor abnormal." Looking at Mrs. Weaver, Short added, "I'll tell you this: As
long as he gets your undivided attention when he wets the bed,
he's likely to continue. He may even be trying unconsciously to
form a relationship with you."

Short once again advised Mrs. Weaver to stop washing the
sheets every day, but she bristled and declared, "Washing is not
the issue."

Neither parent thought much of Short's next suggestion: to
place a potty chair in Larry's bedroom. Rather, they vowed to
continue their present course of limiting his fluids after supper
and taking him to the bathroom at bedtime.

Apart from his bed-wetting, the Weavers said Larry was warm-
ing to the family a little. At first, he had been standoffish with his

mother and sisters. Now he played more with the younger girl, and occasionally, on his own, he climbed up on the couch and sat beside his mother.

Short routinely inquired whether the Weavers had any doubts about their decision to adopt Larry.

"No," they said in unison.

Short visited the Weavers twice in August. Nearly four years old now, Larry seemed to be playing naturally and freely with his sisters. His mother reported, with a trace of pride, that she had spanked him when she caught him decorating everything within reach in the kitchen with a can of whipped cream. It was Larry's first outright naughty behavior during nearly six months in their home; Mrs. Weaver felt it was a natural, inevitable occurrence.

She did not consider his bed-wetting natural. It had continued, and she was at a loss to deal with it. The Weavers were considering taking Larry to a psychologist.

Short once again advised her not to blow it out of proportion, so Larry wouldn't feel it was a big deal. She seemed incapable of grasping his point. He marveled at how in one breath she could say, "I'm the one who has to wash his sheets," then in the next say, "I don't mind, though."

"You've got to understand that bed-wetting is a symptom, not a problem," Short tried to explain. "It's a symptom of his insecurity. His *insecurity* is the problem that you and your husband need to address. His early years were terribly traumatic, and he needs lots of reassurance. If there was some magical way you could stop his bed-wetting, I'm afraid his insecurity would still show up somewhere else—in some other behavior."

When her husband arrived home from work and joined the conversation, Mr. Weaver admitted that he and his wife often quarreled over the bed-wetting.

"You refuse to get involved. You just leave it all to me," his wife complained.

"I'm tired of how you carry on about it," he retorted.

In general, Mary Weaver said, Larry was talking more freely to her, but something still seemed to be missing from their relationship. "He doesn't seem like part of our family yet," she said, looking perplexed. "I don't really know why."

Urging the Weavers to be patient, Short suggested that Larry's adjustment would take time. "I think you're on top of the problem," he said. "Some children who go through what Larry's been through and have his problems, stop talking completely. They withdraw altogether. Be thankful Larry hasn't done that!"

Larry turned four on August 25, six months after he moved in with the Weavers. Outwardly, he was growing more beautiful each year, his heart-shaped face enlivened by dark dramatic eyes. Inwardly he was growing more insecure, his dark eyes marred by a frightened, pained look. He felt deeply confused about who he was and where he belonged. John and Mary Weaver were his fifth set of parents, and his biological parents were fading fast in his mind. He still remembered Sheila, though, and pictured her as being much prettier than Mrs. Weaver.

Larry spent most of his days alone with Mrs. Weaver because his new father went to work and his two new sisters went to school. Larry was uncomfortable around Mrs. Weaver because she screamed so much. She usually started first thing in the morning, when she came into his room and found the bed sheets wet. "You're doing this on purpose!" she would shriek. He would stand in the corner, holding himself still, watching her warily.

"Come with me," she would bark, and he would accompany her silently into the bathroom. Together, they put his sheets and pajamas into the bathtub and rinsed them out while she lectured him about being too lazy to get out of bed.

When the Weavers took a camping vacation in their trailer during Larry's first summer there, they warned him to stop wetting his bed before the trip. Larry felt intensely anxious and was unable to sleep his first night in the trailer. Worried about whether he would wet himself, he slipped out of bed and curled up on the trailer floor. His parents found him asleep there in the morning. His parents took along his potty chair, and Larry managed to use it most of the time. He wet his bed only once or twice during the entire camping trip.

Yet he continued to wet his bed at home all that fall. When the cold weather came, after he'd been there nearly a year, Mrs. Weaver took him into his bedroom one night and announced that he would have to wear new, bulky undergarb until he learned to control his bladder.

Larry hated the new underwear and complained that it was uncomfortable, but Mrs. Weaver insisted that she had to keep the bed dry. "If you stop wetting your bed, you can take them off," she promised. He did manage to stop wetting the bed for a while but inevitably had a relapse.

It wasn't only his bed-wetting that caused her yelling. Nothing he did seemed to please her. She yelled at his father, too, and sometimes he overheard them hollering about his bed-wetting.

Occasionally Larry wondered whether his social worker was going to move him again. Although it frightened him to think about moving, he was so unhappy that sometimes he *wanted* to move. He felt intensely alone and bewildered; hoping to stay out of trouble, he went days without speaking a word to anyone.

Near the end of Larry's first year in the home, John Weaver quit his salesman's job to form a new manufacturing company with a partner. Soon after Weaver sunk his savings into the project, however, he encountered a cash-flow problem: He didn't make enough to pay his bills. So he and his partner parted ways, and early in 1971, he tried a solo business venture.

Larry's caseworker, meanwhile, had visited the Weavers in October 1970 and cheerfully announced that it would be his last home visit before the Weavers signed Larry's final adoption decree in February 1971.

John Weaver immediately demurred. "My income is so unstable right now, it might be better if we postponed the decree," he suggested. "All my money is tied up in this venture. To tell you the truth, at the moment I have no income at all."

Several months later, Weaver stopped by Short's office and said he still felt too financially insecure to sign the adoption decree.

In April 1971, two months after their one-year supervisory period had ended, both Weavers visited Short's office again and said they were still too strapped financially to sign the adoption papers. "Maybe next winter," John Weaver said.

"Maybe, in addition to the money, you're unsure about the

adoption," Short countered. "Maybe that's really why you don't want to sign the papers."

That brought a quick denial from John Weaver, but Mary acknowledged that she had doubts. "For some reason, I haven't been able to bridge the gap with Larry. I just can't seem to get close to him," she said. "It's possible that I never will."

Her husband strongly doubted that. "I *like* Larry," he insisted, looking at his wife. "And I don't think his problems are so serious that we can't work them out."

She shook her head. "What if his problems go on for years? What do we do then?"

"They aren't insurmountable," John Weaver said sharply, "and they won't go on for years."

Short interrupted. "Does this go on at home a lot?"

"Yes," the Weavers confessed.

"Do you get short with each other and lose your temper?"

Glancing sheepishly at each other, the Weavers both nodded. Short let them talk for awhile, venting their obvious frustration. He considered their stress over Larry largely unavoidable. Short knew that couples who adopted older children always seemed to face major adjustment problems. There was little he could do about that. All he could do was offer encouragement and wait, hoping that the Weavers would pull together into a family.

In the summer of 1971, shortly before Larry's fifth birthday, Mrs. Weaver tried a new approach in teaching him to control his bladder. She took him to a toy store and asked him to pick out the toy he wanted most. "If you stop wetting your bed, I'll buy it for you," she said.

For Larry, the pressure was unbearable. He continued to wet his bed a few times each week. Although his foster father didn't yell at him the way his foster mother did, Larry could tell the bed-wetting bothered Mr. Weaver, too.

"Have you grown up enough to stop doing that yet?" Mr. Weaver would ask. He went away frequently on business trips, and when he returned after one particularly long absence, the first thing he said to Larry after he walked in the door was, "Do you still wet the bed?"

Larry nodded and looked down, ashamed.

The family's caseworker visited three times that summer. Each time the family gathered in the living room to talk, Larry was quiet. He couldn't talk about how he felt in front of everyone. He listened for a while, then went to his room.

When Mary Weaver told Short about her ploy of promising Larry a toy if he'd quit his bed-wetting, the social worker frowned. "There are cons to that type of reward, especially if it doesn't work," he warned. "Each time Larry fails, it just focuses more attention on his failure. It will reinforce his failure identity."

During his August visit, Short told the Weavers he would leave them alone indefinitely to sort things out on their own. For the next year, Short paid no more home visits. Although the Weavers occasionally stopped by his office, Short didn't see Larry again until the summer of 1972—a year later.

Inside, Larry felt a gnawing hunger that grew steadily more intense. Sometimes he sneaked into the kitchen and ate a whole box of food—cookies, cereal, whatever he could find. When his mother caught him, she demanded, "Why did you eat all that? What's wrong with you?"

He looked away and said nothing. He could not explain how he felt to her, that he wanted her to stop yelling and be nice to him.

When Larry turned five, the Weavers enrolled him in kindergarten. He enjoyed school and especially looked forward to snack time. After he ate the food his mother packed in his lunch box, he occasionally sneaked food from his classmates' boxes. When his mother confronted him, he pretended he hadn't done it.

His father injured his back one day and had to stay home from work: soon his parents were yelling at each other all the time. Larry grew more and more quiet at home. At school, he grew restless and left his chair to wander around the room, sometimes while the teacher was trying to read stories aloud to the class. She'd holler at Larry to go back to his seat, and he would; but he couldn't stay put for long.

After school, the gnawing in his stomach would return. A neighbor caught him outside rummaging through her trash can, taking out scraps of food. After the neighbor told his mother, Mrs. Weaver demanded an explanation.

"It wasn't me," Larry insisted, looking at his mother with anxious eyes.

In February 1972, John Weaver visited Short's office and reported that he had recovered from his back problem and was working as a salesman again. His independent business venture had gone bust, netting him a total income of $1,700 for 1971. "We're lucky we didn't lose our home," Weaver said.

In March, both Weavers visited Short's office and said they were worried about Larry's abnormal eating. "It's still a day-to-day struggle with him," Mrs. Weaver grumbled. "He wets the bed and hasn't let me through that barrier he's got around him. He just hasn't become a part of the family like we expected him to."

Two years had passed since the Weavers had taken in Larry. Still, they had not signed his adoption decree. Either party—the Weavers or the agency—could call off the adoption before the final papers were signed under the preadoption agreement.

Short asked whether the Weavers could foresee a day when they might call it quits.

"No," Mr. Weaver replied.

His wife was less sure. "I don't see it now," she said, "but two years down the road, if everything is still the same, I don't know how I'll feel."

Deciding not to force the issue, Short let them leave his office without setting a timetable for a decision.

Although Short didn't know it, when the Weavers came to his office in March 1972, Larry was at home with a broken arm. Larry wore a full-length cast on his arm for five weeks that spring. His arm was an unintentional casualty in the escalating hostilities between him and his mother. She could not abide his bed-wetting and yelled ceaselessly at him; he responded with long stretches of silence.

Years later, Larry would recall that he broke his arm during a scuffle with his foster mother. Larry said that she erupted one day, as she often did, and snatched his left arm, twisting it behind his back and screaming at him. Larry cried and squirmed, trying to break free. Suddenly, he heard a crack: The bone in his upper left arm snapped.

Subpoenaed years later for Larry's trial, the emergency room report disclosed that he arrived at the hospital with a "twisted and injured left arm." An X ray revealed a "fractured left humerus and moderate soft tissue injury." When Larry's lawyer finally received the medical records after unsuccessfully combing all the hospitals near the Weavers' home, he wondered whether the Weavers had tried to conceal their abusive treatment of Larry. Why else would Mrs. Weaver have taken him to Franklin Square Hospital in Baltimore County, nearly an hour's drive from their home?

When the Weavers visited Short again on August 2, they asked whether the agency would pay for counseling for Larry. If not, they asked, could the agency place him in a state institution where he could get free psychiatric help? The Weavers were convinced he needed professional help. He was almost six and still wet his bed: something had to be seriously wrong with him.

Yet the Weavers didn't want to give up on him. "If he was one of our own children, we would be seeking the same kind of professional help," John Weaver insisted. Since they were *adopting* Larry, however, they felt the state should bear financial responsibility for his therapy.

Mr. Weaver said his income was stable once again, but he told Short he still didn't want to sign the adoption papers until the expense of Larry's counseling was resolved.

Mrs. Weaver added that she had made no progress in breaking through her son's barrier, after two and a half years of trying. "Larry's got a world of his own where he goes and keeps everyone else out," she said. Then she uttered her standard refrain: "He has not become a real part of the family."

After the Weavers left his office, Short dictated a concise evaluation of the dilemma facing his agency:

> If Larry is removed from the Weaver home and placed in another adoptive home, he must view it as

rejection by the Weavers. Such a move will reinforce his failure identity.

If Larry remains in the Weaver home and outside professional care is arranged, the result cannot be assured. Should no change occur and Larry has to be removed at a later date, the reinforcement of his failure identity will be more severe.

In light of the new stability in the Weaver home, and their open and frank evaluation of the problem, I feel the better choice for Larry is for him to remain in the Weaver home; and that professional assistance be arranged, either through full- or part-time institutional care, and a definite time be planned when all concerned will reevaluate the decision.

It was a crap shoot, and Short was playing to win. He believed Larry's best shot, however poor it might be, lay with the Weavers.

His supervisors disagreed. After a conference in early September, the agency decided to regain custody of Larry and move him again. The agency wanted to uproot Larry from the Weavers while he still stood a chance—even if it was a weak chance—of taking root in another home.

Short summoned the Weavers to his office on September 19 and informed them of the agency's decision.

Mr. Weaver opposed it at once. "It sounds as if you're going to give Larry the help we asked for, only in another home," he said bitterly.

Short said the agency's decision was based chiefly on two facts: After nearly three years, Mary Weaver still had not succeeded in bonding with Larry, and the Weavers still declined to sign the adoption papers.

"There will be less trauma for him to move now than later," Short said.

Mr. Weaver repeated his request for professional counseling. "We had serious money problems last year. You know that's why we delayed the adoption."

"That's only part of it," replied Short. "I think if Larry had become *part of the family,* as you keep saying, you would have managed to find the money for counseling."

"What will you do if we refuse to give him up?" Mr. Weaver asked.

Startled, Short replied, "I can't answer such a speculative question. The agency has requested that you return Larry, and you will have to comply. If you don't, well . . . we'll have to take that into consideration."

Although Mrs. Weaver said she couldn't imagine Larry would fare better in another home, she seemed a little relieved by the agency's announcement. "Maybe the agency knows best," she told her husband. "Maybe it would be better for Larry in the long run."

The Weavers promised to think it over and call Short in a few days. When they hadn't phoned two days later, Short called and reached Mrs. Weaver. She announced that she and her husband had decided they were not going to relinquish Larry. Short hung up, frustrated. He turned the case file over to another worker who was assigned to an Anne Arundel County couple that was trying to adopt their first child.

The new worker visited the Weavers two weeks later. She found Larry friendly and talkative. By then, he had started first grade and was attending a special education class, where he had be-friended a retarded boy and told his worker he was acting as his "big brother."

"He seems to be unaware of the problems the family is having," the worker wrote in her first report. "It would appear that he has adjusted to them, but they are having difficulty adjusting to him."

Although they still hadn't done so, the Weavers said they were going to adopt Larry and would hire their own lawyer if the agency wouldn't help them.

Over the next few months, Larry's new worker tried repeatedly to get the Weavers to attend support meetings with a group of other parents who had adopted older children. Each week, the Weavers found an excuse not to attend.

In December, two months shy of Larry's third anniversary at the Weaver home, Mrs. Weaver told his new worker, "Larry still has not become one of the family."

At school, Larry continued stealing food from other children's lunch boxes. At home, he wet his bed. The Weavers rejected Larry's worker's suggestion that they should try a new anti-bed-wetting product from the Eutone Company. It was too expensive, they said.

Mr. Weaver finally arrived—late—one day at a group meeting for adoptive parents. During the discussion, he revealed that his daughters also were showing behavior problems. Yet he resisted the group's suggestion that the entire family should see a counselor. It was too expensive, he said.

Finally, in May 1973, three years and three months after they took Larry in, the Weavers told the agency they had decided to give him up. They announced their decision at an office visit for which they arrived a half hour late. Mr. Weaver excused himself during the meeting, telling the new social worker, "I have to make a business call that will make me a few thousand."

When he returned, he said the reason they could not keep Larry was the high cost of professional counseling. "We just can't afford it," he said.

Both husband and wife said they believed the problem was Larry, not them. "We were a normal family before Larry came," Mr. Weaver insisted.

Mrs. Weaver echoed Larry's last foster mother, who also had been unable to find in her heart the love that Larry sorely needed. "Maybe a family with no other children would be best for Larry," Mrs. Weaver said.

A few weeks later, Larry's worker took him to the agency for play therapy.

Asked by a counselor to draw pictures of his family, Larry at first refused. Then, at the counselor's insistence, he drew his mother. "That's my meany mother," he declared in a stern voice after he finished drawing a stick figure with a blue crayon.

"Why do you call her meany?" the counselor asked.

"Because she's grouchy all the time."

Studying the picture, the counselor said brightly, "Why don't you draw a picture of yourself?"

Switching to a brown crayon, Larry drew another stick figure.

This one had a big round face with an oversized turned down mouth.

The counselor found the picture sad. "Why don't you have a smile?"

"I'm always sad."

"Why?"

"My mother always yells at me."

The counselor noted that Larry consumed an "unusual" amount of food at lunch. After they ate, the counselor took Larry to a park and watched him play easily and happily with other children.

In a brief report dictated just a few weeks before Larry moved in with Bob and Kay Swartz at the end of June, the counselor drew these conclusions: "It seems that Larry responds well to someone who takes an interest in him and is willing to listen and talk with him. Even though I know that a move from the Weaver home will initially be difficult for Larry, I feel that if he is placed in a home with two very concerned and giving parents, he will be able to put the past behind him and adjust quite well."

5.

The story that sprang to life from the adoption records brought tears to Ron Baradel's eyes. He pored over hundreds of pages of caseworkers' notes in his law office, reading each report carefully, repeatedly, hunting for clues to Larry's psychological makeup. He found it unbearable imagining the heartache Larry must have suffered losing mother after mother in his tender years. For Baradel, it was traumatic enough losing one mother at age ten. By that age, Larry was on his sixth mother. Baradel already identified with Larry because of the alienation they both had felt from their fathers. Now that he understood Larry's profound maternal loss, Baradel identified even more strongly with his client.

He culled hundreds of biographical facts from Larry's records and read them into his Dictaphone, under the title "Significant Events and Observations Re: Natural Mother, Father, Boyfriends, Etc."

His secretary wept as she typed the fifteen-page document. When she told Baradel how it had affected her, he was pleased: If Larry's childhood moved his secretary that deeply, it might break a jury's heart.

ELEVEN

January 1984—April 1985

1.

On the evening of April 17, 1985, fifteen months after the Swartz murders, lawyers on both sides of Larry's case finally were ready for trial. Plea negotiations had stalled long ago; the trial would open in the morning. The lawyers were primed for battle over a contested insanity plea. Ten psychiatrists and psychologists had examined Larry, producing a dizzying array of conflicting diagnoses.

The defense team had devised a two-part legal strategy that focused on Larry's life before and with the Swartzes. They intended to portray the murders as a tragic clash between an emotionally scarred, mentally ill youth and overly strict, controlling parents. One defense psychiatrist would testify that Larry's unstable childhood had led to schizophrenia, which impaired his ability to understand and cope with the world. Another would testify that on the night of the murders, Larry experienced what lawyers called temporary insanity: He exploded in sudden fury and killed his parents before he regained any semblance of control. The defense would argue that the triggering event was inconsequential: The true cause lay in Larry's childhood, in the traumas he suffered in his formative years, which rendered him too emotionally fragile to cope with the disciplinary demands and rejection that his parents heaped upon him. Through adoption and foster-care records, as well as testimony from family friends, the defense would tell the pitiful tale of Larry's childhood in foster care, and follow it with the equally pitiful tale of his life with the Swartzes.

Prosecutor Warren Duckett intended to disprove much of that. Yes, Larry suffered from emotional handicaps and a sorrowful childhood. Certainly, his parents were strict. But that didn't justify cold-blooded murder. Duckett would argue that Larry intentionally murdered his parents to retaliate for their harsh discipline. Moreover, the prosecutor would contend that the evidence suggesting that Larry chased his mother through the snow contradicted his claim that he exploded and killed his parents on the spot. Even if his rage did erupt suddenly, Duckett would remind the jury that Larry had time to reconsider and control his actions during the chase.

Ultimately, though, neither side felt comfortable with its strategy.

The defense lawyers privately worried that the insanity plea might hurt their client. An insanity verdict would send Larry to the Clifton T. Perkins Hospital Center, Maryland's hospital for the criminally insane. Almost everyone found not criminally responsible—thus criminally insane—on a felony charge was committed to the maximum-security hospital in Jessup. Larry would remain there until the Perkins doctors deemed him no longer clinically ill or dangerous. On the average, that took two to three years. Then he would be back on the street, perhaps worse off emotionally than before. His lawyers didn't want him to serve life in prison, but they did want him to get treatment for his emotional problems. They doubted he would get effective treatment in an understaffed state mental hospital.

The state's attorney also had grave doubts about the insanity plea. He felt it served neither Larry nor justice. Duckett did not believe Larry was insane, and he planned to fight the plea in court. Yet he also felt more compassion for Larry than for anyone he had prosecuted and he felt uncomfortable portraying him as a cold-blooded murderer. He hated the thought of seeing the gentle, handsome youth convicted of two counts of Murder One and serving two life terms in the "inner circle of hell," as the state attorney general once called the dilapidated Maryland Penitentiary. Duckett knew that could happen if he proved Larry was sane when he killed his parents. He doubted that Larry would ever recover, even if he won parole after twelve years, the earliest time possible.

The prosecutor believed Larry deserved better than that. The defense lawyers did, too. Yet, curiously, neither side made a serious effort to save Larry from that fate until the last possible moment, at the very end of fifteen long months of intricate legal maneuvering.

The maneuvering had begun immediately after Larry's arrest, when both Baradel and Duckett began searching for a motive. Although it was crucial to each side's legal strategy, Larry's motive in killing his parents was elusive. When Larry confessed to Baradel and Joe Murphy on the day of his arrest, he volunteered no motive and no account of the murders; he just admitted his guilt and wept.

Although Duckett suspected that Larry had confessed to his lawyers, he received no confirmation; the confession was covered by attorney-client privilege. It remained confidential by law unless Larry waived the privilege, and he never did. Duckett had no access to anything Larry told his lawyers during trial preparations or to anything the youth told the defense psychiatrists.

Even the defense lawyers operated in the dark at first, confounded by Larry's claim that he couldn't remember details of the murders. His account was sketchy, incomplete, riddled with holes. "I can't remember," he said when Baradel pressed him on things that made no sense. Psychiatrists told his lawyers that he might be repressing portions of that night, unconsciously defending against the horrible knowledge of what he had done. He may have lost touch with reality during the murders. People who enter psychotic states—if only briefly—sometimes have memory lapses similar to those Larry seemed to be having, the psychiatrists said. Or, he may have been lying, perhaps to make the murders seem sudden and uncontrollable rather than deliberate.

Larry's credibility got a boost two weeks after his arrest when Baradel and Murphy returned to Cape St. Claire to look for the clothes that Larry said he had worn on the night of the murders. "I took my clothes and hid them in the woods across the street," Larry told his lawyers. The wet jeans and T-shirt that police found in his washing machine, Larry said, were clothes he'd been washing earlier in the evening. The lawyers were skeptical; the arrest documents said nothing about clothes being found outside. Surely the police would have mentioned it in their reports if they had found clothes outside.

Larry's story sounded screwy to Baradel. "Why did you take your clothes across the street?"

"I don't know. They were on the floor in my bedroom, and I was thinking, I gotta get rid of these, I gotta get rid of these."

Baradel and Murphy doubted that the clothes would still be in the woods two weeks after the murders, if they'd been there at all, but they wasted no time returning to Larry's neighborhood. Accompanied by a private investigator, the defense team went evidence hunting on February 7, 1984.

The clothes were exactly where Larry had said they would be—in a clearing in the middle of a patch of woods directly across the street from his house. It was the same patch that a fireman had motioned toward the morning the bodies were found. He had told Detective Barr, "There's some spots in the snow that look like blood over there."

The defense attorneys were amazed that the cops had missed evidence this significant. Lab tests would be required to confirm that the clothes were bloody, but Murphy immediately realized that the discovery would make the cops look like blockheads when the case went to trial. Missing the murderer's clothes, right under their noses!

The defense team found seven items—four of them clothes—in three separate piles several yards apart. Stiff, encrusted with what looked like blood, the clothing included a pair of yellow satin gym shorts, a pair of white men's briefs, a casual blue shirt, and a gray pullover sweat jacket with BRUINS printed across the back.

Larry told them it was his wrestling sweat shirt, and Baradel wondered whether that was what Annie had meant when she said she saw a guy walking away from the house wearing a gray sweat shirt that said BROADNECK. Had she really meant Bruins? The shirt the cops found in the washing machine said BROAD-NECK & BRUINS, but it was a T-shirt, and the writing was small and on the front. Annie had said the man was walking *away* from her when she saw him. FBI lab tests would reveal that the T-shirt in the washer contained no trace of blood, while lab tests ordered by the defense would identify human blood on the sweat jacket, briefs, and gym shorts.

The private lab that analyzed the items for the defense detected no blood on the casual blue shirt or on the three non-clothing items found with the clothes: a towel, pillowcase, and blue curtain.

Annie told police that her brother had vomited on his pillow that night, and Larry later told a psychiatrist that after he threw up, he took his pillowcase into the woods with his clothes. However, the lab tested everything for vomit and found no trace of it on the pillowcase or anything else found in the woods. Neither did the pillowcase test positive for blood.

Larry told his lawyers he had no recollection of the towel or the curtain and couldn't imagine why they were found with his clothes. He also couldn't explain why his clothing was scattered in three distinct piles.

"Did you make more than one trip into the woods that night?" Baradel asked.

Larry didn't think so; he only remembered going outside once in front of his house to get rid of his clothes. He remembered tossing the maul and the knife in the swamp behind his house, but he said that was earlier in the evening, immediately after the murders, when he dragged his mother's body outside. He only remembered going outside those two times. He conceded, though, that the whole night was a blur.

Baradel wondered whether the alcohol might have had something to do with the blur. Larry said that shortly before the murders, while his parents thought he was studying in his room, he was drinking rum he had hidden in a Pepsi bottle in his dresser.

"Why were you drinking?" Baradel asked. Supposedly, Larry had been studying for exams.

"I didn't want my parents to find the rum. I wanted to get rid of it," Larry claimed.

What an odd time to decide to "get rid of" his rum. "How much did you drink?" Baradel asked.

Holding up his right hand, Larry extended three fingers—maybe a couple of inches of rum.

Baradel repeatedly questioned Larry about the murders, and Larry repeatedly changed minor details and said, "I can't remember." On key points, though, he remained consistent.

On one point, he never wavered: He never chased his mother outside in the snow, and she never ran from the house. He insisted that he killed both his parents inside the house, then dragged his mother's body into the backyard. He said he had no idea who left the mysterious trail of footprints the police found.

Over the course of many interviews with Baradel and various psychiatrists, based on his limited memory of that night, Larry offered the following account of the murders:

After secretly drinking the rum in his room, he went to the basement laundry room to put clothes in the washing machine. As he left the laundry room and passed through the family room, where his mother was watching TV, she called out without looking at him, "How'd your exams go today?"

Larry knew he had failed Spanish and was in danger of failing two more courses. "I think I did pretty well on one, but I think I flunked Spanish," he said he replied.

"Oh, Larry, knowing you, you probably failed them both," he said his mother retorted. "You'll probably fail them all."

Larry had two more exams the next day, including driver's ed, and was furious with his parents for telling him that he couldn't get his driver's license unless he passed all his courses. As he stood a few feet behind the black Naugahyde chair where his mother sat with her back to him, Larry said he suddenly noticed the maul.

In one confession, he said it was on the floor by the sliding glass door; in another version, it was by the hearth. His lawyers considered it a normal function of memory to change such small details.

Larry told a state psychiatrist at the Perkins hospital, where he was sent for a psychiatric evaluation, that his mother's retort infuriated him. "She was very sarcastic," Larry said. "I was very mad at her sarcasm."

"There was a wood-splitting maul there," he told the same doctor. "She was sitting and watching TV with her blue pajamas on. I got the maul, hit her right in the back of her head, and dropped the maul. She was still sitting there. There was a little table in front of the TV with some silverware and a steak knife on it. She was breathing sharply; I could hear that real loud. I did not care anymore about anything in the world. I picked up the steak knife, stabbed her and got her around the neck. When I saw her blood, I felt, like, good in a sense, because I finally did something about them yelling at me. I did not feel good, because I don't like blood. I had blood on my hands—not much. I started growling like a dog.

"Then I saw my father standing there. He was in his computer room in the basement. He was stunned. I was standing right in front of him with the knife in my right hand. I stabbed him in the left chest around his heart. He screamed and fell back to his room and shut the door. I pushed the door open. He was still standing up. I stabbed him again twice and shut the door. Then I came to my mind and said, 'Oh, God! Oh, God!' about twenty times. Then I thought I wanted to get rid of everything, not to be caught. I took my mother's wrist, dragged her out of the room into the snow, took her clothes off because I wanted to get rid of fingerprints on her clothes.

"I bent over and fingered her twice. I was ready to throw up. I backed up, picked up the maul in one hand and the knife in the other hand. It was a revenge feeling. I took the knife and maul and threw them away in the swampy area.

"Then I thought about Anne, my sister. If she wasn't there, there was no reason in the world to go back to that house. I passed my mother's body. I went in and took off my shirt and shorts. Anne was there and told me she heard a scream. I told her she had been dreaming, and she went back to my bed and slept there.

"I couldn't sleep that night. I wished everything was a dream, but I knew it wasn't. I threw up once on the pillow, then I went to the bathroom and took off my shirt and shorts, and I went to get rid of them."

The state psychiatrist who heard Larry's confession found one grim detail especially puzzling: Why would the youth put his finger inside his mother after he killed her?

Larry didn't have much of an explanation. "I was so mad that I felt I had to do something *real bad* to her," he told the doctor.

Although Larry's memory was fuzzy about where he saw the maul, and he couldn't clearly remember actually walking over to pick it up, he recalled seeing the maul and only the maul, very vividly. The defense psychiatrists said that sounded like tunnel vision, a symptom sometimes associated with psychosis. The next visual memory he had was seeing the maul come down in slow motion on his mother's head.

"He then remembered," Baradel later said, "what he thought was extremely loud breathing by his mother—which I think was not the case—but almost like a roar, and then seeing the knife on the table and being afraid that his mother's loud breathing would wake up Annie. He didn't want Annie to see this, so he had to stop the noise, which is when he started stabbing. He also remembered hearing his father yelling for help. It sounded very distant and far away, and the psychiatrists said, 'There you go.' The breathing of the mother—if she was breathing at all—was probably very shallow, but it sounded like a roar in the head, and the father was probably screaming his head off, but it sounded very faint and distant. All the stab wounds to the mother, by the way, were in her throat. None of them went through the garment. It lends credence to what he said, that he was trying to stop this breathing, this noise. That was, at the time, his sole purpose in stabbing her.

"He told me he saw the maul, went over, hit her in the head, heard the loud breathing. At that point he sees himself like he's on the ceiling, watching a TV program or something. His body was working very quickly; his mind was working very slowly. He would see himself stab her in the throat. His mind would somehow say, God, you've got to stop that! but by the time that thought had formed, he could see himself stabbing her again. He described it to me as, 'My mind never caught up to my body.'

Again, he was viewing himself, seeing the whole scene from somewhere up on the ceiling, or up on the corner of the wall, which again, the psychiatrists tell us, is evidence of psychotic reaction.

"Then he turned around and sensed that his father was there, or somebody was there, and he saw his father standing on the landing with what he called a blank look—as if not comprehending anything. He heard himself, or heard a growl like a wolf or a dog or whatever, and realized it was himself. I think he remembered stabbing his mother once or twice, and stabbing his father maybe two or three times.

"He sensed himself, like taking one giant step, and his father falling back into the computer room, and Larry slammed the door shut. He recalls his father trying to shut the door, and Larry just brushing him aside. Larry slammed the door shut. I think his father was obviously trying to slam the door shut because he'd just been stabbed.

"Larry told me it was like the door wasn't even there: 'I just flicked it.' Again, the psychiatrists and doctors said, 'We have no doubt that's true.' This kid was so pumped up, he probably had superhuman strength at that point because of the adrenaline. He remembers going in and stabbing him again, and his father falling back, and Larry shutting the door.

"He is now standing on the landing. He turns around and looks at his mother. He's got the knife in his hand, and at that point, he said, it started clicking back in. And all he can remember is, 'I must have said it a thousand times, *Oh, my God! Oh, my God! Oh, my God!*'

"Somewhere along the line, he got the idea he had to get rid of everything. His mother was the first thing, so he went to drag her outside.

"There were little things he would say to me that just rang so true. I said, 'What were you thinking?' He said, 'I wasn't thinking, I was doing. I wasn't standing there, planning, This is my next move. I mean, just impulses were coming to me. Thoughts were coming into my mind. Bing—and then another thought would come into my mind: Drag her outside. This is stupid. Then thinking, There are gonna be fingerprints on the sleeper. I gotta take the sleeper off. Naw, that's stupid, and throwing that down.'

"Now I can see that happening. It wasn't like he was going through saying, 'Oh, now I gotta do this, now I gotta do that.' The thoughts he relays don't make any sense, and he admits they don't make sense. That's just what was happening."

Larry's bizarre confession, combined with his memory gaps, persuaded Baradel that he must have had a psychotic reaction during the murders, even though he appeared to regain contact with reality immediately afterward. Some of the ghastly details suggested that he had lost all mental control: swinging the maul over his mother's head, stabbing her neck to stop a noise, stripping her, violating her outside in the snow—they were all telling details, details that Baradel thought might help to convince a jury that Larry was in the throes of a psychosis.

When Duckett received the report from the state doctors at the Perkins hospital, he heaved a sigh of relief. Although he had never really doubted Larry's guilt, he had been sweating his ability to prove it.

Duckett had feared Larry might take the witness stand and try to explain away the circumstantial evidence: "Yes, sir, that was my bloody handprint. I got blood on my hands when I saw my father's body and bent down and touched him. Then I went outside and saw my mother and must have gone into shock." Would that sound so unreasonable to a jury? They wouldn't have to *believe* it, just acknowledge that it *could* have happened that way, that it was a reasonable hypothesis. And how would the prosecutor refute it? "If you examined both your parents' bodies as you claim, Mr. Swartz, then why didn't you say so sooner? Why did you tell police that you didn't know where your father was, and that you *never went downstairs?*"

"I had no idea what I was doing or saying. It was all so shocking," Larry might say. And where would Duckett be? The only evidence that linked Larry to the murders was found inside his own house. The maul had been wiped clean of fingerprints, and no one found the knife. All Duckett really had was proof that Larry had walked in blood and touched things with blood-stained hands in his own house.

The moment Larry opened his mouth at Perkins, however, he banished that nightmarish scenario from the prosecutor's mind.

Duckett couldn't use Larry's confession to the state psychiatrists to establish his guilt in court; that confession was confidential except for the portions dealing with Larry's mental state. The prosecutor could question the state doctors only about Larry's sanity, not his guilt. Yet Duckett viewed the Perkins confession as his guarantee that Larry wouldn't lie in court, because if Larry tried to tell a jury a different story from the one he told the doctors, the rules of evidence would allow Duckett to impeach him with the confession.

While Larry's story eased one headache for the prosecutor, it created new tension elsewhere, for his version of the murders would make the chase more difficult to prove. Larry had to testify to plead insanity effectively, and he surely would tell this spur-of-the-moment tale of whacking his mother over the head, then spinning around and stabbing his father. Duckett thought Larry's tale made more sense than the detectives' bizarre theory; and it could make a difference in the outcome of the trial. If jurors believed Larry's story, they might be less likely to find that his actions were premeditated and deliberate. Given Larry's and the detectives' versions, Duckett doubted that a jury would believe Larry chased his mother around the neighborhood.

Still, the prosecutor had to stand by his investigators. He couldn't ignore the peculiar trail of bare and stockinged footprints they had found. What were the odds of anyone besides Mrs. Swartz walking around in the snow that night with a bare left foot and a sock on the right foot?

In addition, the medical examiner had concluded that Mrs. Swartz was struck on the head with the maul in the backyard where her body was found—not inside the house as Larry claimed. The large pool of blood outside was consistent with her massive head wound, Dr. Thomas Smith told police. The lesser volume of blood on the chair and carpet inside, along with the lack of blood splatters anywhere around the chair, were consistent with the stab wounds in her neck, Smith said.

Detective Barr repeatedly reminded Duckett of these findings. Barr found the lack of blood on the carpet between the chair and sliding glass door particularly revealing: If Larry had dragged his mother over to the door after he cracked her head open, as he claimed, wouldn't he have left a trail of blood? The carpet was clean, except for a few thin streaks by the doorway. So how could Larry's story be true if Mrs. Swartz was killed *outside?* Although it seemed plausible on the surface, Barr contended that Larry's version of the murders had to be false.

Whether he liked it or not, Duckett reluctantly acknowledged that he would have to contest Larry's story at trial. It would confuse the jury, but Duckett couldn't dodge puzzles and contradictions. He had to present the evidence as he found it, argue that it refuted Larry's story, then admit that he wasn't sure what really happened. He would present alternate theories, including the chase, then let jurors make up their own minds about what took place at 1242 Mount Pleasant Drive.

Even though Barr felt the most important investigative work already was done, he continued to plug away on the Swartz murders as a sideline after Larry's arrest. Duckett got Barr reassigned to work full-time in his office on special projects shortly after the murders, and the detective spent the next four months working for Duckett chiefly on white-collar cases. During that time, Barr thought a lot about Larry and his home life, which the detective suspected had resembled his own. It bothered him. He considered himself to be a hard-nosed cop, yet he commiserated with the sequestered life neighbors said Larry had led, never allowed to venture out for ordinary teenage activities. Embittered by his own childhood, Barr felt Larry deserved a break; it seemed the kid had never had one in his sad young life.

The cop in Barr, however, was driven to bring Larry to justice. To do that, Barr felt he needed more evidence to bolster his circumstantial case. He particularly wanted a confession, one that he and Duckett could use in court, one that would rule out any possibility that Larry could proclaim his innocence. He also wanted a confession in which Larry told the *truth:* that he chased his mother through the snow, walked or dragged her back to their yard, then killed her. Barr figured he'd get his confession if he was patient. Sooner or later, Larry would talk: Most murderers did.

Hoping that he had talked already, Barr went to the detention center one day in the spring of 1984 and asked for a list of his cellmates, then called them one by one into a private room. To his disappointment, no one said Larry had confessed.

Still, several inmates offered information that struck Barr as incriminating. The biggest snitch turned out to be Larry's supposed friend John Kemmer, who seemed eager to ingratiate himself with the authorities. Like most inmates, Kemmer knew the best way to hack time off his sentence was to trade information for leniency. The trouble was, Kemmer didn't know anything—yet.

Kemmer said he believed Larry was guilty. "We're fairly close. We share a cell with two other guys. I think Larry has wanted to confess to me several times, but I always tell him not to say anything to me about the murders."

Sure you do, Barr thought. Larry hadn't loosened up yet, but Barr was confident he would. After Barr stirred things up and let inmates know he was interested, he backed off. He would let things settle down, then return to the detention center immediately before the trial. If Larry mouthed off, Barr would learn about it at the last minute, giving the defense little or no time to respond.

"We're in an ax fight, without an ax!" Joe Murphy groaned.

Baradel agreed. Duckett's first round of evidential disclosures looked pretty damning: Larry's bloody fingerprints were found inside his house. His bloody Docksides, caked in mud, were lying in plain view in the basement. The maul—with loose hair still attached—was recovered in the woods behind his house. Although purely circumstantial, the evidence was so overwhelming that the defense lawyers knew they could never refute it. Throw in the bare footprint trail, which supported the cops' nightmarish chase theory, and the lawyers feared Duckett might be able to erase reasonable doubt on count one of Larry's two-count indictment:

COUNT ONE
MURDER

THE GRAND JURY charges that the aforesaid defendant, on or about the aforesaid date, feloniously, willfully, and of deliberately premeditated malice aforethought did kill and murder Kathryn Ann Swartz.

If Duckett could prove that Larry chased his injured mother through the snow before he killed her, then, Baradel believed, a jury surely would convict him of Murder One. Maryland, like most states, required proof that a murder was deliberate and premeditated for a first-degree conviction. Chasing someone a mile through the snow should give anyone plenty of time to think about what they were doing, Baradel thought.

If Duckett prevailed on the first count, Baradel figured it wouldn't matter what the jury decided on the second count, which alleged that Larry killed his father with the same premeditated malice. Murder One automatically would mean a life sentence for Larry, with no possibility of parole for at least twelve years.

Unlike Baradel, Murphy wasn't convinced that the chase evidence would persuade a jury that Larry's actions were deliberate and premeditated. Even if Larry was lying or repressing the memory, and a chase really did occur, Murphy thought it suggested such bizarre behavior that he could turn it around. Ladies and gentlemen of the jury, he could say, I submit to you that this level of unusual behavior is equally consistent with insanity.

Murphy and Baradel were hoping for a diagnosis of psychosis, but they couldn't bank on it. Larry had no history of psychiatric problems and outwardly appeared quite normal. That didn't mean he was normal, but it might make it harder to prove that he *wasn't.*

In addition, Larry couldn't recall a single grievous transgression of his parents, something extraordinary that had provoked his rage and would have created legal grounds to mitigate his crime down to manslaughter. Classic mitigation—a hot-blooded response to reasonable and adequate provocation—clearly was missing.

It would be one thing if Larry claimed his parents had beaten or molested him, but he insisted they had done neither. He claimed he couldn't recall telling his lawyers on the day he first confessed, "He wouldn't stop hitting me!" He said he had no idea what he might have meant. He claimed an explosion went off in his head when his mother made the cutting remark about his exams, and he killed both parents on impulse. His father had yelled at him earlier in the evening about messing up a floppy computer disk, but Larry downplayed the incident, insisting, "It was no big deal." That left nothing but his mother's remark as grounds for provocation, and Murphy knew he could never argue that insulting one's kid over his schoolwork was legally adequate provocation. Mere words, no matter how insulting, were insufficient to reduce murder to manslaughter. On the whole, Larry's confession offered little explanation for the murders. The defense lawyers could only hope that the psychiatrists would coax more out of him.

Murphy knew right away that Larry's motivation would offer the key to his punishment. The trivial provocation, combined with his incredibly brutal response, hinted strongly at mental imbalance. Murphy viewed some kind of diminished mental capacity as a likely defense. The defense team probably would argue that something—a mental disease or defect, perhaps aggravated by the rum—had impaired Larry's ability to form the intent required by law to convict him of murder.

A plea of not guilty by reason of insanity seemed an even better bet. If it succeeded, Larry would go to Perkins, where he might be freed within a matter of a few years—or even sooner—depending on how the hospital psychiatrists viewed his mental state. While Baradel did not want Larry to go unpunished, and he certainly did not want the youth's emotional problems to go untreated, neither did he want Larry to spend decades confined to the state penitentiary. Baradel agreed to pursue the insanity defense with the proviso that if they prevailed, and Larry was released quickly, he would help the youth get private psychiatric treatment the moment he was free.

The defense lawyers decided to shop for shrinks. Murphy knew one forensic psychiatrist who often testified on behalf of criminal defendants: Dr. John M. Henderson, whose bailiwick was schizophrenia. Murphy arranged for Larry to see Henderson and Dr. Spodak, the psychiatrist who had examined Larry the day he was arrested. Spodak wanted to give Larry a battery of tests before rendering an opinion on his mental condition. Under court order, Larry was taken under guard to see the psychiatrists.

While the doctors tested and interviewed him, Murphy and

Baradel considered fallback strategies, legal arguments that might reduce the level of criminal conduct to manslaughter if the jury didn't buy insanity.

The lawyers knew the lone insult from Larry's mother wouldn't do it, but what about repeated insults? What about cruel or abusive treatment over many years? Murphy and Baradel speculated that Larry had experienced long-term harsh treatment at home. They knew that some courts had accepted "cumulative provocation" as an adequate defense in battered-wife cases. In such cases the final provoking incident was trivial, or even absent: The true provocation had occurred over a long period before. Could they apply that theory here?

The defense would be intriguing yet tricky, for it would require extensive research, and it would mean putting Bob and Kay Swartz on trial—something Murphy was extremely reluctant to do. They also might have difficulty citing the traumas Larry suffered before the Swartzes adopted him. "You can't be provoked against your parents by something that happened before you even met them," Murphy said.

Baradel wasn't so sure; he thought the issue merited further study as they explored alternate strategies.

Next, they pursued the hint of brain damage in Larry's childhood medical records. Two defense psychologists said that some of his test responses were commonly seen in persons suffering from epilepsy or other brain "dysrhythmias," irregular patterns of brain activity. Yet his lawyers found no solid evidence of brain damage. His electroencephalogram was within normal limits, revealing no abnormalities in the electrical patterns of his brain. An expert in organic brain syndrome found nothing significant in Larry's responses to a series of neurological or "biological intelligence" tests. The expert, Dr. Dennis J. Madden, a professor at the Institute of Psychiatry and Human Behavior at the University of Maryland School of Medicine, said Larry was functioning within the average range of intelligence. Any impairment in his neuropsychological functioning was too slight to indicate organic brain damage, Dr. Madden concluded.

Dungeons & Dragons was another blind alley. People all over the country had blamed the fantasy game for inciting real-world violence, and the National Coalition on Television Violence had linked more than fifty teenage deaths to the game. Larry's lawyers wondered, could D&D have played a role in these murders? Larry said he played a computer version of the game with his friends. He also said he had argued with his father about the computer on the night of the murders. Even though he insisted the argument was "no big deal," Murphy and Baradel wondered whether he was holding back. Had he played D&D on the night of the murders? The game might be significant if Larry's psychiatrists found that he suffered from schizophrenia, a mental illness that could make it hard for someone to determine where the playing ended and illusion began.

Ultimately, Baradel dismissed the game. Although Larry had played it, he denied that it had anything to do with the murders, and Baradel found no one who was willing or able to contradict him.

The defense suffered a temporary setback on July 27, 1984, when Joe Murphy won an appointment to the circuit court bench.

To discuss his departure from the case, Murphy met Baradel for dinner at Sabatino's, in Baltimore's Little Italy, in early August.

"Who am I going to find to replace you?" Baradel asked glumly, looking across the table at the owlish lawyer. Baradel had counted heavily on Murphy's trial experience and expertise in criminal law. He was pleased for his new friend but crushed to lose him.

Pulling a pen from his jacket pocket, Murphy reached across the red tablecloth, grabbed a cocktail napkin, unfolded it, and scribbled the names of nine criminal defense lawyers. "Any one of these guys could help you," he said. "They're all capable."

Baradel scanned the names without recognizing any of them. "Who do you recommend? Can you give me some priorities?"

"There are nine lawyers there," Murphy replied. "Rich Karceski is Number One. All the rest are Number Two."

Baradel nodded. He had never heard of Rich Karceski, but if Murphy said he was the best, that was good enough for him. "Are you going to call him, or should I?" asked Baradel.

"I'll take care of it."

True to his word, Murphy brought Richard M. Karceski when he met Baradel again for dinner a week later at Dici Naz Velleggia's Italian Restaurant in Towson.

After the introductions, Baradel studied his soon-to-be-partner. Karceski was a somber man with a large build and a sharp booming voice. He wore beige-rimmed glasses over close-set colorless eyes. His thick brown hair hung in a boyish Beatle mop, and his full face looked younger than his thirty-nine years. He spoke and carried himself with considerable poise.

Baradel leaned forward and smiled. "Are you sure you want to get involved in this case? The only thing I can assure you is that you're not going to make any money."

"What the hell," Karceski said, laughing. "There are a lot of cases I never got paid for. Why shouldn't this be one of them?"

Why not, indeed? Although no pot of gold awaited him at the end of this trial, Karceski knew that many criminal defense lawyers would gladly line up to defend Larry Swartz. The case was generating extraordinary publicity, the kind that made lawyers' reputations and offered rare legal challenges. Barely a month away from his fortieth birthday, Karceski was hungry for both. After practicing criminal law for a decade, he only recently had begun to feel that he was achieving the kind of success he deserved. He had defended more than two dozen accused murderers and hundreds of other accused criminals, with mixed results. Yet for reasons he never understood, he had attracted few of the sensational cases that put lawyers on television and front pages.

His biggest break came in 1983 when he won an acquittal for one of three men charged with the contract murders of John and Donna Carback. It was the same drug-related case in Anne Arundel County that came to Barr's mind the morning he went to the Swartz house. While Karceski's client had been acquitted in one courtroom, another defendant, represented by a different lawyer, had been convicted of first-degree murder in a separate trial conducted down the hall. A third defendant was convicted later. Although Duckett handled none of the Carback trials, he sent his top deputies and was not happy when Karceski beat one of them. It especially rankled Duckett that the man Karceski defended had been accused of pulling the trigger.

A native Baltimorean, Karceski attended the University of Baltimore School of Law and had much in common with Murphy and Baradel. All three defense lawyers were within a year of each other in age, all were reared in Catholic families, and all were practicing Catholics. As children, all had absent fathers: Murphy's had died, Baradel's was uncommunicative, and Karceski's was a corporate buyer who traveled nationwide. All three men now had young children of their own and placed their families at the top of their priority lists. In his own way, each found himself deeply moved by Larry Swartz's sorrowful childhood. Although Karceski didn't know Baradel, he and Murphy had become friends more than a decade earlier when they were assistant state's attorneys in Baltimore. Over the years, they had developed strong respect for each other's legal abilities and become close friends. When Murphy went on the bench, Karceski was a natural to inherit the Swartz case, the most celebrated case left in Murphy's portfolio.

Karceski not only appreciated the opportunity to help his friend, he relished the prospect of trying an insanity case. Karceski had taken only one insanity case all the way to a jury verdict before. His client, an accused rapist, had been declared insane. Karceski knew most insanity cases never reached juries. Only one percent of the seventeen thousand defendants charged with felonies each year in Maryland pleaded insanity, and only one in five of those typically prevailed. Most of those who did prevail were uncontested by the state; when state doctors found a defendant insane, prosecutors usually agreed to have the defendant committed to the Perkins hospital. If the state and defense experts disagreed, the defense attorneys often tried to negotiate a plea bargain, for they knew it was tough to win a contested insanity plea. The Swartz case was the first Karceski had seen in ages where the shrinks were in a true deadlock.

When they met for dinner, Baradel brought a fat stack of binders containing his research on the murders, all neatly indexed, and gave them to Karceski to read. As they ate, Murphy and Baradel reviewed the evidence against Larry and everything he had told them about the murders. Karceski immediately saw the conflict between the state's case and Larry's story. "I'm going to have to talk to this kid myself," he told Baradel. "I need to know if he's bullshitting or telling the truth."

The next week, Karceski drove to Annapolis to interview his new client. The guards ushered him into one of the small attorney's booths where lawyers talked to prisoners over telephones. Larry entered the booth on the other side of the large bulletproof window.

After Larry related his story, Karceski questioned him sharply. Larry seemed so nonchalant and unresponsive that the lawyer at first thought he was lying. Karceski figured the cops were right: Larry had chased his mother around the neighborhood, then made up the story about impulsively grabbing the maul to make everyone think he acted spontaneously. His spare tale of two impulsive killings didn't ring true. He couldn't explain any of the contradictory evidence, and he barely made the effort to answer the lawyer's questions.

"The police found a trail of footprints that appear to be one bare foot and one with a sock on," Karceski said. "How do you explain that?"

"I dunno," Larry replied. "All I can tell you is, I didn't take my mother anywhere. It didn't happen that way."

"Were you barefoot when you went outside to throw away the knife and the maul?"

"I dunno. I can't recall."

Karceski continued to grill Larry, and continued to get monosyllabic replies. "Look," the lawyer finally said, "I think it's my obligation to tell you that I've reviewed these police reports, and I've talked to you, and frankly I just don't believe what you're telling me. I think you're lying."

Maybe a direct approach would rile Larry, shake loose the truth. Karceski didn't know what else to do.

Larry didn't blink. "Well, what I've given you is the answer." He looked at Karceski with a blank expression.

Was that it? This kid had just been called a liar and wasn't even offended? Karceski was stunned. Most clients would shout or at least move around in their seats. They'd holler about how their lives were on the line, how their lawyer had to believe them. How could Larry just sit there?

Slowly, Karceski's impression began to change. Maybe Larry wasn't lying. Maybe he truly had blanked out what had happened. Maybe the sketchy details he related were memory remnants of a rage that had exploded without warning, a rage so intense that it might have robbed him, at least temporarily, of his sanity.

In the months that followed, Karceski interviewed Larry several more times and concluded, as Baradel had, that he was telling the truth. The murders either occurred the way he said they did or the memory of what happened was locked away in his mind.

Karceski and Baradel repeatedly questioned Larry about the trail of bare footprints—evidence the lawyers knew could be damaging at trial unless they met it head-on. Each time they questioned Larry, he claimed no knowledge of the tracks. He claimed he couldn't remember what he wore on his feet when he ran out to hide the evidence. However, he did recall two fragments of information that Baradel believed might help refute the cops' chase theory.

"When I came back on the carport, my feet were burning," Larry said. "And the next day, I found a gash on the bottom of my foot. I had no idea where it came from."

"When did you notice the gash?"

"When I was at the police station. I felt this numbness on my toe. I took my sock off and there was a deep gash in my toe. I couldn't remember cutting it."

Baradel found both facts significant. When he got the cut, Larry was probably barefoot; and he didn't remember getting the cut, so he probably was repressing the memory of being outside, Baradel thought.

Given everything else the youth had confessed to—including sexually violating his mother—why would he lie about the chase? Was he smart enough to understand that chasing his mother through the snow could make the difference between first- and second-degree murder? Baradel seriously doubted that.

"What size shoe do you wear?" Baradel asked.

"Nine, usually," Larry said.

Baradel made a mental note to see whether Larry's shoe size matched the bare footprints.

Comparing Larry's foot with his mother's and the bare tracks in the snow would prove difficult, however. Coincidentally, there was barely a half-inch difference in length between Larry's feet and his mother's. Also, the precise length of a footprint in snow can vary that much or more, depending on a person's gait and snow conditions.

The detectives, after conferring with the medical examiner, remained convinced that the snow tracks were Mrs. Swartz's. To them, the most telling detail was that the right footprints were less distinct than the left, suggesting she had worn a sock on her right foot—as Mrs. Swartz was found.

Baradel, on the other hand, grew equally convinced that the bare footprints were Larry's, based on the autopsy photographs. He noticed that the second toe on Kay Swartz's left foot was longer than her big toe, and he didn't see that longer toe in the police photographs of the snow tracks. Baradel also noticed the autopsy report made no mention of any cuts or abrasions to Kay's feet. He wondered, Wouldn't she have cut or scraped her bare left foot if she ran through the woods?

Baradel and Karceski relished the thought of ridiculing the chase theory at trial. It was inconceivable to them that Larry could have stabbed his mother in the neck seven times, stripped off her nightclothes, then chased her around the block. If neighbors heard dogs barking, wouldn't they have heard her screams? And wouldn't a strong, athletic youth like Larry have caught his injured, bleeding mother before she ran more than *half a mile?*

They were convinced that no jury would buy the chase theory.

2.

Larry tore open the envelope, one of hundreds delivered to him at the detention center, and read:

Dear Larry,

I am a 30-year-old mother living in the Annapolis area. I am divorced and work to support me and my child, who is four years old. . . .

Based on what she had read and heard about Larry, the woman said she believed she had "a common bond" with him that he would understand only "as time goes on." After a few vague references to her background, she closed mysteriously, "A Concerned Friend." She gave no name or return address and said that if Larry cared to write back, he should send his letter to Mrs. Smithmyer, who would serve as a go-between. The author had her reasons for remaining anonymous, which she could not reveal.

Larry wrote back, "Thanks for writing."

Larry and the mystery woman soon were engaged in active correspondence, with Larry sending his letters to Mrs. Smithmyer, who forwarded them to his new pen pal. The woman hinted again and again about how alike she and Larry were, yet never explained how. It stumped Larry. Had this woman murdered her parents? His curiosity grew stronger with each letter, all of which bore the same signature: "A Concerned Friend."

Eventually, the woman wrote that it was time for them to talk. She included her phone number in a letter. "Call me," it said.

He did, and found her so charming on the phone that he couldn't wait to meet her in person. She identified herself as Christine Monroe and spoke with a deep southern accent. She told him about her office job with a large corporation, her daughter, and her marriage, which had ended in divorce. Larry talked about his life in jail, the trouble he was having sleeping, his hunger for Dungeons & Dragons books. He pestered Christine about her background. How were the two of them alike?

But Christine was as sly and evasive on the phone as she was in her letters. "When I meet you, I'll tell you," she said. "But I have to see you face to face; I can't tell you on the phone."

He asked her to come to the jail. She said she would eventually but that she wasn't ready yet. When the time was right, she would let him know.

"All right," he said quietly, never guessing what a good friend and source of comfort she would become.

As letters and visitors continued to pour in to the jail, Larry settled into his dreary quarters. He killed time playing chess with other inmates and thumbing through porno magazines that inmates left lying around. Using money provided by Baradel and the Smithmyers, he bought potato chips, toothpaste, and other supplies in the prison store. At four-thirty nearly every after-noon, he switched on the TV to watch "He-Man and Masters of the Universe," a cartoon that featured a brawny space-age hero.

One morning Larry awoke shortly before 5 A.M., to hear a guard hollering at Dean Prince, a cellmate of Larry's, to get his ass off the bunk. Prince was a tier-runner who rose at four-thirty to sweep the concrete floor and deliver breakfast to the inmates. He had overslept, and the guard was roaring at him.

As Prince pulled on his clothes, Larry leaned over and said calmly to John Kemmer, "That's the same damn way my father used to yell at me. My father was a real bastard."

When Larry's curly hair looked shaggy, Kemmer cut it. A born-again Christian, Kemmer earned extra money in jail as a trusty, working for the jail chaplain. He tried to get Larry to attend religious services and Bible study, but after one or two sessions, Larry told Kemmer he didn't want to go again. He'd had enough of organized religion.

Annie couldn't visit because jail policy prohibited children, but Larry spoke to her on the phone when he called the Smithmyers, and he talked about her so much that Kemmer be-gan to wonder whether Larry was more concerned about his sister's welfare than his own. Larry talked about Michael a lot, too. He said Michael had a big-league drug problem, mainly with acid.

Michael had turned eighteen on March 3, 1984, six weeks after the murders. By then, he had been released from the Crownsville Hospital Center and was living in another group home in Anne Arundel County. On his eighteenth birthday, the state lost its commitment power over him; he was free to come and go as he pleased. Because he was not deemed fully capable of supporting himself, however, the state continued to provide caseworker supervision and shelter in a group home. Two weeks after his birthday, Michael visited Larry in jail twice. It was the first time they had seen each other since the funeral. Michael didn't return to the jail for six months.

The Sunday after Easter, Christine Monroe finally worked up enough nerve to meet Larry. Eileen Smithmyer accompanied her to the detention center, but Christine entered the visitors' room alone. Prison rules allowed Christine and Larry only twenty minutes to get acquainted, without much privacy. They stood beside other people and spoke over a telephone, looking at each other through a tiny glass window. On their side of the barrier, inmates stood four to a room and could hear what the others said.

Christine recognized Larry at once from his photographs. He looked even more handsome in person, and she felt attracted to him right away. With one hand leaning against the divider, he cocked his head as she approached. His dark brown eyes locked on hers for an instant and darted away.

"So, you're Christine," he said.

"Yeah, I am," she said, drawling the *I* into an Ahh.

Larry was stunned at how different she was from what he had expected. He could hardly believe she was thirty, thirteen years older than he. She didn't look any older than the girls Larry had liked at school and she was far better looking. At five feet six, Christine was a knockout. She had lively blue eyes surrounded by dramatic blue eyeliner, and strong high cheekbones. Beautiful brown curls bounced down to her shoulders. Her drawling speech and warm, direct gaze were incredibly appealing. Larry could hardly believe this woman was visiting *him.*

He clearly wasn't going to start the conversation, so Christine, devoid of shyness, said, "I don't have long, so I'm going to have to make do with the amount of time I've been given. I don't want to beat around the bush anymore. I want you to know why I got in contact with you in the first place."

Fascinated, Larry looked at her in snatches, never letting his eyes linger on hers for more than a few seconds. She noticed that he kept his head down and angled slightly left, like a cowering puppy. She felt sorry for him, for she, too, had felt whipped as a teenager. At seventeen—Larry's age now—she had come within a few seconds of shooting her father.

"You don't have to say anything," she told him. "All I want you to do is listen. If you want to comment later, go ahead; but I just want you to know about me for your own knowledge."

Christine told her life story in a long run-on narrative, trying to cram as much as she could into the twenty minutes she'd been allotted.

Like Larry, Christine lost her mother before she was two years old. She was the first and only child born to a young couple in a small town in rural Mississippi. Married before they turned twenty, the couple divorced after only a few years, and Christine went to live with her father. How her father gained custody of her would be a mystery to Christine until she grew up and became reacquainted with her mother. Her mother explained that her father had wanted Christine so he could avoid the draft. He was so desperate that he threatened to beat his young wife unless she gave him custody of Christine.

By the time Christine heard the story, she could well imagine how fear of Henry Monroe might have driven a woman to surrender her child. The son of a prominent businessman, Monroe was a six-footer with bright blue eyes and broad shoulders. When he worked, he managed his father's business in the center of town. Several years after his divorce, he remarried a teenager named Jackie. By the time Christine started school, her father and stepmother were fighting constantly. Christine felt closer to her father than to her stepmother, who was only fourteen years older than she.

When she reached the third grade, Daddy got too close to Christine. He liked to give her baths, and one day he slipped his hand between her legs, pushing with his fingers. She squirmed, trying to pull away from him and wondering what he was doing. When she stared at him wide-eyed, he stopped and pretended nothing had happened. He repeated his little game several times, without explanation. Each time, she squirmed and got upset. Each time, he acted as though nothing had happened.

He had an arbitrary temper and whipped Christine over stupid things. "Go get me a hammer," he'd say. Maybe she wouldn't hear the last word—Daddy always mumbled—so she'd say, "Go get what?" and he would pull off his belt and whip her legs until they bled.

He imposed bizarre punishments, too. When she trampled the dandelions in the front yard, he yelled from the front porch, "I told you to stay off the grass! I don't want you on the dandelions! Get back up here!" As she walked up the steps, he continued shouting like a lunatic: When she walked on the dandelions, she spilled the "fuzzies" and spread weeds all over his lawn. He had told her that a hundred times. "Go inside and get the scissors," he hollered. When she brought them out, he made her sit in the grass and cut hundreds of dandelions. He kept her there until nightfall.

When Christine was in the fourth grade, her father went into her bedroom one night and raped her. It happened so fast she didn't have time to think. When she resisted, he forced himself on her. Christine couldn't understand why her stepmother didn't come in and stop him; there was no way Jackie could not hear her cries. By the end, Christine was screaming. Jackie finally summoned the courage to come in, but by then it was too late. "Henry, what in the world are you doing?" Jackie shrieked.

Henry got up calmly and went into his room. Christine could hear them yelling through the wall. She lay perfectly still, crying softly.

When Christine went to school the next day, she felt old and dirty. She felt like a different person, as apart from those around her as if she were in a bubble. Her father hadn't said a word to her at breakfast; neither had Jackie. She had felt pain and she had bled. She thought her parents would take her to a doctor, but they just ignored the episode.

That was the beginning of a long-running nightmare that stretched on and on until Christine began menstruating at age fourteen. Then her father finally decided he didn't want to get her pregnant, so he stopped having intercourse with her. Although his assaults halted, he did not leave her alone. Sometimes he led her into his bedroom and showed her pornographic movies on the screen he kept in there. Once he brought her in and made her watch while he and Jackie had sex.

Her father seemed to get more violent every year. He beat Jackie, he beat Christine, he even beat his dog and locked him in the spare bedroom for months. A germ freak, he washed his hands many times a day and made Christine wash hers after she touched anything that he thought carried germs, which seemed to be just about everything. He refused to let Christine date or wear the miniskirts that her friends wore, and he never let her attend parties.

Her breaking point came at seventeen, when he lost his temper and threatened to rape her again. The incident started when she took a sandwich to him at his office, which was near their home. "Here's your lunch, Daddy," she said as she set the bag down and turned to leave.

"Chris," he said, looking at her back through the sunglasses he always wore.

She stopped but didn't turn around.

"You hate me, Chris, don't you?"

Christine didn't say anything.

"Don't you?"

She turned slowly to face him. "Yeah, I do."

He acted surprised. Rising to his feet, he took off his glasses and stared at her. "What did you say, you little bitch?"

"I do hate you, Daddy." Christine saw the familiar look of rage on his face, a look that turned his handsome face ugly and always terrified her, for it presaged violence. She had never said anything like that to his face before, and she was frightened. "I don't hate you, really, so much as I hate what you have become, and what you do."

Henry could not believe it. "Well, well," he drawled. Grabbing her by the arm, he walked her stiffly into a deserted room, picked up a crowbar, and held it in front of her. "You haven't seen nuthin' yet," he snarled. He led Christine out of the building and turned toward their house, as if to walk her home and do Lord knows what to her.

Christine could not let him get her inside the house. No sooner had they emerged into the sunlight than she broke away and ran. She ran across a field and jumped a fence and was halfway across another field when she realized he was coming after her in his truck. A gunshot sounded behind her. His rifle was out. He would kill her for sure.

Panicked, unsure where to go, she zigzagged off the field,

away from the road, into the woods. She was out of sight but not safe. She'd never be safe as long as he lived. Stopping to catch her breath, she decided to head for the safest place she could think of: her grandfather's house. He loved her and would help her. She took off running again.

She burst into the house ten minutes later and begged her grandfather to save her. "He's gonna kill Jackie! He's gonna kill me! He's gonna kill somebody walking down the street! You've got to help me!"

Her grandfather had no idea what Christine was talking about. His son a *murderer?* Was she deranged? "Honey, you can stay here. It's going to be all right," he said, hugging and trying to comfort her. When her disjointed and bizarre tale came tumbling out, however, her grandfather couldn't believe her. How could Henry rape his own daughter?

Grandpa finally called his son, who came to get her.

Back at home, he reloaded his rifle in front of her and told her he was going to kill her. She ran into her room and slammed the door, hoping he was tormenting her with idle threats. Instead of going after her, he strode suddenly out the back door and drove away in his truck.

Sobbing, Christine climbed into bed and prayed to God to defend her. She told God that if He didn't step in, she was going to renounce Him and defend herself. In case God let her down, she decided she should be prepared. She went into the spare bedroom, where her father kept a trunkful of guns, and pulled out a small, short-handled .38-caliber revolver. He had taught her to shoot in the creek out back, using cans as targets. She loaded the revolver and took it to bed with her. As she lay in the dark, she pictured him coming into her room with the rifle. She pictured him raping her when he came home. What would she do? She wanted it to end. She wanted him dead. There was nothing to do but shoot him. If he stepped foot in her room, she decided she would shoot to kill.

When she awoke, he was standing in the doorway, clutching his rifle. She hadn't meant to fall asleep. Panic rose in her chest.

"I want you to know I'm doing this because of you," he said calmly.

Before she could reach for the pistol, he turned abruptly and

walked into his bedroom, which adjoined hers. He had threatened to kill himself several times before, holding guns to his
head and pulling the trigger. The guns would go *Click! Click!
Click!,* as though he were playing Russian roulette and winning.
She had always thought it was a charade, that the guns weren't
loaded, and she thought so now as she listened to the dry *Click!
Click!* then a sharp explosion, then silence. Christine didn't
move. She didn't trust him. It was probably another of his sick
games.

"Chris! Chris!" Her stepmother's voice sounded weak and far
away.

Christine climbed out of bed and went into the master bedroom. He was slumped on the floor in front of the dresser.
Christine leaned down and saw the .22, then the hole in his
forehead. It was such a tiny hole, she could hardly believe he'd
shot himself. Wouldn't there be more blood? There was just a
trickle.

She went to the phone and called an ambulance.

They flew him by helicopter to the hospital, where, mirac-
ulously, he lived. After several months of treatment for a brain
injury, he went home. Yet he was never the same, never as
abusive or as violent as he was before he shot himself. It was as
though he had performed a lobotomy on his own brain, blowing
out his mental illness with a single well-aimed bullet. He became deeply religious and told everyone how the Lord had
saved his wicked soul and could save theirs, too, if they'd only
open their hearts to Christ.

Christine also became religious, for she believed that God
came through for her that night. If He hadn't, she had been fully
prepared to shoot Daddy herself. She would have to live with
that knowledge for the rest of her life.

"The only difference between you and me was a little quirk of
circumstance," Christine told Larry.

Christine saw his tears and realized that her story had struck
home. Most people were sympathetic when she told them her
story, but rarely did anyone respond with as much emotion as
Larry.

"You know . . . how . . . I feel," he said.

"Yeah, I do."

"I never knew anybody who knew *exactly* how I felt inside until now." Larry struggled not to cry as he spoke. "I look in your eyes and I can see you know where I'm hurting."

Christine smiled sadly. So her hunch had been right: They were kindred souls, with so much to talk about. She hoped she could turn her experience into something positive by helping another abused child work through his pain.

3.

Larry's insanity defense received its first major boost when Dr. Henderson told Baradel and Murphy that Larry suffered from chronic undifferentiated schizophrenia, a mental illness that profoundly distorted the way he perceived, thought, and felt about the world. The disease, which often appears in adolescence, is characterized by such thought disturbances as hallucinations and delusions. Another common symptom is dissociation—a separation of ideas and actions from feelings that normally accompany them.

At the time of the murders, Larry experienced "an acute psychotic episode" caused by his disease, Henderson said. The episode was so severe that Larry was unable to tell right from wrong or conform his conduct to the law—the two legal criteria that Maryland used to determine when a mental disorder was severe enough to relieve a defendant of criminal responsibility. After the murders, the disease went into remission, Henderson said, and Larry currently was sane and competent to stand trial.

As most states did, Maryland used a two-pronged test for criminal responsibility, one that dated to nineteenth century England, when Daniel M'Naghten, a Scottish woodcutter, was acquitted on insanity grounds for shooting the Prime Minister's secretary. In justifying the acquittal, the English common-law judges wrote that a person wasn't responsible for his criminal acts if he didn't understand their nature or know that they were wrong because of "a disease of the mind." Subsequent American court decisions added the element of control to the criminal responsibility test. American judges repeatedly held that a person whose mental disease caused him to lose control shouldn't be held responsible for his crimes, for he lacked intent or mens rea, the so-called guilty mind.

Maryland law incorporated both standards for its insanity test, stating:

> A defendant is not responsible for criminal conduct if, at the time of that conduct, the defendant, because of mental retardation or a mental disorder, lacks substantial capacity:
> 1) To appreciate the criminality of that conduct; or
> 2) To conform that conduct to the requirements of the law.

In 1984, responding to the insanity acquittal of John W. Hinckley, Jr., who shot President Reagan in 1981, Maryland tightened its insanity law. The new law shifted the burden of proof from prosecutors to defendants. Thereafter, defendants had to prove their insanity; prosecutors no longer had to prove defendants were sane. The new law applied only to crimes that occurred after July 1984, though. Larry Swartz would be tried under the old insanity law, and Duckett would have to prove that Larry was sane.

Under either version of Maryland's insanity law, Henderson's finding that Larry couldn't tell right from wrong or control himself was good news for the defense.

The bad news came from Dr. Spodak. Unlike Henderson, Spodak saw no mental disorder that would allow Larry to escape criminal responsibility. In Spodak's opinion, Larry was sane at the time of the murders and was sane now.

Yet Lee Richmond, a child psychologist who occasionally worked with Spodak on cases, disagreed. After testing Larry and interviewing him, she saw evidence of a serious psychiatric disorder, probably schizophrenia. Although she had never testified in court before, Richmond told Larry's lawyers she would be willing to testify on his behalf.

Richmond impressed the defense lawyers as sincere, and they thought a jury might find her credible. Henderson's diagnosis of "chronic" schizophrenia troubled them, however. Larry had no history of mental problems; how was Henderson going to convince a jury that Larry had been mentally ill for years?

The defense lawyers felt they needed more opinions, so Richmond recommended a psychologist in Philadelphia. Although the psychiatric bills were mounting up, Baradel readily assented to another consultation. Richmond sent her test results, along with the reports on Larry's childhood in foster care, to Barry Bricklin, a clinical psychologist and associate professor at the Hahnemann Medical College of Philadelphia.

Bricklin soon concurred with Richmond: There were unmistakable signs of schizophrenia in Larry's test results. Like Richmond, Bricklin believed that Larry's form of schizophrenia allowed him to seem rational most of the time but caused him occasionally to lose control, particularly under the influence of stress or drugs.

Although Richmond based her diagnosis partly on interviews with Larry, Bricklin never laid eyes on him. In a move they knew was risky, the defense lawyers planned to have Bricklin testify in court without interviewing Larry even once. Bricklin would base his testimony entirely on Larry's test responses. The lawyers planned to establish Bricklin's national reputation as an expert on the Rorschach inkblot test, then have him tell the jury, "It doesn't matter if I saw him. I am an expert in the scientific aspect of psychology, and there are measurable things about the responses to these tests. These tests are a lot more objective than people are willing give them credit for being. This test could be Mr. Duckett's; it doesn't matter to me *who* took it. If he took it, he's schizophrenic."

Richmond's tests included many of the same ones Larry took later at the state hospital. Richmond asked him to look at inkblots, tell stories from pictures, draw people and houses. On the Wechsler Adult Intelligence Scale test, he earned a full-scale I.Q. of 102, which placed him in the average range of intelligence. His score later dropped fifteen points on the same test at the state hospital.

Richmond and Bricklin drew nearly identical conclusions from his test responses. Richmond wrote that Larry seemed "affable, likeable, and articulate, but much of this is facade, much like the smile on his picture drawing. He is also frightened, psychologically impoverished, and ill defended. He often feels confused and helpless."

As signs of schizophrenia, she and Bricklin cited Larry's tendency to "personalize" or tell stories about himself from picture cards, and the fact that he drew a transparent house that showed the inside from the outside. They also saw signs of schizophrenia in his Rorschach interpretations. He gave bizarre and incongruous responses, and saw all sorts of primitive insects, including "a dying insect," termites, and "amoebas with green antennae."

Both psychologists noted Larry's denial of an obvious phallic symbol. Larry stared at it for a full forty seconds before saying, "This is nothing. I've never seen it. Oh, it's a flying worm. Here are its flying wings. It has wings, a body, and a head."

The psychologists concluded that Larry relied heavily on repression to defend against anxiety. That impaired his memory and interfered with his ability to learn in school, Richmond said. It probably also led to his being misdiagnosed as learning-disabled.

Richmond saw another theme throughout Larry's test responses: a link among sex, drugs, and violence. The link was clearest when he made up stories from twenty picture cards during the Thematic Apperception Test. His first story was about a "guy who is on drugs" and who "realized that he was wrong." His second story was about a boy caught in a double bind by his mother, who at first wouldn't let him play the violin and then wouldn't let him stop. His sixth story was about a man who loved one woman and fell for another. That hurt the first woman, who then tried to "pull the man back to her." In her report, Richmond said the story was "possibly true and may have been threatening to Larry."

His tenth story was again about someone on drugs. He followed it with a story about a man who raped and killed a woman and then cried because he couldn't believe what he had done. "Drugs and violence are associated in Larry's mind, as are sex and violence," wrote Richmond.

Larry's next few stories were clearly his own, said Richmond. He described a man proposing to a lady "without telling his mother. His mother was upset because she didn't like the lady. The mother couldn't believe that he didn't tell her." After telling the lady that he loved her, the man hugged her as he took her home from a date. On the next card, Larry suddenly shifted and said, "I am dreaming. I am going through a misty town."

"The conflict between sex-violence and sex-love is too much for Larry, and he loses reality contact," Richmond wrote.

Some of his test responses suggested Larry may have been malingering or toying with the doctors. Twice he took the Minnesota Multiphasic Personality Inventory, a test that has built-in scales designed to indicate whether a person is falsely trying to look either good or mentally ill. Both times, Larry gave answers that invalidated his entire profile. The reports concluded that he may have been deliberately trying to make himself look mentally ill.

On another test designed to analyze his social history, Larry reported that he was an unemployed "homemaker" who "currently resides in jail" and was earning between one and two thousand dollars a month "from illegal activities." On the same test, Larry said his adoptive parents were kind but frequently lost their tempers. They excluded him from conversation, severely restricted him, complained about his faults, never praised him for his accomplishments, and made him feel like "an unwanted child."

Larry also said, without elaborating, that his parents had engaged in "unusual sex practices."

Two psychologists and one psychiatrist were enough for Larry's lawyers. On June 26—shortly before Karceski replaced Murphy on the defense team—the defense filed a plea of not guilty, stating that Larry "was insane and therefore not criminally responsible at the time of the alleged offenses." Two weeks later, they waived his right to a speedy trial and petitioned the court to order the state mental examination required of all inmates who raised the insanity defense.

On August 3, Larry was admitted to Perkins. He spent the next week undergoing a battery of psychological and medical tests at the 240-bed maximum-security hospital in Jessup, midway between Washington and Baltimore.

To help the state doctors understand Larry, and to increase the chances of them finding him insane, the defense sent along all Larry's adoption and medical records. "Disclosing this stuff is a gamble," Murphy told Baradel, "but I don't think there's much chance they'll agree with us unless the doctors can see his background."

Baradel recognized the tactical advantage their disclosure might generate if the state doctors proclaimed Larry sane. He relished the prospect of handing the adoption records to the state psychiatrists during cross-examination at trial.

"Did you read this?" Baradel imagined himself saying. Of course, each doctor would have to say yes.

"The fact that this boy was eating garbage out of garbage cans," Baradel would ask, "that didn't seem significant to you? The fact that he was hiding food under his bed, wolfing down lunches he stole from classmates—those things didn't suggest to you that something was seriously wrong with his emotional development?"

Regardless of how the doctors responded, Baradel figured the tactic would build sympathy for Larry with the jury.

Dr. Faramarz Mokhtari, an Iranian psychiatrist on the Perkins staff, was the first state psychiatrist to interview Larry. During their initial meeting, he carefully studied Larry while the youth gave a detailed account of the murders. Mokhtari noticed that he hadn't shaved, but his curly hair was clean and his casual clothes looked neat. After recounting the murders, Larry spoke with restrained bitterness about the constant punishment and sarcasm he had to endure from his parents.

When Mokhtari inquired about his sex life, Larry said his experience with Sarah two nights before the murders was the only time he had had intercourse. He never had had any homosexual experiences, he said.

Mokhtari suspected there was a connection between Larry's sexual encounter with Sarah and the murders, especially after Larry told him that his mother had called Sarah a whore. That probably enraged Larry and triggered a fight with his mother; it may even have triggered the murders, the doctor speculated. Sex, much more than grades, drove people into homicidal rages. The doctor also wondered about Larry's motivation in fingering his mother, but Larry seemed too embarrassed about it to elaborate. He would only say he was "mad" at his mother and wanted to do something "real bad" to her.

In his report, Mokhtari observed that Larry seemed friendly, playful, childish. His thinking was logical and showed no gross distortions or loose associations. He displayed little range of emotion—no depression or elation. He told the doctor he felt depressed about "whatever happened" and had considered suicide but always talked himself out of it. He described a recurring dream of his mother standing on their porch, covered in blood, waving her long pointed finger at him, saying, "You are responsible for whatever happened."

Mokhtari concluded that Larry suffered from a mixed personality disorder, which meant he displayed symptoms of several different personality disorders. Personality disorders are inflexible patterns of behavior that cause people distress and often impair their functioning at work and in social relationships. As a rule, persons with personality disorders remain functional and rarely require hospitalization. For that reason, doctors seldom go into court and testify that such disorders, by themselves, are severe enough to relieve anyone of criminal responsibility.

Specifically, Mokhtari detected symptoms of narcissistic and histrionic personality disorders in Larry, yet he didn't think the disorders were severe enough to render him psychotic.

In Mokhtari's opinion, Larry could tell right from wrong and was capable of controlling his behavior at the time of the murders.

Dr. Carol Kleinman, as a licensed psychiatrist and attorney, was something of a professional oddity. She had gone back to medical school seven years after she received her law degree. When Larry arrived at Perkins for his evaluation, Kleinman, then thirty-nine, had just finished her psychiatry residency and was a relative newcomer to the hospital.

She interviewed Larry five times for a total of eight hours. In the first interview, he gave her the same account of the murders that he had given Dr. Mokhtari, with one omission: He didn't mention that he had sexually violated his mother.

In a subsequent interview, Kleinman told Larry that Mokhtari had mentioned the fingering to her. "Why didn't you tell me about that?"

Larry squirmed, clearly embarrassed. "You're a woman."

Dr. Kleinman figured he was too shy to discuss something such as that with a female doctor. Yet she couldn't help wondering why he did something so demeaning to his mother. She thought it showed utter hatred and a total lack of respect.

"Why did you do it?" she asked gently.

Larry shrugged. He, too, seemed puzzled. "I must have been really *crazy* to do something like that."

Kleinman liked Larry and thought him a beautiful youth with a charismatic, though shy, personality. She didn't think he was lying or consciously trying to persuade her that he was insane. She sensed he was trying to win her over to his side, but that was only natural. Secretly, she hoped she would find a mental disorder, for she wanted to find him legally insane. She was looking for something that might have prevented him from telling right from wrong or from controlling his actions on the night of the murders.

She couldn't find it.

Larry did say a few things that made her wonder whether he was crazy. He only remembered stabbing his mother once, yet the autopsy revealed she had been stabbed seven times. He also remembered stabbing his father only a few times, yet his father had sustained seventeen stab wounds. Those memory lapses troubled Kleinman. They could be the result of repression, but they also were compatible with psychosis. Something else he said made her wonder even more about his mental state during the killings. "I would have done the same thing if a policeman was there," Larry said.

Now *that's crazy!* Kleinman thought.

Nevertheless, she finally decided that Larry was not suffering from any psychotic illness on the night of the murders. He exhibited none of the classic symptoms of schizophrenia: no hallucinations, delusions, bizarre thoughts, or obvious distortions in thinking. He described himself as popular at school and gave no indication that he had ever withdrawn into a private, made-up world. His range of emotional expression was constricted, a symptom often seen in schizophrenics; Mokhtari had commented on that in his report, and all the Perkins doctors had noticed it. That, however, was the only symptom of schizophrenia the state doctors detected. Alone, it was insufficient to warrant a diagnosis of schizophrenia.

If Larry had any mental disorder, Kleinman reluctantly concluded, it was not serious enough to allow him to escape criminal responsibility. On the night of the murders, he seemed aware that his actions were wrong. What else could she conclude when he told her things such as, "I knew what I was doing. I felt mechanical. I was thinking about one thing while doing another. . . . I could appreciate what I was doing was wrong, but I couldn't stop." After the killings, Larry said, "I felt sorry for what I did." Now *that* clearly indicated he was aware his actions were wrong, Kleinman thought.

Neither could she ignore the fact that after the murders he wiped the maul, hid the weapons and his bloody clothes, went home, put clothes in the washer, and persuaded Annie to go to bed—all purposeful acts that indicated an awareness of reality.

Kleinman reluctantly joined Mokhtari in concluding that Larry suffered from mixed personality disorders, but none severe enough to render him legally insane.

Marc J. Tabackman, a clinical psychologist at Perkins, interviewed Larry and gave him the psychologist's stock battery of tests. Although Larry seemed emotionally detached and immature, Tabackman detected no thought or perceptual disorders. His full-scale I.Q. tested at 87, below average, on the Wechsler Adult Intelligence Scale. Yet in conversation his overall functioning suggested a higher I.Q., one that was at least average.

On the ten-card inkblot test, Larry's interpretations were guarded and full of references to animals. He "demonstrates reluctance to disclose thoughts and feelings and a fear that he might 'lose control' of his impulses," Tabackman wrote. "He is able to achieve only fragile self-control" by holding in his emotions, distancing himself from other people, and remaining passive. "This control can break down in the absence of structure or external limits."

Although Larry's ability to perceive reality under stress seemed weak, Tabackman saw no sign of psychosis. The psychologist concluded that Larry suffered from a mixed personality disorder that was wasn't severe enough to render him insane.

Another Perkins psychiatrist, Dr. Jacques Clermont, detected the same emotional flatness that the other doctors observed. But unlike the others, Clermont diagnosed a dysthymic disorder, a depressive neurosis, which meant that Larry suffered from severe depression. That condition could render some patients psychotic, but Clermont did not believe Larry was psychotic now or had been on the night of the murders.

Dagmar S. Parrish, a social worker at Perkins, wrote the most poignant of all the reports filed from the state hospital regarding Larry. In addition to interviewing Larry, Parrish spent hours reading the youth's background file and the police reports, then sat down and tried to piece together the fragments of Larry's sad life in a way that might explain the tragedy:

> Since there is no way to get the Swartz's views on their children's behavior, it is obviously a one-sided view of the family, but this seems to be a pair of apparently well meaning persons who had a somewhat idealized notion of their prospective adoptive family. When met by the realities of dealing with two boys who had led thoroughly disrupted, emotionally distraught early lives, and who came to them with many problems needing support and understanding and a great deal of tolerance, the Swartzes were caught short by the demands of this, plus their careers, and the result was seen by the patient as almost unbearable tension in the family.
>
> The patient saw himself as unable to approach the expectations of his parents, and essentially cut off from any social life by parents, who saw him as untrustworthy, and who constantly informed his acquaintances and friends that he was not to be trusted, and who

rarely let him develop friendships because they found fault either with his associates or with him. He expresses feelings that no matter what he did they would find it wrong, that it was impossible to please them in any way, and that essentially he lived on the razor's edge with the notion lurking in the back of his head that at some point they would give him back like they did Michael. Above all, he was never to express anger, and he is rather proud that he "never gets mad, that no one has really seen him angry." He feels hopeless, inadequate, and worthless and has readily accepted his guilt in any and all things for which he was punished, feeling that it was at least partly his fault and therefore reasonable to accept the blame. He also never quite could be off guard, because every time he thought he knew the rules, someone changed them. . . .

Six days after Larry's admission, the Perkins staff held a forensic conference on his case. Kleinman, Clermont, Mokhtari, Tabackman, Parrish, and Dr. Robin E. Hostetter, another staff psychiatrist, attended. They unanimously concluded that Larry was sane at the time of the murders and was mentally competent to stand trial.

On August 10, Larry was discharged from Perkins and taken under guard back to the detention center.

Twelve days later, the prosecutor filed in court a brief summary of the Perkins findings, alerting the defense to the formidable lineup their psychiatrists would face at trial.

By the fall of 1984, ten psychologists and psychiatrists had examined Larry. As in the Hinckley trial two years earlier, the experts in Larry's case shattered the conventional wisdom that psychiatrists usually agreed on diagnoses. Although the experts on each side offered different opinions, all but one predictably lined up on the side they were supposed to—the one associated with their paychecks. The Perkins doctors were supposed to be neutral, but they drew their pay from the state of Maryland and in the vast majority of cases found defendants sane. All five Perkins doctors sided with the state on the central question of

Larry's criminal responsibility. Just as predictably, four of the five defense doctors lined up on the opposite side: Larry was not responsible for his conduct because of a mental disorder. Only Dr. Spodak—whom the defense naturally would not call as a witness—failed to tell the defense what it wanted to hear.

While three of the defense experts said Larry suffered from schizophrenia, the fifth defense doctor weighed in with yet another view. He was Dr. Neil H. Blumberg, a thirty-three-year-old psychiatrist who recently had left Perkins after nearly three years as a staff psychiatrist, the last ten months as director of forensic evaluation.

When the Perkins doctors unanimously went against them, Larry's lawyers felt they needed another expert. Karceski grew especially worried after he interviewed Dr. Henderson, because Karceski didn't buy Henderson's theory that Larry suffered from chronic schizophrenia. He doubted a jury would, either. Larry was no chronic head case; he'd never shown any symptoms of mental illness before. How could the defense expect a jury to believe that schizophrenia popped up and disappeared like that? Karceski grilled Henderson for more than an hour and didn't like his responses. "Give me the name of one other doctor in the state of Maryland who will agree with you," Karceski demanded.

Henderson suggested Neal Blumberg. When the defense lawyers learned of his background at Perkins, they considered him ideal. He had always represented the state and had never testified for a defendant before. If he found Larry insane, Blumberg could help the defense respond to the Perkins doctors and provide a nice counterpoint for the jury.

Shortly after he began seeing Larry in October, Blumberg rendered an opinion that proved pivotal to the defense. Like Clermont at Perkins, he detected a major depressive illness in Larry. Unlike Clermont, however, Blumberg concluded that Larry suffered an "acute psychotic episode" on the night of the murders. Blumberg categorized the episode as a brief reactive psychosis or atypical psychosis—disorders often used interchangeably by psychiatrists. Lawyers know the disorders as temporary insanity.

Brief reactive psychosis, according to the diagnostic manual used by most psychiatrists, often occurs immediately after a major stress and can last from a few hours to two weeks. Symptoms range from delusions and hallucinations to incoherence and impairment of recent memory. Both brief reactive psychosis and atypical psychosis are catchall labels that doctors sometimes hang on patients when nothing else seems appropriate. Their symptoms are nebulous and varied, which makes them difficult diagnoses for prosecutors to refute.

The diagnosis delighted the defense attorneys.

They had found their ax, Baradel thought, and were back in the ax fight!

TWELVE

April 1985

1.

Patuxent Institution looms like a giant brick fortress on a rural roadside halfway between Washington and Baltimore. Hailed as "Maryland's great experiment" by then-Governor Theodore R. McKeldin, the novel prison opened in 1955 as a place where psychiatrists would try to rehabilitate violent criminals who were considered psychopathic but legally sane. The original guinea pigs were so-called compulsive criminals, men who didn't commit crimes deliberately but because of presumed intellectual or emotional defects. The experiment proved to be highly controversial, and over the next three decades state legislators repeatedly modified the rules governing the prison.

By the time Larry Swartz killed his parents in 1984, Patuxent had acquired a reputation as a humane prison and a fast track to parole. It was a maximum-security prison, but one where prisoners lived in single cells and could do their time with little fear of being raped. It offered an intensive program of psychotherapy, education, and job training to emotionally troubled prisoners such as Larry Swartz.

Conceived in the heyday of psychiatry, when belief in its power to change human behavior was strong, the prison was founded on twin premises: that even violent psychopaths deserved second chances, and that psychiatrists might "cure" them through therapy and the promise of freedom. Those who resisted would stay locked up indefinitely, like incurable psychotics in an asylum.

Jerome Robinson, a compassionate Maryland legislator and one of the prison's founders, had been concerned about compulsive criminals since he witnessed the 1931 murder trial of Herman Webb Duker. The incorrigible son of a wealthy insurance broker, Duker shot and killed a milkman without provocation during a robbery in Baltimore when he was twenty-two. Psychiatrists testified that Duker was legally sane because he understood what he was doing, yet he was psychopathic and lacked impulse control. A judge sentenced him to hang, citing the lack of a state facility to treat him and expert opinion that he would remain "extremely dangerous." Maryland's governor commuted the sentence to life, contending that Duker shouldn't die for mere want of treatment.

A decade later, the apparently unmotivated murder of an eleven-year-old girl by a Baltimore handyman further inflamed political concern about the problem. Robinson, by then a state legislator, chaired a special legislative commission that persuaded the Maryland General Assembly to authorize construction of a new prison to treat "defective delinquents." The 1951 statute defined "defective delinquents" as repeat offenders with a broad range of emotional disorders and intellectual handicaps. It said eligible inmates would go to Patuxent only after they were convicted and sentenced to regular prisons, and then only after a jury committed them at a full-scale hearing.

From the start, Patuxent operated much the same as a hospital for the criminally insane. Psychiatrists led regular therapy sessions and recommended the release of inmates when they considered them no longer dangerous. Committed indefinitely, inmates often remained imprisoned even after their original sentences had expired. Nearly half of the prisoners Patuxent paroled during its first decade were kept beyond their original terms. That changed after a public outcry over the amount of time inmates were being held, often for minor offenses. One inmate told state legislators who visited the prison that he'd been sentenced to two years for unauthorized use of a motor vehicle and was still imprisoned after sixteen years. He described Patuxent as "some Orwellian nightmare."

In 1977, the legislature amended Patuxent's law to prevent inmates from being held beyond their original sentences. The reform bill made other drastic changes to the "great experiment": It opened Patuxent to virtually any prisoner whom the doctors considered a good candidate for rehabilitation. No longer was Patuxent the exclusive domain of psychopathic, repeat offenders. The new law also gave prisoners the right to drop out of Patuxent at any time and return to regular prisons. More significantly, the reform bill gave autonomy to a parole board controlled by Patuxent's top staff. The prison's own parole board—not juries or courts—would decide when inmates would be released. Prison psychiatrists contended they needed parole power as a carrot to motivate criminals to change.

Suddenly, a prison that inmates had feared as a place of no return offered a tantalizing hope of early parole. Murderers and rapists doing life in other state prisons began begging for admission. To win parole, all they had to do was persuade prison psychiatrists that they were sincerely remorseful and willing to change.

Instilling remorse in prisoners became the touchstone of therapy at Patuxent, for the doctors believed many inmates lacked feelings for their victims. If they could learn to feel compassion for their victims, the doctors theorized, inmates would be less likely to repeat their crimes. Inmates met twice a week for group therapy and spent hours discussing what they did wrong, why they did it, what other choices they might have made, what impact their crimes had on their victims. "No one gets out of here until they have lived through their crimes,"

Norma B. Gluckstern, the prison director, told a reporter shortly before Larry's arrest. "Part of our job is to strip through their defenses, to make them feel again." Inmates were encouraged to criticize themselves and talk about their families and childhood. Tears flowed freely, even from "macho" prisoners who wouldn't have dared show such emotion in regular prisons. Some inmates said the experience changed their lives; others claimed it was a verbal con game they played merely to win parole. Regardless, the therapy lasted at least four years and more often, twice that long.

In addition to therapy, Patuxent offered intensive job training and academic education as inmates worked their way up the prison's four housing levels. Each housing level gave inmates greater privileges and responsibilities. At the top level, inmates lived in dormitory-style housing and governed themselves, for the prison's program was designed to help inmates assume responsibility for themselves in preparation for their return to society.

Patuxent officials maintained they had an excellent track record with the inmates they paroled. There were a few notable failures, including a rapist who raped two women within a year after his release in 1980. That case helped to build momentum for a state law enacted in 1982 that required the governor's approval before any lifer could be paroled from Patuxent. Despite the occasional failure, Patuxent officials contended that fewer of their parolees were returned to prison than those paroled from regular prisons—a fact they attributed to Patuxent's unusual therapy program.

State prison officials later would challenge Patuxent's claim to have an extraordinary track record. Its success rate with parolees was nearly identical to that of other Maryland prisons, state prison officials concluded in a hasty study of the prison in 1988.

Patuxent's supporters, however, countered that recidivism statistics didn't consider the prison's impact on the quality of life for successful parolees—which included the vast majority of those who left Patuxent. The unique prison helped many inmates reestablish contact with their families, break from a pattern of crime, and successfully reenter the job market, they contended.

Both Warren Duckett and Richard Karceski knew Patuxent fairly well from years of experience with the criminal justice system. They'd seen criminals enter and leave at varying rates of speed and with varying amounts of success. Prisoners sentenced to life usually stayed at Patuxent about eight years, less than half the time that lifers typically served in other Maryland prisons. Those sentenced to shorter terms, in contrast, sometimes took longer to win parole than they would in the state's regular prisons, because it took at least four years to progress through Patuxent's program.

Considering what Patuxent offered, Duckett felt it was ideal for Larry. Duckett believed the youth had deep emotional problems that needed to be vented through long-term therapy, something that would continue for years. Duckett knew Patuxent would give him that treatment. Most of Patuxent's psychotherapy was in groups, rather than the individual therapy that people got from private practitioners, but it was the only treatment available in Maryland's correctional system. That was more than most states offered criminals. The prosecutor knew that Larry probably could win release from Patuxent within six to eight years, no matter what sentence the court dealt him. That thought didn't disturb Duckett, because he didn't think Larry deserved to spend twenty years behind bars. It actually pleased the prosecutor to think that Larry would return to society while he was young enough to start a new life.

Unlike Duckett, Baradel knew nothing about Patuxent. His clients tended to be corporations and insurance companies, and he had never known anyone who went there. Karceski had, though, and he agreed with Duckett that Larry should go to Patuxent if he had to go to prison. It was no country club, but it was Maryland's best prison.

Still, Karceski was not convinced that Larry had to go to prison. If they prevailed on insanity, Larry would go to Perkins, a hospital where he might win his freedom faster than at Patuxent. As an experienced criminal lawyer, Karceski instinctively thought about how long his client would spend behind bars. He also believed in hard-nosed negotiating from a position of strength, and he wanted to build a solid defense before he considered negotiating a plea that might send Larry to Patuxent. Even if they lost at trial and Larry drew two life sentences for first-degree murder—the worst that could happen—Larry would still have a shot at getting into Patuxent by applying for admission from the regular prison system. For that reason, Karceski thought he had little to lose by aggressively pursuing the insanity defense.

During the eight months after Karceski joined the defense team, he and Baradel sparred repeatedly with the prosecutor. Their hostility escalated beneath a thin veneer of politeness as each side demanded additional psychiatric reports from the other and threatened to file discovery motions to get them. The veneer of politeness was stripped away at a meeting between Duckett and the defense lawyers in October 1984.

Baradel and Karceski had been trying for more than a month to see the state's physical evidence. Barr stalled, prompting them to complain to the prosecutor. Duckett finally told Barr he could delay no longer, so Barr agreed to meet the lawyers at the homicide squad office in Crownsville in mid-October. Without telling the defense lawyers, Duckett decided that he, too, would attend the meeting.

The prosecutor needed to see the evidence before the trial; he decided to watch the defense lawyers as they examined it. This would be his first face-to-face meeting with Karceski, and Duckett wouldn't mind taking him by surprise. He found it helpful to keep his adversaries off guard.

Duckett had not been pleased to see Murphy bow out of the Swartz case; he admired and trusted Murphy and knew his ego would never get in the way of plea negotiations. Duckett knew little about Karceski except that he had beaten his top deputy, Frank Weathersbee, in a sensational drug-related murder trial. Duckett feared that Karceski had an ego as big as Baltimore and would want desperately to win a notorious case such as this. He feared that Karceski would refuse to negotiate a plea that Duckett felt would serve everybody's interests. The last thing Duckett wanted was for Larry to be declared insane. Since the Perkins doctors already had proclaimed him sane, how long would they keep him? A year? Maybe two? Duckett shuddered at the thought. He hoped Karceski would realize that Patuxent had so much more to offer than Perkins.

The prosecutor turned his attention to the offer he should make to open plea negotiations. He felt he couldn't consider manslaughter, given the barbaric nature of the crimes and the fact that two people had been killed. He knew the defense would reject first-degree murder, so the compromise almost had to be second-degree. That carried a prison sentence of up to thirty years. Duckett decided to offer twenty years on each count of second-degree murder. He felt it was rather lenient but also fair, considering the tragic circumstances of the case.

Early on the afternoon of October 15, Detective Barr greeted the defense lawyers in the lobby outside the homicide suite and ushered them back to the lieutenant's office. Bill Meyers, the chief evidence technician on the Swartz case, was carting boxes into the lieutenant's office when the lawyers arrived.

"Why don't you take a seat in here? We're waiting on Mr. Duckett," Barr said.

"Oh? Mr. Duckett didn't tell us he was coming," Karceski replied.

He wasn't invited, either, Baradel thought.

"Well, we told him about the meeting, and he said he would come," said Barr.

As twenty minutes turned into half an hour, the defense lawyers grew visibly annoyed. This was their meeting and they didn't like waiting for an uninvited guest.

Duckett finally strode in and said, "Hi, Ron," without apologizing for his tardiness. He introduced himself to Karceski and extended his hand. "I don't believe we've met."

"Yes, I believe we have." Karceski cited a brief encounter the previous year, which Duckett didn't remember.

After the prosecutor took a seat, he gave Meyers the go-ahead to break out the evidence. Meyers pulled brown paper bags from the cardboard carton, unstapled each one, read the evidence numbers aloud, then handed each item to the defense lawyers. As Karceski and Baradel carefully examined each item, they consulted their own records and jotted descriptive information on legal pads.

"What's that?" Duckett asked when Meyers pulled out a flimsy scrap of plastic from a bag marked "Q14."

"That's the piece that was torn off the kitchen tablecloth," Barr said. "We found it along the footpath in the woods behind the Swartz house."

"What's its evidential value?" Duckett asked.

"The FBI found human blood on it. They also found blood on the kitchen tablecloth it was torn from. We think the killer tore the tablecloth in the kitchen, used the torn piece to wipe his fingerprints off the maul, then used this piece to hold the maul when he carried it outside."

Karceski and Baradel looked at each other. They knew exactly what Q14 was. Baradel had prepared a chart of all the evidence numbers, what the FBI had found on each item, and what the defense wanted to know about it. On the tablecloth scrap, the FBI had found human blood with an enzyme that matched an enzyme in Bob Swartz's blood.

"Q9," Meyers said, handing Mrs. Swartz's blue flannel sleeper to Baradel.

Turning the heavy, zippered jumpsuit around several times, Baradel saw almost no bloodstains on the legs. Most of the stains were in the front and above the waist. Blood also had seeped down her back, but not as heavily as in the front. To Baradel, the blood pattern seemed consistent with Larry's claim that he had first struck his mother on the head with the maul.

Barr, on the other hand, looked at the same blood pattern and thought it consistent with *his* theory that Larry had stabbed his mother in the neck first.

No one spoke as Meyers put away the sleeper and restapled the bag.

When Meyers pulled out the latent lifts—small white paper squares covered with clear plastic—Duckett asked about each fingerprint: "Where was that found? Whose was it?"

Again Baradel and Karceski eyed each other. The prosecutor obviously wasn't familiar with his evidence. Barr and Meyers were leading him by the hand, telling him what everything was, where they had found it. The defense lawyers knew exactly where the fingerprints had been lifted. They also knew about the two doorknobs that Meyers produced next: One had been removed from inside and the other from outside the door to the computer room. The FBI fingerprint report puzzled Baradel, a former FBI agent who had experience reading such reports. It revealed that three prints lifted inside the house didn't match those of Larry or his parents, and the location of at least one print seemed significant—on the inside doorknob to the computer room where Bob Swartz's body was found. It was a partial palm print, and it appeared to be in blood. Baradel wondered, Who besides the killer would have held the doorknob inside that room with a bloody hand? Bob Swartz, maybe, during his struggle with Larry. Unfortunately, however, the FBI couldn't compare Bob or Kay's palm prints with this print, because the police had rolled only their fingers—not their palms—before the Swartzes were buried.

That bloody handprint didn't trouble Barr, though. None of the stray prints did, for he figured almost anyone—the cops, paramedics, even Annie—could have deposited them. It wasn't standard procedure in his department to roll victims' palm prints unless one of particular significance turned up. Barr didn't consider this one significant, not after he identified the bloody handprint on the patio door as Larry's. Once Barr decided that Larry was the killer, all the stray prints became irrelevant to him.

"What's that?" Duckett asked as Meyers pulled out a large metal cone with red splotches on the side.

Karceski couldn't believe that Duckett didn't know what it was. "That's the bullet," he said facetiously.

Baradel smiled, but Karceski stared at the prosecutor, his face deadpan.

"Bullet?" Duckett echoed. "I didn't know there was a bullet in this case."

Baradel burst into laughter. The cone was big enough to come from a cannon! Not wanting to embarrass Duckett, Baradel coughed to control his laughter.

"Oh no, Mr. Duckett, this isn't a bullet," Meyers said. "It's a gatepost we took from the backyard."

"Yeah," Barr added. "The killer probably opened the gate with blood on his hands."

"Whose blood is it?" Duckett asked.

Barr consulted his notes. "There wasn't enough to get a type. It's human, but we don't have a type."

Duckett looked at Karceski, annoyed. He sensed that Karceski was trying to intimidate him.

Duckett quietly watched as Meyers produced more evidence for the defense lawyers to examine. After ten or fifteen minutes, the prosecutor decided it was time to feel out Karceski about a plea. He began by stating the obvious.

"You know, I really don't think a trial would be in your client's best interest," Duckett said suddenly. "I happen to have a lot of compassion for Larry. Personally, I think he belongs in Patuxent. If he goes to trial, you know there's a damn good chance he'll wind up at the pen, or Clifton T. Perkins." That was true; the defense lawyers had to realize it. He paused, looking from Karceski to Baradel. "I'm prepared to accept two counts of second-degree."

Taken aback, the defense lawyers said nothing for a moment. Karceski had barely been on the case a month, and here was a plea offer. "No," Karceski replied. "We're not prepared to negotiate. It's premature to even talk about a plea."

Undaunted, Duckett said, "I think you should take a plea. It would be best for Larry. Just look at what he did to his parents! You know there's a damn good chance a jury will convict him of first-degree."

"There's a damn good chance a jury will find him not guilty by reason of insanity, or guilty of manslaughter," Karceski snapped.

"Maybe, but how's a jury going to feel about him finger-fucking his mother? He does that, then runs around covering up the evidence. The jury's going to see those as the actions of an insane man? Come on! You know a jury will see that as first-degree."

No, Baradel thought; once a jury gets an inkling of the savage attack that Larry committed on his mother, they would probably see him as a raving maniac. Baradel couldn't believe Duckett's storm-trooper act. He obviously was trying to intimidate Karceski.

"We're not prepared to discuss a plea," Karceski repeated. "I don't foreclose the possibility later, but first I have to know more about this case." He shifted in his seat and looked directly at the prosecutor. "If I didn't know you better, Mr. Duckett, I'd think you were trying to intimidate me."

"No, I'm not." Duckett's tone softened, but he refused to retreat. He could feel the spirit of cooperation he had maintained with Murphy slipping away. It was so frustrating having to start from scratch with a new attorney. "You know," he told Karceski, "Joe Murphy always did the right thing for his client, and I admire him so much for that. He and I always dealt aboveboard."

Karceski bristled as Duckett related how Murphy had marched into the prosecutor's office on the day of Larry's arrest and, without actually saying so, implied that Larry had confessed. What a wonderful rapport he had with Murphy; why couldn't he have the same with Karceski? the prosecutor seemed to be saying.

"Look, Mr. Duckett," Karceski said sharply. "Let me say something to you. I have a high regard for Joe Murphy, too. I really do. And I'm sure your dealings with him were as you described them. I hope mine are no *less* than aboveboard. But right now, we have to examine the evidence. That's what we came here to do. Then we're going talk to our witnesses and talk to your witnesses and talk to our client. *Then,* maybe we can begin to talk about a plea. But my first line of defense is never a plea. I think that's the wrong approach."

Realizing that any further attempt at plea discussions would be futile, Duckett fell silent. He watched the defense lawyers finish examining the evidence before he broached the subject of a trial date. He said he didn't want to start the trial on December 11, the tentative date, because several witnesses would be out of town, and he felt the trial could bump up against the Christmas holidays if it started on the eleventh.

The defense lawyers said they didn't want to change the date, but if they had to, Karceski wanted it sooner rather than later because he had a capital-murder trial scheduled for January. None of their schedules was compatible with an earlier trial date, so the meeting broke up without producing a new date. February appeared to be the earliest time possible, even though the defense lawyers were not happy about trying the case more than a year after the murders.

Several weeks later, Duckett reconvened with Baradel and Karceski in the chambers of circuit court judge Raymond G. Thieme, Jr. Although they were there to talk about a technical motion, Duckett took the opportunity to renew his plea offer of second-degree murder.

The defense lawyers told him they still weren't interested in second-degree. "We're willing to talk about manslaughter," Karceski said.

"No," Duckett countered. "I can't accept manslaughter in a case like this. The family would be outraged. Some of them want the *death penalty*. How would manslaughter look to them?"

Karceski was curious about the sentence Duckett had in mind; second-degree carried up to thirty years. "How much time are you talking on second-degree?"

"I'd recommend up to twenty years. I'd ask the judge to limit it to that."

Manslaughter carried a maximum of ten years, half what Duckett was suggesting. No way would Karceski accept twenty years. He had an excellent case to try and could not imagine bargaining it away for twenty years. As a practical matter, Karceski didn't much care *what* Larry pleaded guilty to, so long as he drew a light sentence.

"We would want a ten-year cap on the sentence. No more," Karceski countered.

Duckett shook his head. He couldn't go for ten. "I understand your point of view, but you have to understand where I'm coming from, too. I've got a family who wants that boy executed, or at least put away for a long time. How could I explain a ten-year sentence to them?"

"Then there's no sense discussing a plea," Karceski said briskly. "We would look at manslaughter, or second-degree with a ten-year cap. But that's all."

Duckett was surprised at Karceski's firmness. He thought twenty years was light, given the crimes. It was Duckett's best shot. If they wouldn't take it, he had no choice but to continue trial preparations.

Hostility continued to simmer between the defense and prosecution as both sides shifted their efforts into high gear. The
hostility boiled over in March, three weeks before the trial date
they finally set, when Duckett showed up unannounced at Perkins for a meeting that Baradel and Karceski had arranged with
the psychiatrists.

Duckett did a near repeat of his earlier performance at the
evidence review. Arriving an hour late, he finally strolled down
the hall, casually smoking a pipe, flanked by Barr and an assistant.

His nonchalance infuriated Baradel. "Let me handle this," Baradel muttered to Karceski.

Before the prosecutor could utter a greeting, Baradel yelled,
"What the *fuck* are you doing? Who said you could be here?
This is our meeting, goddammit! There's no reason we can't talk
to these doctors without you butting in. We've got a trial in a
few weeks, and we have better things we could be doing than
waiting on you!"

Pulling his pipe from his mouth, Duckett blanched. He had
never seen Baradel angry before. Even Karceski was surprised.

"I'm sorry you feel this way," Duckett said. "I wasn't late on
purpose. I got held up."

"Why do you even have to be here?"

"Well, if you'll feel better, I'll leave."

"You're goddamn right I'll feel better. I have no intention of
interviewing these doctors with you present." Baradel's voice
was still several decibels louder than normal.

"All right, then. We'll go after I have a word with the doctors." Duckett stepped inside an office to speak with Kleinman
and Mokhtari, then left the hospital.

The defense attorneys spent hours interviewing the Perkins
psychiatrists and left the hospital unimpressed. Dr. Mokhtari
told them he felt so strongly that Larry was sane that he was
convinced Perkins would release Larry within thirty days if he
was acquitted on insanity grounds. Baradel didn't believe
Mokhtari; the doctor had to be saying that for effect. Baradel
actually feared the reverse—that Perkins would keep Larry
medicated and locked up for years, reducing him to a vegetable.
Both defense lawyers doubted that Larry would receive meaningful treatment at Perkins. The hospital housed mostly hard-

core mental cases, many of them violent, and relied heavily on psychotropic drugs to treat them. Patuxent, on the other hand, rejected inmates who were considered insane and relied chiefly on psychotherapy for treatment.

"We could win the battle on insanity, and at the same time lose the war," Baradel said gloomily.

Karceski reluctantly agreed. He had seen other clients go to Perkins and he knew its reputation as a dismal, chaotic place.

After spending a week being evaluated there, Larry knew what Perkins was like, too. He made it through the week unharmed except for a minor scuffle in which a patient struck his left arm with a chair. Larry dreaded going back to live with those lunatics. When Karceski explained that he would be committed indefinitely to Perkins if the jury found him insane, it was one of the few times Larry showed any emotion.

"I don't want to go there," he said in a shaky voice.

"I can understand that," Karceski replied. "But you might not have to stay long. It could be your fastest route to freedom. Think about it."

Larry did, and remained adamant about not wanting to go. Yet when Karceski outlined Duckett's second-degree plea offer, all Larry said was, "Do what you think's best."

After weighing and reweighing their options, Karceski decided to stay with the insanity plea. Although it was risky, he thought it offered Larry his best chance at early release. Karceski did not share Baradel's fear that Perkins would keep Larry locked up for decades and destroy his mind with drugs. He was convinced the hospital would release Larry fairly quickly; and that made the insanity plea preferable to Duckett's twenty-year offer. Karceski felt he could do much better than that at trial.

Mapping their courtroom strategy, the defense lawyers realized that Larry's testimony would be vital. Early on, Joe Murphy had told Baradel that his testimony could make or break their case. After Larry came apart when he confessed in Baradel's law library—a scene that left a deep impression on both lawyers—Murphy and Baradel instinctively believed that Larry had snapped on the night of the murders. They felt the jury would believe it, too, if they could see the raw pain that had gushed out of him that day. "I don't care what questions you ask him or how many times you ask the same ones, you've got to keep him on the stand for three or four days," Murphy told Baradel. Their biggest fear was that Larry would sit up there like an automaton, saying yes and no to every question, showing not one ounce of emotion.

If that happened, the lawyers had a secret weapon: the crime-scene photos. If their strategy worked, Larry would break and weep when they showed him the photographs for the first time. How could he remain detached looking at his mother lying in the snow?

Karceski also was eager to try out the cumulative-provocation theory that Murphy and Baradel had kicked around the previous year. Baradel's law clerk wrote a twenty-page memorandum exploring whether the traumas Larry had suffered in childhood and adolescence might be considered reasonable provocation, which could reduce his murder charge to manslaughter. After reading the case law, Karceski believed he might be able to prove that Larry's sad history constituted cumulative provocation.

Anne Swartz's testimony was almost as crucial to the prosecution as her brother's testimony was to the defense. In an effort to gauge her credibility as a witness and her ability to hold up on the stand, Duckett dispatched her to a clinical psychologist in the summer of 1984. She was the only other person in the house that night. Although her story was sketchy, it was still vital to the case Duckett planned to build against Larry at trial.

Anne was a reluctant patient at first in the office of Anthony B. Wolff, Ph.D. She seemed anxious, depressed, and mildly suspicious of Wolff. She didn't want to talk about much of anything, especially not her parents' death. With prodding, though, she gradually opened up about herself and her fears over the course of six interviews.

Her bland tone and lack of emotion struck Wolff when she repeated the story she had told police about the night of the murders. She expressed ambivalence about her parents, and Wolff noticed that she already was calling the Smithmyers

Mother and Father. When he inquired how she felt about her parents' death, she denied feeling upset at all. He concluded that she hadn't adequately mourned their deaths and was employing "massive denial" to defend against the tragedy.

Compounding the tragedy, Wolff noted, Anne often had wondered about her biological parents, who had given her up for adoption in Korea. "The loss of these parents has haunted Anne for years, making the loss of her second set of parents that much more pointed and incomprehensible to her," he wrote in a report to Duckett.

Wolff concluded that Anne's social judgment and abstract reasoning skills were intact and that she would be a competent witness because she had the ability to accurately observe, remember, and report what she had seen.

Yet Anne did not want to testify against her brother. She repeatedly told Wolff that she would not go to Larry's trial. If she was forced to go, she insisted, she would say nothing. Her reluctance to testify, the doctor concluded, was partly due to her feelings for Larry, whom Wolff described as a "key nurturant and positive" person in her emotional life. She said she expected Larry to live with her at the Smithmyers' after the trial, and the doctor thought it might upset her greatly to see that fantasy shattered.

When he asked about the man she had seen leaving her yard on the night of the murders, Anne denied that she had seen his face. She said his hair resembled Larry's, but she denied that she had identified Larry as the man to police.

"My feeling is that Anne did not in fact see the face of this individual," Wolff wrote, "or if she did, she is defending against what she saw so vigorously that she is not able to come to terms with it."

The doctor suspected that Anne was struggling to repress the knowledge that Larry had murdered their parents, because to admit his guilt would overwhelm her.

When Wolff probed her refusal to testify, she revealed another possible reason besides her loyalty to Larry. She said she was afraid that if she became conspicuous or drew attention to herself, she or the Smithmyers would be killed—presumably by the same person who had killed her parents. "This may in part explain Anne's initial tendency to be withholding and wary of me," Wolff wrote, "and it certainly could explain her reluctance to be placed in the limelight in a court of law."

To spare her the guilt of feeling responsible for sending her brother to prison, Wolff urged the state's attorney not to call her as a witness unless it was "absolutely necessary."

Out of concern for Anne's emotional health, the defense lawyers also lobbied Duckett to spare Anne the trauma of testifying. Baradel suggested that he and Duckett jointly draft a statement of what she saw on the night of the murders and present that to the jury. Duckett agreed.

The defense lawyers thought Anne's testimony was too odd and too inconsistent for a jury to give it much weight. To highlight the inconsistencies, they inserted into the document such details as her claim that she had seen her father "lying in the snow on his back: He was groaning." Obviously, she hadn't seen her father lying in the snow: He was inside the house. Little things like that could discredit her entire testimony, Baradel believed.

2.

During the fifteen months that Larry spent awaiting trial, his friends and supporters never forgot him. He had a half-dozen visitors every week straight through the year, mostly school and church friends. Annie paid her first visit shortly after the jail changed its no-children policy in August and allowed children to visit if an adult accompanied them. Eileen Smithmyer took Annie to the jail ten days later, then didn't take her again for six months. Michael visited only a few more times than Annie. He paid his third visit in September, then didn't see Larry again until the prosecutor personally arranged a lengthy, private visit between the two brothers a few weeks before the trial.

One of Larry's most faithful visitors was a woman he had seen occasionally in church on Sundays. Caryl Sweet was a friend of his parents who had taught Sunday school with Bob. She hadn't known Larry well but decided to visit him after she had a disturbing dream about his mother. Sweet had six children of her own to worry about, yet she felt a maternal urge to help Larry. As she got to know him in jail, Sweet found it increasingly difficult to believe that such a gentle youth could have murdered his parents.

Sweet had a psychic friend she had met on vacation in Maine years earlier who happened to visit Annapolis shortly after the murders. When Sweet told her friend Kay Mora of her concern about Larry, Mora volunteered to do a trance. She thought she might help by channeling, receiving information from beings who were believed to dwell outside the normal range of human perception.

Mora was a professional psychic with her own cable TV show, "Tuning in With Kay," in Jacksonville, Florida. Short and overweight, she had a massive square face framed by short gray hair. She had devoted her entire adult life to the study, practice, and teaching of psychic development. She'd written several books with such titles as *Crystals in Your Life* and *The Seven Levels of Learning.* The FBI and half a dozen local police departments had called on her talents.

Sweet tape-recorded the session in the tiny study of her house. When she channeled, Mora lay back with her eyes closed and spoke in a voice different from her own—a masculine monotone, harsh and guttural. It was the voice of "Sean," one of a dozen spiritual guides that Mora believed spoke through her.

Sweet began by reciting the names of all the Swartz family members and recapping the murder case. The psychic then said, "This boy has an unusual background, has unusual treatment as a small child that goes back to perhaps a year old."

"Could you elaborate on his early life?"

"Yes, this is what we shall do. He was born into a family that did not want this child. . . . He was a crying child, and the crying was out of fear and isolation, for he was left alone much of the time. He was not nurtured or cared for. But he was left lying in his crib or his bed for long periods of time and was neither touched nor loved."

As a small child, she added, he suffered a brain injury that caused an epilepsylike disease. Eventually, it impaired his memory and ability to reason.

"At the age of one and a half to two, we see him in another place, and possibly, in that span of time, in two places. . . . Although his needs were met on the level of taking care of him, his emotional needs were not met due to the fact that there were three or four other children in the same home. He was merely one of many, and there was again the beginning of punishments, or the discipline of the child.

"At the age of three and a half, there were other kinds of treatment, and it appears this may have been another place as well. You will find that there was again the lack of caring, or the lack of attention. . . . By the time the child was five, he was very much into bewilderment or confusion of the soul and not knowing which way to turn, which way to speak, which way to direct. Much punishment was inflicted on things that were not connected to the child."

"Sean" advised Sweet to question Larry about his relationship with his parents: "You will find that there are times that this information has been blocked out. Perhaps through the use of techniques such as hypnosis this child will recall many instances that are at this time blocked from memory. It is only a conscious effort to protect the nervous system of the body, for these are things that the nervous system of the body was unable to deal with."

"Sean," Sweet asked, "is there any possibility that somebody other than this child should be looked for as responsible for this happening? As being the person who actually committed the crime?"

"We would say to you that there is another one involved, yes."

The psychic then offered a series of fragmented clues that seemingly came out of nowhere. She said she saw a man who was twenty-five or twenty-six years old, mustached, and drove a maroon car. It wasn't clear whether "Sean" thought the man was involved in the murders, or was merely a witness to the murders. "You see," the psychic said mysteriously, "there is a witness to all of this, but this one is keeping himself away from it all."

Without being specific, the psychic said that Bob and Kay Swartz's virtuous lifestyle had been an illusion: "There was much going on in the interior of the family that was bad."

She said Larry had built resentment and hatred toward his parents over many years—a passive hatred, not an aggressive one that might have led to premeditated murder. However, she said the resentment could have ignited suddenly, causing his mind "to go berserk." A burst of uncontrollable rage then would have overtaken his conscious mind, giving him superhuman strength: "The subconscious would overtake and block out all events. And then, when it returns to its home, the conscious has no memory whatever."

Sweet found the psychic's clues fascinating but had no idea what to make of them. A few days later, she dubbed a cassette tape of the trance and dropped it off at Baradel's law office. She knew Baradel from church and had told him in advance of her plans to do the trance. Now she figured the clues from "Sean" and his pack of otherworldly friends were the lawyer's problem.

Afterward, Sweet heard nothing from Baradel and didn't know whether he even had listened to the tape.

Baradel did listen but didn't think much of it, even though he couldn't help noticing that the psychic was right about a surprising number of things. She had pinpointed the exact age that Larry left his first home—between a year and a half and two. Her summary of his childhood was also uncannily accurate, according to the adoption records, and her suggestion of a brain injury intrigued him. He marveled, too, at the psychic's claim that Larry was blocking certain memories: Nothing about his memory gaps had appeared in the newspapers.

It was all eerie stuff, but too bizarre and irrelevant for Baradel to pay it much attention. He filed the tape away at the rear of his desk drawer and forgot about the psychic.

Caryl Sweet was not Larry's only eccentric visitor. Christine Monroe had her share of unconventional traits, too. Unlike Sweet, though, Christine proved to be one of Larry's most erratic visitors. She saw him a second time in August, shortly after he returned from Perkins, then abruptly stopped phoning, writing, or visiting.

Larry was crushed. Christine enchanted him, and he wanted to see her again.

The fall of 1984 was bleak for Christine. She had broken up with her boyfriend and questioned where her life was heading. Depression weighed her down, and her visits to Larry had disturbed her. She had never been inside a jail before and couldn't fully grasp why she was going now. She told herself that she was reaching out to an abused child, yet she also knew she was physically attracted to this darkly handsome youth who was so much younger than she. Her ambivalence troubled her. You have no business doing something like this, she told herself angrily. Why are you getting involved with someone accused of murder when you don't even know him? He must think you're some kind of yo-yo. And you *are!*

So she pulled back and tried to put Larry out of her mind. She needed to concentrate on caring for her daughter and putting her own life in order. Yet Larry still pulled on her emotions.

In February 1985, for reasons she didn't fully understand, she finally wrote to him again, apologized for her long silence and asked whether he still wanted contact.

"Yes, I *do* want you to write me!" Larry wrote back.

Not waiting for his letter to arrive, Christine impulsively stopped at the detention center one Sunday while she was running an errand nearby. She could see Larry's delight, but she also sensed his pain.

"I don't understand why you dropped out of sight," he said.

"I just didn't feel right about it," she replied. "I felt like one of those curiosity seekers and wondered if I had a screw loose or something. I'm sorry if I let you down."

Once renewed, their friendship blossomed. Despite their age difference, Christine felt a deep kinship and sense of intimacy with Larry. They talked on the phone almost every night, and she visited twice a week. At first she felt childlike, almost as though they were brother and sister talking in the special language young siblings often develop. As the relationship deepened, she felt like a social worker, sister, and mother rolled into one.

Larry didn't see her as any of the above. He saw her as a beautiful woman, and his growing infatuation was obvious even to Christine. She wasn't oblivious to Larry's physical charms, either. Around the other inmates, Larry was secretive about Christine. He rarely talked about his pretty visitor and shrugged off all questions about her. She had been spooked once; he didn't want it to happen again.

They talked for hours on the phone about their families and childhood. She told him story after story. Gradually, he opened up and begin confiding in her about his experiences. When she told him how she had sneaked down the street as a child and peered in through her cousins' windows, pretending she was part of their family, Larry stared at her openmouthed.

"I don't believe you just said that," he declared.

"Why?"

"I just don't believe you just said that."

She blushed, remembering sneaking around in her cousins' yard at night. "I know it's kind of weird—"

"Weird? I used to do the same thing!"

She giggled, relieved. "Tell me about it," she said softly, and he did.

They carried on like that for weeks, she telling him about her life and he replying, "My God! I did the same thing!" Then he would elaborate on things he'd never told anyone before.

Christine talked for hours about her father. "He was such a pack rat. Our house was always a mess. He liked it so dark, he drew the curtains even in the summer."

Larry was amazed. "My house was like that, too!"

She said her father never wanted her to date and called boys "those filthy things!" Larry said his mother wouldn't let him date the same girl twice and never had a good word for any girl he liked. His mother restricted him at home, watched him at school, and tracked what little freedom he had through the Smithmyers.

Christine avoided talking about the murders, and he never mentioned them. Yet her curiosity was strong, so on the phone one night she said, "Why don't you tell me about that night?"

"I wondered why you never asked," he said, as though he had been waiting for the question. Then he repeated the story he had told the psychiatrists.

Christine could not understand the suddenness of it. "How could you have anger so intense, all at once like that? What set you off, your mother's comment about your exams?"

"I don't know," he said. "It sort of overtook me, like an explosion. It was a spastic thing."

Christine still couldn't fathom what kind of sudden fury would cause a boy to attack his mother with a maul. She could understand a slow rage, for she had felt that herself, yet even a slow rage seemed unlikely to ignite over grades. It would make more sense to her if his mother or father had abused him or done something more than just putting him on restriction.

"Did your parents ever do anything really bad to you to make you want to do something like that?"

"Not really." He spoke in that monotone he used when he talked about things that disturbed him.

"The way Mom and Dad were to Michael got to me," he added. "I hated it. They were so mean to him, I think they hated him. And they started treating *me* like that, for no reason. It wasn't fair."

Larry told her the whole story of Michael. He said that in the end, his mother had threatened to send him to reform school, too.

Still wondering about the tears that her own tale of sexual abuse had evoked, she asked whether he had ever been molested.

"No," he replied.

She knew all too well how traumatic such an experience could be, especially when it involved a parent. The more she thought about it, the more she sensed that something was missing from his story. "It's normal to feel guilty about something like that," she said gently. "I know I did."

"Well," Larry said suddenly, "there was something like that, but it was a long time ago." He admitted that he had been molested when he was eight years old by a man who lived in his neighborhood.

Christine nodded. "More than once?"

"Yes," Larry said softly. He was uncomfortable talking about it. He refused to elaborate, even when she tried to get him to tell her more.

"I don't see how it's going to help with *this,*" Larry said.

She dropped the subject, doubting that the old incident with a neighbor would shed any light on the murders.

3.

In December, Duckett had requested the reassignment of Barr to his office again, this time to work exclusively on the Swartz case. By January, Barr was reporting to Annapolis and meeting daily with Duckett.

The trial was postponed yet again, until April 18, after Duckett was hospitalized in February for a neck fusion. While the prosecutor was laid up for a week, Barr continued working full time on trial preparations.

In March, Barr won his sergeant's stripes. He was moving up the departmental ladder so quickly that his wife, Pat, was convinced he would wind up as chief.

Barr helped the prosecutor interview witnesses, review evidence, and pore over maps of the Swartz neighborhood. He and Duckett went to Perkins for lengthy interviews with the state psychiatrists, then visited the FBI's forensic laboratory in Washington, D.C. At Barr's request, an FBI agent photographed the soles of Larry's Docksides and compared the photograph with a bloody shoe print that police had photographed in the snow near Mrs. Swartz's body. The two shoeprints matched.

Duckett grew obsessed with Larry's palm print, the one police had lifted from the sliding glass door frame. It was outlined in red, but that wasn't enough for Duckett. He felt his entire evidentiary case hung on that palm print. "I need to prove that it's *blood,*" he said. "What the hell good does it do me if it's an ordinary print?"

"We can't prove that it's blood," Barr warned. "You'll destroy the whole thing if you try."

Barr had sent the print to the FBI for chemical analysis the previous spring, but the FBI didn't do extensive blood work on it. An FBI serologist had warned that the blood work might destroy the print. Barr argued that it wasn't worth destroying crucial evidence for a one-in-a-million crap shoot. Duckett wouldn't listen, however. He figured expert testimony would establish that it was Larry's handprint, even if the serologist blurred it beyond recognition. At Duckett's insistence, an FBI blood expert opened the lift, rubbed it with a saline-coated swab, and analyzed it.

As Barr had predicted, the blood test was inconclusive, and it smeared beyond recognition the one piece of evidence he deemed most crucial to their case.

In February, Barr decided to see whether Larry had talked in jail. He went to the detention center and summoned Larry's cellmates for private interviews at the state's attorney's office. John Kemmer—Larry's supposed friend—recounted a vague, semiconfession that he claimed Larry had made only a few months after he went to jail.

Barr also interviewed two other inmates who shared Larry's cell, and they offered a confession that Barr found more convincing that Kemmer's. Mark Staab, a twenty-one-year-old convicted thief, was hoping to trade his cooperation in a big murder case for leniency on his own theft case. Staab told Barr that he and Larry became good friends while they shared a cell, and that Larry had confessed. Staab's knowledge about Larry's home life gave him some credibility with Barr, and the detective hoped it would give him credibility with a jury, too.

Staab said Larry had confessed at four o'clock in the morning as they lay in their bunks. Larry related what happened in a low voice and drew a diagram to demonstrate where the murders took place, the inmate said.

Barr found Staab's account of the murders interesting, for in it, Larry said he stabbed his mother with the knife first, then she ran out through the patio door, and Larry struck her with the maul outside. Barr was convinced that Larry had told Staab the truth and had lied to the psychiatrists.

"At the same time while this was happening," Staab continued, "his father walked out of the computer room and Larry went over and backed him into the room and started to beat on him with his fists. Larry told me that he couldn't get him down, that his father was pretty strong. Larry then took the knife and stabbed him. I asked Larry what it was like to stab somebody, and he told me that it was just like cutting a chicken. I asked him why he did it, why did he kill them. Larry told me that he was tired of their shit, and them always picking on him and putting him down, particularly around his girlfriend."

A few days later, another inmate gave Barr a statement that seemed to corroborate Staab's. Thomas W. Johnson, Jr., a twenty-six-year-old who was charged with altering the identification number on a pistol, said he was lying on his bunk when he overheard Larry talking to Staab and another inmate. Johnson repeated much of what Staab had said, then added some other things he said he overheard. "His mother would always call his girlfriends whores and would only let him go out with a girl one time," Johnson said. "His mother also hassled him about his grades, and on the night that the murders happened, the two of them argued about grades and his girlfriend, Sarah, and her being a whore. When his mother called his girlfriend a whore, he zapped out and started to stab her. I believe he said stabbed, but I'm not exactly sure. He also said something about using a maul or an ax on her. . . ."

Barr thought a jury might find it credible that Larry's mother had called his girlfriend a whore immediately before the murders. That might remove some of the mystery about his motive.

4.

"Have you talked to Christine?" Eileen Smithmyer asked.

Baradel raised his bushy eyebrows. "No. Who is she?"

"She talks to Larry for hours almost every day. Maybe she could help you," Eileen said.

With the trial barely a month away, Baradel and Karceski were visiting the Smithmyers to review their testimony about

the Swartzes' family life. After the attorney related how withdrawn and reticent Larry still was after months of interviews,
Eileen suggested that Baradel should contact Christine.

Maybe this woman could help, Baradel thought. He decided
to meet her.

Setting down his wineglass, Baradel stared at Christine Monroe.
"That was *you*?"

"Yeah," she said softly. "That was me."

He shook his head. "I am *so sorry*. I can't believe I didn't
listen to you." Baradel was surprised to realize that this was the
woman who had called him the year before and said she was a
"concerned person" who wanted to help Larry. He had brushed
her off without giving her a second thought.

"You probably thought I was some off-the-wall nut, calling
out of the blue like that," she reassured him. "You couldn't possibly have known what I was going to tell you. Don't worry
about it."

They were sitting in the cocktail lounge of the Chart House, a
piertop restaurant in front of Baradel's law office overlooking
Spa Creek. At Baradel's request, Christine had met him at his
office after work. He had asked her to explain her involvement
with Larry, and her whole life story tumbled out—how she had
been sexually abused as a child and had come close to shooting
her own father. The story deeply moved Baradel.

He took another sip of wine and looked across the table. She
was intriguing, this attractive brunette. He decided to be frank.
Eileen had said she had gotten close to Larry; maybe he had
confided things about his home life to her that could help his
defense.

"The truth is, I'm having trouble getting anything out of
Larry," Baradel said. "He's not very forthcoming. I think it might
be helpful to his case if you and I could talk about some of the
things he's told you."

She nodded. "I don't want to betray any confidences, but if
you really think it might help, I'll do what I can."

"What has he told you about his parents? Has he talked about
why he wanted to kill them?"

"Yeah"—she nodded—"but I still wonder if what he tells me

is the truth." She related Larry's complaints about his parents' strictness and how they had humiliated him. Judging by his strong reaction to her story of incest, Christine said she didn't completely believe his claim that his parents had never abused him.

She wondered whether she should mention Larry's sexual encounter with the man in his neighborhood. Larry would be angry if she did, but she felt it was in his best interest because Baradel was trying to defend Larry, to keep him out of prison for life. Taking a deep breath, she blurted it out.

"He said *that*?" Baradel gasped.

"Yeah."

"Damn! I've been trying to get things like that out of him for months. Go on."

After she related several other things Larry had told her about his home life, Christine returned to the murders. "Do you think there's any possibility he didn't do it?"

"No, but I've got to admit, a lot of things don't add up." Baradel took another sip of wine. "It's frustrating talking to him, because he keeps changing his story around. There are so many inconsistencies, things he can't remember."

Baradel had spent dozens of hours at the detention center questioning Larry. Larry distorted things, omitted things, denied things that obviously were true. Baradel sensed that the youth was protecting his parents by downplaying how harshly they had treated him. His attitude seemed to say, Well, I killed them once, why kill them again?

Most frustrating were his memory gaps about that night, especially the puzzling footprints. Baradel wanted to nail down who had left those bare footprints in the snow. He worried that Larry really had chased his mother and had repressed the memory. The defense lawyers didn't want that memory suddenly returning when Larry was on the witness stand. A detail such as that could seriously undermine their defense.

Karceski and Baradel had considered hypnotizing Larry but rejected the idea because of the possibility that it would contaminate his testimony. Although police often used hypnosis to develop leads and jog witnesses' memories, hypnotically induced testimony was rarely admissible in American courts. The defense attorneys considered Larry's testimony too crucial to risk having it ruled inadmissible.

Other stray details puzzled Baradel, too, little things such as Michael's custody and juvenile delinquency papers, which the detectives had found strewn around the foyer of the Swartz house. Larry couldn't or wouldn't say why they were there. The cops thought Larry had placed them there to cast suspicion on Michael. However, Baradel wondered, Could his parents have waved the papers in Larry's face that night and threatened to give him back to the state, as they had Michael?

Baradel had had no luck solving any of these mysteries. Maybe Christine would. He looked at her thoughtfully. "If he's more comfortable talking to you, maybe you can help us."

She smiled. "I'll certainly try."

Christine continued talking to Larry almost daily over the next few weeks, and phoned in regular reports to Baradel. Much of what she reported the lawyer already knew, either through interviews with family friends or from Larry himself. Still, the attorney hoped she would make a breakthrough, that Larry would suddenly remember taking his shoes off after the murders and walking outside barefoot, or that he would reveal new details about how his parents had mistreated him.

She approached Larry slowly, cautiously. He was so timid that she chastised him, trying to goad him into becoming more assertive. He prefaced remarks with "You're gonna think I'm crazy," or "You're gonna think I'm weird."

"Don't *do* that," she replied. "Don't start out apologizing. I want to know what you think and feel. Just say it."

They talked about how his family had closed in on him, and she asked, "Why didn't you just run away? If it was that bad at home, why did you stay?"

"I don't know. I guess I figured the rest of the world was like that, too. I was scared, and I didn't know anything about the rest of the world. They never let me go anywhere."

Christine spent hours explaining her religion to him, hoping it would afford him solace. At first, she was reluctant to talk about her relationship with Christ. "Don't think I'm a goody-two-shoes," she begged. Although she wasn't a regular churchgoer, she recounted how she had developed a personal relationship with her Lord and Savior when she was an adolescent. Christ had guided her through some terrible times and He had helped her to see the world from beyond the confines of her own pain.

Larry said that even though he had attended church regularly, he never felt close to God. He used to hide outside church to be alone and to escape the long tedious services.

"Larry, why is it that you have to go to church to talk to God?" she asked. "Why can't you just talk to God by yourself and have a relationship without all this formality the Catholic Church makes you go through?"

"I don't know."

Christine could tell it was a new idea to Larry, that he might speak directly to God. She wanted it to sink in. "Read the Bible," she suggested. "Find out how *you* feel about religion, not how you've been taught to feel. Learn how to think and feel for yourself. You don't realize how much you've been controlled."

"Yeah," he replied. "But you know, it's so hard to break away and feel like I have real freedom, because I've never had it before."

Some nights she strummed her guitar over the phone and sang songs she'd written, or read her poems aloud. Other nights, she read from the Bible. She told Larry that if he ever wanted to accept Christ into his heart and pray directly to Him, she'd help. All he had to do was ask.

"You know why I think you came into my life?" Larry asked.

"No, why?"

"I think God sent you."

Christine chuckled softly. "Only certain people can go to certain people, because those are the only ones they'll listen to. We're all kind of missionaries. And because I've been through an experience similar to yours, I can get through your barriers. And you know what? That shows you how much God loves you, because I don't know why else I ever got involved in this thing. It must have been the Holy Spirit sending me to you."

As the trial approached, Larry asked Christine on the phone one night to help him accept Christ into his heart. They prayed together, and Christine thought she detected a new note of enthusiasm in his monotone. She was pleased.

Larry occasionally talked about the many people who visited him, and he mentioned that one woman who visited regularly knew a psychic who had done a trance on him.

Christine was curious. "Who is she?"

"Her name's Mrs. Sweet," Larry said.

Larry couldn't answer any of Christine's questions; he knew nothing about the psychic. So Christine decided to do some snooping. She got the phone number from Larry, called Mrs. Sweet the next evening, and introduced herself as a friend of Larry's.

Standing in her kitchen, stirring vegetables on the stove and trying to coordinate dinner for her large family, Caryl Sweet was annoyed. Who was this woman, and why didn't she give her name?

"What are you looking for?" Sweet asked suspiciously.

"I'm not sure, exactly." Christine mentioned the psychic and said she hoped the psychic could answer some questions that had been bothering her.

"Look," Sweet said, exasperated, "if you're hoping the psychic will help with Larry's defense, forget it. I've already tried that."

"You mean a trance?"

"Yes."

"What did the psychic say?"

"I'm not at liberty to discuss it. It's in the attorney's hands."

"Ron Baradel?"

"Yes. He has a tape of the trance."

Oh, he *does,* does he? Christine thought. "All right, then, thanks," she said, and hung up.

She called Baradel immediately.

"You nosy, nosy little thing!" he cried. "How did you find out about that?" It had been so long ago, Baradel had forgotten about the silly psychic tape.

"I have my secrets." She laughed. "So where is the tape? Can I hear it?"

Baradel was quiet for a minute. "It's in my office, and no, you can't. It's not going to do any good. It's just a psychic."

"Oh, come on. It can't hurt. I really want to hear it."

She badgered him for ten minutes, and Baradel resisted. Finally, he relented.

Christine went to his office the next evening, and he handed her a recorder with the trance tape inside. At the same time, he gave her a binder containing Larry's adoption records. "If you're going to listen to the tape, I suppose you should read this, too."

While Baradel went to work in another room, Christine sat in his office for more than an hour, listening to the psychic's low strange monotone and flipping through Larry's adoption records.

"I can't believe this!" she told Baradel after she finished. "This woman is right on the money about Larry's childhood. Don't you think that's weird?"

"Yeah, I do," he reluctantly conceded, "because there is no way she could have read that stuff. Those are confidential agency reports. They're sealed by law."

With the trial barely a week away, Baradel considered the psychic's vague clues a distraction he didn't need. He had never entertained the possibility that Larry might be innocent: Larry had *confessed*—why would he make up such a gruesome confession?

Baradel once again put the trance tape in his desk drawer and forgot about the seance.

Although they were curious, the otherworldly clues led to no new revelations or discoveries in the case.

When Christine ate dinner with Baradel and Karceski at the Chart House in Annapolis a few days before the trial, both lawyers vented frustration over Larry's hazy memory. They feared that he was withholding information about the murders, and they worried about trying the case around such potentially damaging gaps as the footprints.

Although Baradel had dismissed the psychic, Christine had not. The weird tape had strengthened her suspicions that Larry knew more than he was saying. As incredible as it might seem, she wondered, What if the psychic was right about someone else being involved in the murders? The idea appealed to her partly because she *wanted* Larry to be innocent; she had grown deeply fond of the shy, handsome youth. As she listened to the lawyers discuss their legal strategy, she made up her mind to have one last talk with Larry. She hoped to uncover information that might help his defense before it was too late.

The next day, she went to the detention center determined to confront Larry as she never had before. She told the guard that she had injured her back and couldn't stand up in the visiting room where she usually saw Larry. Just this once, could she have a private room?

The guard acquiesced and ushered her into one of the attorney's booths. They were still separated by a large glass window and still had to talk by phone, but they could sit down and didn't have to share the room with other people. For the first time, Larry and Christine had privacy.

She came right to the point. "I didn't want the other guys in there to hear me. I've got to talk to you about what is going on." She looked directly into his eyes. "Larry, I know you are not being truthful with me. You have got to stop this bullshit. You're going to trial now. You've got to tell the truth."

"No, I am. I am telling the truth," Larry stammered. "I don't know what you mean." His eyes looked pained, as though he'd been slapped.

"I've talked to you all this time, and you are still being silent on so many things. It doesn't add up. I don't believe you."

Larry's eyes avoided hers. "Christine, I don't know what you're talking about." He was fidgety and could not understand the abrupt change in her. She had never been confrontational before. "What are you talking about?"

"There's someone else involved, isn't there?"

Larry stared at her. "In the murders?"

"Yeah. There is, isn't there?"

"No way," he said, shaking his head. "I don't know what you're talking about."

Christine was disappointed. She had upset him, deliberately, without producing the intended effect. She had thought he might come undone and tell her the truth. The whole experience upset her tremendously. Her eyes burned with tears, yet she plowed on.

"Are you totally sure you have these blackouts? Are you sure you can't fill in some of these voids you're not talking about? I think there was more going on in that house than you're telling anyone."

"I've told everything I remember. I don't understand why you're doing this. Why don't you believe me?"

"I'm sorry I'm upsetting you, but it's just that we're *here* now. We are *here*. This is the wire. If you have any leads you can give me, anything you can tell me at all, no matter how bad it is, no matter if *you* think it won't help you, *I* want to hear it."

Larry shook his head no.

"Okay. So this is how you want to leave it?"

"Yeah."

"Look, I know I upset you, and I'm sorry. I just felt I had to do this."

Larry's face resumed its familiar blank expression. "That's okay," he said flatly.

On the phone the next night, Larry told Christine that her visit had upset him so much that he returned to his cell after she left and tried as hard as he could to concentrate on whatever it was he was blocking out.

"I passed out sitting on my bed," Larry said. "I was concentrating and I just blacked out. Nothing like that ever happened to me before."

5.

Detective Barr climbed into his cruiser and looked at the few names remaining on the defense witness list. Most of them were crossed off; he'd done a lot of interviewing in the last week. Few of the witnesses had much to say. Glancing at his watch, Barr wondered whether he should call it a day. It was late Wednesday afternoon, the day before Larry's trial. Barr still felt a little nervous and Duckett did, too. The prosecutor had asked him to find out what the defense witnesses had to say, so Barr decided to track down one last witness. Scanning the list, he picked Dolores Price, a name he thought he recognized from the log of Larry's jail visitors.

Acting friendlier than most witnesses, Mrs. Price opened her door in downtown Annapolis and invited Barr inside. She talked freely about the Swartzes, who had been close family friends for four years. She was still talking when her husband, Sam, arrived home.

Sam Price spoke at length about Larry's poor relationship with his father. He seemed sympathetic to the youth, and Barr wondered whether Larry had confided in him about the murders.

"You visited Larry at the detention center a lot, didn't you?" Barr asked.

"That's right," Sam Price replied.

"You and he must be fairly close, then."

"Yeah. I feel like Larry trusts me and can confide his problems to me."

Suddenly, Price brought up Dungeons & Dragons. "That game has demonistic qualities," he said. "I think those demonistic qualities were transposed into Larry. They should ban that game because it's sacrilegious and dangerous. It's the devil's game."

Price said Larry had told him about a dream involving Dungeons & Dragons, and Barr asked when.

"Last October," replied Price. "He called me from the detention center one night. He said he was playing Dungeons & Dragons in his dream and came upon a big strong monster. The monster was superpowerful, and he couldn't overpower him. So Larry took a knife and stabbed the monster in the chest, but the monster was really tough to get down. Then Larry advanced to the next level in the game, where he encountered a long slender snake. It had a long neck, and he had to hit the snake about its head and neck with a maul to overpower it."

"Well, of course I thought about the murders right away. The dream was so similar to the murders that I knew it was something very significant. It was that demonistic game. I can't understand why they don't take it off the market. It's poisoning the minds of our youth."

Barr could barely conceal his excitement. He thought the symbolism in the dream was unmistakable. If Larry went this far with Price, could he have gone one step further?

"After this conversation about the dream, did Larry confess to you?"

"Yes."

"What did he actually say?" Barr tried to keep his tone neutral, but it was difficult. He was excited. This could be the confession he had sought for so long, the one he and Duckett could use in court.

"The next time I saw him at the detention center, I told him that I knew the dream was his way of telling me about the murders. I told him he needed to clear his conscience and come clean. And then he just looked at me and said, 'I killed them.'"

"Did he tell you why?"

"He didn't have to. I told him I already knew that he'd done it, and I also knew why."

Afraid that he might spook the Prices, Barr had refrained from taking notes throughout the interview. Now he was eager to leave so he could call Duckett and write it down while the conversation was fresh in his mind. They talked for a few more minutes, then Barr excused himself and left.

"This brief reactive psychosis thing is what worries me the most," Duckett said.

"Why?" asked Patrick J. Bell, an assistant state's attorney.

"Because I think Dr. Blumberg will be able to pull it all together with this diagnosis, and the jury will buy it. We were all right before this came in. Damn. I just don't like it."

Duckett reread the supplemental response the defense had belatedly filed to Duckett's discovery motion. The response disclosed that Dr. Blumberg had rendered an oral opinion that Larry suffered from "a brief reactive psychosis" at the time of the murders.

"We used to call that temporary insanity," Duckett said. "Juries can relate to it. This kid had all he could take and blew up one night—lost all control and literally went out of his mind. That's what they're going to say. And dammit, it makes sense, especially after the jury hears Dr. Henderson talk about how the kid's childhood made him schizophrenic. Henderson can be a spellbinder on the stand. Then Blumberg will come in and tie it all together somehow with brief reactive psychosis."

It was Wednesday afternoon. Duckett was nervous about the Swartz trial, which was scheduled to start the next day. He had gone to Bell's office for advice, and Bell was quizzing his boss, helping to crystallize his thoughts.

For months, Duckett said, he had believed he could beat Dr. Henderson one on one with either of his two lead doctors from Perkins—Kleinman or Mokhtari. Now, however, he feared that Blumberg had tipped the balance in the battle of the shrinks: The defense seemed to have the edge.

"Either they'll be able to convince the jury that he's insane," Duckett grumbled, "or, in the alternative, it will be a big mess like the Hinckley case. And the jury will go back in the jury room and say, Jesus Christ, the fucking doctors can't even agree on what occurred! The judge told us about reasonable doubt, and if that's not reasonable doubt, what is?"

Duckett had spent much of the day agonizing over whether he should go through with the trial. The more he talked, the more he leaned toward renewing plea negotiations. He did not want to lose a big case like this. He didn't think the defense really believed it was in Larry's best interest to stand trial; not if Duckett was willing to negotiate a reasonable sentence and recommend Patuxent.

"What happened the last time you talked about a plea?" Bell asked.

Duckett explained that Karceski had insisted on a light sentence, something around ten years. Karceski had suggested manslaughter, which Duckett could not accept. The prosecutor wanted Larry to plead guilty to second-degree murder, for he believed these killings were crimes of passion, not premeditated first-degree acts. Duckett thought that a second-degree plea would result in a moderate sentence, and that Larry would serve his sentence at the Patuxent Institution, where he would get the treatment Duckett believed he deserved. The hang-up, Duckett explained, had been the length of the sentence. Duckett wanted at least twenty years, and the defense had insisted on no more than ten.

Karceski was convinced that if he tried the case, he could win on insanity and that Larry would be freed fairly quickly. Karceski did not want Larry locked up in prison for any length of time, even at Patuxent. Duckett agreed that an insanity verdict would be Larry's shortest path to freedom, and the idea disturbed him. An insanity verdict would be a major loss for the prosecutor and would outrage the victims' families.

"Well, what do the sentencing guidelines say on second-degree?" Bell asked.

"I'm not sure."

"Let's take a look."

Reaching over to the wall shelf beside his desk, Bell pulled down the Maryland Sentencing Guidelines. He filled out a worksheet to determine what the recommended sentencing range would be if Larry pleaded guilty to second-degree. The system was based on a matrix with two variables: the seriousness of the offense and the offender's criminal background. Bell asked Duckett a series of questions about each variable: What type of weapon did he use? Did he have a juvenile record?

"It looks like twelve to twenty years," Bell said finally.

"Twelve to twenty?" That seemed shorter than what Duckett had offered during plea negotiations last fall. It certainly gave him room to negotiate. "Maybe I'll try again, using that as a starting point."

Returning to his office, Duckett picked up the phone and tracked the defense lawyers down at Karceski's law office in Baltimore. When Karceski got on the line, Duckett went right to the point.

"I don't remember exactly what sentence I mentioned the last time we talked about a plea," Duckett said, "but the guidelines call for twelve to twenty. If your client will plead guilty to second-degree, I'll modify my sentence recommendation. I'm willing to stay within the guidelines."

The prosecutor caught Karceski by surprise. Karceski knew Duckett hadn't forgotten his first offer of twenty years. He figured this was just Duckett's way of relenting, of saying, Hey, I'm willing to consider a lighter sentence.

That was fine with Karceski. It was fine with Baradel, too.

The defense lawyers both wanted to try the case. They were confident, prepared. Yet how could they, in good conscience, ignore an overture such as this? Duckett was backing down from twenty years. The only question was, how far would he go? Karceski knew they would have to bring Judge Bruce C. Williams into the discussion. He recently had been named to handle the case in place of Judge Thieme, who had a scheduling conflict. They would have to obtain a commitment on the length of sentence and a referral to Patuxent from Judge Williams.

"We're interested," Karceski said, "but we need to be more specific about the sentence, and we need a commitment from Judge Williams. Why don't we meet in chambers first thing tomorrow?"

THIRTEEN

Thursday, April 18, 1985

"Will you say a prayer for me?" Larry asked.

"Sure," John Kemmer replied. "Let's join hands." As Kemmer took Larry's hand, a few inmates followed suit, forming a circle and bowing their heads. Kemmer prayed: "Lord, please watch over Larry today, and give him strength. Guide him through his trial and make everything work out good for him. In Jesus's name we pray. Amen."

"Amen."

The inmates were in a holding cell near the entrance to the detention center, waiting for the police van to take them to the courthouse. Six inmates were going to court that morning.

Larry had donned his tan western boots and gray suit, the one his parents had given him for Christmas. Beneath his silver-framed aviator glasses, his rich olive complexion had lost its coloring and turned a pale institutional gray. His curly hair was a few inches shorter than it had been when police arrested him fifteen months earlier.

Kemmer watched Larry chewing furiously on a piece of gum. He'd never seen his friend so nervous before. "Stay cool, man," Kemmer said. "Just stay cool and calm."

When Larry said he was nervous about his court appearance, Kemmer relayed some advice: "Don't give any facial expressions when you testify. Just hold yourself still and look straight at your lawyer. Do what my drama teacher told me for my trial: Pretend you're accepting an Academy Award."

It was a bright sticky morning in Annapolis, unusually warm for April. The police van stopped beside the courthouse at 9 A.M. Larry Swartz stepped out, shackled to another inmate. A dozen photographers and television cameras closed in on them. The other inmate covered his head with a cloth, but Larry held his erect and looked straight ahead, a dazed expression on his face. Two sheriff's deputies led the inmates down a brick staircase and whisked them into the courthouse basement, where Baradel, Karceski, Mrs. Smithmyer, and Christine Monroe waited in a small office adjacent to a row of holding cells.

"Everything is going to be all right. I just know it," Christine said, hugging Larry for the first time.

"The prosecutor has made a plea offer," Karceski announced. "You're going to have to decide whether you want to accept it." He detailed Duckett's offer: plead guilty to two counts of second-degree murder, and the prosecutor would recommend a sentence of twelve to twenty years. Larry would go to Patuxent, which the lawyers explained was the best prison that Maryland had to offer.

"We're going to see the judge now," Karceski added. "We'll do our best to get you something on the low end, as close to twelve as we can. Think it over while we're gone, because it's your decision. After we see the judge, we'll come back and talk."

Larry stayed behind with Christine and a deputy sheriff in the small office. He ambled past a desk and over to the lone window, where he saw people walking along the sidewalk outside.

They were so close, he could almost reach out and touch them. "It's so weird," he muttered.

Christine walked over beside him. "What?"

"These people. Look at them, going about their business." Larry stared absentmindedly out the window. "It's so weird to see life going on as usual, just an arm's length away."

"Yeah, I guess it is." She thought how fifteen months in prison must seem like a lifetime to an eighteen-year-old. No wonder the sidewalk scene mesmerized him.

He watched for a while longer, then walked back to the chair and sat down. "Christine, I don't know what to do."

"Don't ask me. I can't tell you." Even though she had fantasized about an acquittal, Christine hoped Larry wouldn't let this opportunity slip by. The offer seemed so logical, so right, and the alternatives seemed so risky. The attorneys had explained to her about Patuxent's psychotherapy program. She thought Larry desperately needed therapy. His emotions were locked up so tight; maybe the prison's group therapy would teach him to express his feelings. Like his lawyers and the prosecutor, she suspected that if Larry had been able to vent his feelings toward his parents—to a counselor or any adult whom he trusted—the explosion might never have occurred.

"Well," she said, "practically speaking, you know if you're tried, you could get two thirty-year sentences for second-degree murder. Or even two life sentences for first-degree. You could get sent to one of the hard-core places, or to Perkins—"

"I don't want to go to Perkins!" he said sharply.

"That's what you're going for if you plead insanity. You know that, Larry."

He was quiet; she sensed his tension. During the past few weeks, he had seemed calmer than she, calmer even than his lawyers. Now the pressure seemed to be getting to him. He chewed on his gum, then released it and rested his head in his hands, lost in thought.

"You know, sometimes all God needs is a little window," Christine said softly. "Sometimes all He needs is for you to open a window, sit back, and let Him do the rest. You have confessed and repented, and I believe you meant it. God does not want your life destroyed. You are His child. Maybe God wants an opportunity to show you how much He loves you. Why don't you let Him show you?"

"I'm going to do it," Larry declared, raising his head.

She was relieved; she wasn't sure he'd been listening. "Are you sure?"

"Yeah."

"You feel good about it?"

"Yeah."

"Listen to your heart. Tell me what your heart says."

Larry looked at her and smiled. "It tells me it's okay. I'm going to do it."

Karceski and Baradel entered Judge Williams's second-floor chambers confident that they would reach a plea agreement. They required only two things: a firm commitment from the judge to cap the sentence somewhere lower than twenty years, and a guarantee that Larry would go to Patuxent. It would have to be a conditional plea. If the Patuxent admission team rejected Larry after his evaluation, the deal was off. He would withdraw his guilty plea and they would try the case. Those were their minimum terms. Karceski was too shrewd a negotiator, however, not to go for as short a sentence as he could get. He would push for twelve years, the minimum sentence under the guidelines as Duckett had calculated them.

Actually, Karceski believed Duckett had miscalculated the guidelines. After he had talked to the prosecutor the previous evening, Karceski had turned to Baradel and said, "I don't know where he's getting twelve to twenty. It was eighteen to thirty when I did it." Karceski had followed the provision that said when a person commits two crimes in a single incident, the sentence goes up on the second count because the first crime counts as a prior offense in the calculations. By Karceski's count, the guidelines were twelve to twenty on Larry's first murder count, then jumped to eighteen to thirty for the second count; but he wasn't going to object to Duckett's calculations.

Duckett arrived in chambers at ten o'clock, accompanied by Barr and a law clerk. He took a seat to one side of Judge Williams.

The fifty-four-year-old judge, six two on his feet, slumped forward in his chair and placed both elbows on the desk. He leaned his square rugged face on his hands and listened intently as Duckett explained where plea negotiations stood.

Sitting across the desk from Duckett, Karceski and Baradel also listened intently. When the prosecutor finished, Karceski told the judge that any plea would have to be conditioned upon Larry's acceptance at Patuxent. He wanted to reserve the right to try the case if the special prison rejected his client and sent him back to the regular prison system.

Judge Williams wasn't worried about Larry getting into Patuxent; he thought the youth's psychological evaluations made him a perfect candidate. The judge volunteered to phone Patuxent's director to try to expedite Larry's evaluation, but when he placed the call, the director was out.

Karceski looked from the prosecutor to the judge. "We want a sentence at the low end of the guidelines," he said.

Duckett shook his head. "No." It was up to the judge, but the prosecutor didn't want Larry to receive too light a sentence. Half a dozen family members had flown in for the trial. "The family will raise a tremendous ruckus if Larry receives twelve years," he warned the judge. "I'm trying to keep them informed, but they want the maximum. Some of them even want the death penalty."

The Patuxent director returned the judge's phone call a few minutes later and said that she could expedite Larry's evaluation, but the prison couldn't determine his eligibility until after he was found guilty and sentenced to the state Division of Correction: That was state law.

Judge Williams was so confident of Larry's acceptance that he felt the evaluation was a mere formality. He said he would make Larry's plea and sentence contingent upon his acceptance at Patuxent.

That left only one unresolved question: the length of the sentence.

Without being specific, Duckett again recommended twelve to twenty, and again told the judge he preferred a sentence closer to the high end.

"I'll tell you all, I'm contemplating a sentence somewhere between twelve and fifteen years," Judge Williams announced.

"Twelve to fifteen?" asked Karceski. "Can you be more specific?"

The judge shook his head. He was still undecided.

Fifteen years sounded pretty good to Baradel, who was willing to accept that as the best they were going to get. Karceski, however, haggled, trying to make the judge commit himself to twelve.

"You're saying twelve to fifteen, but what you really mean is fifteen, isn't it?" Karceski asked.

"That's right," the judge said. "I'm really thinking fifteen."

In truth, Judge Williams had twenty years in mind, with five suspended. That would look stronger to the public than a straight sentence of fifteen years, although as a practical matter, they were the same. He considered fifteen years lenient for a double murder, but he also knew that Larry's sentence would be moot at Patuxent. The prison's parole board made release decisions independent of court-imposed sentences. Yet Williams knew the sentence would not seem moot to the public or to the victims' relatives. Like the prosecutor, he had to be able to explain his disposition to the public. He well remembered the outcry that followed Stuart Kreiner's commitment to Patuxent, for he had presided over Kreiner's plea bargain seven years earlier. The last thing he wanted was a repeat.

At the same time, he wanted to avoid a trial and an insanity acquittal. He thought Larry had been pushed to his breaking point and had gone temporarily insane on the night of the murders. As cruel as it might sound, Williams believed that when Larry killed his parents, he had cured himself by correcting the problem that drove him to kill. Like Baradel and Duckett, the judge was convinced that Larry would not kill again. The likelihood of Larry being so trapped again, and so mistreated emotionally, at such a vulnerable point in his life—right on the edge of adulthood—seemed slim to none. Neither the judge nor the attorneys wanted to see the prison system turn Larry into the hardened criminal they didn't think he was. Williams, especially, hoped the defense attorneys would have enough sense to drop the insanity plea. The judge wanted Larry to undergo therapy at Patuxent while he was still young and had a reasonable chance of resuming a normal life.

After two hours of haggling failed to produce an agreement, Baradel rose to stretch his legs. Karceski stood up at precisely the same moment.

Startled, Judge Williams glanced at the defense lawyers, who appeared to be getting ready to leave. Were they going to try the case, after all? He looked expectantly at Karceski.

Karceski said nothing.

"Okay," the judge said suddenly. "I'll give him twenty years and suspend all but twelve."

Karceski smiled.

He had won.

A breeze wafted in through the tall open windows of Courtroom Number 1 as construction machinery beeped outside. A hundred potential jurors squeezed against one another on the long mahogany spectator benches, where they had spent all morning waiting for voir dire to begin. Fifteen reporters, three courtroom artists, and dozens of spectators had found seats before the bailiff closed the packed courtroom to the public.

At 1:30, moments after the jurors returned from lunch, the bailiff walked down front and announced, "You're all free to go."

Michael Swartz, sitting in the front row with his social worker, stood up with the jurors. Obviously, there was to be no trial. His brother must have struck a plea bargain, and Michael didn't want to watch. He turned and walked out of the courtroom with the social worker.

After the jurors filed out, a deputy sheriff escorted Larry through the door at the rear of the courtroom and watched him sit down at the defense table between his lawyers. Baradel put a reassuring hand on Larry's shoulder.

During the lunch recess, Larry had met privately with them and had accepted the final plea offer. He would take the twelve-year sentence and go through Patuxent's treatment program. It was an exceptionally lenient sentence, the attorneys assured him. Karceski told him he could expect to serve perhaps half his sentence, six years. At the worst, so long as he behaved himself, Larry would earn good time and get out in about nine years.

The most important thing, though, was the therapy Patuxent

would offer. The judge, prosecutor, and defense attorneys believed that the social system had let Larry down as a child. They thought he not only needed but deserved psychotherapy for his deep emotional problems. He also needed to continue his high school studies and receive job training; Patuxent offered more training than any other Maryland prison.

During the lunch break, Judge Williams deemed a presentence report unnecessary and told the lawyers he would sentence Larry immediately.

Sixty spectators milled inside the courtroom after lunch, waiting for the judge's arrival. John Riely glared at the defense table, his anger almost uncontrollable. He wanted to hurt his cousin, for Larry had inflicted incredible pain on Riely's mother and the rest of their family, pain so intense that Riely doubted the scars would ever heal. He imagined himself walking up to Larry and saying something spiteful, something hateful. But what? Detective Barr had told him of an unsubstantiated rumor that Larry had taken a male lover in jail.

Riely rose from his seat, strode past the mahogany gate toward the defense table, and leaned down beside his cousin. *"I hear you've been sucking a lot of cock lately,"* he whispered in Larry's ear.

Larry drew back, shocked. He turned to stare at his cousin, but Riely already was walking away.

Baradel saw Larry's flushed face and leaned over. "What did he say?"

Larry repeated the remark; Baradel just shook his head.

Judge Williams entered the courtroom and everybody rose. After Duckett announced that they had reached a plea agreement, Karceski told Larry to take the witness stand so he could walk him through the plea.

To each question regarding waiver of his constitutional rights to a jury trial, the voluntariness of his plea and all its ramifications, Larry answered with a soft but firm yes or no. He stared straight ahead, never taking his eyes off Karceski, while Baradel sat at the defense table with his arms crossed, looking vaguely relieved.

When Karceski finished, Judge Williams, sitting behind a wide dark-paneled bench high above everyone else, leaned forward and peered down at Larry. "Is it still your desire to enter a guilty plea to two counts of second-degree murder?"

"Yes."

"You may step down."

Larry walked back to the defense table and flashed a quick smile at Baradel before he sat down.

Duckett stood to read a statement of the evidence he would have presented if the case had gone to trial. As he recounted how paramedics had found the bodies of Bob and Kay Swartz, Larry listened intently, alternately chewing on his lip and pushing on his cheek with his tongue. Larry expressed no emotion except when the prosecutor quoted a paramedic as saying that Larry had told him to put the family dog to sleep. Larry shook his head, as if he couldn't believe he would have said such a thing.

Reading from notes, Duckett gave an incredibly detailed account of the state's case, from the cops' discovery of tracks in the snow to the FBI analysis of the hairs found on the maul. When Duckett was still reading twenty minutes later, Baradel leaned behind Larry and whispered to Karceski, *"God, this will be the first two-day guilty plea I've ever seen!"*

When he reached the insanity issue, Duckett explained that a panel of state doctors had concluded that Larry was sane, and a panel of defense experts had disagreed. "It would have been one psychiatrist against another psychiatrist, saying, Yes, he is! and No, he's not!"

Duckett listed the witnesses he would have called to rebut the defense doctors: a string of teachers and friends who would have described Larry as outwardly normal, with no apparent history of psychosis. "It's obvious that he"—Duckett turned to look at Larry—"is a very troubled person, and is sick and needs treatment. Patuxent is the only institution that can provide him with the treatment he needs to hopefully return to our community one day and assume a meaningful role. I think a finding of two counts of murder in the second degree is exactly what this case warrants. The state urges that this is in the best interest of justice."

At exactly 2:50 P.M., after more than half an hour of oration, Duckett sat down.

Judge Williams summoned Larry to the bench for a brief conference. Larry walked back to the defense table and stood behind it, facing the judge with his hands folded primly in front of him.

"I will accept his plea of guilty to two counts of second-degree murder," the judge declared.

Karceski requested a recess to speak privately with Larry. Ten minutes later, Larry again stood behind the defense table with his lawyers, facing the judge.

Karceski said that Larry's background was "a most unfortunate one." He described the murders as "an insane reaction to what must have been an insane situation" in Larry's life. Then he asked Williams to give Larry a sentence "at the low end of the guidelines, around twelve years."

The judge looked at Larry. "Mr. Swartz, is there anything you would like to tell me?"

"No, sir." Larry spoke so softly Williams couldn't hear him.

"Excuse me?" said the judge, leaning forward.

"No, sir," Larry repeated, louder.

Williams turned to the prosecutor.

Never one to pass up a speechmaking opportunity, Duckett said, "I didn't know Kay and Bob Swartz, but like everyone in this courtroom—I hope including the defendant—I am terribly sorry for what happened. There's nothing I can do now, nothing anyone can do, to correct the horrible wrong. Nothing in this world, including all the psychological testimony, can ever justify the type of death that Kay and Bob Swartz suffered.

"But if indeed we are a civilized society, we look forward instead of backward. I hope there is some good that comes out of this. The message I would like for this courtroom to teach us is that all of us, in our everyday lives, don't accept things without question, without concern. Maybe some things could have been done to relieve this situation and keep it from occurring. That's hindsight. If we all take that out of the courtroom, maybe there won't be as many Bobs and Kays and Larry Swartzes."

As Duckett sat down, the judge sat up straight behind the dark wooden bench, the American and Maryland flags crossed majestically behind him. Williams knew the community was shocked by this case and had waited more than a year for the catharsis of a trial. The plea bargain would be a letdown, not only for the lawyers but for the community as well. Aware that he would be widely quoted, Williams chose his words carefully:

"This is one of the most tragic cases that has ever occurred in this county, and perhaps that has ever occurred in the State of Maryland. Rightfully, there has been a lot of media attention."

The judge recapped the plea negotiations, then said, "This is not a case that really fits in with the standard behavior of a criminal. This is a young man who had a very troubled childhood. There are some disputed facts in his background, but the picture that comes through is that of a strict family, at least not a very understanding family. The communication was not very good between Larry and his father. For some reason or another, something happened on the night of January sixteen that no one has been able to explain.

"Larry was seventeen years old. . . . He had never been in prior trouble. By all appearances, he was an average, normal seventeen-year-old boy. Psychological evaluation by a series of doctors indicates that under this facade of normality there was a great deal that was abnormal, a great deal that needs treatment, and a great deal that perhaps explains what happened."

Williams acknowledged "a real possibility" that Larry would have been declared insane, but said he personally believed "there was a greater chance for him to be found sane and responsible for what happened." Had the case been tried, he predicted Larry would have been convicted of "at least second-degree murder."

"The real issue," the judge said, "is what the court can do to protect society, punish Mr. Swartz for what he has done, and yet rehabilitate him. I don't think time itself has any great significance: Whatever time the court imposes will be questioned by someone. More significant is the length and type of treatment Mr. Swartz will get, so that when he is released, he will be able to begin his life anew without being a danger to himself or others. Often the reason for something like this is resolved by commission of the act itself, and I suspect this is the case here. I believe Mr. Swartz would not act out like this against anyone else in the world."

Larry stood with his hands rigidly locked behind his back as the judge solemnly imposed two concurrent twenty-year sentences and suspended all but twelve years of each. The afternoon sun poured in through the high windows, highlighting his curly black hair and pallid skin over his cheekbones. Larry displayed no emotion when Williams meted out the sentence, and none when his lawyers turned to tell him good-bye.

Baradel had brushed away tears during the judge's speech, and his eyes glistened now. He was sad that Larry was going to prison, and he prayed that they had done the right thing. Larry seemed so vulnerable, so exposed to the judicial system. Baradel prayed that his short wrecked life would be rebuilt.

With dry eyes and a blank face, Larry turned, as a deputy sheriff approached to shackle his hands, and asked Karceski to relay a message of thanks to Christine Monroe.

Tears streaming down her face, Christine pushed her way through the crowd. As the deputy turned to lead Larry away, she reached out, squeezed his arm, and smiled.

Larry smiled back but said nothing as he walked down the center aisle of the courtroom and disappeared through the rear door.

AFTERWORD

Larry Swartz still is the only one who knows exactly what happened that snowy night in January 1984, and the details may stay locked forever in his memory. Despite intensive psychotherapy at Patuxent, he has never shared with those closest to him any new information on the killings.

Barr and Baradel still disagree about whose footprints were found in the snow, and Larry's supporters continue to wonder what sparked his smoldering rage. Baradel always found the details of the murders more puzzling than the larger question of why they happened.

Asked after the plea to explain Larry's motive, Baradel replied, "I'll tell you the bottom line. I've done a lot of thinking about it, a *lot* of thinking about it. I think you had well-meaning and well-intentioned people; I *know* you had that. I think that they were peculiarly ill equipped because of their own personalities to deal with the problems that Larry had. I also know that they never knew of the problems that Larry had. They were doing what they felt was best to motivate a child. And I think their approach to discipline, and their attempts to motivate, were unfortunately and tragically exactly the wrong thing for this child."

Karceski, joining Baradel and Duckett at an unusual two-hour news conference after the plea, said, "I think the best analogy we can draw is that this was comparable to a balloon that was being pumped up, and it just happened to burst on this night. The event was not so significant as the fact that it was about to happen; I think Larry Swartz had pent up within him as much as he could hold."

Deprived of the emotional release that trials provide, all the lawyers in the case suffered what Duckett called "postplea blues." Duckett spent months thinking about the tragedy and what kind of lesson it might offer other families. When the Arundel Senior High School asked the prosecutor to deliver the commencement address in June 1985, the Swartz murders seemed a natural topic. He told the crowd that he couldn't remember the speakers or the speeches at his graduations years ago. He wanted to tell a story that they would never forget, one that would be meaningful to their lives.

"It is a story about a young man about your age. He should be graduating this year, but he's not. He's in prison. He'll be there for the next year and a half to twelve years. He was convicted of murdering his parents." Duckett recounted the murders in graphic, gruesome detail and recapped Larry's chaotic childhood and restrictive life with the Swartzes. "It's not just a horrible story," he concluded. "It's a story we can learn from. What we have to do in all relationships is reach out and communicate. Do not assume anything."

Baradel expressed his pent-up feelings in a letter to the *The Capital,* which the newspaper printed across the top of page one. He listed the good things he thought had come out of the Swartz tragedy, including the fact that "the judicial system worked as it was meant to work." He concluded:

My hope is that as a result of Larry Swartz' story, parents will perhaps take another look at how they treat their own children, that children will have the strength and courage to talk to *somebody* about the problems they might be experiencing, and that friends and neighbors who see families with problems will come forward, get involved, and not simply close their eyes. And, my prayer is that this community will never again be faced with a tragedy such as this.

Baradel and Monroe spent most of 1985 talking to Larry and interviewing others about the case. No matter how often they asked the same questions, Larry still claimed he couldn't remember anything more. Baradel's obsession with the mystery persisted for a long time, and friends told him he was "possessed." He had trouble sleeping, and his religious faith waned.

"I still have difficulty seeing how things could stay locked up for so long," he said late in 1985. "There are certain things that at least I *surmise* must have happened, that Larry either cannot or will not remember. All I get is, 'I don't know.' I could see where you could lock things away in your mind, but there was never a necessity for bringing it up. There was never the probing like I've probed. I don't know whether it's curiosity or what. I don't have the whole picture yet and that bothers me. The missing pieces drive me bonkers."

The missing pieces bothered Monroe, too. Still haunted by the psychic's suggestion that someone else was involved in the murders, she suspected for a while that it was Michael Swartz. During a visit to Patuxent, she confronted Larry with her suspicions about Michael. Larry vehemently denied that his brother had anything to do with the murders and insisted that he had acted entirely on his own.

More than anything, Monroe wanted to understand Larry's motivation. "It took some kind of fury, and I have a real hard time with it," she said in September 1987. "I want to know the ammunition for it. What gave him that kind of gusto?"

Her constant grilling finally elicited one small confession from Larry: His original story had been, at least in part, a lie. He told

Christine that he had made up the conversation he claimed to have had with his mother before the murders. She never made the sarcastic crack about his exams, he disclosed. She never said anything to him at all.

"What happened?" Monroe asked.

"Nothing," Larry replied. "I just came downstairs and killed them."

Michael Swartz walked out of court rather than watch his brother plead guilty in April 1985, and for months insisted that he believed his brother was incapable of murder.

In an interview later that summer, he freely acknowledged that many people suspected he was involved in his parents' murders. He said those suspicions never troubled him. "I got, like, a hundred witnesses saying where I was at," he said.

He denied that he had ever threatened to harm his parents, as relatives claimed, and scoffed at the thought that they had feared him. "I think they'd have a right to be afraid of me, though," he added bitterly. "All that stuff they did. I think if I treated my child that way and he grew up to be twenty-some years old, and I was an old man, I'd be scared of him. He's gonna slap his old man around now."

He said he was certain that Larry had loved, not hated, their parents, even if he had killed them. "Did you ever see *Old Yeller*?" he asked. "Did they like that dog? They loved that dog, didn't they? They had to shoot it."

As Michael struggled to cope with the loss of the family that had briefly been his, his relationship with Larry grew strained. He visited Larry at Patuxent twice during the summer of 1985, but the visits so disturbed Larry that he took Michael off his list of approved visitors. Larry told friends that his brother made him uncomfortable because he was "fidgety" and wouldn't meet his eyes when they talked.

Michael worked at various jobs, and bounced between apartments and houses, before he settled into a career as a cabdriver in Annapolis. By the summer of 1987, Michael was driving a cab and working with an army recruiter. He said he wanted go to the Army's "sniper school" to study small-arms repair. Asked why, he smirked and said, "I'm going to become a sniper—learn to kill and get away with it."

The two brothers finally had a reunion in the summer of 1988 when Warren Duckett personally called Patuxent to arrange it. Michael went to the prosecutor to seek his assistance in getting into the army. Duckett, then on the verge of winning an appointment to the circuit-court bench, wrote a letter of recommendation to Michael's army recruiter and called Patuxent to arrange a visit.

The reunion went so well that Larry put Michael back on his visitors list.

By the fall of 1988, Michael had been rejected by the army and continued to drive his cab. He laughingly acknowledged that some people still suspected he was involved in the murders. "Even my *girlfriend* thinks I did it," he said. Asserting that he had nothing to hide, he freely agreed to the author's request to be fingerprinted so that police could compare his prints with the stray prints found inside the Swartz house—including the bloody partial palm print found on the inside doorknob to the computer room, which didn't match either Larry's or his parents' hands. None of Michael's prints matched, either.

Early in 1989, Michael began searching for the natural parents and siblings he had left behind when he was four. "I'd like to know where I'm from. All I know is I'm an Indian from somewhere," he explained.

He said he loved Larry deeply but still harbored anger toward him for killing their parents and robbing him of any hope of reconciliation. The murders had occurred at a time when Michael still had been hoping to win his parents' forgiveness and return to the family fold. "I still fight it," he said. "It's hard to accept, because there's no chance for a reunion now."

While Michael made his own way in the world, Anne Swartz continued to live with the Smithmyers on the Eastern Shore.

In June 1985, two months after Larry went to Patuxent, the Smithmyers sought permanent custody of her through a court petition. Helen and James Rodden of Indianapolis, the aunt and uncle named as her guardians in the Swartzes' wills, filed an opposing petition, claiming they were her legal guardians.

The Roddens grew worried that spring when they discovered that Anne was having problems in school and might have to repeat another grade. They feared that Anne, then eleven, would suffer from the notoriety of her brother's murder conviction if she stayed in Maryland. They also worried that John and Eileen Smithmyer, with seven children of their own, wouldn't be able to give Annie the special attention she needed.

"She is one sweet little girl and she deserves to be out of that environment," Helen Rodden, Kay Swartz's older sister, told a reporter for *The Capital* that summer. "I know my sister would want that."

Judge James C. Cawood ruled that Anne would remain with the Smithmyers while the two families fought over her custody. Cawood, however, never had to decide which home offered Anne her best chance at happiness: The Roddens soon withdrew their custody request and agreed to let her stay with the Smithmyers.

Larry's sad life—and his parents' violent deaths—continued to trouble people in the small community where he lived. Parents asked themselves how they were different from Bob and Kay Swartz, and many tried to become better parents, including all the attorneys involved in the case.

"I really did do a turnabout, because I'm a yeller, I'm a screamer, and I didn't hesitate to take off on my children verbally," Karceski said. "After this, I see the significant effect that has. Not that I believe that either one of my kids are going to do what Larry Swartz did, but I really think it has a lasting effect on them. And I hope that what I did in the past isn't irreversible."

So many people identified with the Swartz story that Baradel thought it would make a good book. When he mentioned that to Larry, to Baradel's surprise Larry agreed that someone should write his story. Baradel recalled: "He said, 'I want *you* to do it.' I said, 'You've got to be kidding me!' He said, 'You'll be the only one I talk to about it.'" Baradel had some journalism experience in college and decided to take a stab at it. He recruited Christine Monroe as his collaborator, and they began a routine of visiting Larry and meeting at night to organize their thoughts. Baradel's law practice consumed so much time, however, that he found it difficult to schedule regular work sessions with Christine. The sessions grew more infrequent, and after one publisher rejected their book proposal, they abandoned the project in 1986.

During 1987, Baradel, worn out from an ordeal that had lasted three years, retreated to rebuild his own life. He stopped visiting Larry and channeled his energy back into his civil-law practice. Occasionally, he sent Larry money and wrote letters promising to visit, but he didn't visit Patuxent once during 1987 and 1988.

By early 1989, Baradel was feeling guilty and melancholy about the whole experience. "We all had the best intentions," he said. "Kay and Bob did. I did. We all did in trying to get him into Patuxent. I viewed the legal case as a prologue for what I was going to do for Larry: I was going to be more than his lawyer; I was going to visit him once a week. I didn't follow through.

"It has changed me fundamentally. I am less willing now to accept things or people as they appear to be. And though it may sound contradictory, I'm also more willing to accept human frailties, because I think people may have the best intentions, but they don't always follow through."

In 1985, Larry went to Patuxent eager to embark on a program he hoped would improve his life. His first week there, he wrote an upbeat letter to his former cellmate John Kemmer. Besides demonstrating his borderline illiteracy, the letter showed his growing infatuation with Christine, and a buoyancy that would serve him well in prison. Larry wrote that his new cell was small and the prison was boring.

"John, I didn't tell you how serious Christine and I are," he added. "Were talking about Marriage when I get out. . . . Have you ever had anybody who thinks the same thoughts as you do is talking at the same level as you at all times can make you upset or cry because they are? If so then you have some understanding of what we are about."

Not surprisingly, considering the deep emotional reserve he had developed in childhood, Larry did not shine in Patuxent's psychotherapy program. He was slow to express himself in group therapy, both to other inmates and to the psychiatrists. He told friends he was too intimidated by the doctor who headed his program to approach him.

Partly due to his reserve, Larry worked his way through Patuxent's tier system a little more slowly than some inmates. Yet by the end of 1988, he had earned his high school equivalency diploma, completed several college courses, and reached the prison's third tier, the next-to-the-last stop on his way to parole. He told friends he was contemplating getting a degree in psychology so he could become a counselor and help other people when he got out of prison.

Larry's release date, and his future outside of prison, remain uncertain. He told friends he plans to leave Maryland when he gets out so that he can put his tragic past behind him. With credit for good time, he should become eligible for mandatory release by the end of 1992 at the latest—nearly nine years after he was incarcerated. He is already eligible for parole, however, and Patuxent's parole board could grant him parole sooner.

Patuxent officials said his release may have been delayed by the public uproar that erupted over Maryland's unusual prison after the 1988 presidential election, prompting the General Assembly to revamp the parole board and enact reforms that will drastically alter the prison's character.

George Bush set the backdrop for the uproar with his campaign ads spotlighting Willie Horton, the convict who raped a woman in Maryland while he was on furlough from a life-without-parole term for murder in Massachusetts. Marylanders grew outraged immediately after the election when they learned that one of their own prisons—Patuxent—was giving unsupervised furloughs to a triple murderer who had served only twelve years of three consecutive life terms. Public outrage intensified when a rapist escaped from Patuxent's work release program and raped another woman in late November 1988.

Reacting swiftly, Patuxent froze all inmate releases while the General Assembly enacted emergency reforms to tighten the prison's parole policies and strip the parole board of its autonomy. The reforms were designed to halt early paroles at the prison and keep out many of the murderers and rapists whom Patuxent originally was built to treat. The new law took effect in March 1989, but its full impact will not be known for several years because it calls for a lengthy study that will lead to a new treatment program, as well as new eligibility and release rules at the prison.

Larry, meanwhile, delighted Christine Monroe and Caryl Sweet with his progress. "Larry has changed so much," said Sweet, who became his most faithful visitor. "He talks so much more freely about himself and how he operates."

Monroe also saw striking changes in Larry after she left Maryland in the fall of 1987 and returned occasionally to visit. "His statements are stronger," she said after one visit to the prison. "He's point-blank now and meets your eyes all the time. He said before, if somebody else loved him, *he* could love him. Now he says he's learning to love himself."

ACKNOWLEDGMENTS

Many people contributed generously to this book, and many shared painful thoughts and memories with hopes of conveying a worthwhile message. My appreciation runs deep to those who spent hours re-creating for me the lives of their loved ones. Special thanks to the relatives of Bob and Kay Swartz who invited me into their homes and spoke candidly about the family's strengths and weaknesses.

Words cannot express my gratitude to Ron Baradel, whose contribution to the book, and benevolence to Larry Swartz, were simply extraordinary. Many others gave freely of their time, especially Warren B. Duckett, Jr., and Gary Barr. Thanks to them and to all the characters in the book who spoke with me. For sharing their professional expertise, I am particularly obliged to Dr. John Smialek, chief medical examiner of Maryland; Dr. William Gormley, a former deputy medical examiner; and Dr. Mallory Eisenman, a Philadelphia podiatrist.

For research, moral support, and editorial insight, I am thankful to my friend Kaye Thompson Peters, who stayed with the project from start to finish. Many thanks also to my agent, Esther Newberg, whose persistence helped make the book a reality, and Charles Spicer at St. Martin's Press, who did a thorough job of editing and, with his infectious enthusiasm, kept me going through some difficult times. I am also indebted to three friends: Kelly Gilbert and Ellyn Hunt, who spent nights and weekends reading the copy with sharp eyes; and Jonathan Coleman, who pointed me in the right direction and offered inspirational advice.

For assistance and support too varied to explain, I am equally thankful to Stacey Hinrichs, Lewis W. Walker, III, Cathy Mentzer, Jonathan Massie, Linda and Joyce Church, Steve Feinstein, Caryl Sweet, Janet Davidson, Sue Kopen, Gwen Ifill, Melody Simmons, and everyone on The Row, Bill Thomas at St. Martin's Press, Jamie Grubb, Vicky Hilvety, and especially, Daphne Brennan.

Above all, I thank my parents, who provided me with so much more than the computer used to write this book. To them, for their endless encouragement and indomitable spirit, I am eternally grateful.